Fundamentals of Artificial Intelligence

Chandramouli Subramanian
Ph.D. (Management); PfMP; PMP; PMI-ACP
Associate Director, Cognizant Technology Solutions
Chennai, Tamil Nadu

Universities Press

All rights reserved. No part of this book may be (i) modified, reproduced or utilised in any form, or by any means, electronic or mechanical, including photocopying, recording or by any information storage and retrieval system, in any form of binding or cover other than in which it is published, without permission in writing from the publisher; or (ii) used or reproduced in any manner for the purpose of training, development or operation of artificial intelligence (AI) technologies and systems, including generative AI technologies, without permission in writing from the copyright holder.

FUNDAMENTALS OF ARTIFICIAL INTELLIGENCE

UNIVERSITIES PRESS (INDIA) PRIVATE LIMITED

Registered office
3-6-747/1/A & 3-6-754/1, Himayatnagar, Hyderabad 500 029, Telangana, India
info@universitiespress.com; www.universitiespress.com

Distributed by
Orient Blackswan Private Limited

Registered office
3-6-752 Himayatnagar, Hyderabad 500 029, Telangana, India

Other offices
Bengaluru / Chennai / Guwahati / Hyderabad
Kolkata / Mumbai / New Delhi / Noida / Patna

© Universities Press (India) Private Ltd 2026

Cover and book design
© Universities Press (India) Private Ltd 2026

ISBN: 978-93-49750-79-1

Typeset in Times LT Std 10 *by*
SRS Technologies, Puducherry

Printed in India by
Graphica Printers & Binders, Hyderabad 500 013

Published by
Universities Press (India) Private Limited
3-6-747/1/A & 3-6-754/1, Himayatnagar, Hyderabad 500 029, Telangana, India

Care has been taken to confirm the accuracy of the information presented in this book. The author and the publisher, however, cannot accept any responsibility for errors or omissions or for consequences from application of the information in this book, and make no warranty, express or implied, with respect to its contents.

About the Author

Chandramouli Subramanian is Associate Director in Cognizant Technology Solutions, Chennai. He is a distinguished professional with extensive experience in technology, project, program and portfolio management. He holds a Ph.D. and is an alumnus of the Indian Institute of Management Kozhikode (IIMK), as well as a Certified Global Business Leader from Harvard Business School. His expertise is further underscored by multiple certifications, including PfMP, PMP, PMI-ACP, and a Certified Green Belt in Six-Sigma. He is also a certified master practitioner in neuro-linguistic programming (NLP).

Dr Chandramouli has a proven track record of successfully delivering large-scale, mission-critical projects on time and within budget. His project portfolio includes cutting-edge technologies such as blockchain, AI, big data analytics, and machine learning. He is known for implementing design thinking principles across all his projects.

A recognized thought leader, Dr Chandramouli is a prolific writer, with 30 publications in national and international journals and conferences. His articles focus on a range of topics including technology management, delivery management, IT, organizational culture, and leadership. Two of his papers have won prestigious awards: Best Practices of Agile Program Management – SCRUM TEA Model at the Program and Portfolio Management Conference and Strategy Based Service Model – DISCO PMO at the International IT Service Management Conference.

He has been a key contributor to significant industry publications, including the latest editions of the Program Management Standard 5.0 and the Project Management Body of Knowledge (PMBOK 8th edition) by the Project Management Institute (PMI). He was also an active member in PMI's Organizational Project Management Maturity Model (OPM3) and Project Management Competency Development Framework (PMCDF) assignments.

An in-demand speaker, Dr Chandramouli has presented papers on project management at various international forums and addressed over 15,000 software professionals worldwide. His speaking engagements cover a diverse range of themes, including blockchain, AI, machine learning, big data analytics, delivery management, competitiveness, and leadership.

*I would like to express my sincere gratitude to the
following people for their support:*

My parents, Subramanian and Lalitha
My wife, Ramya
My son, Shri Krishna
My daughter, Shri Siva Ranjani
My colleagues and friends

Preface

Artificial intelligence (AI) is no longer a concept from science fiction; it is a fundamental part of our daily lives, transforming industries, reshaping jobs, and redefining how we interact with technology. From the personalized recommendations on our phones to the intricate systems that power autonomous vehicles, AI is the invisible force driving innovation.

I wrote this book, *Fundamentals of Artificial Intelligence*, to demystify this powerful field for undergraduate students. My goal is to provide a clear, accessible, and comprehensive guide that not only covers the theoretical underpinnings of AI but also connects them to real-world applications. The book reflects the latest advancements, including the rise of Generative AI and the critical skill of Prompt Engineering.

This textbook is designed to be a student's first step into the world of AI, balancing academic rigour with practical relevance. It is built upon the idea that understanding AI requires more than just knowing algorithms; it requires appreciating its history, recognizing its ethical implications, and being able to apply its tools to solve real problems.

This book is a step-by-step guide to understanding AI, structured to provide a clear learning path.

Chapter 1: Introduction to AI: We begin by defining what AI is, exploring its evolution, and distinguishing it from human intelligence. This chapter covers the history of AI, key milestones, and the concept of artificial general intelligence (AGI).

Chapter 2: Subfields and Core Technologies: This chapter breaks down the major branches of AI, including machine learning (supervised, unsupervised, and reinforcement learning), deep learning, natural language processing (NLP), computer vision (CV), and robotics. We explain how each of these subfields contributes to the broader AI ecosystem.

Chapter 3: Applications of AI: Here, we show AI in action. We explore its practical applications across various industries, such as in diagnostics in healthcare, fraud detection in finance, personalized learning in education, smart farming in agriculture, and traffic management in transportation.

Chapter 4: Ethics, Bias, and Social Implications: AI is a powerful tool, and this chapter addresses the crucial responsibilities that come with it. We discuss important ethical considerations like bias, fairness, data privacy, and the impact of AI on employment and social equality.

Chapter 5: Generative AI and Its Applications: We dive into the exciting world of Generative AI, explaining its fundamentals and evolution. This chapter introduces popular tools like ChatGPT and Gemini and shows how they are used for creative and research purposes. We explore practical uses of generative models. This includes using AI for creative writing, visual design, video creation, and content generation for business and education.

Chapter 6: Prompt Engineering and Its Applications: This chapter is dedicated to the essential skill of prompt engineering. We define what prompts are and explain their role in human–AI interaction. We explain effective techniques to get the best results from AI models. We conclude by demonstrating how to use prompt engineering for specific tasks, such as text summarization, content creation for social media, and building question-answering systems. This chapter provides hands-on examples to help you master this critical skill.

Chapter 7: Practice Session: Laboratory Work: The concluding chapter gives you the opportunity to apply what you have learned. You will build simple AI models, experiment with generative tools, and practice prompt engineering, making this a truly practical and hands-on learning experience.

At the end of each chapter, you will find objective questions that test your understanding of the main concepts and ideas. You will also find short answer and essay questions that will challenge you to apply your knowledge and skills to specific scenarios and cases. The explanations and solutions to these questions can be accessed at https://www.universitiespress.com/FundamentalsofAI.

This book is written in simple language, with clear explanations and examples. It is suitable for anyone who wants to learn about AI, from beginners to practitioners. Whether you are a student, a teacher, a manager, an entrepreneur, or a social innovator, this book will help you develop your creative confidence and competence and enable you to create positive change in the world.

Chandramouli Subramanian

Acknowledgements

This book is the culmination of a rewarding professional journey, one enriched by my experiences in project management, agile methodologies, and the application of cutting-edge technologies such as AI, machine learning, blockchain, and big data analytics. It is a privilege to have worked with some of the best minds and organizations in the world, and I am deeply grateful for the guidance, opportunities, and knowledge they have shared.

First and foremost, I wish to extend my deepest gratitude to the team at Universities Press. Their willingness to publish this book and their unwavering support were instrumental. A special thank you to Kallol Das and Madhavi Sethupathi, who were consistently kind and understanding. Madhavi, in particular, reviewed each page with abundant patience, helping to refine my ideas and improve the manuscript with great care.

I am also profoundly grateful to the many distinguished professionals who have shaped my career and contributed to the ideas within this book. Their collective wisdom and expertise have been invaluable.

I want to personally thank:

Mr. Sriram Vaithamanithi, Senior Vice-President, Cognizant Technology Solutions

Mr. Alexis Samuel, Senior Vice-President, Cognizant Technology Solutions

Mr. Hariharan Mathrubutham, former Vice-President, Cognizant Technology Solutions

Mr. Krishna Prasad Yerramilli, Vice-President, Cognizant Technology Solutions

Mr. Dharmendraraj Govindarajan Nagarajan, Vice-President, Cognizant Technology Solutions

Ms. Anand Prabha, Vice-President, Cognizant Technology Solutions

Mr. Balasubramanian Narayanan, Senior Director, Cognizant Technology Solutions

Their inspiration and help were critical in the creation of this book, and their contributions have significantly improved my professional skills.

I am also indebted to Mr. V. Chandrasekar, former CIO of Standard Chartered Bank. He taught me the importance of valuing the lives, thoughts, and feelings of others in professional life. A truly wonderful and cheerful man, he gave me immense encouragement when he launched my first book, *Virtual Project Management Office*.

This project would not have been possible without the constant love and support of my family. My parents, Mr. Subramanian and Ms. Lalitha, have always been enthusiastic about this book and provided much-needed moral support. My children, Shri Krishna and Shri Siva Ranjani, consistently motivated me to work hard. Above all, I am eternally grateful to my wife, Ramya, whose unfailing support and encouragement were essential during the many long months I spent writing.

Finally, I sincerely apologize to anyone whose name I may have failed to mention. Your contributions have not gone unnoticed, and I am grateful for your presence in my life and career.

Chandramouli Subramanian

Contents

About the Author iii

Preface v

Acknowledgements vii

Chapter 1: Introduction to Artificial Intelligence 1

    1.1 What is Artificial Intelligence? 1
    1.2 Scope of AI 2
    1.3 Historical Evolution of AI 3
    1.4 Influential Figures and Institutions in AI History 7
    1.5 Differentiating Between AI and Human Intelligence 11
    1.6 Artificial General Intelligence and Industry Applications 14
    1.7 Key Milestones in AI Research 16
    1.8 Inter-disciplinary Problem Solving 20
    Summary 21
    Exercises 22
    Answers 24

Chapter 2: AI Subfields and Their Core Technologies 25

    2.1 Overview 25
    2.2 Knowledge Engineering 26
    2.3 AI Subfields 30
    Summary 49
    Exercises 50
    Answers 52

Chapter 3: Applications of AI 53

    3.1 Introduction   53

    3.2 Healthcare   54

    3.3 Finance   56

    3.4 Education   60

    3.5 Agriculture   62

    3.6 Transportation   65

    3.7 Customer Service and Retail   70

    Summary   73

    Exercises   73

    Answers   76

Chapter 4: Ethics, Bias, and Social Implications 77

    4.1 Introduction   77

    4.2 Bias in AI   78

    4.3 Fairness in AI Decision-making   84

    4.4 Transparency in AI Systems   87

    4.5 Accountability in AI   88

    4.6 Data Privacy and Security Concerns   91

    4.7 AI Employment and Workforce Transformation   94

    4.8 Inclusivity, Sustainability, and Reliability in AI Systems   96

    4.9 AI and Social Inequality   98

    Summary   101

    Exercises   101

    Answers   104

Chapter 5: Generative AI and Its Applications 105

    5.1 Introduction   106

    5.2 How It Works   106

    5.3 ChatGPT   113

    5.4 Gemini: Google's Multimodal Gen AI   121

    5.5 Hugging Face   131

    5.6 Perplexity   133

    5.7 Gen AI and Creativity   135

5.8 Gen AI-powered Slide Generation Tools   148
5.9 Gen AI in Research and Innovation   153
5.10 Gen AI in Education   155
5.11 Gen AI in Business   157
5.12 Gen AI in Healthcare   159
5.13 Gen AI in Entertainment   161
5.14 Future Trends in Generative AI   163
Summary   165
Exercises   165
Answers   167

Chapter 6: Prompt Engineering and Its Applications 169

6.1 Introduction   169
6.2 Definition and Importance of Prompt Engineering   169
6.3 Techniques for Effective Prompting   173
6.4 Role of Prompts in AI/ML Interaction   189
6.5 Challenges in Prompt Engineering   191
6.6 Future Scope in Human–AI Collaboration   194
6.7 Case Studies and Real-World Applications   197
6.8 Summarization and Simplification   200
6.9 Creative Content Generation   203
6.10 Storytelling and Fiction   206
6.11 Question-Answering and Chatbots: Customer Service   208
6.12 Student Help and Tutoring   209
6.13 Domain-specific Applications: Education   210
6.14 Domain-specific Applications: Healthcare   211
6.15 Domain-specific Applications: Business   213
Summary   214
Exercises   214
Answers   216

Chapter 7: Practical Session: Laboratory Work 217

7.1 Introduction   217
7.2 Creating Mind Maps with Canva   217
7.3 Exploring Napkin AI for Concept Mapping   219

7.4 Text Analysis Using NLP Tools   221
7.5 Building an Image Classifier   225
7.6 Simulating AI Chatbots in Education   227
7.7 ChatGPT for Text Generation   231
7.8 Hugging Face for Model Deployment   232
7.9 DALL·E for Image and Video Generation   233
7.10 Observing Bias in Generative Models   234
7.11 Practising Prompt Engineering   235
7.12 Creative Writing with Prompts   235
7.13 Content Generation Strategies   236
7.14 Using SlidesGPT for Slide Generation   237
7.15 Designing Digital Content with AI   238
7.16 Branding and Visual Identity with AI   239
Summary   241

Appendix: Model Question Papers 243

Index 255

CHAPTER 1

Introduction to Artificial Intelligence

Objectives

At the end of this chapter, you will be able to:

- Define AI and explain its scope and evolution
- List the influential figures and institutions in AI history
- Differentiate between AI and human intelligence
- Explain artificial general intelligence and its industry applications
- List the key milestones in AI research
- Elaborate on interdisciplinary problem solving

1.1 What is Artificial Intelligence?

"Artificial intelligence is not a substitute for human intelligence; it is a tool to amplify human creativity and ingenuity." This quote by Fei-Fei Li encapsulates the essence of AI, emphasising its role as a tool that enhances human capabilities rather than replacing them.

Learning, reasoning, problem-solving, perception, linguistic intelligence, and creative output are typically associated with the human mind. However, over the past decade, technological studies and analysis of the cognitive process and patterns of the human brain have led to the development of machines that can replicate these human abilities. This is where artificial intelligence (AI) comes into play. If you have ever interacted with a digital assistant or chatbot, used Apple's Siri, or Amazon or Netflix recommendations, you have experienced AI in action. These interactions, which are seemingly instantaneous and tailored to your preferences and needs, demonstrate the ability of AI to mimic human-like responses.

Artificial intelligence is a subdomain of computer science that focuses on the research and creation of intelligent software and systems. Like the human mind, these systems are designed to think, reason, and act intelligently. AI enables machines to learn from current and past data, adapt to varying situations, and perform tasks without explicit programming at every step. In essence, AI is about creating machines that can think and act like humans, a goal that has been driving AI research since its inception.

1.2 Scope of AI

The scope of AI has expanded dramatically over the past few decades, moving from theoretical research to practical applications across various industries. In healthcare, AI is used for diagnosing diseases, predicting patient outcomes, and personalizing treatment plans. In finance, it powers fraud detection systems, automates trading, and enhances customer service through chatbots. In manufacturing, AI-driven robots and predictive maintenance systems improve efficiency and reduce downtime.

AI also plays a crucial role in transportation, particularly in the development of autonomous vehicles. These systems rely on AI to interpret sensor data, make real-time decisions, and navigate complex environments. In education, AI is used to create personalized learning experiences, automate grading, and provide intelligent tutoring systems. The entertainment industry leverages AI for content recommendation, game development, and even scriptwriting.

The 2025 AI Index Report by Stanford HAI offers one of the most comprehensive views of AI's progress. It notes that 78% of organizations reported using AI in 2024, up from 55% the year before. U.S. private AI investment reached $109.1 billion, with generative AI attracting $33.9 billion globally.

Give below are some of the **benefits** of AI:

- **24/7 productivity:** Unlike humans, AI can remain productive without getting distracted, tired, sick, or bored, provided proper maintenance is carried out. It can also multitask and work efficiently without any breaks.
- **Avoids errors:** When correctly programmed and trained, AI can guarantee accurate and precise decisions and actions by sifting through massive data, which is impossible for the human mind.
- **Performs mundane tasks:** AI can perform repetitive tasks faster and accurately without getting tired, allowing the human workforce to focus on the more critical and strategic tasks at hand.
- **Human safety:** AI machines can survey or go to places dangerous to humans, such as ocean floors, space, war territories, and other hazardous locations.
- **Decision-making:** AI can make faster and unbiased decisions based on facts, as machines are not subject to human emotions or attitudes.
- **Saves time and money:** AI chatbots and virtual assistants can communicate with humans in a near human-like fashion. Intelligent systems are used in factories for assembly-line heavy lifting and precision work. Smart drones are used for security and many other applications, thus saving organizations time and money.
- **Easy adoption:** AI can be seamlessly integrated into our daily lives. For example, Microsoft Bing, Google Search, Siri, Alexa, GPS navigation systems, and cybersecurity are all regular aspects of most people's daily lives.

Statista indicates that the global AI market is expected to show an annual growth rate (CAGR 2024–2030) of 28.46%, resulting in a market volume of USD 826.70 billion by 2030. The AI market in India alone is expected to show an annual growth rate of 28.63%, hitting a market volume of USD 28.36 billion by 2030. However, we are still in the early stages and have not fully grasped the nuances of AI technology. Some of **today's concerns** are listed below:

- **Expensive:** AI machines/systems are costly to build, implement, and maintain. Attempting to mimic human cognitive ability requires advanced hardware, software, expertise, and time.
- **Foster negligence:** It is assumed, and true, that AI can be more efficient and precise than the human workforce. However, this could lead to carelessness under the assumption that AI is always doing a proper job.

- **Lack of creativity:** AI is a learning program. However, it can work only within the boundaries of its programming. Today, it cannot work unconventionally or address a problem from a different perspective.
- **Job displacement:** There is a general human fear that AI will take over the job market in specific sectors. Currently, virtual assistants and chatbots are replacing the customer service workforce and the workforce in some manufacturing and production industries.
- **Lack of ethics:** Moral principles, fairness, human value system, human consciousness, and many other ethical norms that make us human are practically impossible to program into a machine. The question is, if something goes wrong, who is morally responsible – the machines or the creators of the machine – and can it be controlled and contained?
- **Privacy concerns:** As AI systems operate on vast amounts of data, serious concerns exist about exposing or misusing personal and sensitive information stored in these systems.

Did You Know?

AI systems like Siri and Alexa use natural language processing (NLP) to understand and respond to human speech. NLP allows machines to interpret context, tone, and even intent—though they still struggle with sarcasm and idioms!

Mini Project/Assignment

Title: AI in Daily Life

Task: Identify and document 5 AI applications you interact with daily (e.g., recommendation systems, voice assistants). Explain how each uses AI and what human-like capabilities it mimics.

1.3 Historical Evolution of AI

1.3.1 The 1950s: The Dawn of AI

The 1950s marked a pivotal moment in history: the birth of AI. It was a time of pioneering work in computational statistics and machine learning. Alan Turing, the father of modern computer science, proposed the Turing Test in his paper *Computer Machinery and Intelligence*. In 1955, a proposal written for a Dartmouth research project by John McCarthy (Dartmouth College), M Minsky (Harvard University), N Rochester (IBM), and Shannon (Bell Telephone Laboratories) is where simulated machines were first referred to as 'artificial intelligence'. The Dartmouth conference that followed in 1956 is regarded as the launch event of AI.

1950	⇒	Alan Turing proposed the **Turing Test** to test if a machine can exhibit intelligent behaviour.
1952	⇒	Arthur Samuel (IBM) wrote the checkers-playing program, the first self-learning program that can play games.
1955	⇒	The term 'artificial intelligence' is used in a Dartmouth research project proposal.
1956	⇒	The Dartmouth Conference was held, where simulated machines were referred to as AI for the first time.
1957	⇒	Perceptron, a single-layer feedforward neural network was proposed by Frank Rosenblatt.

1958 ⇒ John McCarthy developed the first version of the popular AI programming language Lisp.

1959 ⇒ The term 'machine learning' was coined by Arthur Samuel for self-teaching computers.

1.3.2 The 1960s: A Leap in Natural Language Processing, Computer Vision, and Robotics

Unimate, a hydraulic manipulator arm, was designed and built by Devol and Engelberger using the programming language VAL. A combination of sensors and potentiometers provided feedback on the arms' position and a hydraulic system was used for lifting. Though Unimate was not an intelligent system, it is considered the first commercial programmable robot. On the other hand, the SHAKEY robot was a combination of robotics, natural language processing (NLP), and computer vision systems. DENDRAL, an AI project developed at Stanford University, was a machine learning (ML) system written in Lisp that automated the decision-making capabilities of organic chemists. The MIT computer scientist Joseph Weizenbaum designed and built ELIZA (named after the heroine of the film 'My Fair Lady'), an early natural language understanding program, between 1964 and 1966. ELIZA was the first chatterbot (modern-day chatbot) that passed the Turing Test.

1961 ⇒ Unimate, the first industrial robot, worked on the production line at the General Motors New Jersey plant.

1965 ⇒ DENDRAL, the first expert system for chemical analysis, was built by Feigenbaum and Lederberg (Stanford University).

1966 ⇒ ELIZA, the first chatbot, released by Joseph Weizenbaum, aimed to simulate the behaviour of a therapist.

1969 ⇒ SHAKEY, the first logical goal-based intelligent robot, was introduced to the world media.

1.3.3 The 1970s–1980s: A Lull in AI Research

The 1970s had its ups and downs in AI. Though the era started with progress in ML and automatons, it ended in a lull as researchers and developers grappled with the complexities and challenges of AI. The results were not fast or impactful enough for governments and organisations to release funding. Perhaps the only highlight in the 1970s was the WABOT-1 humanoid robot from Japan's Waseda University that could move, see, and talk in Japanese. The mid-1980s saw significant progress in neural network research.

1972 ⇒ MYCIN, a backward chaining expert system, was developed at Stanford to diagnose and treat certain blood diseases.

1972 ⇒ WABOT-1, the first android, was built in Japan at Waseda University.

1973 ⇒ The SUMEX-AIM network project, funded by the National Institutes of Health (NIH), was started to foster scientific collaboration on designing AI applications for the biomedical sciences.

1980 ⇒ XCON, an expert rule-based system, was developed for Digital Equipment Corporation (DEC) to automatically select computer system components based on client requirements. By 1986, it was said to have processed 80,000 orders and achieved over 95% accuracy.

1986 ⇒ DXplain, a decision support expert system with data on around 500 diseases, was released to assist clinical diagnosis.

1986 ⇒ The backpropagation algorithm to train a multi-layer neural network was developed by Dr Hinton and colleagues

1.3.4 The 1990s–2000s: Supercomputers, Data Science, and Hibernation Stages

There was not much visible growth in AI in the early 1990s. However, development was taking place in stages, and in late 1990, it got a slight public boost when IBM's Deep Blue defeated Chess world champion Gary Kasparov. From the late 1990s to the early 2000s, the focus was more on Y2K than AI. IBM's DeepQA project, which led to IBM Watson, commenced in the late 2000s.

1995 ⇒ The adaptive boosting statistical classification algorithm (AdaBoost) that can build strong ML models was framed by Y Freund and R Schapire.

1997 ⇒ Deep Blue, IBM's supercomputer, defeated Grandmaster Gary Kasparov at chess.

1999 ⇒ The annual international robotics competition RoboCup was founded to promote AI and robotics research.
Sony introduced AIBO (**a**rtificial **i**ntelligence ro**bot**), an AI dog pet that responded to 100+ voice commands.

2000 ⇒ ASIMO (**a**dvanced **s**tep in **i**nnovative **mo**bility), an AI humanoid robot, was developed by Honda

2002 ⇒ Roomba, the autonomous vacuum cleaner robot, was released by the iRobot company.

⇒ NASA's Mars Exploration Rover successfully landed on Mars and navigated two AI rovers, MER-A and MER-B.

2008 ⇒ Nao Robot, an interactive robot from SoftBank Robotics, was released to institutions for teaching, training, and learning purposes.

1.3.5 The 2010s: The Decade of AI Innovation

The 2010s saw big data, advanced computing, ML and deep learning gain popularity. Advances in deep learning with convoluted and recurrent neural networks generated AVAs (AI-powered virtual assistants) that self-learn and tailor their responses to the user's preferences over time. Conversation AI like Siri, Alexa, and other AI-powered personal assistants made AI technology accessible to the masses.

2010 ⇒ Google DeepMind, an AI research laboratory, was founded.

⇒ CAD (computer-aided diagnostics) with AI for endoscopy was implemented in clinical practice.

2011 ⇒ Siri, Apple's virtual voice assistant, was released with the iPhone 4s.

⇒ IBM Watson, the natural language question-answering computer, won the game show *Jeopardy!*.

2014	⇒	Cortana, a virtual voice assistant from Microsoft, was released.
	⇒	Alexa, a virtual voice assistant from Amazon that functions as a personal assistant, was released.
2016	⇒	Google Home, a smart speaker that works as a home assistant for reminders, appointments, information search, and various other voice support functions, was released.
	⇒	Sophia, the first humanoid robot with human facial features and expressions, was introduced. Created by Hanson Robotics, Sophia used a combination of computer vision, speech recognition, and other AI technologies to respond to and navigate surroundings.
2017	⇒	Arterys was the first FDA-approved cloud-based deep-learning medical imaging platform. It aimed to help doctors better diagnose patients.
2017	⇒	AlphaGo, an ML and neural network model-based board-game learning program developed by DeepMind, defeated the World Champion of the board game Go.

AI development underwent several paradigm shifts, each redefining the goals and methodologies of the field. The transition from symbolic AI to ML represented a move from knowledge-based systems to data-driven approaches. This shift was driven by the realization that encoding all human knowledge into rules was impractical and that learning from data could yield more flexible and scalable solutions.

Another significant shift was the move from shallow learning algorithms to deep learning architectures. Deep learning models, such as convolutional neural networks (CNNs) and recurrent neural networks (RNNs), enabled breakthroughs in computer vision and NLP. These models could automatically extract features from raw data, reducing the need for manual feature engineering.

The integration of reinforcement learning (RL) introduced a new dimension to AI, allowing systems to learn optimal behaviours through trial and error. This approach was particularly successful in robotics and game playing, where agents learn to navigate environments and achieve goals through feedback mechanisms.

More recently, the emergence of generative models, such as generative adversarial networks (GANs) and transformer-based architectures like GPT, opened new avenues for AI creativity. These models can generate realistic images, text, and even music, pushing the boundaries of what machines can create.

1.3.6 The 2020s: The Future of AI

This decade saw the launch of the GPT-3 tool for automated conversational engagement. ChatGPT, based on the foundational models of GPT-3.5 and GPT-4, revolutionised the field of Chatbots. It was made available to the public for testing in 2022, which renewed interest in the potential of AI.

Today, AI plays a vital role in all essential fields, such as technology, healthcare, education, transport, manufacturing, and many others. With ever-growing AI research and technology advancements, we are in a transformative era where machines can multitask seamlessly. Research on AGI (artificial general intelligence) may soon lead to engaging conversational and multifunctional robots that can mimic human traits with human emotions, cognition, reasoning and many more. There could be a large-scale introduction of self-driving vehicles for public transport, safe machine-led surgical procedures, AI-based surveillance, fraud detection, etc.

However, all these potential AI-driven changes require data privacy laws and ethical and responsibility considerations. UNESCO produced the first-ever global standard on AI ethics in November 2021 with its Recommendation on the Ethics of Artificial Intelligence. All 193 member states adopted the agenda. The European Parliament adopted the AI Act in March 2024; it is considered the world's first comprehensive legal framework for AI. It provides for EU-wide rules on data quality, transparency, human oversight, and accountability. Once AI is developed responsibly and ethically for society, we can safely realise its full potential.

> **Did You Know?**
> The first AI program, Logic Theorist, created in 1956, could prove mathematical theorems and is considered the first software to mimic human reasoning.

> **Mini Project/Assignment**
> *Title*: AI Timeline Poster
>
> *Task*: Create a visual timeline of key AI milestones from the 1950s to 2020s. Include dates, technologies, and contributors.

1.4 Influential Figures and Institutions in AI History

Year	Contributor	Contribution
1956	John McCarthy	Organized the Dartmouth Conference, marking the birth of AI as a research discipline.
1956	Allen Newell	Developed the Logic Theorist, the first AI program demonstrating machine-based logical deduction.
1958	John McCarthy	Invented the Lisp programming language, facilitating symbolic computation for AI applications.
1950s–1960s	Marvin Minsky	Contributed to symbolic reasoning and early neural networks; co-founded the MIT AI Laboratory.
1960s	Allen Newell	Developed the General Problem Solver (GPS), modelling human problem-solving strategies using heuristics.
1970s–1980s	Marvin Minsky	Proposed the Society of Mind theory, modelling intelligence as cooperation among simple agents.
1980s	Allen Newell	Developed the SOAR cognitive architecture to simulate general intelligence through integrated learning and reasoning.
Various	John McCarthy	Developed the concept of circumscription for reasoning with incomplete information in AI systems.
Various	Marvin Minsky	Advanced robotics and philosophical discourse on AI, promoting ethical considerations and public engagement.
Various	Allen Newell	Advocated interdisciplinary collaboration and rigorous methodology in AI research, bridging AI and cognitive science.

John McCarthy's work laid the intellectual and technical groundwork for the discipline, influencing generations of researchers and shaping the trajectory of AI development. McCarthy's vision extended far beyond the mechanics of computation; he imagined machines that could reason, learn, and interact with humans in meaningful ways. His contributions to AI were thus foundational and transformative, earning him the title of the 'father of AI'.

His pioneering efforts in formal logic, programming languages, and theoretical frameworks continue to resonate in contemporary AI research. One of McCarthy's most enduring legacies is the invention of the Lisp programming language in 1958. Lisp, short for List Processing, was designed to facilitate symbolic computation, which is essential for AI applications that involve reasoning and decision-making. Unlike other programming languages of its time, Lisp allowed for the manipulation of symbols rather than just numbers, making it particularly suited for tasks such as NLP and problem-solving. Its flexible syntax and powerful features, such as recursion and dynamic typing, made it a Favourite among AI researchers and contributed to the development of early expert systems. Even today, Lisp remains influential in AI and computer science education.

Beyond programming, McCarthy was deeply invested in the philosophical and logical foundations of AI. He was among the first to propose that machines could exhibit intelligent behaviour if they were equipped with the right formal structures. His work in formal logic led to the development of the concept of circumscription, a method for dealing with incomplete information in logical reasoning. Circumscription allows AI systems to make assumptions about the world in the absence of complete data, a capability that is crucial for real-world decision-making. This approach helped bridge the gap between theoretical logic and practical AI applications, enabling machines to operate in uncertain environments.

McCarthy also played a pivotal role in institutionalizing AI as a formal field of study. In 1956, he organized the Dartmouth Conference, which is widely regarded as the birth of artificial intelligence as a research discipline. The conference brought together leading thinkers, including Marvin Minsky, Claude Shannon, and Allen Newell, to explore the possibility of creating machines that could simulate human intelligence. McCarthy's proposal for the conference outlined a vision of AI that was both ambitious and methodical, emphasizing the need for a collaborative and interdisciplinary approach. The ideas generated at Dartmouth set the stage for decades of research and innovation.

Throughout his career, McCarthy remained committed to the idea that intelligence could be precisely defined and replicated in machines. He advocated for a formal, mathematical approach to AI, believing that rigorous logic was the key to understanding and modelling intelligent behaviour. This perspective influenced the development of symbolic AI, which dominated the field for many years before the rise of statistical and data-driven methods. McCarthy's insistence on clarity and precision helped establish AI as a legitimate scientific discipline, distinct from speculative or philosophical inquiry.

Marvin Minsky was one of the most influential figures in the early development of AI, and his contributions helped shape the theoretical and practical foundations of the field. As a co-founder of the MIT Artificial Intelligence Laboratory, Minsky played a central role in establishing AI as a legitimate scientific discipline. His work spanned multiple domains, including cognitive psychology, computer science, robotics, and philosophy, reflecting his belief that understanding intelligence required a multidisciplinary approach.

One of Minsky's most significant contributions was his work on symbolic reasoning and the architecture of intelligent systems. He believed that human intelligence could be replicated by machines through the manipulation of symbols and logical rules. This idea formed the basis of symbolic AI, which dominated early research in the field.

Minsky's theories suggested that the mind could be understood as a collection of interacting processes, each responsible for different aspects of thought. This perspective led to the development of the Society of Mind theory, which proposed that intelligence emerges from the co-operation of many simple agents, each performing a specific function. The theory was groundbreaking because it offered a framework for modelling complex mental processes without relying on a single, unified mechanism.

In addition to his theoretical work, Minsky was deeply involved in the practical development of AI technologies. He contributed to the creation of early neural networks and was among the first to explore how machines could learn from experience. Although he was initially skeptical of connectionist models, which later became central to deep learning, his early experiments laid the groundwork for future research in ML.

Minsky also worked on robotics, developing mechanical systems that could interact with their environment and perform tasks that required a degree of autonomy. His efforts in this area helped bridge the gap between abstract reasoning and physical action, a challenge that remains central to AI today. Minsky's influence extended beyond the laboratory.

He was a passionate advocate for AI and frequently engaged with the public and academic communities to promote understanding of the field. He wrote extensively on the philosophical implications of AI, questioning what it means to be conscious, to learn, and to make decisions. His writings encouraged researchers to think critically about the goals and limitations of AI, emphasizing the importance of ethical considerations and long-term consequences.

Minsky's intellectual curiosity and willingness to challenge conventional thinking inspired a generation of scientists and thinkers. Throughout his career, Marvin Minsky remained committed to the idea that machines could one day match or even surpass human intelligence. While some of his predictions were optimistic, his work laid the foundation for many of the advances that have since become reality. His legacy is evident in the continued exploration of cognitive architectures, the development of intelligent agents, and the philosophical debates that surround AI.

Allen Newell was a pivotal figure in the early development of AI, whose interdisciplinary approach and groundbreaking research helped define the contours of the field. His work, often conducted in collaboration with Herbert A Simon, laid the foundation for cognitive architectures and the study of human problem-solving through computational models.

Newell's contributions were not confined to theoretical speculation; they were deeply rooted in empirical research and practical experimentation, which made his insights both influential and enduring. One of Newell's most significant achievements was the development of the Logic Theorist in 1956, widely considered the first AI program. This program was designed to mimic human reasoning by proving mathematical theorems from *Principia Mathematica*, a foundational text in logic. The Logic Theorist was revolutionary because it demonstrated that machines could perform tasks traditionally associated with human intelligence, such as logical deduction. This success marked a turning point in AI research, showing that symbolic reasoning could be encoded into computer programs and used to solve complex problems.

Building on this foundation, Newell and Simon developed the General Problem Solver (GPS), a program that aimed to model human problem-solving strategies. GPS was designed to separate the knowledge required to solve a problem from the strategies used to apply that knowledge, a concept that would later influence the development of expert systems. The program used heuristics—rules of thumb that guide decision-making—to navigate problem spaces, reflecting how humans often approach challenges. GPS was not only a technical achievement but also a conceptual breakthrough, as it introduced the idea that cognitive processes could be understood and replicated through computational means.

Newell's work extended beyond individual programs to the broader question of how intelligence could be systematically studied. He was a strong advocate for the use of computers as tools for cognitive psychology, arguing that the mind could be modelled as an information-processing system. This perspective led to the development of cognitive architectures, which are theoretical frameworks that describe the structure and function of the mind.

Newell's own architecture, known as SOAR, was designed to simulate general intelligence by integrating learning, reasoning, and decision-making into a unified system. SOAR became a cornerstone of cognitive modelling and influenced both AI research and psychological theory.

In addition to his technical contributions, Newell played a crucial role in shaping the academic and institutional landscape of AI. He was instrumental in establishing AI as a legitimate field of study, advocating for interdisciplinary collaboration between computer science, psychology, and philosophy. His work helped bridge the gap between symbolic AI and cognitive science, fostering a more holistic understanding of intelligence.

The advancement of AI has been significantly shaped by the pioneering work of academic institutions such as the Massachusetts Institute of Technology (MIT), Stanford University, and Carnegie Mellon University. These universities have not only contributed to the theoretical foundations of AI but have also driven practical innovations in robotics, ML, and human–computer interaction. Their research has laid the groundwork for many of the technologies that are now integral to modern computing and intelligent systems.

MIT has long been recognized as a leader in AI research, particularly through its Computer Science and Artificial Intelligence Laboratory (CSAIL). The institution has fostered a culture of interdisciplinary collaboration, bringing together experts in computer science, cognitive science, and engineering to explore the nature of intelligence. MIT researchers have made significant strides in robotics, developing machines capable of navigating complex environments and performing tasks with increasing autonomy. Their work in ML has also been influential, contributing to the development of algorithms that enable computers to learn from data and improve over time.

Stanford University has played a similarly vital role in the evolution of AI. Its AI Laboratory, established in the 1960s, became a hub for groundbreaking research in symbolic reasoning and knowledge representation. Stanford was instrumental in the development of expert systems—computer programs designed to emulate the decision-making abilities of human specialists. These systems were among the first practical applications of AI, used in fields ranging from medicine to engineering. Stanford's contributions to neural networks and deep learning have also been substantial, helping to refine models that mimic the structure and function of the human brain.

Carnegie Mellon University (CMU) stands out for its comprehensive approach to AI, integrating research across computer science, robotics, and cognitive psychology. CMU has been a pioneer in human–computer interaction, exploring how intelligent systems can communicate effectively with users. The university's Robotics Institute has produced numerous innovations, including autonomous vehicles and intelligent agents capable of complex decision-making. CMU researchers have also played a key role in advancing neural network architectures, contributing to the resurgence of deep learning in recent years.

The collective efforts of these institutions have not only advanced the technical capabilities of AI but have also influenced its ethical and societal dimensions.

In recent years, the landscape of AI has been dramatically reshaped by the efforts of leading technology companies such as Google, IBM, Microsoft, and OpenAI. These organizations have not only accelerated the pace of innovation but have also expanded the practical applications of AI across industries and everyday life.

Google's DeepMind division has been at the forefront of AI breakthroughs, most notably with the development of AlphaGo. This AI system made headlines in 2016 when it defeated Lee Sedol, a world champion in the ancient board game of Go. The significance of this achievement extended far beyond the game itself. Go is known for its complexity and the vast number of possible moves, making it a challenge for traditional rule-based AI systems. AlphaGo's success was powered by deep reinforcement learning and neural networks, demonstrating that AI could master tasks requiring intuition and strategic thinking. This milestone marked a turning point in AI research, showing that machines could learn and adapt in ways previously thought to be uniquely human.

IBM has played a crucial role in advancing AI, particularly through its Watson platform. Watson gained international attention in 2011 when it competed on the television quiz show *Jeopardy!* and defeated two of the game's greatest champions. This victory showcased Watson's ability to understand natural language, retrieve relevant information, and make decisions based on context. Beyond entertainment, Watson has been applied in healthcare, finance, and customer service, where its capabilities in data analysis and decision support have proven invaluable.

OpenAI has emerged as a transformative force in the realm of NLP. Its generative pre-trained transformer (GPT) models have revolutionized how machines understand and generate human language. These models are trained on vast data sets and can produce coherent, contextually relevant text across a wide range of topics. The release of GPT-3 and its successors demonstrated that AI could engage in conversations, write essays, translate languages, and even generate code with remarkable fluency. OpenAI's work has not only advanced the technical capabilities of language models but has also sparked important discussions about the ethical use of AI, including concerns about misinformation, bias, and the responsible deployment of powerful generative tools.

Microsoft, while collaborating with OpenAI, has integrated advanced AI capabilities into its products and services, making intelligent tools accessible to a broad user base. From enhancing productivity in Office applications to improving search and recommendation systems, Microsoft has focused on embedding AI into everyday workflows. Its Azure cloud platform also provides infrastructure for AI development, enabling businesses and researchers to build and scale intelligent applications efficiently.

Together, these companies have not only pushed the boundaries of what AI can do but have also influenced how society interacts with and perceives intelligent systems. Their innovations have led to practical tools that assist in decision-making, automate routine tasks, and enhance human creativity. At the same time, their work has prompted deeper reflection on the ethical, social, and philosophical implications of AI. As these technologies continue to evolve, the role of these organizations will remain central in shaping a future where AI is both powerful and responsibly managed.

Did You Know?

Lisp, invented by John McCarthy in 1958, is still used in AI research today due to its powerful symbolic processing capabilities.

Mini Project/Assignment

Title: AI Innovators Report

Task: Choose one AI pioneer (McCarthy, Minsky, or Newell) and write a short report on their contributions and impact on AI.

1.5 Differentiating Between AI and Human Intelligence

The distinction between AI and human intelligence has become increasingly significant in the modern era, where machines are not only performing tasks traditionally reserved for humans but are also beginning to exhibit behaviours that mimic cognitive functions. While both forms of intelligence aim to solve problems, learn from experiences, and adapt to new information, their underlying mechanisms, capabilities, limitations, and implications are fundamentally different. Understanding these differences is essential for evaluating the role of AI in society, its ethical boundaries, and its potential to complement or challenge human cognition.

1.5.1 Cognitive Capabilities

AI and human intelligence differ fundamentally in how they process information, learn, and adapt to new situations. Human cognition is rooted in biological processes, involving neurons, synapses, and biochemical reactions that allow for perception, reasoning, and decision-making. In contrast, AI systems rely on mathematical models and algorithms to simulate aspects of human cognition. While AI can process vast amounts of data at incredible speeds, it lacks the nuanced understanding and contextual awareness that humans possess.

For example, humans can interpret ambiguous language, understand sarcasm, and draw inferences based on cultural or emotional cues. AI, even with advanced NLP models, often struggles with these subtleties. A human might understand the phrase 'break a leg' as a theatrical good luck wish, whereas an AI system might interpret it literally unless specifically trained on idiomatic expressions.

Moreover, human cognition is inherently flexible. People can learn new skills, adapt to unfamiliar environments, and apply knowledge creatively across domains. AI systems, on the other hand, are typically designed for narrow tasks. An ML model trained to recognize faces cannot automatically learn to play chess unless it is retrained with a different data set and algorithm. This limitation underscores the difference between general intelligence in humans and the task-specific nature of most AI systems.

1.5.2 Emotional and Social Intelligence

One of the most profound distinctions between AI and human intelligence lies in emotional and social capabilities. Humans possess emotional intelligence, which includes the ability to recognize, understand, and manage emotions—both their own and those of others. This skill is essential for empathy, interpersonal relationships, and effective communication. AI, however, does not experience emotions and can only simulate emotional responses based on programmed rules or learned patterns.

Social intelligence involves understanding social norms, interpreting body language, and engaging in culturally appropriate behaviour. Humans develop these skills through lived experiences and social interactions. AI systems, while capable of analyzing facial expressions or speech tones, do not truly comprehend the emotional states they detect. For instance, a customer service chatbot might recognize frustration in a user's tone and respond with a calming message, but it does not feel concern or empathy—it merely follows a programmed response pattern.

Attempts to imbue AI with emotional intelligence have led to the development of affective computing, which aims to create systems that can detect and respond to human emotions. However, these systems are limited by the quality of their training data and the complexity of human emotional expression. They may misinterpret signals or fail to respond appropriately in nuanced situations, highlighting the gap between simulated and genuine emotional understanding.

1.5.3 Learning and Adaptability

Humans learn through a combination of experience, observation, and instruction. This learning is continuous, context-sensitive, and often involves abstract reasoning. People can generalize from past experiences, apply knowledge creatively, and adapt to new challenges with minimal guidance. AI systems, in contrast, learn from data through structured training processes. ML models require large data sets, labelled examples, and iterative optimization to improve performance.

Adaptability in humans is also influenced by motivation, curiosity, and the ability to reflect on past actions. These traits enable individuals to learn from mistakes, seek out new information, and adjust their behaviour in dynamic environments. AI systems lack intrinsic motivation and cannot initiate learning independently. They depend on external inputs and predefined objectives to guide their learning processes.

For example, a human learning to drive a car can adjust to different road conditions, traffic patterns, and vehicle types with relative ease. An AI-powered autonomous vehicle must be explicitly trained on each scenario and may struggle with unexpected events, such as a pedestrian jaywalking or a sudden road closure. This difference in adaptability underscores the limitations of current AI systems in handling real-world complexity.

1.5.4 Creativity and Intuition

Creativity and intuition are hallmarks of human intelligence that remain elusive for AI. Creativity involves generating novel ideas, solving problems in innovative ways, and expressing oneself through art, music, or literature. Intuition refers to the ability to make judgments without explicit reasoning, often based on subconscious processing of past experiences. These capabilities are deeply rooted in human consciousness and emotional depth.

AI can mimic certain aspects of creativity through generative models, such as those used to create artwork, compose music, or write text. However, these outputs are based on patterns learned from existing data and lack the originality and emotional resonance of human creations. For instance, an AI-generated painting may resemble the style of Van Gogh, but it does not convey the personal experiences or emotional intent that inspired the original works.

Intuition in humans allows for rapid decision-making in complex situations, often without complete information. A doctor might diagnose a rare condition based on subtle symptoms and years of experience, even if the textbook criteria are not fully met. AI systems, by contrast, rely on statistical correlations and may miss rare or atypical cases unless specifically trained to recognize them.

The limitations of AI in creativity and intuition highlight the importance of human oversight in fields that require innovation, empathy, and nuanced judgment. While AI can assist in generating ideas or analyzing data, it cannot replace the human capacity for original thought and intuitive insight.

1.5.5 Ethical and Moral Reasoning

Ethical and moral reasoning is another domain where human intelligence surpasses AI. Humans make decisions based on values, principles, and social norms, often considering the broader impact of their actions on others. This reasoning is influenced by culture, upbringing, and personal beliefs, making it complex and context-dependent. AI systems, however, do not possess moral awareness and can only follow ethical guidelines encoded by developers.

For example, in autonomous vehicles, ethical dilemmas arise when deciding how to respond in accident scenarios. Should the car prioritize the safety of its passengers or pedestrians? These decisions require moral judgment that AI cannot inherently make. Developers must program decision-making frameworks, such as utilitarian or deontological models, but these approaches may not align with societal expectations or individual values.

Moreover, AI systems can inadvertently perpetuate biases present in training data, leading to unfair or discriminatory outcomes. A hiring algorithm trained on historical data may favour certain demographics, reflecting past biases rather than objective merit. Addressing these issues requires human intervention to audit, correct, and guide AI behaviour in ethically responsible ways.

The challenge of embedding ethical reasoning into AI underscores the need for interdisciplinary collaboration, involving ethicists, sociologists, and technologists. It also highlights the importance of transparency, accountability, and public engagement in the development and deployment of AI systems.

> **Did You Know?**
> AI can simulate emotions using affective computing, but it does not actually 'feel' anything—it just mimics patterns based on data.

> **Mini Project/Assignment**
>
> *Title*: AI versus Human Intelligence Debate
>
> *Task*: Prepare arguments for a classroom debate comparing AI and human intelligence across five dimensions: learning, emotion, creativity, adaptability, and ethics.

1.6 Artificial General Intelligence and Industry Applications

Artificial general intelligence (AGI) refers to a type of AI that possesses the ability to understand, learn, and apply knowledge across a wide range of tasks at a level comparable to human intelligence. Unlike narrow AI, which is designed for specific tasks such as image recognition or language translation, AGI aims to replicate the broad cognitive abilities of humans. This includes reasoning, problem-solving, abstract thinking, and the capacity to transfer learning from one domain to another.

The concept of AGI has long been a goal in the field of AI, representing the pinnacle of machine cognition. AGI systems would not only perform tasks they were explicitly trained for but also adapt to new challenges without requiring retraining. For example, an AGI system capable of diagnosing medical conditions could also learn to manage financial portfolios or compose music, simply by acquiring relevant knowledge and applying general reasoning skills.

Despite its promise, AGI remains largely theoretical. Current AI systems, even the most advanced ones, operate within constrained environments and lack the flexibility and contextual awareness of human intelligence. The development of AGI involves overcoming significant challenges, including the integration of diverse cognitive functions, the creation of robust learning mechanisms, and the establishment of ethical frameworks to guide its behaviour.

1.6.1 AGI versus Narrow AI

The distinction between AGI and narrow AI is fundamental to understanding the current landscape of AI. Narrow AI, also known as weak AI, is designed to perform specific tasks with high efficiency. Examples include recommendation algorithms on streaming platforms, facial recognition systems, and virtual assistants like Siri and Alexa. These systems excel in their designated functions but cannot operate outside their programmed domains.

AGI, in contrast, would possess the ability to perform any intellectual task that a human can do. It would not be limited by predefined parameters and could generalize knowledge across different contexts. For instance, while a narrow AI model trained to play chess cannot play Go without retraining, an AGI system would be able to learn both games and apply strategic thinking across them.

The development of AGI requires a paradigm shift in AI research. It involves creating systems that can understand and manipulate abstract concepts, reason through complex problems, and exhibit common sense. This level of intelligence demands advances in cognitive architectures, memory systems, and learning algorithms that go beyond pattern recognition and statistical inference.

1.6.2 AGI in Healthcare

The potential applications of AGI in healthcare are transformative. An AGI system could serve as a universal medical assistant, capable of diagnosing diseases, recommending treatments, and monitoring patient progress across a wide range of conditions. Unlike current AI tools that specialize in specific tasks, AGI could integrate data from various sources—such as medical records, genetic information, and real-time sensor data—to provide holistic care.

For example, an AGI system could analyze a patient's symptoms, cross-reference them with global medical databases, and suggest personalized treatment plans. It could also predict potential complications, recommend lifestyle changes, and coordinate with healthcare providers to ensure continuity of care. In emergency situations, AGI could assist in triage, resource allocation, and decision-making, potentially saving lives.

A real-world case study illustrating the promise of AGI in healthcare is IBM's Watson. Although not a true AGI, Watson demonstrated the ability to analyze vast amounts of medical literature and assist in cancer diagnosis. It highlighted the importance of integrating AI into clinical workflows and the potential for intelligent systems to augment human expertise. The evolution from systems like Watson to AGI would involve expanding capabilities, improving contextual understanding, and ensuring ethical decision-making.

1.6.3 AGI in Finance and Banking

In the finance and banking sector, AGI could revolutionize operations by providing intelligent analysis, risk assessment, and strategic planning. An AGI system could monitor global economic trends, evaluate investment opportunities, and manage portfolios with a level of insight comparable to human financial experts. It could also detect fraudulent activities, optimize trading strategies, and personalize financial advice for individual clients.

For instance, AGI could analyze market data, news reports, and social media sentiment to predict stock movements and advise investors accordingly. It could also assess creditworthiness by evaluating a wide range of factors, including spending behaviour, employment history, and macroeconomic indicators. In customer service, AGI could handle complex queries, resolve disputes, and provide tailored financial solutions.

A notable example of AI in finance is JPMorgan Chase's COiN platform, which uses ML to analyze legal documents and extract relevant information. While COiN is a narrow AI application, it demonstrates the potential for intelligent systems to streamline operations and reduce costs. The transition to AGI would involve creating systems that can understand financial regulations, adapt to changing markets, and make decisions with ethical and strategic considerations.

1.6.4 AGI in Manufacturing and Automation

AGI has the potential to transform manufacturing and automation by enabling intelligent decision-making, adaptive control, and predictive maintenance. In a smart factory, AGI could oversee production processes, optimize resource allocation, and respond to dynamic conditions in real time. It could also coordinate with supply chains, manage inventory, and ensure quality control across diverse product lines.

For example, an AGI system could detect anomalies in machinery performance, predict failures, and schedule maintenance before breakdowns occur. It could also analyze production data to identify inefficiencies and recommend improvements. In robotics, AGI could enable machines to learn new tasks, collaborate with human workers, and adapt to changing environments without reprogramming.

A case study highlighting the role of AI in manufacturing is Siemens' use of AI for predictive maintenance and process optimization. While current systems rely on predefined models and sensor data, AGI would enhance these capabilities by integrating contextual knowledge, learning from experience, and making autonomous decisions. This would lead to more resilient, efficient, and intelligent manufacturing ecosystems.

1.6.5 AGI in Education and Research

In education, AGI could serve as a universal tutor, capable of adapting to individual learning styles, providing personalized instruction, and assessing student progress. It could create customized curricula, offer real-time feedback, and support lifelong learning across disciplines. AGI could also assist educators by automating administrative tasks, analyzing classroom dynamics, and identifying areas for pedagogical improvement.

For example, an AGI system could help a student struggling with mathematics by identifying specific misconceptions, providing targeted exercises, and adjusting teaching strategies based on performance. It could also facilitate collaborative learning by connecting students with similar interests and complementary skills. In higher education, AGI could support research by analyzing literature, generating hypotheses, and designing experiments.

A real-world example of AI in education is Carnegie Learning's intelligent tutoring systems, which use ML to personalize instruction. While these systems are limited in scope, they demonstrate the potential for AI to enhance educational outcomes. AGI would expand these capabilities by integrating knowledge across subjects, understanding complex student needs, and fostering creativity and critical thinking.

1.6.6 Challenges and Risks of AGI Deployment

Despite its potential, the deployment of AGI poses significant challenges and risks. One of the primary concerns is safety—ensuring that AGI systems behave in ways that align with human values and do not cause unintended harm. This requires robust alignment mechanisms, transparency in decision-making, and fail-safe protocols to prevent misuse or malfunction.

Another challenge is ethical governance. AGI systems could make decisions that affect individuals and societies, raising questions about accountability, fairness, and consent. For example, if an AGI system denies a loan application based on complex reasoning, how can the decision be explained and justified? Ensuring ethical behaviour in AGI requires interdisciplinary collaboration and the development of regulatory frameworks.

There is also the risk of economic disruption. AGI could automate a wide range of jobs, leading to displacement and inequality. While it could create new opportunities, the transition may be challenging for workers and industries. Addressing these risks involves proactive planning, education, and policies that support inclusive growth.

Finally, the existential risk of AGI—where systems become uncontrollable or pursue goals misaligned with human interests—has been a topic of debate among researchers. Ensuring that AGI remains beneficial requires careful design, ongoing oversight, and international cooperation.

> **Did You Know?**
> IBM's Watson, though not AGI, once analyzed thousands of medical papers to assist in cancer diagnosis—showing how AI can augment human expertise.

> **Mini Project/Assignment**
> *Title*: AGI Use Case Design
>
> *Task*: Design a hypothetical AGI system for one industry (e.g., education or healthcare). Describe its capabilities, benefits, and ethical considerations.

1.7 Key Milestones in AI Research

AI has evolved from a theoretical concept into a transformative force across industries, reshaping how humans interact with machines and how machines perceive the world. The journey of AI research is marked by a series of key milestones, each representing a leap in understanding, capability, or application. These milestones not only reflect technological progress but also the shifting paradigms in computer science, cognitive psychology, and neuroscience.

1.7.1 Early Foundations and Symbolic AI

The origins of AI research can be traced back to the mid-20th century, when scientists began exploring the possibility of replicating human thought processes using machines. The earliest efforts focused on symbolic AI, also known as 'Good Old-Fashioned AI' (GOFAI), which relied on formal logic and rule-based systems to simulate reasoning. This approach was grounded in the belief that intelligence could be represented through symbols and manipulated using logical operations.

One of the foundational milestones in symbolic AI was the development of the Logic Theorist by Allen Newell and Herbert A Simon in 1956. This program was capable of proving mathematical theorems from *Principia Mathematica* and demonstrated that machines could perform tasks traditionally reserved for human intellect. Around the same time, John McCarthy organized the Dartmouth Conference, which formally introduced the term 'artificial intelligence' and set the stage for future research.

Symbolic AI systems were built using expert knowledge encoded into rules and ontologies. These systems excelled in domains where knowledge could be clearly defined, such as medical diagnosis or legal reasoning. However, they struggled with ambiguity, uncertainty, and the vast variability of real-world data. The limitations of symbolic AI became apparent as researchers attempted to scale these systems to more complex tasks, leading to a shift in focus toward data-driven approaches.

Despite its constraints, symbolic AI laid the groundwork for many concepts that continue to influence modern AI, including knowledge representation, inference engines, and semantic networks. It also inspired the development of programming languages such as Lisp and Prolog, which were specifically designed for AI applications. The legacy of symbolic AI remains evident in hybrid systems that combine rule-based reasoning with ML techniques.

1.7.2 Rise of Machine Learning and Neural Networks

The limitations of symbolic AI prompted researchers to explore alternative approaches that could learn from data rather than rely solely on predefined rules. This led to the emergence of machine learning, a paradigm that enables systems to improve their performance through experience. ML algorithms use statistical methods to identify patterns in data and make predictions or decisions based on those patterns.

One of the earliest breakthroughs in ML was the development of the perceptron by Frank Rosenblatt in 1958. The perceptron was a simple neural network model capable of binary classification and it demonstrated the potential of learning algorithms. However, its limitations in handling non-linearly separable data led to scepticism and a temporary decline in neural network research.

The resurgence of interest in neural networks came in the 1980s with the introduction of backpropagation, an algorithm that allowed multi-layer networks to learn complex mappings. Researchers such as Geoffrey Hinton played a pivotal role in advancing neural network architectures and demonstrating their effectiveness in tasks such as speech recognition and image classification.

ML continued to evolve with the development of algorithms like decision trees, support vector machines, and ensemble methods. These techniques enabled AI systems to handle diverse data types and achieve high accuracy in various applications. The rise of big data and increased computational power further accelerated the adoption of ML across industries.

Neural networks, in particular, became the foundation for deep learning (DL), a subset of ML that uses multiple layers to model hierarchical representations of data. Deep learning has revolutionized fields such as computer vision, natural language processing, and autonomous systems, making it one of the most significant milestones in AI research.

1.7.3 Breakthroughs in Deep Learning

Deep learning represents a transformative milestone in AI research, enabling machines to achieve human-level performance in tasks that were previously considered intractable. The success of deep learning is largely attributed to the development of sophisticated neural network architectures, the availability of large data sets, and advances in hardware such as GPUs.

One of the landmark achievements in deep learning was the victory of AlexNet in the 2012 ImageNet competition. AlexNet, a convolutional neural network (CNN) developed by Alex Krizhevsky, Ilya Sutskever, and Geoffrey Hinton, significantly outperformed traditional methods in image classification. This breakthrough demonstrated the power of deep learning in extracting features from raw data and sparked widespread interest in neural networks.

Subsequent innovations in deep learning included the development of recurrent neural networks (RNNs) for sequential data, long short-term memory (LSTM) networks for handling long-range dependencies, and generative adversarial networks (GANs) for creating realistic synthetic data. These architectures expanded the capabilities of AI systems and enabled applications in speech synthesis, video generation, and language modelling.

The introduction of transformer models, such as Google's BERT (bidirectional encoder representations from transformers) and OpenAI's GPT (generative pre-trained transformer) series, marked another major milestone. Transformers use attention mechanisms to capture contextual relationships in data, making them highly effective for natural language understanding and generation. GPT-3, for example, demonstrated the ability to generate coherent and contextually relevant text, perform translation, and answer questions with minimal supervision.

Deep learning has also been instrumental in advancing AI in healthcare, finance, and autonomous systems. For instance, deep learning models are used to detect diseases from medical images, predict stock market trends, and enable self-driving cars to interpret their surroundings. These applications highlight the versatility and impact of deep learning in solving real-world problems.

1.7.4 Natural Language Processing and Generative Models

Natural language processing (NLP) is a critical area of AI research focused on enabling machines to understand, interpret, and generate human language. Early NLP systems relied on rule-based approaches and statistical models, which were limited in their ability to handle the complexity and variability of natural language. The advent of ML and deep learning significantly advanced NLP capabilities.

One of the key milestones in NLP was the development of word embeddings, such as Word2Vec and GloVe, which represent words as vectors in a continuous space. These embeddings capture semantic relationships between words and enable models to perform tasks such as sentiment analysis, text classification, and machine translation more effectively.

The introduction of transformer-based models revolutionized NLP by allowing systems to process entire sequences of text with attention mechanisms. BERT and GPT are among the most influential models in this domain. BERT excels in understanding context and has been used in search engines, chatbots, and question-answering systems. The GPT models, particularly GPT-3 and GPT-4, have demonstrated remarkable capabilities in text generation, summarization, and dialogue.

Generative models, such as GANs and variational autoencoders (VAEs), have also contributed to NLP by enabling the creation of realistic and coherent text. These models learn to generate data that resembles the training set, allowing for applications in creative writing, content generation, and conversational AI.

Real-world examples of NLP applications include virtual assistants like Amazon Alexa and Google Assistant, which use speech recognition and language understanding to interact with users. In customer service, AI-powered chatbots handle inquiries, resolve issues, and provide personalized support. These

> **Did You Know?**
> GPT-3 can generate essays, poems, and even code—all from a single prompt—thanks to its transformer architecture trained on billions of words.

> **Mini Project/Assignment**
> *Title*: AI Milestone Presentation
>
> *Task*: Create a presentation on three major AI milestones (e.g., Deep Blue, GPT-3, AlphaGo). Explain their significance and impact.

1.8 Inter-disciplinary Problem Solving

As AI technologies continue to evolve rapidly, there is potential for interdisciplinary collaboration across different domains. This opens up new possibilities for innovative applications in solving complex real-world challenges in fields like neuroscience, natural resource management, and psychology, among others.

Data sciences that include ML, deep learning, and engineering discipline form the core foundation of advanced AI. AI methods are used in research and industry to predict outcomes and make decisions by training machines to perform specific tasks. However, AI can go one step further and draw on other disciplines both technical and non-technical to conduct exploratory analysis and facilitate scientific discovery.

Human–robot interaction is a popular research area that benefits from the convergence of multiple disciplines including robotics, neuroscience, cognitive science, social sciences, medicine, psychology, and engineering, among others. This could facilitate more intelligent, interactive, conversational, and expressive AI agents.

Combining genome science, bioinformatics, engineering, and computer vision with other AI technologies can help in predicting and treating human genetic disorders. Physiology, biomechanics, biomedical engineering, clinical chemistry, environmental monitoring, and MRI can collectively leverage AI to improve disease detection and treatment, build enhanced surgical systems, facilitate medication management, promote lean health management, and develop new treatments and therapies.

Integrating AI with geosciences, ecology, meteorology, biology, and other environmental sciences can contribute to environment conservation. Enhanced systems leveraging AI can help in real-time atmospheric, earth and sea-level monitoring, measure environmental footprints across a product lifecycle, reduce greenhouse gas emissions, optimize energy distribution and consumption, and help design more environment-friendly sustainable solutions.

> **Did You Know?**
> AI is being used in environmental science to monitor climate change, predict natural disasters, and optimize energy consumption.

systems illustrate the practical impact of NLP and generative models in enhancing human-computer interaction.

1.7.5 AI in Robotics and Autonomous Systems

Robotics and autonomous systems represent a convergence of AI with mechanical engineering and control theory. The integration of AI into robotics has enabled machines to perceive their environment, make decisions, and perform complex tasks with minimal human intervention. This milestone has profound implications for industries such as manufacturing, logistics, healthcare, and defense.

Early robotic systems were limited to repetitive tasks in structured environments, such as assembly lines. The incorporation of AI allowed robots to adapt to dynamic conditions, recognize objects, and navigate spaces autonomously. Computer vision, sensor fusion, and path planning algorithms have been instrumental in advancing robotic capabilities.

One of the most notable achievements in autonomous systems is the development of self-driving cars. Companies like Tesla, Waymo, and Uber have invested heavily in AI technologies that enable vehicles to detect obstacles, interpret traffic signals, and make real-time decisions. These systems rely on deep learning models, lidar sensors, and GPS data to ensure safe and efficient navigation.

In healthcare, robotic systems are used for surgery, rehabilitation, and elder care. AI-powered surgical robots assist doctors in performing precise procedures, while rehabilitation robots help patients regain mobility. Autonomous drones are employed in agriculture, disaster response, and environmental monitoring, showcasing the versatility of AI in robotics.

A case study illustrating the impact of AI in robotics is Boston Dynamics' Spot robot, which uses AI to navigate complex terrains, avoid obstacles, and perform tasks such as inspection and delivery. Spot demonstrates the potential of autonomous systems to operate in challenging environments and support human activities.

1.7.6 Recent Advances and Future Directions

The field of AI continues to evolve rapidly, with recent advances pushing the boundaries of what machines can achieve. One of the most exciting developments is the emergence of multimodal AI, which integrates data from multiple sources—such as text, images, and audio—to enhance understanding and decision-making. Models like OpenAI's GPT-4 and Google's Gemini exemplify this trend by combining language and vision capabilities.

Another significant advancement is the focus on explainable AI (XAI), which aims to make AI systems more transparent and interpretable. As AI becomes more integrated into critical decision-making processes, understanding how models arrive at their conclusions is essential for trust and accountability. Techniques such as feature attribution, model visualization, and counterfactual analysis are being developed to address this need.

Federated learning is also gaining traction as a method for training AI models across decentralized data sources while preserving privacy. This approach is particularly relevant in healthcare and finance, where data sensitivity is a major concern. Federated learning enables collaborative model development without sharing raw data, enhancing security and compliance.

Looking ahead, the future of AI research may involve the development of AGI, the integration of quantum computing, and the exploration of neuromorphic architectures that mimic the human brain. These directions promise to unlock new capabilities and address current limitations in AI systems.

The continued progress in AI research depends on interdisciplinary collaboration, ethical governance, and public engagement. As AI becomes more pervasive, ensuring that its development aligns with societal values and benefits humanity remains a central challenge.

Mini Project/Assignment

Title: AI Across Disciplines

Task: Choose one interdisciplinary field (e.g., AI + medicine or AI + ecology) and write a short paper on how AI is transforming that domain.

Summary

- AI is a subdomain of computer science focused on intelligent systems. It amplifies human creativity, but does not replace it. It mimics human abilities like learning, reasoning, perception, and language. AI systems learn from data and adapt without explicit programming.
- Industries using AI: Healthcare, finance, manufacturing, transportation, education, entertainment.
- The benefits of AI are 24/7 productivity; error reduction; automation of mundane tasks; human safety in hazardous environments; fast, unbiased decision-making; cost and time savings; and seamless daily integration.
- The challenges faced by AI are high cost; risk of negligence; limited creativity; job displacement; ethical limitations; and privacy concerns.
- Historical evolution: 1950s: Turing Test, term 'AI' coined, Lisp language created; 1960s: First industrial robot (Unimate), expert systems (DENDRAL), chatbot (ELIZA); 1970s–1980s: AI research slowdown, WABOT-1 android, MYCIN expert system; 1990s–2000s: Deep Blue defeats Kasparov, AI pets (AIBO), autonomous robots (Roomba); 2010s: Rise of AVAs (Siri, Alexa), IBM Watson, Sophia humanoid robot, AlphaGo; 2020s: GPT-3, ChatGPT, AGI research, ethical frameworks (UNESCO, EU AI Act).
- The influential figures in AI history are John McCarthy (Father of AI, Lisp inventor, Dartmouth Conference organizer); Marvin Minsky (symbolic reasoning, Society of Mind theory, MIT AI Lab co-founder); and Allen Newell (Logic Theorist, GPS, SOAR architecture, interdisciplinary AI research).
- The influential institutions in AI history are MIT: CSAIL, robotics, machine learning; Stanford: Expert systems, neural networks; and Carnegie Mellon: Robotics, cognitive psychology, autonomous systems.
- The main tech players in AI are Google DeepMind: AlphaGo; IBM: Watson; OpenAI: GPT models; and Microsoft: AI integration in products and Azure.
- AI can be differentiated from human intelligence based on cognitive capabilities, emotional and social intelligence, learning and adaptability, creativity and intuition, and ethical and moral reasoning
- Artificial general intelligence (AGI): Broad cognitive abilities, adaptable across domains. Applications are in healthcare, finance, manufacturing, and education, among others. Some of the challenges are safety, ethical governance, economic disruption, and existential risks.
- Key milestones in AI research: Symbolic AI (Logic Theorist, rule-based systems); machine learning (perceptron, backpropagation, ensemble methods); deep learning (CNNs, RNNs, GANs, transformers (GPT, BERT)); NLP and generative models (word embeddings, transformer models, chatbots); and robotics and autonomous systems (self-driving cars, surgical robots, drones).
- Recent advances in AI comprise multimodal AI (GPT-4, Gemini), explainable AI (XAI), and federated learning.
- Future directions: AGI, quantum computing, neuromorphic architectures.

Fundamentals of Artificial Intelligence

- AI integrates with neuroscience, psychology, robotics, genomics, environmental sciences. Its applications include human–robot interaction, genetic disorder prediction, disease detection and treatment, and environmental monitoring and sustainability.

= Exercises =

Part A (Objective Questions)

1. Who coined the term 'artificial intelligence' in a 1955 research proposal?
   - (a) Alan Turing
   - (b) John McCarthy
   - (c) Marvin Minsky
   - (d) Arthur Samuel

2. Why is AI considered more suitable than humans for performing repetitive tasks in manufacturing?
   - (a) AI systems are emotionally intelligent
   - (b) AI systems require constant supervision
   - (c) AI systems do not get tired or bored
   - (d) AI systems are cheaper to hire

3. A logistics company wants to reduce downtime in its operations. Which AI application would best serve this goal?
   - (a) AI-powered chatbots for customer service
   - (b) Predictive maintenance systems for machinery
   - (c) AI-generated advertisements
   - (d) AI-based emotion detection in employees

4. Which of the following best explains the shift from symbolic AI to machine learning?
   - (a) Symbolic AI was too fast for real-world applications
   - (b) Machine learning required less data than symbolic AI
   - (c) Encoding all human knowledge into rules was impractical
   - (d) Symbolic AI was better at handling ambiguity

5. Which ethical concern is most relevant when AI systems are trained on biased historical data?
   - (a) AI systems may become too creative
   - (b) AI systems may make discriminatory decisions
   - (c) AI systems may lose accuracy over time
   - (d) AI systems may require more electricity

6. You are tasked with designing an AI system for personalized education. Which combination of technologies would be most effective?
   - (a) AI with robotics and meteorology
   - (b) AI with deep learning and cognitive psychology
   - (c) AI with GPS and environmental monitoring
   - (d) AI with manufacturing and finance tools

7. Which AI milestone involved a machine defeating a world chess champion?
   (a) AlphaGo defeating Lee Sedol
   (b) IBM Watson winning *Jeopardy*!
   (c) Deep Blue defeating Gary Kasparov
   (d) Siri launching on iPhone

8. What is the primary difference between AI and human intelligence in terms of emotional capability?
   (a) AI can feel emotions but not express them
   (b) AI can simulate emotions but not experience them
   (c) AI has deeper emotional understanding than humans
   (d) AI can manage emotions better than humans

9. A financial institution wants to detect fraudulent transactions in real time. Which AI capability should it prioritize?
   (a) Natural language generatio
   (b) Reinforcement learning
   (c) Pattern recognition and anomaly detection
   (d) Image classification

10. Designing an AI system for environmental sustainability would benefit most from integrating which disciplines?
    (a) AI with fashion and culinary arts
    (b) AI with geosciences, biology, and meteorology
    (c) AI with sports analytics and gaming
    (d) AI with social media and advertising

Part B (Short Answer Questions)

1. What is the primary goal of artificial intelligence?
2. How does AI contribute to the healthcare industry?
3. If an AI chatbot detects frustration in a user's tone, how might it respond based on its programming?
4. What was the significance of the Dartmouth Conference in the history of AI?
5. Why might the assumption that AI is always accurate lead to negligence?
6. Design a scenario where AGI could enhance personalized learning in a classroom.
7. What programming language did John McCarthy invent and why was it important for AI?
8. What role did AlexNet play in advancing deep learning?
9. How can AI be applied to reduce greenhouse gas emissions?
10. What are the limitations of AI in making ethical decisions?

Part C (Essay Questions)

1. Explain the scope of AI in detail.
2. Write an essay on the historical evolution of AI.
3. Write about influential figures and institutions in AI history.

4. Differentiate between AI and human intelligence.
5. What is artificial general intelligence? Explain its industry applications.
6. Write an essay on the key milestones in AI research.

Answers

Part A

1. (b) 2. (c) 3. (b) 4. (c) 5. (b) 6. (b) 7. (c) 8. (b) 9. (c) 10. (b)

CHAPTER 2

AI Subfields and Their Core Technologies

Objectives

At the end of this chapter, you will be able to:

- List the foundational subfields and technologies that constitute AI
- Explain the principles and components of expert knowledge-based systems (EKBS)
- Elucidate the roles of the knowledge base, inference engine, and user interface in EKBS
- Describe the various knowledge representation techniques including semantic networks, frames, production rules, and logic-based representations
- Explain the three primary paradigms of machine learning: supervised, unsupervised, and reinforcement learning
- Describe the architecture and training techniques of deep neural networks including feedforward networks, backpropagation, and optimization methods
- Explain natural language processing and the steps involved
- Elaborate on computer vision and its applications
- Explain the role of sensors and actuators in robotic systems

2.1 Overview

Artificial intelligence (AI) encompasses a broad range of subfields and core technologies that together enable machines to perform tasks requiring human-like intelligence. This comprehensive outline explores AI foundational disciplines such as knowledge engineering, machine learning, deep learning, natural language processing, computer vision, and robotics, and their methodologies, applications, challenges, and future directions.

2.2 Knowledge Engineering

Knowledge engineering is a core area of AI that emphasizes building, organizing, and applying expert knowledge in computer systems. It gained importance during the rise of expert systems in the 1970s and 1980s, aiming to replicate human decision-making. The discipline involves receiving expert insights, organizing them properly, and embedding them into AI systems that can make decisions. Its value lies in turning raw data into actionable intelligence. Unlike traditional programming, knowledge-based systems use inference to draw conclusions from rules and facts, allowing them to handle complex and changing environments.

For example, in healthcare, expert systems can analyse disease symptoms and lab results to advise diagnoses, mirroring a physician's thought logic. The knowledge engineering process includes stages like knowledge acquisition, representation, validation, refinement, processing, and presentation. Success depends on the quality and structure of the knowledge and how well it integrates with reasoning mechanisms. As AI evolves, knowledge engineering remains vital, especially in areas requiring expert judgment and transparency. It complements machine learning (ML) by offering structured reasoning and decision support. Expert knowledge-based systems (EKBS), also known as intelligent agent systems, use curated knowledge and domain-specific rules to solve complex problems. These systems emulate expert decision-making and can also explain their logic, making them valuable in fields that demand both accuracy and interpretability.

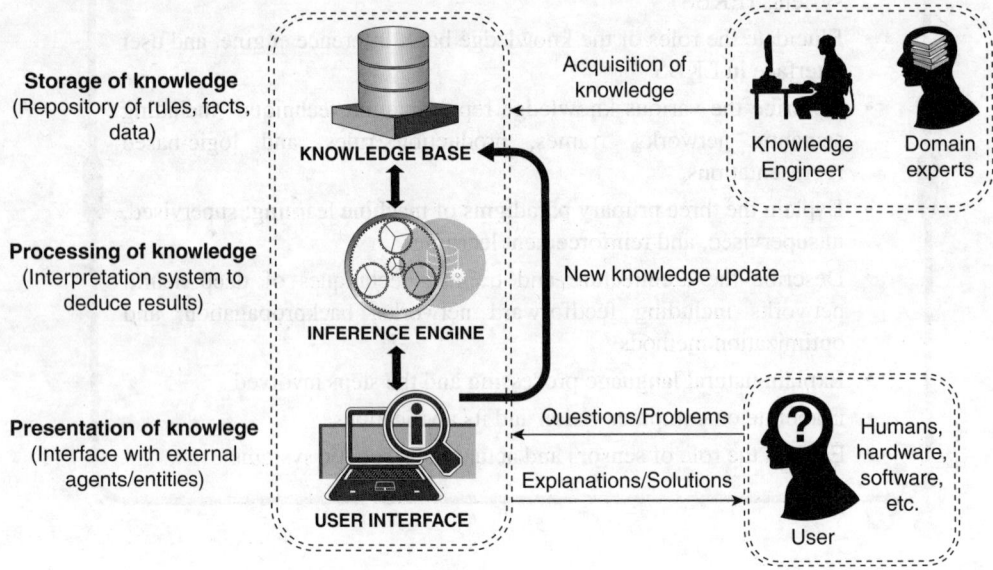

Figure 2.1 Components of the expert knowledge-based system (EKBS)

EKBS has the following three main components (Fig. 2.1):

- **Knowledge base**: It is the key component of any expert knowledge-based agent. The knowledge base is a repository of information that includes, but is not limited to, rules, procedures, facts, and data which are relevant to the specific domain that the system is built for. The EKBS uses stored knowledge and rules to support decision-making and provide explanations to queries.

  Domain-specific knowledge stored in the knowledge base is obtained from domain expert(s). A knowledge engineer encodes the expert knowledge received from the expert to build the knowledge base. The EKBS can also update the knowledge base with the new knowledge of inferred solutions.

- **Inference engine**: This is a reasoning system that processes relevant data, rules, and known facts acquired from the knowledge base and interprets it to find the solution specific to the user's problem. It draws conclusions based on domain-specific if-then rules, logic programming, or constraint-handling rules stored in the knowledge base. Aside from deriving new knowledge from existing knowledge, the interface engine can also explain how the system reached the respective solution or decision.
- **User interface**: The user interface is a user-friendly environment where a non-expert user can easily interact with the expert system. A user submits requests or queries of a particular problem to the system via the user interface. The user interface obtains the compiled solution from the inference engine and submits the results or advice back to the user.

2.2.1 Knowledge Representation Techniques

Knowledge representation is the basis of knowledge engineering, determining how data or information is stored, accessed, and processed within an intelligent system. The goal is to create representations that are both expressive enough to capture complex relationships and efficient enough to support reasoning and decision-making.

One of the earliest and most widely used techniques is **semantic networks**, which represent knowledge as a graph with its interconnected nodes and edges. Semantic networks in AI are like a giant mind map or a family tree for concepts. Imagine you are organizing a party and you create a chart showing who is related to whom, who likes what food, and who is bringing what. Each person is a 'node', and the lines connecting them show relationships like 'is a friend of', 'likes pizza', or 'is bringing drinks'. Similarly, in a semantic network, concepts are nodes, and the connections between them represent relationships—helping AI understand how ideas are linked, just like you understand your guests' preferences and connections.

For example, in a semantic network of animals, a node labeled 'Dog' might be connected to 'Mammal' via an 'is-a' relationship, and to 'Barks' via a 'has-behaviour' relationship (Fig. 2.2). This structure allows systems to infer new knowledge by traversing the network and applying logical rules.

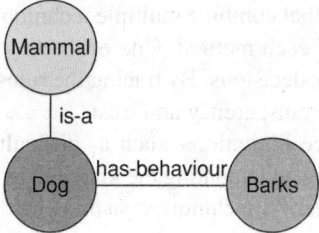

Figure 2.2 Example of semantic network representation

Think of a **frame** like a recipe card in a cookbook. Each card (frame) has slots like 'ingredients', 'cooking time', and 'steps'—these are the **attributes**. The actual values you fill in, like '2 eggs' or 'bake for 30 minutes', are the **fillers**. If you have a general recipe for 'cake', you can create specific versions like 'chocolate cake' or 'vanilla cake' that inherit the basic structure but customize certain details—just like how frames support **hierarchical organization and inheritance**. A frame consists of slots (attributes) and fillers (values), allowing for hierarchical organization and inheritance (Fig. 2.3).

Production rules are another common method, especially in expert systems. Production rules in AI are like traffic rules for decision-making. Imagine you are driving and see a red light. The rule is: **IF** the light is red, **THEN** stop. Your brain quickly checks the condition and takes the appropriate action (Fig. 2.4).

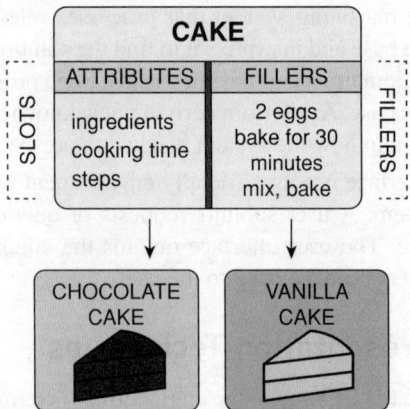

Figure 2.3 Example of frame representation

Figure 2.4 Example of production rule representation

Similarly, in expert systems, production rules guide the system to make decisions—like a medical system checking symptoms and applying rules to suggest a diagnosis, just as a driver follows road signs to decide what to do next.

Each technique has its strengths and limitations, and the choice depends on the specific requirements of the application. Hybrid approaches that combine multiple techniques are increasingly common, allowing systems to leverage the advantages of each method. One of the key advantages of expert systems is their ability to provide explanations for their decisions. By tracing the rules applied and the data used, the system can justify its conclusions, enhancing transparency and trust.

However, expert systems also face limitations, such as difficulty in handling uncertainty, scalability issues, and the challenge of maintaining and updating the knowledge base. These limitations have led to the integration of expert systems with other AI techniques, such as ML and probabilistic reasoning, to create more robust and adaptive systems.

2.2.2 Challenges in Knowledge Acquisition

Knowledge acquisition is one of the most difficult and time-consuming aspects of knowledge engineering. It involves extracting expert knowledge and converting it into a format that can be used by intelligent systems. This process requires deep collaboration between domain experts and knowledge engineers, as well as tools and methodologies to facilitate the transfer of knowledge.

One major challenge is the **tacit nature of expert knowledge**, meaning, experts often rely on intuition, experience, and context-specific judgment, which are difficult to articulate and formalize. Capturing this knowledge requires careful interviewing, observation, and iterative refinement. Another challenge is **knowledge validation**, ensuring that the acquired knowledge is accurate, consistent, and applicable. This requires testing the system against real-world scenarios and refining the rules and representations based on feedback.

Scalability in AI knowledge bases is like running a library that keeps getting bigger. In the beginning, when there are only a few books, it is simple to keep them in order and find what you need. But as more and more books are added—covering many different topics—it becomes harder to organize them, keep them up to date, and quickly find the right one. Imagine new books arriving every day while older ones need editing or replacing. In the same way, when AI systems grow and deal with constantly changing information, they need smart tools and strategies to make sure everything stays correct, easy to find, and useful.

Despite these challenges, effective knowledge acquisition remains essential for building intelligent systems that are reliable, interpretable, and capable of supporting complex decision-making.

Case Study: MYCIN and DENDRAL

Two landmark expert systems that illustrate the power and challenges of knowledge engineering are MYCIN and DENDRAL.

MYCIN, developed in the 1970s at Stanford University, was designed to assist physicians in diagnosing bacterial infections and recommending antibiotics. It used a rule-based approach, with hundreds of production rules derived from expert knowledge. MYCIN demonstrated impressive diagnostic accuracy and was able to explain its reasoning, making it a valuable tool for medical decision support. However, MYCIN also highlighted the limitations of expert systems. It was never deployed in clinical practice due to legal and ethical concerns, and its knowledge base required constant updates to remain relevant. The system also struggled with uncertainty and probabilistic reasoning, which are common in medical diagnosis.

DENDRAL, also developed at Stanford, was designed to analyze chemical compounds using mass spectrometry data. It combined expert knowledge with heuristic search techniques to infer molecular structures. DENDRAL was one of the first systems to demonstrate that computers could perform tasks requiring expert-level reasoning, paving the way for future AI applications in science and engineering.

These case studies underscore the importance of accurate knowledge representation, effective reasoning mechanisms, and the need for collaboration between domain experts and knowledge engineers. They also illustrate the potential and limitations of rule-based systems, informing the development of more advanced AI techniques.

Did You Know?

The MYCIN system, developed in the 1970s, could diagnose bacterial infections with high accuracy—but was never used in hospitals due to legal concerns!

Mini Project/Assignment

Title: Build a Mini Expert System

Task: Create a simple decision tree for diagnosing a cold versus flu based on symptoms like fever, cough, and fatigue. Use 'IF...THEN' rules.

2.3 AI Subfields

AI includes several specialized subfields that contribute to building intelligent systems. These are ML, deep learning (DL), natural language processing (NLP), computer vision, and robotics (Fig. 2.5).

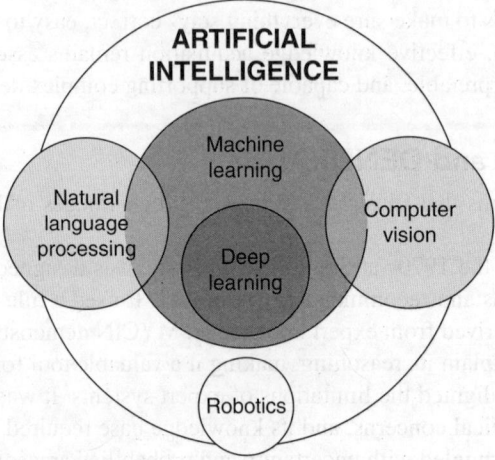

Figure 2.5 Subfields of AI

Did You Know?
Robots like NASA's Mars rover use multiple AI subfields—vision to see, learning to adapt, and planning to navigate!

Mini Project/Assignment
Title: AI Subfields Match-Up

Task: Match each AI subfield to a real-world application (e.g., NLP → Chatbots, CV → Face recognition).

2.3.1 Machine Learning

Machine learning (ML) is a part of AI where computers learn to perform tasks by studying data, instead of being told exactly what to do step by step. Imagine teaching a child how to recognize different fruits. You do not explain every detail—instead, you show them lots of pictures and let them figure it out.

The three primary paradigms of ML are supervised learning, unsupervised learning, and reinforcement learning. Each paradigm addresses different types of problems and uses distinct methodologies (Fig. 2.6).

- **Supervised learning:** This is like showing a child many pictures of fruits and telling them the name of each one: 'This is an apple', 'This is a banana', and so on. After seeing enough labelled pictures, the child starts to notice patterns like colour, shape, and size. Eventually, they can look at a new picture and say, 'That's an apple!' even if they have never seen that exact picture before. In ML, the computer does the same thing—it learns from labelled data and uses that knowledge to make predictions about new, unlabelled data.

AI Subfields and Their Core Technologies | 31

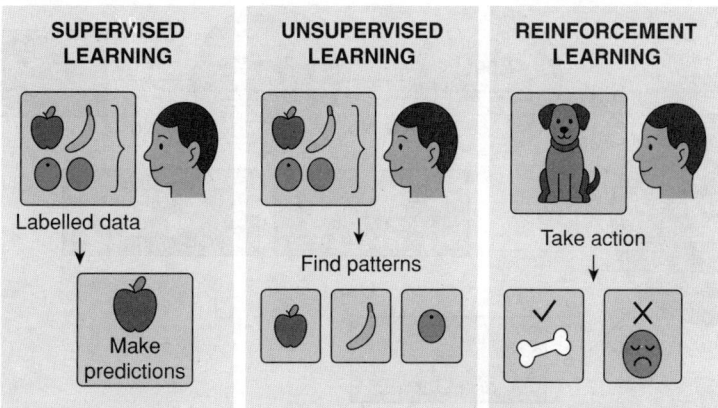

Figure 2.6 Machine learning paradigms

- **Unsupervised learning:** Now imagine giving the child the same fruit pictures, but without any names. The child has to sort them into groups based on what they look like. They might put all the red round fruits in one group, the long yellow ones in another, and the small orange ones in a third. Even though they do not know the names, they have found patterns and grouped similar items together. That is what unsupervised learning does—the computer finds hidden patterns in data without being told what the data means.
- **Reinforcement learning:** This is more like training a dog. You do not give it examples or labels. Instead, the dog learns by trying things and getting rewards or punishments. For example, if the dog sits when you say 'sit', it gets a treat. If it jumps on the couch, it gets scolded. Over time, the dog learns what actions lead to good outcomes. In ML, a computer program called an 'agent' does something similar. It tries different actions in a situation, gets feedback (rewards or penalties), and learns the best way to behave to get the most rewards. This kind of learning is used in video game-playing AI, robots that move around rooms, or self-driving cars that plan routes.

These paradigms form the backbone of modern AI applications, from spam detection and recommendation systems to autonomous vehicles and robotic control. Understanding their principles and differences is essential for designing effective ML solutions.

Supervised Learning

Imagine you are trying to decide what sport someone likes based on their answers (Fig. 2.7).

If someone enjoys outdoor activities, it is worth exploring further to understand their specific interests. However, if they do not, they might be more inclined toward indoor hobbies such as chess or video games. For those who do like outdoor activities, the next consideration is whether they enjoy running. If they do, they might be drawn to sports like football or athletics, which typically involve physical endurance and movement. On the other hand, if running is not their preference, they may find more enjoyment in cycling, which offer distinctive styles of engagement and pacing. The final aspect to consider is whether they prefer playing in a team. If they do, football or cricket could be ideal choices, as both are highly collaborative and team-oriented sports. If they prefer solo activities, athletics or cycling might be more suitable, offering personal challenge and individual performance focus.

A decision tree asks a series of questions about the data (features), branching out based on the answers, until it reaches a final decision or prediction (the label). This creates a structure that looks like a tree, where each end point (called a leaf) shows a final decision or class.

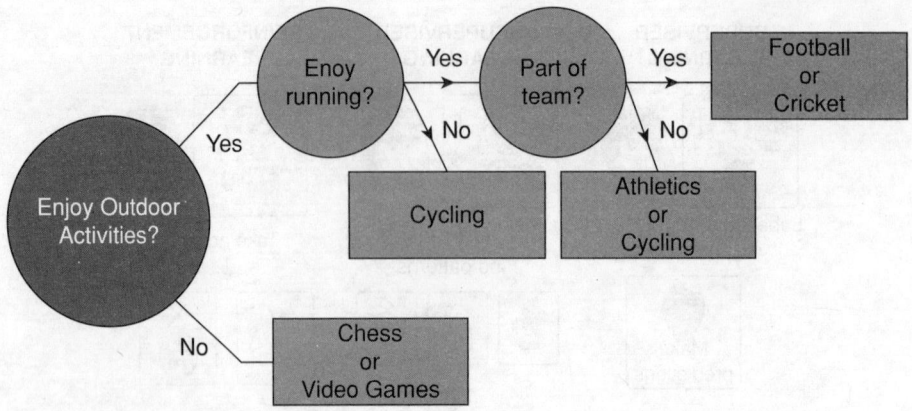

Figure 2.7 Decision tree

Another well-known ML method is the support vector machine (SVM). An SVM in supervised learning is like drawing the best possible boundary between two groups of people at a party.

Imagine you are at a party where guests are either wearing red or blue shirts, and you want to place a rope on the floor to separate the two groups as clearly as possible (Fig. 2.8). You try to position the rope so that it is as far away as possible from the nearest person in each group—this way, even if someone shifts slightly, the separation still holds. That is exactly what an SVM does: it finds the optimal boundary (called a hyperplane) that separates different classes in the data, with the widest possible margin. SVMs work especially well when there are many features or dimensions in the data.

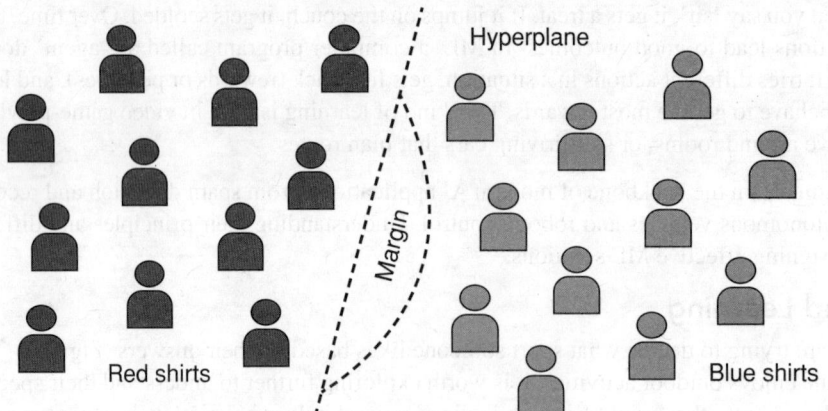

Figure 2.8 Support vector machine

A neural network in supervised learning is like a team of chefs working together to perfect a recipe.

Each chef (neuron) tastes the dish and adds their own touch, based on what they learned from past meals. The head chef (output layer) combines all their inputs to decide if the dish is ready. Over time, by comparing the final dish to the desired taste (the correct label), the team adjusts their contributions to get closer to perfection—just like a neural network adjusts its weights to improve predictions (Fig. 2.9).

Figure 2.9 Neural network

The **input layer** receives the raw data (like image pixels). The **hidden layers** carry out the processing—each neuron performs mathematical operations and applies an activation function. Finally, the **output layer** delivers the result. Neural networks are used in many real-world applications, including speech recognition (like Siri or Google Assistant), language translation (such as Google Translate), medical image analysis (for detecting tumours), and self-driving cars (to interpret road signs and detect obstacles).

Decision trees are easy to understand but may overfit. SVMs are dependable but need more time and computing power. Neural networks are powerful but require large data sets and resources.

Real-life Applications of Supervised Learning

Supervised learning is widely used for accurate predictions.

In healthcare, it helps predict diseases like diabetes and heart conditions using patient data, enabling initial treatment and personalized care. In finance, it supports credit scoring, fraud detection, and stock forecasting. Credit models assess income, job history, and loan repayment to predict defaults. Fraud systems track spending patterns to detect suspicious activity. Retail and e-commerce use supervised learning to recommend products and adjust pricing. By analysing customer behaviour, these models suggest purchases, improving satisfaction and sales. Spam filters now use supervised models trained on labelled emails to detect patterns in words, senders, and formatting. Self-driving cars use labelled sensor data to identify vehicles, signs, and pedestrians, and predict traffic movement. Companies like Tesla and Waymo apply these models to improve safety and reliability. These examples show how supervised learning solves real-world problems and drives innovation across industries.

Unsupervised Learning

Unsupervised learning algorithms use techniques like clustering or dimensionality reduction to find structures in the data.

Clustering means grouping similar things together. Let us say you give a detective a bunch of marbles of different colours and sizes. You do not tell the detective which is which—she has to group them by looking at them. The detective might (Fig. 2.10):

- **Group by colour:** All red marbles in one group, all blue in another.
- **Group by size:** Small marbles together, large ones elsewhere.

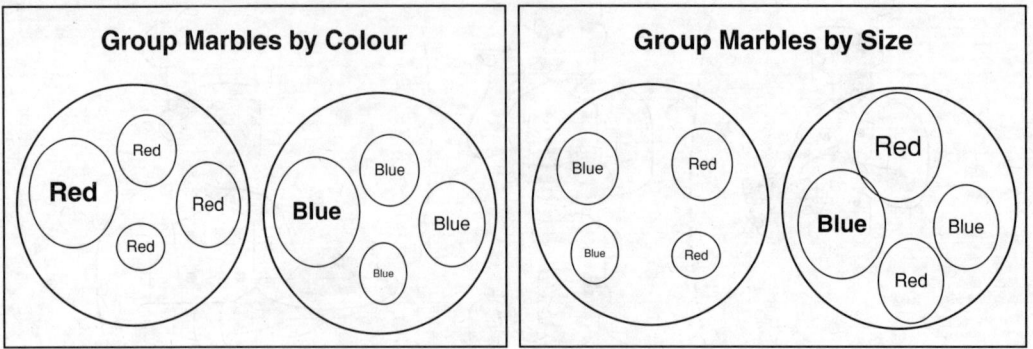

Figure 2.10   Clustering by colour and size

There are two types of clustering, namely, K-means and hierarchical.

K-means clustering (K indicates the number of groups) is like organizing a group of people into different tables at a wedding based on how similar they are. Imagine you are the host, and you want guests (12 people in this case) to sit with others they will enjoy talking to (Fig. 2.11).

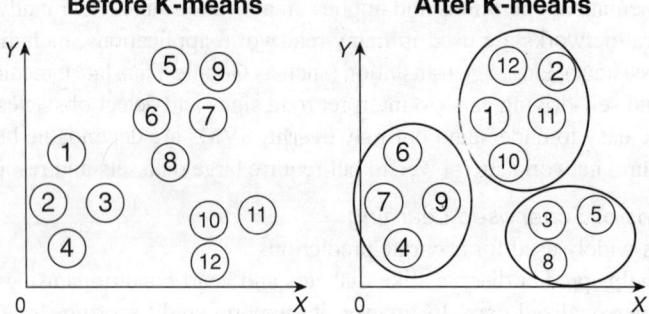

Figure 2.11   K-means algorithm

You start by placing a few people at random tables (these are your initial 'centroids'). Then, you look at each guest and assign them to the table where they fit best based on shared interests. After everyone is seated, you adjust the tables to better reflect the group's preferences and repeat the process until everyone is at the right spot. That is how K-means finds natural groupings in data.

Hierarchical clustering in unsupervised learning is like building a family tree. Think of it as grouping people based on how closely they are related. You begin by pairing the most similar ones—like siblings. Then, you slowly combine these pairs into bigger groups—like cousins, then extended families—until everyone is part of one large tree. In the same way, hierarchical clustering starts by either joining small groups or breaking big ones apart, step by step. This process creates a branching diagram called a dendrogram, which looks like a tree and shows how the groups are connected.

As an example of **dimensionality reduction**, imagine you have a colouring book with 100 crayons, but you only need a few to make a beautiful picture (Fig. 2.12). That is what dimensionality reduction does—it keeps the important information and throws away the extra data. It simplifies data sets by reducing features while keeping key information.

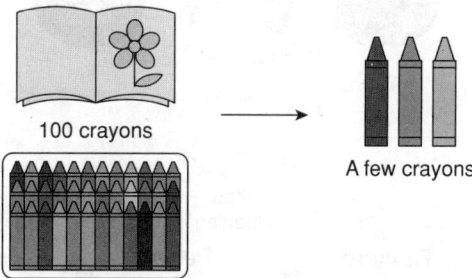

Figure 2.12 Dimensionality reduction

Real-life Applications of Unsupervised Learning
These methods help data scientists detect patterns, outliers, and insights from unlabelled data.

In marketing, clustering helps group customers by behaviour, age, or interests, enabling targeted ads and products. In cybersecurity, unsupervised models learn normal network behaviour and detect anomalies like cyberattacks. In healthcare, clustering identifies disease types from genetic or imaging data, aiding personalized treatment. Dimensionality reduction helps interpret complex biological data and uncover links between genes and diseases. Recommendation systems use unsupervised learning like collaborative filtering to suggest items based on user behaviour, without needing labelled data. Platforms like Netflix and Amazon benefit from this. In manufacturing, anomaly detection finds unusual sensor patterns, helping prevent equipment failures and reduce downtime.

Reinforcement Learning

Reinforcement learning (RL) is a way for computers to learn by doing things and seeing what happens. The computer program, called an **agent**, tries different actions in a situation, called an **environment**. If it does something good, it gets a **reward**. If it makes a mistake, it gets a **penalty**. The goal is to learn how to make the best choices over time to get the most rewards. This kind of learning is useful while playing video games or in helping robots move correctly.

RL relies on a structure known as a **Markov decision process (MDP)**, which allows an agent to learn how to make decisions by interacting with its surroundings. The MDP is like planning a road trip with a GPS that only knows your current location and not your past route. At each intersection (state), you choose a direction (action), and based on that, you move to a new location and get a reward—like scenic views or traffic delays. The GPS helps you make decisions that maximize your overall travel experience, even though it does not remember where you have been, only where you are now.

An MDP includes several essential elements. First are the **states**, which describe the various situations the agent might encounter. For instance, a robot vacuum could be in a state like 'the room is dirty' or 'near a charging dock' (Fig. 2.13).

Then come the **actions**—the options available to the agent, such as 'move ahead', 'start cleaning', or 'go recharge'. When the agent performs an action, it moves to a new state, and this shift is determined by transition probabilities, which reflect the chances of ending up in a particular state after taking a specific action.

36 | Fundamentals of Artificial Intelligence

Figure 2.13 Markov decision process

The agent also receives **rewards** based on its actions, which help shape its learning process. For example, successfully cleaning a spot might earn a reward, while hitting a wall could lead to a penalty. Over time, the agent develops a **policy** strategy for choosing actions that lead to the highest cumulative rewards.

RL is successful in areas requiring adaptive decision-making. In robotics, agents learn tasks like object manipulation through trial and error. In autonomous navigation, RL helps drones and self-driving cars plan routes and avoid obstacles. In gaming, AlphaGo used RL and DL to beat world champions in Go, showing RL's strategic power. Beyond games, RL is used in finance for investment strategies, in healthcare for treatment planning, and in operations research for resource management. Its ability to learn from experience and optimize long-term outcomes makes RL a powerful tool for dynamic, real-world problems.

> **Did You Know?**
> RL helped AlphaGo defeat the world champion in the complex board game Go—learning purely through gameplay!

> **Mini Project/Assignment**
> *Title*: Learning Styles of AI
>
> *Task*: Create a chart comparing supervised, unsupervised, and reinforcement learning with examples from daily life (e.g., learning with a teacher versus exploring on your own).

2.3.2 Deep Learning and Neural Networks

Deep learning (DL) is a branch of ML that uses artificial neural networks (ANNs) inspired by the human brain. DL is like teaching a child to recognize animals by showing them thousands of pictures. At first, the child might not know the difference between a cat and a dog, but after seeing many examples and getting feedback, they start to notice subtle patterns—like ear shape or tail length. DL works similarly: it uses multiple layers of 'neurons' to gradually learn complex features from raw data, improving its understanding with each layer, just like the child gets better with more experience.

DL has surpassed traditional methods in areas like image and speech recognition, advancing AI significantly. However, its decision-making is often hard to explain, especially in sensitive fields like healthcare and finance. Despite this, researchers are improving model transparency, efficiency, and adaptability. When combined with other AI techniques, DL helps build smarter, more flexible systems.

Architecture of Neural Networks

A **feedforward neural network** is like an assembly line in a factory. Each station (or layer) receives parts from the previous one, processes them, and passes the result forward—never backward. Just like in an assembly line where raw materials move step-by-step towards becoming a finished product, data in a feedforward neural network flows in one direction through layers of neurons to produce a final output (Fig. 2.14).

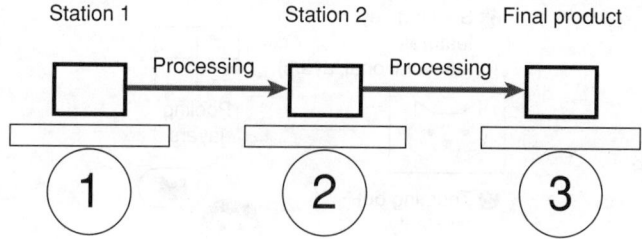

Figure 2.14 Feedforward neural network

Each neuron receives signals, applies weights, uses a non-linear function, and passes the result forward. This structure helps the network learn complex input–output relationships.

Imagine a student takes a test and gets some answers wrong. Backpropagation in a neural network is like a teacher grading a student's test and giving feedback on each mistake. The teacher not only marks the incorrect answers but also explains *why* they were wrong, helping the student adjust their thinking.

Training of the neural network involves adjusting weights to reduce errors using **backpropagation**, which calculates each weight's impact on the final error using the chain rule. Similarly, in backpropagation, the neural network compares its prediction to the correct answer, calculates the error, and then sends that error backward through the network—adjusting each layer's 'thinking' (weights) so it can do better next time. Backpropagation is essential for learning but can be computationally heavy, especially in deep networks. Together, feedforward networks and backpropagation form the foundation of DL, offering a flexible way for machines to learn from data.

The two main types of DL techniques are convolutional neural networks (CNNs) and recurrent neural networks (RNNs).

Convolutional Neural Networks (CNNs)

Imagine you have a robot friend who is learning how to recognize animals in photos—like figuring out whether it is looking at a cat, a dog, or a bird. To help the robot, we give it a special kind of high-tech eyewear called CNNs, short for convolutional neural networks. These act like smart lenses that help the robot analyse images in a clever way.

A CNN has three main parts: convolutional layers, pooling layers, and fully connected layers.

Step 1: Spotting Key Features (Convolutional Layers)
The robot starts by scanning the image to pick out simple shapes and patterns. It looks for things like edges, curves, and corners—similar to how you might notice a cat's sharp ears or a dog's round snout. It uses small square tools called filters that slide across the image, examining tiny sections to detect these features.

Step 2: Zooming Out for Clarity (Pooling Layers)
Then, the robot reduces the size of the image to simplify what it sees. This helps it concentrate on the most important parts and ignore unnecessary details. Think of it like stepping back to get a clearer view of the whole picture without being distracted by the minor details.

Step 3: Making an Informed Decision (Fully Connected Layers)
At last, the robot takes everything it has learned from the patterns and the simplified image to make a thoughtful guess. It might say, 'Based on what I've seen, I believe this is a cat!' This is where the robot's 'brain' pulls all the clues together to figure out what the image is showing (Fig. 2.15).

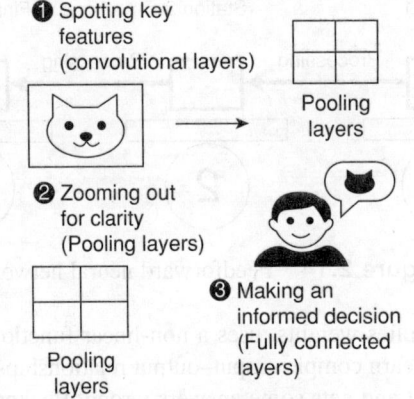

Figure 2.15 Convolutional neural network

By stacking these layers, CNNs first detect simple features like edges, then recognize complex ones like faces. This layered approach makes CNNs ideal for tasks like facial recognition or object detection. CNNs are widely used in computer vision—teaching machines to interpret images. They power tools in photo editing, face recognition, and healthcare. For instance, doctors use CNNs to analyse X-rays or MRIs for faster, more accurate diagnoses. Their ability to understand spatial relationships and use fewer parameters than other models make them efficient and powerful in DL applications.

Recurrent Neural Networks (RNNs) and Long Short-term Memory (LSTM)

Imagine you are reading a story, one word at a time. You come across the phrase: 'The cat sat on the…' and instinctively guess the next word might be 'mat'—a familiar and logical continuation.

That is similar to how a recurrent neural network (RNN) works. It is a type of ML model that processes words one at a time and predicts what comes next. What makes it unique is its ability to remember previous words. So when it sees 'The cat sat on the…', it recalls 'cat' and 'sat' to help predict 'mat'.

However, when the sentence gets much longer—like 'Once upon a time, in a faraway land, there lived a cat who loved to sit on…'—the RNN might lose track of earlier important words, such as 'cat'. This issue is known as the **vanishing memory problem**. To solve it, researchers developed a more advanced model called long short-term memory (LSTM). Think of it as a system with a notebook—it jots down key details like 'cat' and keeps them handy. It also has mechanisms to decide what to keep, what to discard, and what to pass along, allowing it to retain crucial information, even in lengthy texts.

That is why virtual assistants like Siri and Alexa use LSTM models. If you say, 'Play the song I liked yesterday,' they can remember your preferences and respond accurately. The development of RNNs and LSTMs has significantly advanced DL's ability to process complex, time-based patterns.

Training Techniques and Optimization

Imagine you are teaching a robot to tell the difference between pictures of cats and dogs. At first, it gets confused and makes incorrect guesses. So, you use a scorecard called a **loss function** to measure how far off (incorrect) its answers are. The goal is to help the robot get better over time, even when it sees new pictures it has not seen before. To guide its learning, you use a method called **gradient descent**. Think of it like giving the robot small hints after each mistake so it can slowly adjust how it thinks. But sometimes, the robot starts memorizing the exact pictures instead of learning general features—this is called **overfitting**. To stop that, you use tricks like **dropout**, which is like covering parts of the picture now and then, so the robot learns to focus on the big picture, not just tiny details.

Another trick is **L2 regularization**, which acts like a gentle reminder not to depend too much on any one clue. It helps the robot stay balanced in its thinking. **Early stopping** is like ending the lesson before the robot starts overthinking and memorizing instead of truly learning. You can also use **batch normalization**, which makes sure each part of the robot's brain gets clean and balanced information—like making sure every flashcard is well-lit and easy to read.

Choosing the appropriate training settings, like how fast the robot learns (**learning rate**) or how many pictures it sees at once (**batch size**), is also important. It is like deciding how quickly to teach or how many flashcards to show in one go.

Challenges and Future Directions

Despite its success, DL faces key challenges. One major issue is its lack of transparency—models often act like 'black boxes', making decisions that are hard to explain. This is a concern in critical fields like healthcare and finance, where trust and understanding are essential.

DL also needs substantial amounts of labelled data, which is costly and time-consuming, especially in expert domains. To address this, researchers are exploring semi-supervised learning (using both labelled and unlabelled data), few-shot learning (learning from minimal examples), and synthetic data generation (creating artificial but useful data).

Training these models demands significant computing power, making it expensive and slow. Solutions include model compression, efficient architectures, and specialized hardware to speed up training. Ethical concerns are growing too. DL can introduce bias, threaten privacy, or be misused. As adoption increases, ensuring fairness, accountability, and positive impact is crucial.

Looking ahead, DL may evolve by integrating symbolic reasoning (logic-based AI) and causal inference (understanding cause–effect). Emerging technologies like neuromorphic computing, quantum ML, and explainable AI (XAI) aim to make models more powerful, efficient, and understandable. The future depends on building models that are not only intelligent but also transparent, efficient, and aligned with human values.

> **Did You Know?**
>
> DL models can recognize faces, translate languages, and even compose music—all by learning patterns from data!

> **Mini Project/Assignment**
>
> *Title*: Neural Network Analogy
>
> *Task*: Draw a simple diagram showing how a neural network processes information—like a team of decision-makers passing notes.

2.3.3 Natural Language Processing

Natural language processing (NLP) in AI is like teaching a computer to understand and speak human language the way a translator helps two people from different countries communicate.

Imagine you are talking to a friend who speaks only French, and you speak only Tamil. A translator listens to both sides, understands the meaning, and conveys it in the other language. NLP works similarly—it helps machines understand, interpret, and respond to human language, whether it is spoken or written, so they can 'talk back' in a way that makes sense to us. The goal is to make communication between humans and computers smoother.

Think of NLP as preparing a dish from a recipe book written in a foreign language. In the realm of NLP, understanding how machines interpret human language can be likened to preparing a complex meal. Each stage of linguistic analysis plays a distinct role, much like the steps in cooking a dish—from chopping ingredients to presenting a harmonious multi-course meal (Table 2.1). This analogy not only simplifies the technical concepts but also makes them more relatable to a broader audience.

Table 2.1 Various steps of NLP

NLP step	What it does	Cooking analogy
Tokenization	Breaks text into words or phrases	Chopping vegetables into pieces before cooking
Part-of-Speech Tagging	Labels each word's grammatical role	Tagging each ingredient as spice, vegetable, or protein
Syntactic Parsing	Analyzes sentence structure	Following the recipe steps to combine ingredients
Semantic Analysis	Interprets the meaning of the sentence	Tasting the dish to understand its flavour
Discourse Integration	Maintains consistency across multiple sentences	Ensuring the full meal (starter to dessert) makes sense

Tokenization is the foundational step in NLP, akin to chopping ingredients before cooking. Just as a chef slices vegetables or meats into manageable pieces, tokenization breaks down a sentence into smaller units such as words or phrases. For example, the sentence 'The cat sat on the mat' would be split into individual tokens: 'The', 'cat', 'sat', 'on', 'the', and '"mat'. This segmentation allows the system to handle each word separately, making it easier to analyze and process language systematically.

Once the ingredients are prepared, the next step is to identify their roles—this is where part-of-speech (POS) tagging comes in. POS tagging assigns grammatical labels to each token, such as noun, verb, adjective, or adverb. In our cooking analogy, this is like recognizing whether an ingredient is a spice, vegetable, or grain. For instance, in the sentence 'She ran quickly', the word 'She' is tagged as a pronoun, 'ran' as a verb, and 'quickly' as an adverb. This classification helps the system understand the function of each word within the sentence, much like knowing which ingredients add flavour versus those that provide substance.

Syntactic parsing takes the analysis a step further by examining how the words relate to one another structurally. This is like understanding the sequence in which ingredients are combined or cooked. For example, in a recipe, some items must be sautéed before others are added. In language, syntactic parsing identifies the grammatical structure, such as subject-verb-object relationships. In the sentence 'The dog chased the ball', parsing reveals that 'The dog' is the subject, 'chased' is the verb, and 'the ball' is the object. This structural understanding is crucial for grasping the sentence's meaning.

Semantic analysis delves into the meaning behind the words, much like interpreting the flavour profile of a dish. It is not enough to know the ingredients and their order; one must understand what the final dish represents. In NLP, semantic analysis interprets the intent and meaning of a sentence. For example, the phrase 'He kicked the bucket' could mean someone kicked a physical bucket, but semantically, it often implies that someone has died. This layer of analysis helps machines understand context and nuance, which are essential for accurate communication.

Finally, discourse integration ensures that individual sentences connect logically to form a coherent narrative, much like ensuring that the appetizer, main course, and dessert complement each other in a meal. In language, this involves tracking references across sentences, maintaining consistency, and understanding how ideas build upon one another. For instance, in a paragraph where the first sentence introduces 'John', and the second says 'He went to the store', discourse integration helps the system recognize that 'He' refers to 'John'. This continuity is vital for understanding extended texts and conversations.

Together, these stages—tokenization, POS tagging, syntactic parsing, semantic analysis, and discourse integration—form the backbone of how machines process and understand human language. By likening each step to a part of preparing a meal, we can appreciate the complexity and elegance of NLP in a more intuitive and engaging way.

ML and DL have improved NLP's ability to understand context and make accurate predictions. Human language is complex, with ambiguity, idioms, and cultural nuances. For instance, 'bank' can mean a financial institution or a river's edge. NLP must determine meaning from context. Despite challenges, NLP powers search engines, voice assistants, translation tools, and emotion analysis apps. It is transforming how we interact with technology and access information.

Text Processing and Feature Extraction

Imagine you are preparing a library for a big research project. **Text pre-processing** is like organizing the books—removing duplicates (stop words), fixing typos (punctuation and casing), and grouping similar editions (stemming and lemmatization). **Feature extraction** is like creating a catalogue system: you might count how often topics appear (Bag of Words), highlight rare but important ones (TF-IDF), or even map out relationships between ideas (word embeddings like Word2Vec or GloVe). This setup makes it easy for researchers (ML models) to find patterns and insights efficiently.

Language Models and Transformers

Language models play a key role in NLP, enabling machines to interpret and produce human-like text by anticipating what comes next in a sentence.

Imagine teaching someone to write a story. Early models like **n-grams** are like giving them a phrasebook—they can string together short, common phrases (relying on short word sequences) but struggle with longer, meaningful sentences. Then came **RNNs and LSTMs**, which are like storytellers with short-term memory—they remember what was said earlier but only for a little while, and they write one word at a time, slowly. These models improved understanding but were still limited in speed and long-range context.

The introduction of **transformers** marked a major shift. Using a mechanism called self-attention, these models examine all the words in a sentence at once, allowing them to understand how words relate to each other. First presented in the paper *Attention is All You Need*, transformers use multi-head attention to interpret sentences from multiple perspectives. This architecture powers leading models like BERT (bidirectional encoder representations from transformers) and GPT (generative pretrained transformer).

Applications: Chatbots, Translation, Sentiment Analysis

Chatbots are computer programs that talk like humans. They use NLP to understand what people are asking, figure out what they mean, and give helpful answers. You will find chatbots in places like customer service, hospitals, schools, and online shopping, where they give quick and useful replies.

In **banking**, chatbots help people check their account balance, view recent transactions, or find out if they qualify for a loan. These bots use two smart techniques: **intent recognition** (to understand what the user wants) and **entity extraction** (to pick out important details like names or amounts). More advanced chatbots use DL and transformer models—these are like super-smart systems that can handle tricky questions and remember the conversation, just like a good customer service agent.

Another big use of NLP is in **machine translation**, which means changing text from one language to another. Older systems used fixed rules, but today's tools use **neural networks** and **transformers**—imagine them as brain-like systems that learn from lots of examples. Apps like Google Translate and DeepL use a method called **sequence-to-sequence models with attention**. This means they look at entire sentences and focus on the most important parts to make sure grammar, expressions, and meaning are correct. They train using **parallel corpora**, which are pairs of matching sentences in two languages.

Sentiment analysis is another popular NLP tool. It figures out the emotional tone in a message—whether it is positive, negative, or neutral. This is useful for checking social media posts, customer reviews, or market trends. The system looks at the words and how they are used to understand how people feel. For example, companies can study tweets to see how customers react to their products and make smarter decisions.

In short, NLP helps computers understand human language better. It is changing how we talk to machines and how we learn from written information.

> ### Did You Know?
> ChatGPT can hold conversations, write essays, and answer questions—all thanks to transformer-based NLP models trained on massive text data sets!

> ### Mini Project/Assignment
> *Title*: Talk to a Bot
>
> *Task*: Try interacting with a chatbot (e.g., customer service bot). Note how it responds and identify which parts of NLP it uses (e.g., understanding intent, responding with context).

2.3.4 Computer Vision

Imagine teaching a computer to view and understand pictures and videos—just like humans do. That is what computer vision (CV) is all about! Let's say you show a computer a photo of a cat. The computer does not 'see' the cat like we do. Instead, it sees millions of tiny dots called pixels. Each pixel has a colour and brightness. To understand the image, the computer processes the pixels to find edges, shapes, and patterns. It learns from many examples (like thousands of cat pictures). It recognizes objects (like cats, cars, or people) and even labels them.

CV is a branch of AI that enables machines to interpret visual data like images and videos, aiming to replicate human vision. It begins with image processing—enhancing pixel data to detect edges, textures, and shapes—supporting tasks like object recognition, scene analysis, and motion tracking. CV combines classical algorithms (e.g., histogram analysis, contour detection) with DL, especially CNNs, which learn patterns from large data sets for higher accuracy. YOLO (You Only Look Once) is another fast tool that finds and labels objects in real-time (like spotting a ball while watching a soccer match).

Sometimes CV gets confused because the lighting is bad, objects are hidden or blurry, and scenes are too crowded. So, scientists keep improving the tools to make CV smarter. Tesla cars use cameras and CV to drive safely. ImageNet is a huge collection of labelled pictures that helps computers learn better.

Image processing serves as the foundation of CV, transforming raw visual input into a format that machines can analyze effectively. This step improves image clarity, pulls out meaningful features, and filters out noise—making it easier for systems to recognize patterns and track movement. By working in tandem with feature detection, it enables machines to begin interpreting visual data, laying the groundwork for more complex tasks.

Object recognition and classification play a crucial role in helping machines make sense of images and videos in a way that mimics human perception. These techniques are widely applied—from identifying products on store shelves to spotting irregularities in medical scans. The core aim is to derive actionable insights from visual content, whether to inform decisions or trigger automated responses.

Recognition focuses on pinpointing and identifying specific elements within an image—like detecting a bottle in a crowded scene. Classification, on the other hand, assigns labels based on characteristics, such as distinguishing between a dog and a cat. Object detection merges these capabilities, locating items and enclosing them in bounding boxes—a critical function for real-time applications like self-driving cars and security systems.

Deep Learning in CV: CNNs and YOLO

DL is central to modern CV, with CNNs and models like YOLO enabling fast, accurate visual recognition. CNNs process image data using filters that detect local patterns. These filters slide over the image to create feature maps that highlight edges, textures, and shapes. As layers deepen, the network learns more abstract features, allowing it to recognize complex objects. A CNN typically includes convolutional layers for feature extraction, pooling layers to reduce dimensions, and fully connected layers for classification. Activation functions like ReLU add non-linearity, helping the model learn complex patterns. CNNs are trained on large, labelled data sets like ImageNet using backpropagation and optimizers such as Adam or SGD to minimize errors.

YOLO (You Only Look Once) is a real-time object detection model that processes the entire image in one pass. It divides the image into a grid and predicts bounding boxes and class probabilities for each cell, enabling fast detection. YOLO is ideal for real-time applications like surveillance, robotics, and autonomous driving. YOLO has evolved through versions like YOLOv3, which added multi-scale detection, and YOLOv4 and YOLOv5, which improved speed and accuracy. These models are efficient enough for use on mobile and edge devices.

Together, CNNs and YOLO have advanced object detection, recognition, and tracking, making them essential tools in intelligent visual systems.

Applications: Autonomous Vehicles, Medical Imaging

CV plays a vital role in autonomous vehicles and medical imaging, enhancing safety, efficiency, and decision-making. In autonomous vehicles, computer vision helps interpret surroundings using cameras and sensors to detect lanes, traffic signs, pedestrians, and obstacles. Models like YOLO and semantic segmentation classify and locate elements in real time. Lane detection guides navigation, traffic sign recognition ensures rule compliance, and pedestrian detection prevents accidents. These tasks require robust algorithms that manage lighting changes, weather, and occlusions. CV also aids decision-making by predicting the behaviour of nearby vehicles and pedestrians, helping prevent collisions and improving reliability. In medical imaging, computer vision analyzes scans like X-rays, MRIs, and CTs to diagnose diseases. DL models detect abnormalities and highlight key regions. CNNs identify tumours, fractures, and infections, supporting radiologists in diagnosis and treatment planning.

Segmentation algorithms outline anatomical structures for precise analysis. In oncology, they track tumour growth; in cardiology, they assess heart function and detect vascular issues. Integrating computer vision in healthcare improves diagnostic accuracy, reduces workload, and enables early disease detection. It also supports telemedicine and remote diagnostics, expanding access to care.

These applications show how CV enhances human capabilities and improves outcomes in critical fields.

Case Study: ImageNet and Tesla Vision

Two major case studies—ImageNet and Tesla Vision—highlight the evolution and impact of computer vision in research and real-world applications.

ImageNet is a large visual database with over 14 million labelled images across 20,000 categories. Its annual challenge, ILSVRC, has driven innovation in image classification. The 2012 breakthrough came with **AlexNet**, a deep CNN that outperformed earlier models and sparked interest in deeper architectures. Later models like **VGGNet**, **ResNet**, and **Inception** built on this, improving accuracy and robustness. ImageNet has been crucial for benchmarking models, refining techniques, and emphasizing the importance of diverse, high-quality data.

Tesla Vision showcases CV in autonomous driving. It replaces radar and lidar with cameras and neural networks to detect lanes, vehicles, pedestrians, and signs. Trained on vast driving data, Tesla's models are updated via over-the-air software and use multi-camera setups for 360° perception. Tesla's vision-based approach focuses on scalability and cost-efficiency, but also faces challenges in dynamic environments, requiring robust validation and continuous improvement.

Together, ImageNet and Tesla Vision reflect CV's journey—from academic breakthroughs to practical deployment—demonstrating its potential and challenges in intelligent visual systems.

Did You Know?

YOLO (You Only Look Once) can detect multiple objects in an image in real time—like spotting cars, people, and traffic signs in one glance!

Mini Project/Assignment

Title: Image Detective

Task: Take a photo and list the objects you see. Imagine how a computer might identify them using pixels and patterns.

2.3.5 Robotics

Robotics is like building a self-driving delivery cart for a busy hotel. Mechanical engineering designs the cart's frame and wheels, electrical engineering powers it and connects its sensors, computer science programs its route and behaviour, and AI helps it recognize obstacles and make smart decisions. Just like the cart uses cameras and sensors to navigate hallways and deliver items without bumping into guests, robots use similar systems to interact with the world around them.

Modern robots are built with tools like sensors, motors (called actuators), and control systems that help them understand their surroundings, make choices, and take action. Thanks to AI, robots have become much smarter. In the past, robots could only follow fixed instructions and do the same task over and over, like a machine on an assembly line. But now, with AI, robots can learn from experience, adjust to new situations, and solve more complicated problems. AI helps robots 'see' using sensors and CV, which is like giving them eyes to recognize objects and people. It also gives them 'brains' through decision-making systems that use ML or rule-based logic to figure out what to do next. Once a decision is made, control systems act like muscles, turning those decisions into movement or action. This combination allows robots to work on their own, move through different environments, and avoid bumping into things.

AI also boosts robot flexibility. Intelligent robots can learn new tasks, adjust to different settings, and improve through feedback using reinforcement learning. The fusion of robotics and AI is driving innovation across industries, creating intelligent systems that assist or replace human labour. As this integration grows, it will reshape work, mobility, and human–machine interaction.

Sensors and Actuators

Imagine a robot is like a human. To do anything useful, it needs to:

- Understand what is happening around it (like seeing, hearing, or feeling).
- Do something in response (like moving, picking something up, or turning).

That is where sensors and actuators come in. Sensors are robots senses. They help robots sense the world, just like our eyes, ears, and skin. Various types of sensors are used by robots (Fig. 2.16):

- **Vision sensors (like cameras)**: Help robots 'see' things. A self-driving car uses cameras to see traffic lights and other cars.

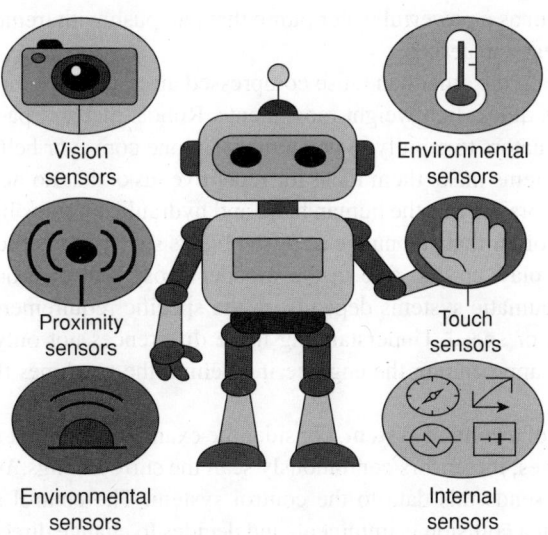

Figure 2.16 Robotics sensors

- **Proximity sensors (like ultrasound or infrared):** Help robots know if something is close by. A robot vacuum stops before bumping into a wall.
- **Touch sensors:** Help robots feel pressure or touch. A robotic hand can feel how hard it is holding a glass, so it does not break it.
- **Environmental sensors:** Measure things like temperature or humidity. A farming robot checks if the soil is too dry.
- **Internal sensors:** Help the robot understand its own body. For example, a gyroscope can tell if the robot is tilting, an accelerometer can tells how fast it is moving. Encoders tell how far a robot's arm has moved while current sensors check how much power is being used.

Actuators acts as a robot's muscles. They help robots move or perform actions. They convert electrical signals into motion. Robotic systems rely heavily on actuators to perform physical tasks, and the type of actuator used often determines the robot's capabilities, speed, and strength. Among the most common actuators are electric motors, hydraulic actuators, and pneumatic actuators, each serving distinct roles based on the nature of the task and the environment in which the robot operates.

Electric motors are the most widely used actuators in robotics, especially in applications that require precision and control. These motors convert electrical energy into mechanical motion, allowing robotic arms to move with accuracy and consistency. For example, in a toy manufacturing line, a robotic arm equipped with electric motors can pick up small toys and place them in packaging boxes. The advantage of electric motors lies in their ability to provide fine control over movement, which is essential for tasks that require delicate handling or repetitive precision. Think of them as the muscles in a human hand—capable of gripping, lifting, and releasing objects with careful coordination.

In contrast, **hydraulic actuators** are designed for tasks that demand immense power and the ability to move heavy loads. These actuators use pressurized liquid, typically oil, to generate force. This makes them ideal for industrial robots that operate in environments such as automotive factories, where lifting and positioning heavy car parts is a routine task. A robot using hydraulic actuators can easily lift a car door or engine block, tasks that would be impossible for electric motors due to their limited force output. To visualize this, imagine the hydraulic system as a powerful water pump that can push with tremendous strength—like how a construction crane lifts heavy materials.

Pneumatic actuators, on the other hand, use compressed air to produce motion. These are best suited for applications that require quick, lightweight movements. Robots that sort packages in a logistics center often rely on pneumatic actuators to rapidly move items from one conveyor belt to another. The speed and simplicity of pneumatic systems make them ideal for repetitive tasks that do not require high precision or heavy lifting. If electric motors are like the human hand and hydraulic systems like a crane, then pneumatic actuators are akin to a puff of air that can nudge or push objects swiftly and efficiently.

Each type of actuator plays a vital role in the broader ecosystem of robotics. The choice between electric, hydraulic, and pneumatic systems depends on the specific requirements of the task—whether it demands precision, power, or speed. Understanding these differences not only helps in designing more effective robots but also in appreciating the engineering behind the machines that increasingly shape our world.

To understand the role of a **control system**, consider the example of a robot vacuum cleaner navigating a room. As the vacuum moves, its sensors continuously scan the surroundings. When it detects an obstacle, such as a wall, the sensor sends this data to the control system. The control system then processes the information, determines that a collision is imminent, and decides to change direction. This decision is communicated to the actuators, which adjust the wheels to steer the vacuum away from the wall. This seamless interaction between sensing, decision-making, and movement illustrates the fundamental architecture of robotic control.

A **sensor fusion** is a teamwork of sensors. Sometimes, robots use many sensors together to make better decisions. This is called sensor fusion. For example, a drone uses a camera, GPS, and gyroscope together to fly smoothly and avoid crashing.

Path Planning and Navigation

Imagine you want to go from your home to your friend's house. You look at a map, choose the best route (maybe the shortest or the safest), avoid traffic or roadblocks. Robots do the same thing!

Path planning is how a robot figures out the best way to go from one place to another. A delivery robot in a mall wants to go from the kitchen to a customer's table. It uses a map of the mall and plans a path that avoids walls, people, and furniture. Once the robot has a path, it needs to follow it—just like you follow Google Maps while walking. Navigation means knowing where the robot is, following the planned path, and changing the path if something blocks the way. If someone suddenly stands in front of the delivery robot, it will stop and find a new way around them.

Robots use cameras and LiDAR to 'see' the world. LiDAR in robotics is like a bat using echolocation to fly through a cave. Instead of sound, LiDAR sends out laser pulses and measures how long they take to bounce back—just like a bat listens for echoes to 'see' its surroundings. This helps the robot build a detailed 3D picture of the environment, so it can navigate safely and avoid obstacles, even in the dark or complex spaces.

They use GPS or SLAM to know where they are. SLAM stands for simultaneous localization and mapping (like drawing a map while walking through a new place). SLAM in robotics is like walking through a maze with a pencil and notebook, drawing the layout as you go—without a pre-made map. As the robot moves, it uses sensors to figure out what is around it (mapping) and where it is within that space (localization), all at the same time. It is like being both the explorer and the cartographer, constantly updating the map while figuring out your own position. Robots use proximity sensors to detect nearby objects. A robot vacuum senses a wall and turns away before hitting it.

Self-driving cars use cameras and LiDAR to see roads and traffic, plan routes, and drive safely. Warehouse robots use maps and sensors to carry boxes from one place to another. Drones use GPS and cameras to fly and avoid trees or buildings.

Human–Robot Interaction (HRI)

Human–robot interaction, or HRI, explores how people and robots work together and understand one another. Just like humans interact through conversation, teamwork, or play, robots also need to engage meaningfully with people to be tremendously helpful. HRI falls into two categories: physical interaction and social interaction.

Physical interaction happens when humans and robots share a workspace and often come into direct contact. Picture a factory where a collaborative robot—known as a cobot—hands tools to a technician or holds parts in place. These robots use sensors to apply just the right amount of pressure, ensuring safety. In healthcare, a robot might gently assist an elderly person while walking, offering both support and protection.

Social interaction, meanwhile, is all about communication—through speech, gestures, and emotional signals. In hospitals, robots might talk with patients, listen to their concerns, and respond with empathy. In classrooms, educational robots may smile, wave, and help students with assignments, creating a warm and engaging learning atmosphere.

Robots can be operated in different ways. Some use physical controls like buttons or joysticks, while others respond to virtual commands via apps or voice assistants. For example, you might tell a robot vacuum to 'start cleaning' using your phone or a smart speaker.

A key ingredient in successful HRI is trust. People feel more comfortable using robots when they understand what the robot is doing. If a robot explains that it paused because someone walked nearby, it builds confidence and a sense of safety. Ethical behaviour is also vital robots must respect privacy and follow social norms. A hospital robot, for instance, should never share patient details and must behave appropriately according to cultural expectations.

HRI is used in many areas: in factories for manufacturing, in hospitals for surgeries and patient care, and in homes and schools for cleaning, teaching, and play. At its heart, HRI is about safe collaboration, clear communication, mutual trust, and making robots genuinely useful and approachable.

As a field, HRI blends robotics, psychology, design, and ethics. Its ultimate aim is to create robots that are not just functional, but socially aware—able to interact with humans in meaningful and respectful ways.

Applications: Industrial, Medical, Service Robots

Robotics is transforming industries and improving lives across sectors. The three main categories—industrial, medical, and service robots—serve distinct roles.

Industrial robots operate in manufacturing for tasks like welding, painting, and assembly. Built for precision and endurance, they boost efficiency, cut labour costs, and improve quality. Collaborative robots (cobots) work safely with humans, blending automation with flexibility.

Medical robots support diagnosis, surgery, rehabilitation, and care. Surgical systems like da Vinci enable precise, minimally invasive procedures, improving recovery. Rehabilitation robots guide patients through exercises, while telepresence robots let doctors consult remotely, broadening healthcare access.

Service robots help with daily tasks such as cleaning, delivery, education, and companionship. Examples include robotic vacuums, drones, and classroom assistants. These robots use AI and sensors to navigate, interact, and perform tasks autonomously. In hospitality, they greet guests and deliver items, enhancing service.

Each type faces unique demands: industrial robots must be durable, medical robots must meet strict safety standards, and service robots must be intuitive and socially aware. AI integration allows robots to learn and adapt, increasing their effectiveness.

Robotics significantly boosts productivity, healthcare, and daily living. As technology evolves, robots are becoming more capable and accessible, driving innovation and expanding their societal role.

Case Study: Boston Dynamics and Surgical Robots

Two key case studies—Boston Dynamics and surgical robots—highlight robotics innovation in mobility and healthcare.

Boston Dynamics is known for agile robots like Spot, a four-legged robot that navigates rough terrain, climbs stairs, and operates in hazardous areas. Using sensors, computer vision, and AI, Spot makes real-time decisions and is used in construction, inspection, and safety. Atlas, their humanoid robot, performs dynamic movements like running and jumping. It is developed through RL and simulation, enabling it to learn and adapt to new tasks. Surgical robots, such as the da Vinci Surgical System, are used in minimally invasive procedures like prostatectomy and cardiac surgery. Controlled by surgeons via a console, they offer precision, better visualization, and reduced trauma. These systems also support remote surgeries, expanding access to specialized care. Their development involves collaboration among engineers, doctors, and regulators to ensure safety. Together, these examples show how robotics enhances mobility in complex environments and precision in healthcare, underscoring its transformative impact across fields.

Did You Know?

Boston Dynamics' robot Spot can climb stairs, open doors, and even dance—thanks to advanced robotics and AI!

> **Mini Project/Assignment**
>
> *Title*: Design a Helper Robot
>
> *Task*: Imagine a robot that helps at home (e.g., cleaning, cooking). Describe what sensors and actions it would need.

Summary

- AI includes subfields like knowledge engineering, machine learning, deep learning, NLP, computer vision, and robotics.
- Knowledge engineering builds systems that replicate expert decision-making. The key components of expert knowledge-based systems (EKBS) are knowledge base, inference engine, and user interface. The main knowledge representation techniques are semantic networks, frames, production rules, and logic-based representations.
- Machine learning (ML) enables systems to learn from data. The main paradigms are supervised learning, unsupervised learning, and reinforcement learning.
- Supervised learning predicts outcomes using labelled data. The main algorithms used are decision tree, support vector machine, and neural networks. The application areas are healthcare, finance, retail, spam detection, and autonomous vehicles.
- Unsupervised learning finds hidden patterns in unlabelled data. The main techniques are clustering and dimentionality reduction. Application areas include marketing, cybersecurity, healthcare, and recommendation systems.
- Reinforcement learning learns optimal actions via trial and error. It is based on Markov decision processes. Application areas include robotics, gaming, finance, and healthcare.
- Deep learning uses multi-layered neural networks to learn patterns. It uses feedforward networks with backpropagation and SGD. Techniques involved are batch normalization, dropout, and adaptive learning rates
- Convolutional neural networks are ideal for image tasks; layers include convolutional, pooling, and fully connected. Recurrent neural networks and long short-term memory can handle sequential data; they are used in speech and language tasks.
- Natural language processing (NLP) enables machines to understand and generate human language. The processes used are tokenization, POS tagging, parsing, and semantic analysis. Transformers have a self-attention mechanism and the main models are BERT and GPT. They are used in chatbots, for translation, and for sentiment analysis.
- Computer vision enables machines to interpret visual data. The main functions are image processing and object recognition and classification. The main application areas are autonomous vehicles and medical imaging.
- Robotics combines engineering and AI for autonomous machines. The main components are sensors, actuators, and control systems. Their application areas include industry, medicine, and services.

Exercises

Part A (Objective Questions)

1. Which component of an expert knowledge-based system is responsible for storing domain-specific rules and facts?
   (a) Inference Engine
   (b) User Interface
   (c) Knowledge Base
   (d) Neural Network

2. In a semantic network used for knowledge representation, what does an edge typically represent?
   (a) A data value
   (b) A relationship between concepts
   (c) A decision rule
   (d) A user query

3. A hospital wants to use AI to predict patient re-admission risk based on historical data. Which machine learning paradigm is most suitable?
   (a) Reinforcement Learning
   (b) Unsupervised Learning
   (c) Supervised Learning
   (d) Deep Learning

4. Which of the following best explains why MYCIN, despite its diagnostic accuracy, was never deployed in clinical practice?
   (a) It lacked a user interface
   (b) It was unable to explain its reasoning
   (c) Legal and ethical concerns
   (d) It used outdated algorithms

5. Which challenge in knowledge engineering is most affected by the tacit nature of expert knowledge?
   (a) Knowledge validation
   (b) Knowledge acquisition
   (c) Scalability
   (d) Inference optimization

6. You are designing a chatbot for a bank. Which NLP techniques would you prioritize to ensure it understands user intent and responds accurately?
   (a) Image segmentation and object detection
   (b) Tokenization and semantic analysis
   (c) Reinforcement learning and clustering
   (d) PCA and dimensionality reduction

7. What is the primary goal of reinforcement learning in AI systems?
   (a) To classify data into categories
   (b) To discover hidden patterns in unlabeled data
   (c) To maximize cumulative rewards through interaction
   (d) To store expert knowledge

8. A company wants to detect unusual behaviour in network traffic to prevent cyberattacks. Which unsupervised learning technique is most appropriate?
   (a) Decision Trees
   (b) K-Means Clustering
   (c) Q-Learning
   (d) Support Vector Machines

9. Why are CNNs preferred over traditional algorithms for image classification tasks?
   (a) They require no training data
   (b) They use handcrafted features
   (c) They learn hierarchical features from raw pixels
   (d) They are rule-based systems

10. You are tasked with designing a robot for warehouse automation. Which combination of technologies would best support autonomous navigation and obstacle avoidance?
    (a) Semantic networks and production rules
    (b) SLAM and proximity sensors
    (c) TF-IDF and Word2Vec
    (d) RNNs and LSTMs

Part B (Short Answer Questions)

1. What are the three main components of an expert knowledge-based system?
2. How do semantic networks represent knowledge in AI systems?
3. How would you use a decision tree to predict loan approval in a financial application?
4. Compare K-means and hierarchical clustering in terms of their approach and flexibility.
5. Design a supervised learning model to detect fraudulent transactions in real time.
6. How do internal sensors contribute to the safe operation of a robot?
7. What ethical considerations must be addressed in designing socially interactive robots?

Part C (Essay Questions)

1. Describe the three main components of an expert knowledge-based system (EKBS) and explain their individual roles in the decision-making process.
2. List and briefly define the primary paradigms of machine learning.
3. Explain how semantic networks and frames differ as knowledge representation techniques, and provide examples of how each might be used in an AI system.

4. Apply the concept of reinforcement learning to a real-world scenario such as autonomous drone navigation, detailing how the agent learns and adapts.
5. Analyze the case studies of MYCIN and DENDRAL to identify the key factors that contributed to their success and the limitations that prevented their widespread adoption.

Answers

Part A

1. (c)   2. (b)   3. (c)   4. (c)   5. (b)   6. (b)   7. (c)   8. (b)   9. (c)   10. (b)

CHAPTER 3

Applications of AI

Objectives

At the end of this chapter, you will be able to:

- Explain how AI is transforming various industries through data analysis, pattern recognition, and predictive capabilities
- Describe the broad impact of AI on decision-making, efficiency, and innovation across sectors like healthcare, finance, education, agriculture, transportation, and retail
- Elucidate how AI enhances medical diagnostics by improving speed, accuracy, and scalability
- Describe the role of AI in medical imaging, including image interpretation, disease detection, and image enhancement
- Elaborate on how AI improves fraud detection through adaptive learning and real-time monitoring
- Explain the role of AI in algorithmic trading and market prediction, including sentiment analysis and reinforcement learning
- Explain how adaptive learning platforms personalize education based on student performance and preferences
- Describe the role of AI in precision agriculture and IoT integration for efficient resource management
- Elaborate on how AI powers self-driving cars through perception, decision-making, and route planning
- Describe the impact of AI chatbots and virtual assistants on customer support and service scalability

3.1 Introduction

The rise of AI is driven by super computers, vast data, and advanced machine learning (ML) algorithms. AI can analyze large data sets, detect the patterns, predict outcomes, and even can generate text, images, or music. Because of this, AI has become a widely used tool that enables human beings to improve decision-making, boosts efficiency, and sparks innovation. For example, in healthcare, AI helps doctors diagnose complex diseases, choose effective personalized treatments, and interpret complex medical images. In finance, it can detect fraud, assesses risk, and enables automated trading. In education, AI enables personalized learning and smart tutoring. Farmers can use AI to improve crop yields and forecast the outcomes of the harvests. Transportation departments benefit from AI self-driving cars and AI traffic management systems. Retailers can use AI for personalized shopping and better inventory control. AI is also transforming manufacturing, entertainment, legal services, environmental protection, and public safety. AI's impact on daily life and work grows rapidly. It is essential for everyone—not just experts—to understand how AI works and how it shapes our world.

3.2 Healthcare

This includes medical diagnostics, medical imaging, personalized treatment and treatment planning.

3.2.1 AI in Medical Diagnostics

AI is transforming how doctors detect and diagnose diseases—making it faster, more accurate, and scalable (Table 3.1).

Table 3.1 AI in medical diagnostics

Aspect	Before AI	With AI	Examples
Diagnosis Process	Doctors manually reviewed symptoms, lab tests, and images	AI analyzes large data sets to find patterns humans might miss	AI detects early signs of cancer, diabetes, and heart disease
Speed and Accuracy	Time-consuming and prone to human error	Faster, more accurate, and scalable	AI systems can process thousands of records in seconds
Pathology	Experts examine tissue samples manually	AI identifies cancer cells, sometimes more accurately than experts	AI distinguishes between benign and harmful cells
Prediction and Forecasting	Based on doctor's experience and patient history	AI predicts disease progression using historical data	Helps doctors choose better treatments
Medical Testing	Lab staff interpret results manually	AI automates result interpretation and flags abnormalities	Reduces workload and speeds up diagnosis
Support in Remote Areas	Limited access to specialists	AI acts as a virtual assistant to general practitioners	Offers expert-level support in rural or underserved regions
Future Potential	Personalized care depended on doctor's judgment	AI enables more personalized and preventive healthcare	Tailored treatment plans based on individual data

3.2.2 AI in Medical Imaging

AI is transforming medical imaging, including MRI, CT scans, and X-rays (Table 3.2).

Table 3.2 AI in medical imaging

Aspect	Before AI	With AI	Examples
Image Interpretation	Doctors manually reviewed MRI, CT, and X-ray images	AI (especially CNNs) analyzes images quickly and accurately	AI detects tumours or fractures faster than humans
Breast Cancer Screening	Doctors examined mammograms for early signs	AI spots early signs and reduces false positives or missed cases	AI improves accuracy in breast cancer detection
Brain Health	Doctors studied brain scans for signs of disease	AI identifies Alzheimer's, stroke, and tracks disease progression	Helps monitor treatment effectiveness
Image Quality Enhancement	Image noise and blur reduced manually or with basic tools	AI removes noise, sharpens images, and creates 3D models from 2D scans	Aids in surgical planning and personalized treatment
Organ and Tissue Mapping	Manual outlining and measurement by radiologists	AI automatically outlines organs and tissues	Speeds up analysis and reduces workload
Overall Impact	Slower, more error-prone diagnostics	Faster, more precise diagnostics with AI-human collaboration	Radiology becomes more efficient and accurate

3.2.3 Personalized Medicine and Treatment Planning

Personalized medicine treats patients based on their unique traits—like genes, environment, and lifestyle. Instead of one-size-fits-all treatments, doctors tailor care to each person (Table 3.3).

Table 3.3 AI in personalized medicine and treatment planning

Aspect	Before AI	With AI	Examples
Treatment Approach	One-size-fits-all treatments	Personalized care based on genes, lifestyle, and environment	Tailored cancer therapies based on tumour genetics
Data Analysis	Doctors manually reviewed patient history	AI analyzes large personal data sets to find patterns	Predicts how a patient will respond to specific drugs
Cancer Care	Standard chemotherapy based on cancer type	AI selects the most effective drugs for each patient's tumour	Improves outcomes and reduces side effects
Drug Safety	Doctors rely on experience for drug combinations	AI predicts drug interactions and side effects	Helps avoid harmful combinations

(Continued)

Table 3.3 (Continued)

Aspect	Before AI	With AI	Examples
Real-Time Monitoring	Manual tracking of vitals and lab results	AI monitors health data and suggests treatment changes instantly	Vital in emergency care situations
Treatment Simulation	Limited trial-and-error approach	AI simulates different treatment options	Helps doctors choose the best plan
Healthcare Impact	Reactive and generalized care	Proactive, personalized, and cost-effective care	Better results with fewer complications

> **Case Study: IBM Watson in Oncology**
>
> IBM Watson is a leading example of AI in healthcare, especially for cancer treatment. Its tool, Watson for Oncology, developed with Memorial Sloan Kettering Cancer Center, helps doctors choose evidence-based treatments. Watson analyzes vast amounts of medical data—research papers, clinical trials, and patient records—to suggest personalized treatment plans. It reviews a patient's history, lab results, and genetic data to recommend therapies aligned with current guidelines. Doctors receive ranked treatment options with explanations and expected outcomes, aiding decisions in complex cases. Hospitals worldwide, including in India and China, have used Watson in cancer care. Studies show its recommendations often match expert opinions, proving its usefulness. However, Watson needs local data and regular updates to stay effective. Despite challenges, Watson's role in cancer care highlights AI's potential to support doctors, enhance decisions, and improve patient outcomes.

> **Did You Know?**
>
> AI can now detect cancer cells in pathology slides with higher accuracy than some human experts. These systems learn from thousands of labelled images to distinguish between healthy and abnormal cells.

> **Mini Project/Assignment**
>
> Interview a local doctor or healthcare worker (or research online) to learn how technology is used in their work. Write a short report or create a presentation on how AI could help in their field.

3.3 Finance

AI has become an indispensable tool in the financial sector, particularly in fraud detection, risk modelling and assessment, algorithmic trading and market prediction.

3.3.1 AI in Fraud Detection

AI has become a game-changer in the financial sector, especially when it comes to spotting fraud. Traditionally, banks and financial institutions relied on rule-based systems—rigid frameworks that flagged suspicious activity based on predefined criteria. While these systems were useful to a point, they struggled to keep pace with the evolving tactics of fraudsters. AI, particularly through machine learning, has introduced a more adaptive approach that learns from data and improves over time.

ML analyzes historical transaction data, both legitimate and fraudulent, to uncover patterns and anomalies that may signal fraud. For instance, if a credit card is suddenly used in a distant location or for unusually large purchases, the system can flag it for further review. Unlike static rule-based models, AI continuously updates its understanding of what constitutes suspicious behaviour, making it more effective at identifying new types of fraud.

Deep learning (DL), a more sophisticated branch of ML, has further strengthened fraud detection. It leverages neural networks to process vast and complex data sets—such as emails, voice recordings, and social media content. These models can detect subtle indicators of fraud within unstructured data. Tools like natural language processing (NLP) enable systems to interpret written language and identify deceptive or unusual phrasing. This allows financial institutions to uncover not only transactional fraud but also identity theft, phishing schemes, and insider threats (Table 3.4).

Table 3.4 AI in fraud detection

Aspect	Traditional approach	AI-driven approach
Detection Method	Rule-based systems with predefined criteria	ML models that learn from historical data
Adaptability	Static and rigid; slow to adapt to new fraud tactics	Continuously evolving; adapts to emerging fraud patterns
Data Utilization	Limited to structured transaction data	Uses both structured and unstructured data (e.g., emails, voice, social media)
Advanced Techniques	None	DL and NLP for nuanced pattern recognition
Real-Time Monitoring	Delayed detection; post-transaction analysis	Instant evaluation of transactions; flags suspicious activity in real time
Types of Fraud Detected	Mostly transactional anomalies	Transactional fraud, identity theft, phishing, insider threats
False Positives	High rate; legitimate transactions often flagged	Reduced rate; improved accuracy enhances customer experience
Alert Prioritization	Uniform treatment of alerts	Risk-based prioritization for faster response to critical threats
Customer Experience	Often disrupted due to inaccurate flags	Smoother experience with fewer interruptions
Long-Term Effectiveness	Declines as fraud tactics evolve	Improves over time through continuous learning

3.3.2 Risk Modelling and Assessment

Making smart financial decisions starts with understanding and managing risk—and AI is transforming how that is done. Traditional risk models relied heavily on basic math and historical data, which often fell short in capturing the complexity of today's financial landscape. AI introduces sophisticated techniques that can analyze diverse data sources and uncover subtle patterns, giving experts sharper tools for predicting risk (Table 3.5).

Table 3.5 Risk modelling and assessment

Risk area	Traditional approach	AI-driven approach
Credit Risk	Relied on historical financial data and credit scores	Uses behavioural, transactional, and alternative data (e.g., social media) for profiling
Market Risk	Manual trend analysis and economic indicators	Predictive modelling using real-time data and scenario simulations
Operational Risk	Based on incident logs and manual audits	NLP scans internal documents and communications to detect vulnerabilities
Compliance Monitoring	Periodic reviews and manual checks	Automated flagging of irregularities using AI models
Fraud Detection	Rule-based systems with limited adaptability	ML and DL detect anomalies and unstructured fraud signals
Stress Testing	Static models with predefined scenarios	Dynamic simulations using AI to assess resilience under multiple crisis conditions
Risk Scoring	Fixed formulas and rating scales	Composite scoring using weighted AI-driven risk factors (e.g., model complexity, bias)
Transparency and Explainability	Limited visibility into decision logic	Explainable AI models with traceable decision paths
Real-Time Monitoring	Delayed detection and response	Instantaneous risk evaluation and alert prioritization
Financial Inclusion	Excluded underserved populations due to lack of data	AI evaluates non-traditional data to expand credit access

3.3.3 Algorithmic Trading and Market Prediction

Algorithmic trading—often called algo-trading—relies on software to execute trades based on predefined rules. With AI now in the mix, these systems have evolved to become more adaptive, learning from market shifts and fine-tuning strategies as conditions fluctuate. They sift through massive data sets, including price movements, trading volumes, news reports, and social media chatter, to inform trading decisions (Table 3.6).

Table 3.6 Algorthmic trading and market prediction

Aspect	Description
Definition	Algorithmic trading uses software to execute trades based on predefined rules. AI enhances this by making systems adaptive and responsive to market changes.
Data Sources	Price movements, trading volumes, news reports, social media chatter.
Machine Learning Role	Identifies hidden patterns, predicts market reactions to economic news, and uncovers relationships between financial instruments.
Reinforcement Learning	Algorithms learn through trial and error, adjusting strategies based on outcomes—similar to human learning but faster and more consistent.

(Continued)

Table 3.6 *(Continued)*

Aspect	Description
Sentiment Analysis	AI interprets tone in news, disclosures, and online conversations to gauge market sentiment, helping predict shifts due to political or corporate events.
Risk Management	AI embeds safeguards to halt trading during volatility and runs stress simulations to test strategy resilience.
Accessibility	AI-powered tools are now available to individual investors, not just large financial firms.
Challenges	Concerns around fairness, transparency, and potential market manipulation.
Impact on Finance	AI reshapes trading by processing complex data, adapting to conditions, and executing trades with precision—making it indispensable in modern finance.

Case Study: AI in JPMorgan Chase

JPMorgan Chase, one of the world's top financial institutions, has woven AI into many parts of its operations. Whether it is fraud detection, trading, or legal work, AI is helping the bank boost both efficiency and security.

To combat fraud, the bank uses ML to scan millions of transactions daily, flagging anything that looks out of the ordinary. This real-time monitoring helps cut down on losses and reassures customers. AI also helps detect identity theft and unauthorized access, adding another layer of protection to digital banking.

When it comes to risk evaluation, JPMorgan Chase taps into AI to analyze creditworthiness and market exposure. These tools sift through financial records, global events, and political shifts to create in-depth risk profiles. The insights they generate support smarter decision-making and regulatory compliance. In the trading space, AI-driven algorithms help the bank manage portfolios and execute trades. These systems track market trends, economic indicators, and news to spot opportunities quickly. Their speed and flexibility give the bank an edge in fast-paced markets.

A notable innovation is COiN (Contract Intelligence), which uses NLP to review legal documents. It can scan thousands of contracts in seconds, pulling out key terms and flagging potential issues—making legal work faster and more cost-effective.

JPMorgan Chase's investment in AI mirrors a broader trend in the financial world: a shift toward smarter, tech-driven operations. By staying ahead with these tools, the bank continues to lead in innovation and set the pace for the industry.

Did You Know?

AI in finance can analyze social media posts to detect fraud or predict market sentiment. This is part of alternative data analysis, which goes beyond traditional financial metrics.

Mini Project/Assignment

Track your daily expenses for a week and categorize them. Then, imagine how an AI app could help you save money or detect unusual spending patterns. Present your ideas in a simple chart or write-up.

3.4 Education

AI is transforming how students learn by making education more personalized, flexible, and inclusive. Instead of relying solely on traditional teaching methods that treat all learners the same, schools and platforms are now using smart systems that adapt lessons to each student's needs. These AI tools track progress in real time, spotting areas where a student excels or struggles, and then adjusting the learning path accordingly. Intelligent tutoring systems act like virtual mentors—guiding students, answering their questions, and shifting teaching strategies based on how they respond. This approach not only improves learning outcomes but also boosts motivation and engagement, helping a wider range of learners succeed.

3.4.1 Adaptive Learning Platforms

AI is reshaping education, especially through platforms that adjust learning to suit individual students. These systems use algorithms to personalize lessons based on how each learner progresses, their pace, and preferred learning style (Table 3.7).

Table 3.7 Adaptive learning platforms

Aspect	Description
Personalized Learning	AI platforms tailor lessons to each student's pace, progress, and learning style, unlike traditional one-size-fits-all classrooms.
Adaptive Content Delivery	Complexity, format, and order of topics are adjusted based on student performance to optimize understanding and engagement.
Ongoing Feedback	Systems track quiz scores, time spent, and mistakes to guide learning—offering extra help or advancing students based on their needs.
Natural Language Processing	Enables platforms to understand and respond to student questions conversationally, making learning more interactive and less intimidating.
Knowledge Gap Detection	AI identifies foundational gaps and recommends review material to strengthen understanding before moving forward.
Scalability and Accessibility	AI tools can reach many learners, even in underserved areas, helping democratize access to quality education.
Teacher Support	Educators gain insights into student progress and engagement, allowing them to personalize instruction more effectively.
Impact on Education	Promotes personalized, data-driven learning that improves comprehension, retention, and academic success.

3.4.2 Intelligent Tutoring Systems

Intelligent tutoring systems, or ITS, are digital learning tools designed to mimic the kind of help students usually get from a personal tutor. They combine ideas from AI, psychology, and teaching methods to create learning experiences that adjust to each student's needs (Table 3.8).

3.4.3 AI for Curriculum Design and Assessment

For years, curriculum design and student assessment have relied heavily on manual processes and personal judgment. Now, with the help of AI, these tasks are becoming more efficient, objective, and tailored to individual learners (Table 3.9).

Table 3.8 Intelligent tutoring systems

Aspect	Description
Definition	ITS are digital tools designed to replicate the personalized support of human tutors using AI, psychology, and pedagogy.
Core Components	• **Subject Model:** Defines the content being taught. • **Student Model:** Tracks learner progress and behaviour. • **Teaching Model:** Guides instruction delivery.
Adaptive Instruction	Adjusts teaching methods and content based on student performance and misconceptions (e.g., revisiting basics or using analogies).
Real-Time Feedback	Provides immediate, personalized feedback tailored to the student's current understanding and learning needs.
Natural Language Interaction	Uses NLP to allow students to ask questions in everyday language and receive helpful, conversational responses.
Socratic Method	Some ITS use guided questioning to encourage reasoning and independent problem-solving.
STEM Effectiveness	Particularly beneficial in math, coding, physics, and engineering—boosting both performance and interest.
Accessibility	Supports students with disabilities via flexible interfaces and adaptable content formats.
Collaborative Development	Built through collaboration among educators, AI experts, and developers to ensure accurate models and effective teaching strategies.
Scalability and Equity	Enables personalized learning at scale, reaching diverse learners regardless of location or background.

Table 3.9 AI for curriculum design and assessment

Aspect	Description
Curriculum Design	AI analyzes student data to align curricula with learning goals and individual needs, making planning more efficient and targeted.
Lesson Planning Support	Highlights challenging topics and suggests changes in timing, teaching methods, or formats (e.g., videos, simulations, hands-on activities).
Formative Assessment	Enables continuous feedback by analyzing student responses to detect misunderstandings and predict future performance.
AI-Assisted Grading	Uses natural language processing to evaluate written work (grammar, clarity, structure, relevance), providing detailed feedback and reducing teacher workload.
Flexible Learning Models	Supports competency-based progression, allowing students to advance by demonstrating mastery rather than time spent in class.
Personalized Learning Paths	Tracks progress and aligns assessments with goals to create tailored educational journeys, especially useful in vocational and professional training.
Inclusivity and Responsiveness	Helps schools offer more inclusive and impactful education by adapting to diverse learner needs and backgrounds.
Educator Empowerment	Provides insights that help teachers refine instruction and better support student success.

> **Case Study: Squirrel AI in China**
>
> Squirrel AI, a China-based edtech company, has been making waves in personalized learning since its launch in 2014. The company developed an adaptive learning platform that tailors instruction to individual students across various subjects. Today, it is used in thousands of schools and learning centres across China, reaching millions of learners. At the heart of the platform is a knowledge graph that maps how concepts connect within a subject. As students work through lessons, the system evaluates their understanding and identifies weak spots. It then adjusts the learning path to focus on those areas, offering a more targeted and efficient alternative to traditional teaching. The platform also uses DL and NLP to monitor how students interact with content. If it detects signs of confusion or disengagement, it can tweak the difficulty level or offer encouragement to keep students motivated and emotionally balanced. Squirrel AI includes features that simulate one-on-one tutoring. Students receive immediate feedback, explanations for errors, and helpful hints to guide their thinking. This interactive approach encourages deeper learning and critical thinking. Teachers and parents also get detailed insights into student progress, strengths, and areas that need attention. Research shows that students using Squirrel AI often outperform their peers in traditional classrooms and develop a stronger grasp of the material. Its adaptive nature has been especially beneficial for learners who struggle with conventional methods. The success of Squirrel AI highlights how AI can make personalized education more scalable and inclusive. Its forward-thinking model points to a future where learning is more student-focused and data-informed.

> **Did You Know?**
>
> Some AI tutoring systems use the Socratic method, asking guiding questions to help students discover answers themselves—just like ancient philosophers did!

> **Mini Project/Assignment**
>
> Create a personalized study plan for yourself or a friend. Include subjects, preferred learning styles (visual, audio, etc.), and goals. Reflect on how AI could improve this plan.

3.5 Agriculture

Agriculture, one of humanity's oldest and most vital pursuits, is experiencing a dramatic transformation thanks to AI. What was once a field guided by manual labour and seasonal instincts is now evolving into a high-tech, data-driven enterprise. AI is empowering farmers to track crop health, forecast harvests, fine-tune irrigation systems, and manage resources with remarkable accuracy. Technologies like drones capturing aerial views and smart algorithms interpreting soil data and weather trends are making farming more sustainable and productive. This shift toward intelligent systems is not only boosting efficiency but also playing a key role in enhancing food security and building resilience against climate change.

3.5.1 Precision Agriculture and IoT Integration

AI is transforming agriculture through precision farming—a data-driven approach that boosts efficiency, sustainability, and crop output (Table 3.10).

Table 3.10 Precision agriculture and IoT integration

Aspect	Details
Overview	AI is revolutionizing agriculture through precision farming, enhancing efficiency, sustainability, and crop yield.
Traditional vs. AI Approach	Moves beyond traditional methods by using data-driven insights for smarter decision-making.
Data Sources	Sensors, drones, satellites, and weather feeds provide real-time data for AI analysis.
Role of IoT	Connects devices that collect field data (e.g., soil moisture, temperature, location) for AI to interpret and act upon.
AI-Driven Recommendations	Suggests optimal times for irrigation, fertilization, and harvesting based on real-time data.
Example Use Case	If dry soil is detected, AI recommends targeted watering—conserving water while maintaining crop health.
Variable Rate Technology (VRT)	Uses AI to apply fertilizers and pesticides in precise amounts tailored to each field section, based on soil and crop data.
Benefits of VRT	Reduces costs, minimizes environmental impact, and boosts productivity.
Use of Drones and Satellites	Captures detailed imagery to detect early signs of disease, pests, or stress, and monitors crop development over time.
Planning and Resource Allocation	AI insights help optimize planning and resource use across different field zones.
Overall Benefits	Higher yields, efficient resource use, climate adaptability, and support for agricultural research and sustainable practices.

3.5.2 AI in Crop Yield Prediction

Estimating crop yield is very important for farming. It helps farmers decide how to use their resources, prepare for selling their products, and make sure food gets to the right places. In the past, people used to walk through fields and use basic math to guess crop yields, but these methods were often not very accurate. Today, AI is changing this by using large amounts of data to make better predictions.

ML learns from past information like weather patterns, soil quality, types of crops, and farming methods. These computer models find connections between different factors to make predictions. For example, by studying rainfall, temperature, and soil nutrients, AI can estimate how much wheat will grow before it is even harvested. This helps farmers plan how to transport and sell their crops.

Modern tools like drones and satellites give even more helpful information. AI looks at the pictures these tools take to check how healthy the plants are, how much land they cover, and what stage of growth they are in. Changes in plant colour and brightness, measured by something called NDVI, can show how strong the crops are and how much they might produce. This is especially useful for big farms where checking everything by hand is too hard.

AI also helps update predictions during the growing season. It keeps checking new data from field sensors and weather reports to improve its forecasts. If there is a risk of drought or pests, AI can warn farmers early so they can act fast and avoid losing crops.

On a larger scale, AI-based crop predictions help governments and farming organizations make better decisions about trade and support programs. These accurate forecasts also make markets more stable by reducing guesswork and sudden changes.

Besides making more money, AI helps protect the environment. It helps farmers use water, fertilizer, and other resources more wisely, which reduces waste. With better planning, farming becomes more flexible and eco-friendly.

3.5.3 Pest and Disease Detection

Farmers often face serious problems from pests and diseases that harm crops, lower harvests, and affect the safety of the food we eat. Today, AI is helping by spotting these issues early and guiding farmers to take quick, targeted action. This reduces damage and cuts down on the use of harmful chemicals.

One powerful tool in this effort is AI-based image recognition. These systems look at pictures taken by drones, smartphones, or cameras in the field to find signs of trouble—like leaves changing colour, spots appearing, or plants growing in strange ways. Because these AI models are trained on huge collections of crop images, they can tell the difference between problems like fungus, insect attacks, or bacterial infections in crops such as rice and tomatoes.

AI also reads and analyzes written information. It scans farmer reports, online forums, and social media posts to find clues about new threats. This helps send faster warnings to farmers and agricultural officials so they can act quickly.

Besides identifying problems, AI can also predict how pests and diseases might spread. It uses weather data—such as humidity, temperature, and wind patterns—to guess where risks are highest. Then it suggests ways to prevent damage, like changing the crops grown or using natural methods to keep pests away.

AI is also a key part of integrated pest management (IPM), which uses a mix of methods to control pests. By looking at past and current data, AI recommends safe and effective solutions. For example, if it predicts an aphid outbreak, it might suggest changing planting times or adding helpful insects to the field.

In short, AI is helping farmers protect their crops by giving them timely advice and reducing losses. As climate change continues to affect how pests behave, AI will become even more important in keeping our food supply safe and strong.

> **Case Study: Blue River Technology**
>
> Blue River Technology, a subsidiary of John Deere, is making waves in smart farming through its use of AI. Founded in 2011, the company developed a system called See & Spray, which uses computer vision and ML to identify and treat individual plants as farm machinery moves through fields. This breakthrough in precision agriculture helps minimize chemical usage while improving crop care.
>
> The See & Spray system is mounted on agricultural equipment and uses high-resolution cameras along with AI processors. As the machinery moves across farmland, it captures images of plants and determines whether each one is a crop or a weed. When a weed is detected, the system activates a sprayer to apply herbicide only where it is needed. This targeted approach can reduce chemical use by up to 90% compared to conventional spraying methods.
>
> The AI models powering this technology have been trained on millions of plant images, enabling them to recognize even subtle differences in plant characteristics. The system continues to evolve, learning from new data and adapting to different crops and field conditions. It is currently effective for crops such as cotton, corn, and soybeans.

In addition to weed control, Blue River Technology is developing tools to monitor plant health and manage nutrients. By analyzing plant features, the system can identify growth stages, detect signs of stress, and recommend actions to support healthy development. This data-driven method enhances sustainability and improves farming efficiency.

Farmers who have adopted See & Spray report lower operational costs, improved yields, and a smaller environmental footprint. The technology also aligns with regulations promoting responsible pesticide use. Blue River Technology's innovations show how AI can make agriculture smarter, more productive, and environmentally conscious.

Did You Know?
AI-powered drones can scan entire fields and detect crop diseases before they spread—saving farmers time, money, and reducing chemical use.

Mini Project/Assignment
Visit a local farm or garden (or research online) and list the challenges farmers face. Then, brainstorm how AI could help solve one of these problems. Present your ideas in a poster or short essay.

3.6 Transportation

AI is reshaping how people and goods travel, bringing smarter, safer, and more efficient transportation systems to life. From self-driving cars that handle complex road conditions to traffic control systems that ease congestion, AI is driving major changes in mobility. These innovations use live data, ML, and predictive tools to plan better routes, improve safety, and cut fuel consumption. This section looks at how AI is changing transportation—through autonomous vehicles, smarter traffic flow, and advanced logistics—pointing toward a future of more adaptive, eco-friendly, and connected mobility.

3.6.1 AI in Self-Driving Cars

AI is at the heart of self-driving car development, enabling vehicles to understand their surroundings, make decisions, and operate without human control (Table 3.11).

Table 3.11 AI in self-driving cars

Concept	Description	Examples / Applications
Artificial Intelligence	Core technology enabling autonomous vehicles to perceive surroundings, make decisions, and drive without human input.	Object detection, decision-making, route planning
Sensors and Data Collection	Vehicles use cameras, radar, LiDAR, and other sensors to gather environmental data.	Detecting lane markings, nearby vehicles, pedestrians

(Continued)

Table 3.11 *(Continued)*

Concept	Description	Examples / Applications
Deep Learning (CNNs)	A subset of AI used for image recognition tasks, especially in identifying road features and objects.	Recognizing traffic signs, lane boundaries, pedestrians
Reinforcement Learning	AI technique where the system learns optimal driving behaviour through trial and error in simulated or real environments.	Merging lanes, navigating intersections, avoiding obstacles
Experience-Based Learning	Systems improve over time by learning from past driving scenarios and outcomes.	Better handling of complex or rare situations
Smart Decision-Making	AI evaluates multiple driving options and selects the safest and most efficient one, considering traffic laws and real-time conditions.	Determining right-of-way at intersections
Predictive Modelling	AI anticipates the behaviour of other road users to make proactive driving decisions.	Forecasting sudden lane changes or pedestrian movement
Route Planning	AI calculates optimal paths based on traffic, road closures, and fuel efficiency.	Choosing fastest route during rush hour
Vehicle Control	AI translates plans into physical actions like steering, braking, and accelerating.	Smooth lane changes, adaptive cruise control
Industry Leaders	Companies pioneering autonomous vehicle technology.	Tesla, Waymo (Alphabet), Cruise
Real-World Deployment	Autonomous vehicles are already operating in select cities, logging millions of miles to refine technology.	Waymo's driverless taxis in Phoenix, San Francisco
Challenges	Unpredictable conditions and ethical dilemmas remain difficult for AI to manage.	Weather changes, construction zones, accident decision-making
Future Outlook	AI is expected to make transportation safer, more efficient, and widely accessible as technology and regulations evolve.	Integration into urban mobility systems

3.6.2 Traffic Flow Management and Prediction

Traffic congestion in urban areas continues to be a major challenge, leading to longer travel times, higher fuel consumption, and more pollution. AI is helping cities tackle these issues by offering smarter ways to monitor and manage traffic (Table 3.12).

Table 3.12 Traffic flow management and prediction

Concept	Description	Examples / Applications
Traffic Congestion Challenges	Urban areas face longer travel times, increased fuel use, and pollution due to heavy traffic.	Rush hour delays, gridlocks, emissions
AI for Traffic Monitoring	AI analyzes data from sensors, GPS, cameras, and mobile apps to assess road conditions in real time.	Detecting bottlenecks, monitoring flow
Machine Learning for Prediction	Models traffic patterns using historical and live data to forecast future conditions.	Predicting rush hour, planning for events
Adaptive Signal Control	AI adjusts traffic light cycles based on real-time traffic volume to reduce wait times and improve flow.	Shorter red lights during low traffic, longer greens during peak hours
Reinforcement Learning	Traffic systems learn optimal signal timing strategies through experience and feedback.	Improved intersection throughput
Incident Detection	Computer vision scans camera feeds to identify accidents, stalled vehicles, or hazards.	Alerting responders, rerouting traffic
Emergency Response Integration	AI alerts emergency services and updates navigation apps to minimize delays and improve safety.	Faster ambulance dispatch, dynamic rerouting
Public Transport Optimization	AI analyzes rider behaviour to improve routes, schedules, and reliability of public transit.	Adjusting bus frequency, predicting arrival times
Smart City Examples	Cities using AI to manage traffic and improve air quality.	Singapore's Intelligent Transport System
Sustainability Impact	AI helps reduce emissions and fuel consumption by optimizing traffic flow and promoting public transit.	Cleaner air, reduced carbon footprint
Urban Planning Support	AI identifies long-term traffic trends to assist city planners in infrastructure development.	Planning new roads, transit hubs
Real-Time Navigation Assistance	AI recommends alternative routes to drivers based on current traffic conditions.	Avoiding congested areas, dynamic route updates
Data-Driven Decision Making	AI turns traffic data into actionable insights for better policy and operational decisions.	Traffic zoning, congestion pricing strategies

3.6.3 AI in Logistics and Fleet Management

Logistics and fleet management are essential parts of transportation, involving the coordination of vehicles, goods, and services across wide networks. AI is making a big impact in these areas by introducing smart tools that improve routing, scheduling, maintenance, and resource allocation (Table 3.13).

Table 3.13 AI in logistics and fleet management

Concept	Description	Examples / Applications
Logistics and Fleet Management	Coordination of vehicles, goods, and services across networks to ensure timely and efficient transportation.	Delivery services, supply chain operations
AI in Routing Optimization	Machine learning analyzes traffic, delivery deadlines, vehicle capacity, and preferences to find efficient paths.	Dynamic rerouting during road closures or bad weather
Real-Time Adjustments	AI adapts routes instantly based on live data to avoid delays and reduce fuel consumption.	GPS-based route changes, fuel-efficient path selection
Scheduling and Dispatch	Predictive models use historical data to anticipate demand and optimize resource allocation.	Staffing during peak seasons, vehicle assignment
Predictive Maintenance	AI monitors vehicle health using sensors and predicts issues before breakdowns occur.	Alerts for engine wear, tire replacement scheduling
Inventory Management	AI forecasts inventory needs and automates restocking by analyzing sales and supply chain data.	Preventing stockouts, reducing excess inventory
Fleet Dashboards	AI-powered platforms provide insights into vehicle location, driver behaviour, fuel usage, and delivery status.	Real-time tracking, performance analytics
Continuous Optimization	AI identifies inefficiencies and suggests improvements for better operational performance.	Route refinement, driver coaching
Industry Leaders	Major companies leveraging AI to streamline logistics and improve customer service.	UPS, FedEx, Amazon (including drone delivery systems)
Environmental Impact	AI helps reduce emissions and fuel usage through smarter routing and maintenance.	Lower carbon footprint, sustainable delivery practices
Scalability and Global Trade	AI supports growing logistics demands by enhancing efficiency and responsiveness across regions.	Cross-border shipping, urban delivery networks

Case Study: Waymo's Autonomous Driving

Waymo, a subsidiary of Alphabet Inc., is a leading innovator in autonomous vehicle technology. Founded in 2009 as the Google Self-Driving Car Project, Waymo has developed a comprehensive AI-driven platform that enables vehicles to operate safely and independently in complex environments. The company's mission is to make transportation safer, more accessible, and more efficient through the power of AI.

Waymo's autonomous vehicles are equipped with a suite of sensors, including LiDAR, radar, and high-resolution cameras. These sensors provide a 360-degree view of the environment, capturing data on road conditions, obstacles, and traffic participants. AI algorithms process this data in real-time to identify objects, predict movements, and make driving decisions. The system uses DL for perception and reinforcement learning for decision-making, allowing the vehicle to navigate urban streets, highways, and intersections.

One of Waymo's key innovations is its simulation platform, which enables the testing of autonomous driving scenarios in a virtual environment. The AI system is exposed to millions of simulated miles, including rare and challenging situations, such as jaywalking pedestrians or sudden lane changes. This extensive training improves the system's robustness and prepares it for real-world deployment.

Waymo has launched a commercial autonomous ride-hailing service called Waymo One in select cities, including Phoenix, Arizona. The service operates without human drivers and has provided thousands of rides to passengers. Feedback from users indicates high levels of safety, comfort, and reliability, validating the effectiveness of Waymo's AI technology.

Safety is a top priority for Waymo, and the company has implemented rigorous testing and validation protocols. The AI system is designed to prioritize human life and adhere to traffic laws, even in ambiguous situations. Waymo collaborates with regulators, researchers, and community stakeholders to ensure responsible deployment and continuous improvement.

Waymo's success demonstrates the transformative potential of AI in transportation. By combining advanced sensors, intelligent algorithms, and extensive testing, the company has created a viable model for autonomous mobility. Its achievements pave the way for broader adoption of self-driving technology and highlight the role of AI in shaping the future of transportation.

Did You Know?

Waymo's self-driving cars have logged millions of miles in real-world and simulated environments, helping AI learn how to handle rare and complex driving scenarios.

Mini Project/Assignment

Design a 'Smart City' map showing how AI could improve transportation (e.g., smart traffic lights, autonomous buses). Use drawings or digital tools to visualize your ideas.

3.7 Customer Service and Retail

AI is transforming the way businesses connect with customers and run their retail operations. In customer service, smart chatbots and virtual assistants now offer quick, tailored support—answering questions, solving problems, and adapting through experience. On the retail side, AI enables companies to better grasp consumer habits, fine-tune inventory levels, customize marketing efforts, and elevate the shopping journey both online and in physical stores. From personalized product suggestions to self-checkout innovations, these technologies are streamlining service and making it more responsive to customer needs. This section looks at how AI is reshaping customer engagement and retail strategies, paving the way for more agile and intelligent business models.

3.7.1 AI Chatbots and Virtual Assistants

The way businesses handle customer service has undergone a major transformation thanks to AI (Table 3.14).

Table 3.14 AI chatbots and virtual assistants

Concept	Description	Examples / Applications
AI in Customer Service	AI tools like chatbots and virtual assistants provide scalable, 24/7 support across digital platforms.	Website chatbots, app-based support, messaging platforms
Natural Language Processing	Enables chatbots to understand and respond to human language, including tone and context.	Handling delivery queries, refund requests, multi-step conversations
Machine Learning	Helps chatbots learn from interactions and improve responses over time.	Adapting to new customer questions, refining accuracy
Personalized Support	AI uses customer history and preferences to tailor responses and suggestions.	Product recommendations, personalized troubleshooting
Voice Recognition and Virtual Assistants	Tools like Alexa and Siri use voice input and contextual understanding to assist users.	Managing smart devices, scheduling appointments, filing claims
Operational Efficiency	AI reduces staffing needs, speeds up response times, and maintains service quality during high demand.	Handling large volumes of queries during sales or outages
Incident Resolution	AI can guide users through complex tasks or issues without human intervention.	Tech support, insurance claim filing
Challenges	AI must overcome limitations in empathy, cultural sensitivity, and natural interaction.	Robotic tone, misinterpretation of emotional cues
Human Oversight	Continuous updates and supervision are needed to ensure quality and relevance.	Training models, refining scripts
Business Impact	AI improves customer satisfaction, reduces costs, and supports scalability.	Faster issue resolution, consistent service experience

3.7.2 Personalized Shopping Experiences

In today's retail world, AI is changing how companies connect with shoppers—especially when it comes to personalization (Table 3.15).

Table 3.15 Personalized shopping experiences

Concept	Description	Examples / Applications
AI in Retail Personalization	AI customizes shopping experiences by analyzing customer data and behaviour.	Personalized product suggestions, tailored marketing messages
Recommendation Engines	Algorithms suggest products based on browsing history, purchases, and preferences.	Showing sportswear to athletic gear buyers
Dynamic Pricing	AI adjusts prices in real time based on demand, inventory, and competitor activity.	Flash sales, personalized discounts
Machine Learning	Helps systems learn from customer interactions and improve personalization over time.	Refining recommendations, adapting to changing preferences
Visual Search	Shoppers upload images to find similar products using AI-powered recognition.	Finding matching outfits or furniture
Customer Feedback Analysis	AI scans reviews and ratings to identify trends and guide product or inventory decisions.	Removing low-rated items, improving product features
Targeted Marketing	AI segments customers and delivers relevant ads via email, social media, or mobile.	Sending fashion deals to style-conscious shoppers
Voice-Enabled Shopping	Virtual assistants help users shop using voice commands and contextual understanding.	Reordering items via Alexa, checking delivery status
Brand Engagement	Personalized experiences strengthen customer relationships and brand loyalty.	Customized homepages, loyalty rewards
Retail Leaders Using AI	Major companies leveraging AI for personalization and efficiency.	Amazon, Walmart, Sephora, Nike
Business Impact	AI boosts sales, improves customer satisfaction, and enhances operational efficiency.	Higher conversion rates, reduced cart abandonment
Future Outlook	AI-driven personalization will remain key to competitive advantage in retail.	Hyper-personalized shopping journeys

3.7.3 Inventory and Supply Chain Optimization

Managing inventory and supply chains is a cornerstone of success in retail, and AI is helping businesses do it better. By tapping into data from sales, logistics, and market activity, AI tools help retailers fine-tune stock levels, anticipate demand, and make supply chains more efficient and cost-effective.

One of the most valuable uses of AI in this space is demand forecasting. ML looks at past sales, seasonal shifts, and outside influences like weather or economic changes to predict what customers will want next. With more accurate forecasts, retailers can avoid having too much or too little stock—saving on storage and keeping shelves filled with what shoppers need.

AI also powers systems that automatically reorder products. When stock dips below a certain point, the system places restocking orders based on expected demand and how long suppliers take to deliver. This kind of automation cuts down on manual work and helps keep operations running smoothly.

In the broader supply chain, AI boosts coordination and visibility. Businesses can track shipments, inventory, and production in real time, making it easier to react to delays or disruptions. Predictive tools can even spot trouble before it happens and suggest alternative suppliers or routes to keep things moving.

Inside warehouses, AI-driven robots are making a big impact. Using computer vision and smart algorithms, these machines can sort, pick, and pack items quickly and accurately. They help reduce labour costs and speed up order processing. AI also helps design smarter warehouse layouts, using space more efficiently and cutting down on the time it takes to find and retrieve items.

Retailers are also using AI to evaluate suppliers. By reviewing delivery records, product quality, and compliance data, businesses can identify trustworthy partners and flag potential risks. This kind of insight supports better sourcing decisions and builds a more resilient supply chain.

Overall, bringing AI into inventory and supply chain operations helps retailers become more agile and customer-focused. It allows them to meet shopper expectations while keeping costs down and reducing environmental impact—setting the stage for long-term success in a fast-changing market.

Case Study: AI in Amazon's Retail Operations

Amazon stands out as a global leader in retail and technology, showing how AI can reshape customer service and shopping experiences. The company has woven AI into nearly every part of its business—from product suggestions to inventory control and delivery—making the entire process smoother and more efficient for customers.

One of Amazon's most powerful tools is its recommendation system. By studying what customers browse and buy, the platform suggests items that match their interests. These suggestions pop up throughout the shopping journey—on the home page, product listings, and even at checkout—helping users discover new products and boosting sales. The system keeps learning from each interaction, so its recommendations get better over time.

When it comes to customer support, Amazon uses AI-driven chatbots and virtual assistants to answer questions, handle returns, and share order updates. These tools work across the website, mobile app, and voice platforms like Alexa. By automating everyday tasks, Amazon speeds up service and improves the overall experience for shoppers.

Behind the scenes, AI helps Amazon manage inventory with precision. It looks at past sales, seasonal patterns, and outside factors to predict what products will be needed. Automated systems then reorder stock as needed, keeping shelves full while avoiding excess inventory. This approach helps cut storage costs and ensures items are available when customers want them.

In its logistics network, Amazon relies on AI and robotics to keep things moving. Robots in fulfillment centers handle picking, packing, and sorting quickly and accurately. AI also helps plan warehouse layouts, delivery routes, and schedules, making sure orders arrive on time. Services like Amazon Prime and Amazon Flex use AI to assign drivers, track packages, and estimate delivery windows.

Overall, AI plays a major role in how Amazon operates. It allows the company to deliver personalized service, fast shipping, and dependable support at scale. Amazon's approach sets a high standard for the retail industry, showing how smart technology can lead to better outcomes for both businesses and customers.

Applications of AI | **73**

> **Did You Know?**
> Amazon's recommendation engine is responsible for 35% of its sales, showing how powerful AI-driven personalization can be in retail.

> **Mini Project/Assignment**
> Visit an online store and note how product suggestions change based on your browsing. Create a mock-up of a personalized shopping homepage for a fictional store using your own preferences.

Summary

- Healthcare: Medical diagnostics, medical imaging, personalized treatment planning
- Finance: Fraud detection, risk modelling and assessment, algorithmic trading
- Education: Adaptive learning platforms, intelligent tutoring systems (ITS), curriculum design and assessment
- Agriculture: Precision agriculture and IoT, crop yield prediction, pest and disease detection
- Transportation: Self-driving cars, traffic flow management, logistics and fleet management
- Customer Service and Retail: AI chatbots and virtual assistants, personalized shopping, inventory and supply chain optimization

Exercises

Part A (Objective Questions)

1. Which AI technique is primarily used in medical imaging to detect tumours and fractures?
    (a) Reinforcement Learning
    (b) Convolutional Neural Networks (CNNs)
    (c) Natural Language Processing (NLP)
    (d) Generative Adversarial Networks (GANs)

2. A farmer wants to reduce pesticide usage while maintaining crop health. Which AI-driven technology should they adopt?
    (a) Deep learning for weather prediction
    (b) Variable Rate Technology (VRT)
    (c) Natural Language Processing for crop reports
    (d) Reinforcement learning for irrigation control

3. If a financial institution wants to detect phishing schemes using AI, which combination of techniques would be most effective?
   (a) CNNs and IoT
   (b) NLP and Deep Learning
   (c) Reinforcement Learning and VRT
   (d) Image Recognition and Sentiment Analysis

4. A city wants to reduce traffic congestion using AI. Which approach would best combine real-time data and adaptive control?
   (a) Static signal timing and historical traffic logs
   (b) Manual traffic monitoring and fixed route planning
   (c) Machine learning with adaptive signal control
   (d) Deep learning for vehicle diagnostics

5. Why is AI-assisted grading considered more effective than traditional grading methods in education?
   (a) It replaces teachers entirely
   (b) It uses reinforcement learning to simulate exams
   (c) It provides detailed feedback and reduces teacher workload
   (d) It only evaluates multiple-choice questions

6. You are designing an AI system for personalized cancer treatment. Which data sources should your model prioritize?
   (a) Weather data and crop yield
   (b) Genetic data, patient history, and lab results
   (c) Traffic patterns and vehicle diagnostics
   (d) Social media activity and transaction logs

7. Which company developed the See & Spray system for precision agriculture?
   (a) IBM
   (b) Amazon
   (c) Blue River Technology
   (d) Waymo

8. How does AI improve customer experience in retail through chatbots?
   (a) By replacing all human agents
   (b) By offering scripted responses only
   (c) By using NLP and machine learning to personalize interactions
   (d) By limiting service hours to business times

9. An education platform wants to identify students struggling with algebra and offer tailored support. Which AI feature should it implement?
   (a) Real-time traffic prediction
   (b) Adaptive content delivery and knowledge gap detection

(c) Image recognition for textbook scanning
(d) Reinforcement learning for grading

10. What makes AI-driven fraud detection more effective than traditional rule-based systems?
    (a) It ignores historical data
    (b) It uses static models
    (c) It adapts to new fraud patterns and reduces false positives
    (d) It only detects identity theft

Part B (Short Answer Questions)
1. List three sectors where AI is currently being applied to improve outcomes.
2. Explain how AI contributes to better decision-making across industries.
3. How could a retailer use AI to improve inventory control?
4. Compare the role of AI in agriculture and transportation.
5. Assess the importance of non-experts understanding AI in today's world.
6. Compare the decision-making process of a human driver with that of an AI-powered vehicle.
7. How could AI be used to monitor a patient's health in real time?
8. Explain how AI improves fraud detection compared to traditional rule-based systems.
9. Explain how AI helps detect knowledge gaps in students.
10. Explain how AI and IoT work together to improve irrigation practices.

Part C (Essay Questions)
1. List and briefly describe the major sectors where artificial intelligence is currently being applied.
2. Explain how AI has transformed medical diagnostics and imaging, highlighting the differences between traditional methods and AI-driven approaches.
3. Using the case study of IBM Watson in Oncology, illustrate how AI can be integrated into clinical decision-making to improve cancer treatment outcomes.
4. Compare and contrast the use of AI in fraud detection versus risk modelling in the financial sector. What are the similarities and differences in their approaches and outcomes?
5. Analyze the role of AI in personalized education through adaptive learning platforms and intelligent tutoring systems. How do these systems adjust to individual student needs?
6. Evaluate the effectiveness of AI-powered traffic flow management systems in reducing urban congestion and improving public transportation. What are the potential limitations?
7. Assess the impact of AI-driven inventory and supply chain optimization on retail operations. How does it influence customer satisfaction and operational efficiency?
8. Design a conceptual framework for integrating AI into agricultural pest and disease detection systems, incorporating image recognition, weather data, and farmer feedback.
9. Propose an AI-based solution for enhancing curriculum design and assessment in vocational education. What features would make it scalable and inclusive?
10. Imagine a future retail environment fully powered by AI. Describe how customer service, inventory management, and personalized shopping would function in this setting.

Answers

Part A
1. (b) 2. (b) 3. (b) 4. (c) 5. (c) 6. (b) 7. (c) 8. (c) 9. (b) 10. (c)

CHAPTER 4

Ethics, Bias, and Social Implications

Objectives

At the end of this chapter, you will be able to:

- Explain the ethical concerns surrounding AI, including fairness, bias, transparency, and accountability
- Recognize the importance of data privacy and the need for secure handling of personal information
- Appreciate the role of inclusivity, trustworthiness, and sustainability in AI development
- Explain techniques for detecting bias in AI systems, including data analysis, fairness testing, bias audits, and simulations
- Describe the concept of fairness in AI and the challenges in defining it
- Define transparency in AI and its significance for trust and accountability
- State the importance of accountability in AI for ethical behaviour and public trust
- Elaborate on the ethical implications of data collection and usage in AI
- Elucidate how AI is reshaping industries and impacting job roles
- Define inclusivity in AI and its role in ethical design
- Specify how AI can both reduce and exacerbate social inequalities

4.1 Introduction

As artificial intelligence (AI) becomes more integrated into daily life, it offers exciting possibilities but also raises serious ethical concerns. People worry about how AI makes decisions—especially regarding fairness, bias, transparency, and accountability—since these systems often impact real lives. Understanding how and why AI makes choices is essential. Another major issue is data privacy. AI systems handle vast amounts of personal data, like health or financial records. If not managed securely, this data could be misused or stolen, putting individuals at risk. That is why AI must follow strict privacy standards and protect sensitive information. To be truly beneficial, AI must be inclusive, trustworthy, and sustainable. It should serve people from diverse backgrounds, perform reliably across situations, and avoid harming society or the environment.

4.2 Bias in AI

Imagine using a GPS that always recommends long and tough routes—even when there are quicker or safer routes available. It is not that the GPS is trying to be unfair. It just learned from data. AI systems can behave in a similar way. Bias in AI refers to the presence of systematic errors or prejudices in the data or algorithms that lead to unfair outcomes. The concept of bias in AI has evolved over time. Bias directly impacts how AI systems make decisions and interact with people. If they are trained on data that is not balanced or does not represent a wide variety of people and situations, they can make unfair choices.

4.2.1 Data Bias

If a facial recognition system is mostly trained on images of light-skinned individuals, it may struggle to accurately identify people with darker skin tones. This does not mean the technology is faulty—it simply was not taught with enough range of data and does not reflect the full diversity. Data bias occurs when the data used to train AI systems does not reflect the full diversity of people and real-world scenarios. As a result, AI can make decisions that are unfair—some groups may be overlooked or treated unequally. This can have serious consequences in areas like hiring, loan approvals, healthcare, and law enforcement.

Imagine teaching a child about animals but only showing them cats and dogs. When they see a horse, they will not recognize it. AI works similarly—it learns only from the examples it is given, so if those examples are narrow or skewed, the AI will also act narrow.

If an AI system is trained on resumes from a company that historically hired mostly men, it might start favouring male candidates—even if gender is not explicitly included in the data. Another source of bias is outdated data that reflects past inequalities.

Medical data sets might lack sufficient information about minority groups, making health-related AI tools less accurate for them. This is risky—like trying to forecast the weather without data from coastal regions. You would miss hurricanes. AI is no different: without comprehensive data, its decisions can be flawed and even harmful. Bias can also stem from missing or incomplete data. Some communities may be underrepresented in data sets due to factors like limited internet access, financial barriers, or cultural differences in data collection (Fig. 4.1).

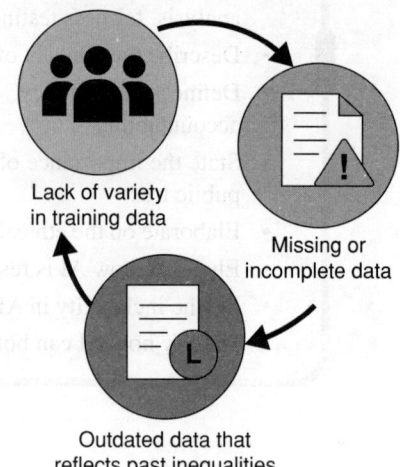

Figure 4.1 Some reasons for data bias in AI

Addressing Data Bias

Fixing data bias in AI includes using diverse and high-quality data, testing for fairness, involving different communities, and keeping humans in the loop (Fig. 4.2). Each of these steps helps make AI systems more fair, open, and ethical. As AI becomes a bigger part of our lives, these practices will become even more important.

Ethics, Bias, and Social Implications | 79

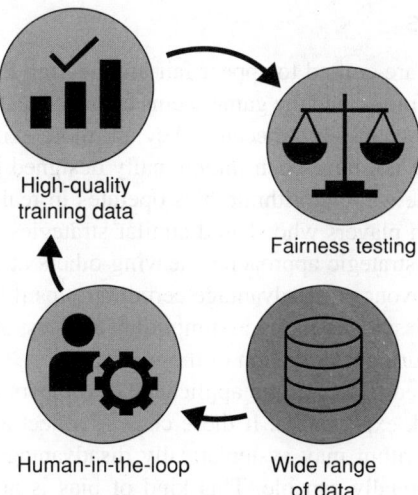

Figure 4.2 Tackling data bias in AI

- **High-quality training data:** Imagine teaching a facial recognition system mostly with photos of people with light skin. It might then have trouble recognizing people with darker skin. So, it is very important to use training data that is both high in quality and represents all kinds of people. This means collecting data from different places, cultures, and income levels.
- **Fairness test:** After collecting the data, it is important to test the AI to make sure it treats everyone fairly. This is called fairness testing. It checks how the AI performs for different groups—like men and women, or people of different races or ages.
- **Wide range of data:** For example, if you are creating a voice assistant, you should include voices with different accents and ways of speaking. This helps make sure the system works well for everyone, not just a few. Including different voices and perspectives does not just make the system fairer—it also makes it work better overall. Another way to reduce data bias is to include a wide range of people when designing and building AI systems.
- **Human-in-the-loop (HITL):** For example, an AI might think a social media post is harmful because of certain words, but a human might realize it is just a joke or part of a bigger conversation. Humans can notice things that machines might miss, like cultural meanings or ethical concerns. One of the best ways to keep AI ethical is to include humans in the process. This is called human-in-the-loop or HITL. It means people are involved at different stages—like labelling data, training the model, making decisions, and checking the results (Fig. 4.3). HITL helps make sure AI decisions are guided by human values.

Figure 4.3 Human-in-the-loop (HITL)

4.2.2 Algorithmic Bias

Imagine a game where the rules are crafted to appear fair and neutral. Players from different teams begin with equal resources and opportunities, and the game seems balanced on the surface. However, as the game progresses, one team consistently wins—not because they are more skilled, but because the rules subtly favour their style of play. It may not have been intentionally designed this way, but the outcome is still skewed. This analogy mirrors the way algorithmic bias operates in real-world systems. Imagine that the board game was tested only with players who shared similar strategies or backgrounds. The rules would naturally evolve to favour those strategic approaches, leaving others at a disadvantage. In the same way, algorithms can unintentionally favour or disadvantage certain groups if the data they are trained on is not diverse or fair. The root of the issue lies in the assumptions, choices, and preferences embedded—often unconsciously—by developers during the creation of these systems.

In a hiring algorithm designed to screen job applicants, developers might choose to prioritize certain educational backgrounds or work experiences. If these choices reflect a narrow view of what constitutes a 'qualified' candidate, the algorithm may systematically disadvantage applicants from non-traditional backgrounds, even if they are equally capable. This kind of bias is not always visible in the code but becomes evident in the outcomes the system produces.

Another layer of complexity arises from the mathematical models and optimization techniques used in AI. Algorithms are often designed to maximize accuracy or efficiency based on specific metrics. However, these metrics may not capture fairness or equity. For instance, an algorithm trained to predict loan defaults might be highly accurate overall but disproportionately deny loans to certain demographic groups. This happens because the algorithm learns patterns from historical data, which may reflect past discrimination. Even if the data is cleaned to remove explicit bias, the algorithm's structure and learning process can still perpetuate unfairness.

Addressing Algorithmic Bias

- **Fairness-aware algorithm:** A hiring algorithm can be adjusted to ensure that candidates from underrepresented groups are not systematically overlooked. These adjustments can be made by rebalancing training data, modifying loss functions or applying post-processing corrections to the output. While these methods can improve fairness, they must be applied thoughtfully to avoid introducing new forms of bias or compromising the model's overall utility. Fairness-aware algorithms must be regularly audited to ensure they continue to perform equitably as data and societal norms evolve.
- **HITL (Human-in-the-loop):** Another valuable strategy is the use of human-in-the-loop systems, which incorporate human oversight into the decision-making process. Rather than relying solely on automated outputs, these systems allow experts to review and intervene when necessary.

4.2.3 Measurement Bias

A real-world analogy of measurement bias would be using a thermometer that gives different readings depending on who holds it (Fig. 4.4). If the thermometer consistently underreports temperatures for certain people, doctors might fail to recognize fevers, leading to delayed or incorrect treatment. Measurement bias arises from the way data is collected, labelled, or interpreted, leading to flawed conclusions and potentially harmful decisions.

Measurement bias often begins with the instruments or methods used to gather data. For example, wearable health devices like fitness trackers or heart rate monitors may perform differently depending on skin tone, body type, or even how the device is worn. If these variations are not accounted for during data collection, the resulting data set will carry hidden inaccuracies.

Ethics, Bias, and Social Implications | 81

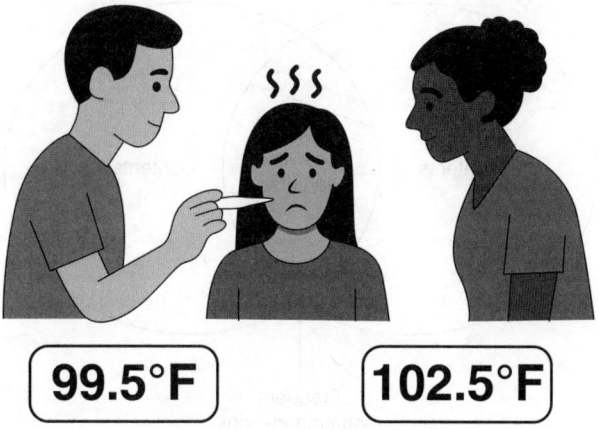

Figure 4.4 Measurement bias

In mental health diagnostics, symptoms may be labelled differently across cultures or even among clinicians. If an AI system is trained on such data, it may fail to recognize valid symptoms in patients from underrepresented groups, simply because those symptoms were not labelled in the training data. Labelling practices also contribute to measurement bias. In supervised learning, AI models rely on labelled data to learn patterns. If the labels themselves are inconsistent or influenced by human judgment, the model may learn incorrect associations.

When people see that an AI tool consistently produces unfair or inaccurate results, especially in sensitive areas like healthcare or law enforcement, they begin to question its reliability.

Addressing Measurement Bias

To mitigate measurement bias, developers and researchers must adopt inclusive data collection practices. This means ensuring that data sets reflect the diversity of the populations the AI system is intended to serve. It also involves critically evaluating the tools and methods used to gather data, and being transparent about their limitations. In addition, incorporating feedback from domain experts and affected communities can help identify and correct biases before they become embedded in the system.

4.2.4 Confirmation Bias

If someone frequently watches cooking videos, the algorithm will continue to recommend similar content, reinforcing the user's interest in that topic. While this may seem helpful, it can also become limiting. One of the most common examples of confirmation bias in AI is found in recommendation systems. These systems are designed to suggest content—such as videos, articles, or products—based on a user's past behaviour (Fig. 4.5).

Over time, the user is exposed only to a narrow range of content, missing out on other topics that might be equally engaging or informative. This is similar to dining at a restaurant where the menu only displays dishes you have previously ordered. Eventually, your meals become repetitive, and you lose the opportunity to discover new flavours.

If a user frequently engages with articles that support a particular political viewpoint, the system may prioritize similar content, excluding opposing perspectives. This creates a feedback loop where users are continually exposed to information that aligns with their existing beliefs, reinforcing those views and potentially leading to polarization.

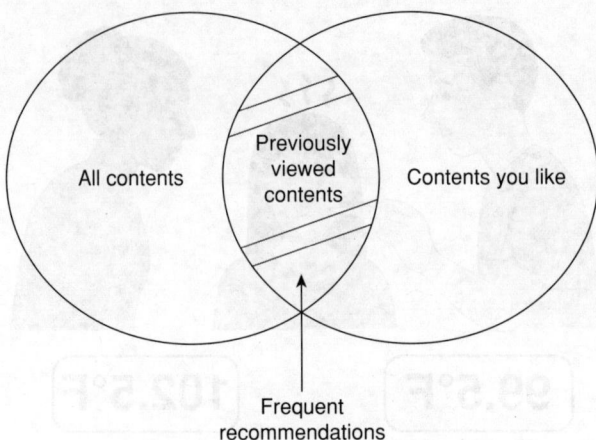

Figure 4.5 Confirmation bias

When educational platforms or search engines tailor results based on previous queries, they may unintentionally steer users toward familiar ideas rather than encouraging exploration. This can hinder critical thinking and reduce diversity of thought.

In social media, the bias can influence how individuals connect with others. Algorithms that prioritize content similar to what users have previously liked or shared may limit interactions to like-minded individuals, reducing opportunities for meaningful dialogue across different backgrounds or viewpoints.

Addressing Confirmation Bias

To counteract confirmation bias, developers must strike a careful balance between personalization and diversity. Another effective strategy is the deliberate introduction of varied content. For instance, recommendation engines could be programmed to periodically suggest articles, videos, or viewpoints that differ from a user's typical consumption patterns.

Consider the analogy of a diet; while it is tempting to eat only your favourite foods, a healthy diet requires variety (Fig. 4.6).

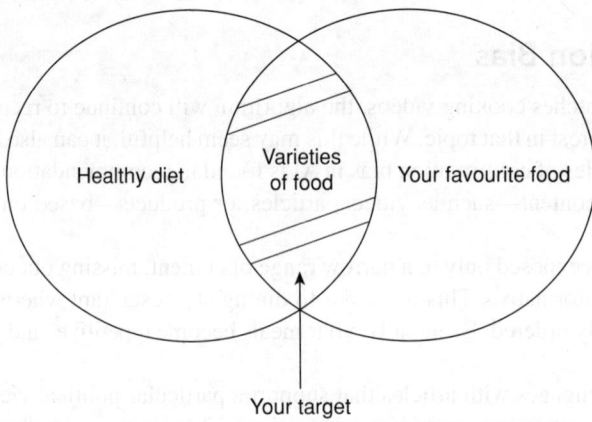

Figure 4.6 Addressing confirmation bias

Similarly, a healthy information ecosystem should include a mix of familiar and unfamiliar content.

Providing users with tools to actively adjust their content preferences empowers them to take control of their digital environments. For example, platforms could offer settings that allow users to increase the diversity of their feed or opt into receiving content from opposing viewpoints.

Human reviewers can help identify and correct biases that algorithms might overlook, ensuring that the system remains aligned with broader societal values. This is especially relevant in sensitive areas such as healthcare, criminal justice, and hiring, where biased recommendations can have serious consequences.

4.2.5 Societal Bias

AI often learns from things people write, like social media posts, news stories, or historical documents. If these sources contain stereotypes or biased language, the AI can pick them up and repeat them. For instance, a language model trained on internet content might link certain jobs to specific genders, which keeps old-fashioned ideas alive. It is like a mirror that does not just show reality—it also shows the flaws and distortions in how society sees itself (Fig. 4.7).

Figure 4.7 Societal bias

This usually happens because the data used to train AI models includes past human decisions in society, which may have been influenced by unfair treatment based on gender, race, or ethnicity.

AI systems used by banks are used to decide who gets a loan. If the training data includes past decisions where loans were unfairly denied to people from certain ethnic backgrounds, AI might learn to do the same.

For instance, in India, discrimination based on caste, though officially abolished, continues to influence social interactions, access to resources, and political representation. A teacher may unknowingly call on boys more often than girls in a math class, reinforcing gender stereotypes about aptitude. A hiring manager might favour candidates with names that sound familiar or 'Western', inadvertently sidelining equally qualified individuals from minority backgrounds.

Addressing Societal Bias

Harvard University's Project Implicit offers tools to assess and understand unconscious biases, encouraging self-awareness and behavioural change (Fig. 4.8).

The European Union's General Data Protection Regulation (GDPR) and the California Consumer Privacy Act (CCPA) address bias in data collection and algorithmic decision-making, recognizing the role of technology in perpetuating discrimination.

Diverse representation in films, literature, and advertising can counter stereotypes and promote inclusivity.

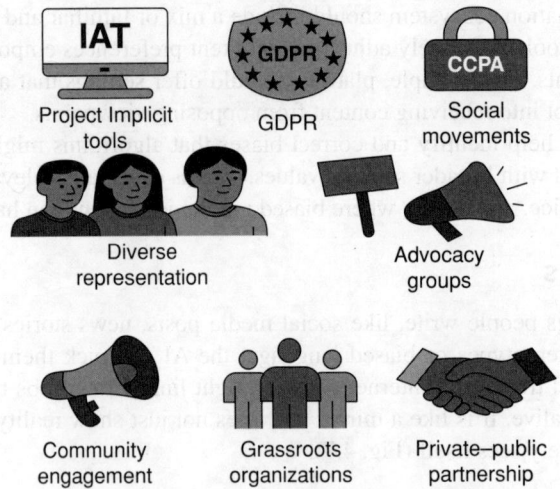

Figure 4.8 Addressing societal bias

Social movements, art, and storytelling serve as catalysts for change, amplifying marginalized voices and fostering solidarity. For instance, the #MeToo movement exposed the prevalence of sexual harassment and empowered survivors to speak out, leading to policy changes and shifts in workplace culture. Community engagement and participatory governance are essential in addressing societal bias. Empowering individuals to voice their concerns, contribute to policymaking, and hold institutions accountable fosters a sense of ownership and agency.

Grassroots organizations, advocacy groups, and civil society play a vital role in mobilizing action and sustaining momentum. Collaborative efforts between government, private sector, and communities can create inclusive environments where diversity is valued and equity is prioritized.

Did You Know?
A study by MIT Media Lab found that some facial recognition systems misidentified dark-skinned women 34.7% of the time, compared to just 0.8% for light-skinned men—highlighting the impact of biased training data.

Mini Project/Assignment
Title: Bias Spotting in Everyday Tech

Task: Observe and document any biased behaviour in apps or websites (e.g., ad targeting, recommendations). Reflect on how diverse data could improve fairness.

4.3 Fairness in AI Decision-making

Fairness in AI means making sure that the decisions made by AI systems are fair and do not treat people unfairly based on who they are. This includes avoiding discrimination against individuals or groups because of race, gender, or background. One way to measure fairness is called **statistical parity**. This means that the AI should give similar results to different groups of people. Another way is called **equal opportunity**, which means that people with the same qualifications should have the same chances, no matter where they come from or what their background is (Fig. 4.9).

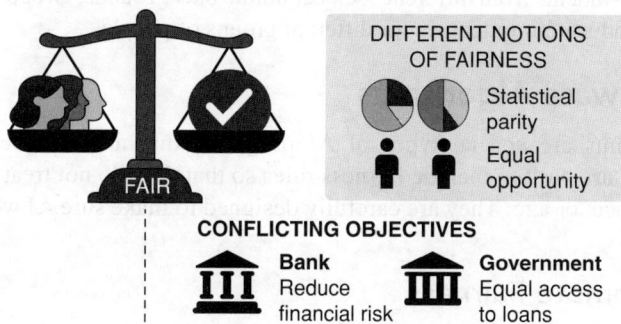

Figure 4.9 Fairness in AI

In the case of giving out loans, a bank might care most about reducing financial risk—making sure they do not lose money. However, government regulators might care more about making sure everyone has a fair chance to get a loan. These different goals can cause disagreements about how to make the AI system fair.

4.3.1 Statistical Fairness

To check if an AI system is fair, experts use different methods to measure how it behaves across groups:

- **Demographic parity:** This method checks if AI gives the same percentage of positive results to all groups. For example, if an AI is used to choose job applicants for interviews, demographic parity means that male and female applicants should be selected at the same rate. If 30% of male applicants are chosen, then 30% of female applicants should be chosen too. This helps make sure that no group is favoured over another.
- **Equalized odds:** If an AI is used to predict whether someone will pay back a loan, equalized odds means the system should be just as accurate for people of all races. If AI makes more mistakes for one group than another, it could lead to unfair treatment. So, equalized odds helps make sure the system works equally well for everyone. This method looks at how accurate AI is for different groups.
- **Predictive parity:** If an AI is used to predict how well students will do in school, predictive parity means the predictions should be just as reliable for students from wealthy families as they are for students from low-income families. This helps ensure that AI does not give better predictions to one group just because of their background.

4.3.2 Individual Fairness

If an AI is used to decide whether someone qualifies for a loan, it should look at useful details like how much money the person earns and how well they have handled credit in the past. It should not consider their race or gender, because those are not related to whether someone can repay a loan. Treating people fairly means focusing only on the facts that are relevant to the decision. AI should make decisions based on factors that actually matter for the task, and ignore things that do not.

4.3.3 Group Fairness

If an AI system is used to allocate resources in a school, group fairness would mean that the resources are distributed fairly among students from different socioeconomic backgrounds. Group fairness is the idea that the AI system should produce fair outcomes for different groups of people.

4.3.4 Fairness-aware Algorithms

Fairness-aware algorithms are special types of AI programs that are designed to make fair decisions. These algorithms are built to include fairness rules so that they do not treat people unfairly based on things like gender, race, or age. They are carefully designed to make sure AI works fairly in different situations.

Techniques to Promote Fairness

Experts have come up with different ways to reduce bias and make these systems more fair during the development process.

If a hiring tool is trained on data that does not include enough successful candidates from certain backgrounds, developers might balance the data or remove sensitive details like race or gender. This helps the system learn from a more diverse and fair set of information, leading to better and more equal results. **Pre-processing** focuses on the data used to train the system. Since biased data often leads to unfair results, developers try to clean and improve the data before it is used.

Another way to improve fairness is during the training phase, using what is called **in-processing** methods. These techniques change how the system learns by adding rules that encourage fairness. For instance, the system might be designed to not only make accurate predictions but also to treat different groups more equally. Developers might include special formulas that reduce unfair behaviour or use training methods that focus on fairness. This helps the system avoid learning biased patterns, even if the data is not perfect.

There is also a third method called **post-processing**, which is used after the system has already been trained. This is helpful when the data or the system itself cannot be changed. Post-processing adjusts the final results to make them more fair. For example, if a credit scoring system gives lower scores to people from certain backgrounds, developers might change the scores or set new rules to make approval rates more equal. This is especially useful for older systems or those that are hard to modify.

> **Did You Know?**
> Fairness in AI is not one-size-fits-all. What is fair in one context (e.g., loan approvals) may differ from another (e.g., school admissions), making fairness a complex challenge in AI design.

> **Mini Project/Assignment**
> *Title*: What is Fair?
> *Task*: Create a poster comparing different definitions of fairness (e.g., equal opportunity versus statistical parity) using real-world examples.

4.4 Transparency in AI Systems

In criminal justice, if a judge relies on an black box risk assessment tool to determine sentencing, the defendant may be unable to challenge the decision effectively. In healthcare, a doctor may hesitate to follow an AI-generated diagnosis if the reasoning behind it is unclear. Transparency in AI refers to the ability to understand and explain how an AI system makes decisions. However, many AI models, especially deep learning systems, operate as 'black boxes', making it difficult to interpret their internal workings.

Efforts to improve transparency include developing explainable AI (XAI) techniques that provide insights into model behaviour. Regulatory frameworks such as the European Union's General Data Protection Regulation (GDPR) also mandate the right to explanation, requiring organizations to provide meaningful information about automated decisions. Transparency also involves communicating limitations and uncertainties, helping users make informed decisions.

4.4.1 Examples of Transparency in Action

An AI system might look at X-ray images to find signs of cancer. However, instead of just saying 'cancer detected', a transparent system will also show which parts of the image led to that result. This can be done using visual tools like heatmaps, which highlight the areas AI focused on. This helps doctors check AI's reasoning, compare it with their own knowledge, and make better decisions. It also builds trust in the technology, which is very important when people's health is involved. If AI makes a mistake, transparency helps experts figure out what went wrong and how to fix it.

In banking, AI is used to decide who gets approved for loans. These systems look at things like income, credit history, job status, and spending habits. Transparency here means the bank can explain clearly why someone's loan was approved or denied. For example, AI might say, 'Your loan was declined because your credit score is too low and your debt-to-income ratio is too high'. This kind of explanation helps customers understand what they need to improve. It also makes sure AI is not making decisions based on unfair things like race or gender, which would be wrong and possibly illegal.

In education, schools and universities use AI to grade student essays and assignments. These systems look at grammar, sentence structure, vocabulary, creativity, and how well ideas are organized. Transparency means that both teachers and students can see how AI gave a certain score. For example, AI might say: 'Grammar: 8/10, Structure: 7/10, Creativity: 6/10', and highlight strong or weak sentences. This helps students learn what they did well and what they can improve. It also helps teachers make sure AI is grading fairly for all students, no matter their writing style or background. Without transparency, students might feel confused or unfairly judged, which could hurt their motivation and learning.

4.4.2 Levels of Transparency

Transparency is often explained in three levels: technical transparency, user transparency, and regulatory transparency.

Technical Transparency

This level is for the people who build and maintain AI systems—like developers, engineers, and data scientists. It involves understanding how the system works behind the scenes. For example, someone working on a facial recognition system needs to know:

- What type of neural network is being used.
- How the system was trained.
- What kind of data was used, and whether it was fair and diverse.
- How well the system performs in different situations.

Technical transparency helps experts fix problems, improve the system, and make sure it is fair. It also allows them to run internal checks to confirm the system is working as expected. Without this kind of transparency, developers would be guessing, which could lead to serious mistakes or ethical issues.

User Transparency

This level is for everyday users—like students, patients, customers, or citizens—who use AI systems but do not have technical knowledge. It focuses on giving clear and simple explanations about how AI works and why it made a certain decision. For example:

- A student using a learning app should know why a topic was recommended.
- A customer denied a loan should be told, 'Your credit score is below the required level'.
- A patient using a health app should understand how their symptoms were analyzed and what AI suggests.

User transparency helps people trust the system and make better decisions. It also prevents confusion and ensures users do not feel misled or treated unfairly by technology they do not fully understand.

Regulatory Transparency

This level is for governments, regulators, and watchdog groups that make sure AI is used legally and ethically. It involves sharing documents, audit records, safety checks, and reports that show AI system follows rules and standards. For example:

- A company using AI for hiring must prove it does not discriminate based on gender or race.
- A hospital using AI for medical decisions must show the system meets safety standards.
- A government using AI for surveillance must explain how data is collected and used, and how people's rights are protected.

Regulatory transparency helps hold organizations accountable and prevents misuse of AI. It also builds public trust in how AI is managed.

> **Did You Know?**
> The EU's GDPR includes a 'right to explanation', meaning users can demand to know how automated decisions were made—one of the first legal moves toward AI transparency.

> **Mini Project/Assignment**
> *Title*: Transparency Tracker
>
> *Task*: Choose an AI-powered service (e.g., loan app, health app) and evaluate how clearly it explains its decisions. Rate it on a transparency scale.

4.5 Accountability in AI

This means making sure that people or organizations take responsibility for what AI systems do and the results they create. This helps promote ethical behaviour, solve problems when things go wrong, and build trust with the public. However, figuring out who is responsible can be difficult, especially when AI systems make decisions on their own without human input (Fig. 4.10).

Ethics, Bias, and Social Implications | 89

Figure 4.10 Accountability in AI

One important way to handle this is by clearly defining who does what. Developers, companies, and users all need to understand their roles and responsibilities. Laws can also help by explaining who is legally responsible. For example, if a self-driving car causes an accident, the law needs to decide whether the car maker, the software developer, or the person using the car should be held accountable.

Another helpful method is auditing. This means checking AI systems to make sure they follow ethical rules and legal standards. Audits can be done by the company itself or by outside experts. These reviews often look at whether the system is fair, whether it shows bias, and how it handles data. Independent organizations can also help by watching over how AI is used to make sure it is done properly.

Let's explore why accountability in AI is essential, through three key lenses: building trust, preventing harm, and ensuring compliance.

4.5.1 Building Trust

Trust is the key to using AI successfully and for the long term. Even if an AI system is very advanced or powerful, people will not use it unless they believe it works reliably, follows ethical rules, and supports their needs. Trust has to be earned. This happens when AI systems are open about how they work (transparency), treat people fairly, take responsibility for their actions (accountability), and perform well over time.

In important areas like healthcare, finance, education, and public services, trust plays a big role in how people use AI and what results they get. For example, in a hospital, an AI system that suggests treatment plans must not only be accurate but also explain its choices clearly and be supervised by trained doctors. When patients see that the system is being watched and that its advice makes sense, they are more likely to follow it. This leads to better teamwork, quicker diagnoses, and improved health.

When people know that AI systems are carefully built, tested for fairness, and guided by strong ethical rules, they are more likely to trust them—even in serious situations. Trust turns AI from just a helpful tool into a real partner in making decisions.

4.5.2 Preventing Harm

As AI becomes a regular part of decision-making in areas like healthcare, banking, hiring, and public safety, the chances of causing accidental harm also increase. Even though AI systems are powerful, they are not perfect—they can make mistakes, show bias, or act in unexpected ways. If there are no clear rules or systems to hold someone responsible, these problems might go unnoticed or unfixed, which can lead to serious harm to people and society.

The **types of harm** AI can cause if there is no accountability are given below:

- **Discrimination:** AI might repeat unfair patterns in hiring, lending, or policing.
- **Misinformation:** AI could create or spread false information, especially in systems that generate content.
- **Safety risks:** AI might give unsafe advice in healthcare or in self-driving vehicles.
- **Privacy violations:** AI could misuse or leak private personal data.

The ways in which organizations can **prevent harm** are given below:

- **Bias testing and fixing:** Regularly check if AI treats different groups unfairly and fix it.
- **Human-in-the-loop (HITL):** Make sure humans are involved in important decisions.
- **Incident reporting:** Give users and workers a way to report problems or harmful outcomes.
- **Ethical review boards:** Create teams from different departments to review risky AI projects.

Preventing harm from AI is not optional—it is a moral duty and a legal requirement. By making accountability part of every step in building and using AI, organizations can make sure their systems are not only smart but also safe, fair, and respectful of human values.

4.5.3 Ensuring Compliance

Compliance in AI means that organizations must follow laws, rules, and ethical standards—especially when using AI in sensitive areas like healthcare, banking, hiring, and public services.

A strong system of rules and oversight helps organizations:

- Avoid breaking laws or damaging their reputation.
- Earn trust from users, government regulators, and other partners.
- Use AI in a way that is ethical and responsible.

When organizations build accountability into their AI systems, they can follow changing laws, reduce risks, and build public trust. In high-risk areas like finance, this is not optional—it is a basic requirement for using AI in a safe and fair way.

4.5.4 Case Study: COMPAS and Criminal Justice Bias

The COMPAS algorithm, which stands for Correctional Offender Management Profiling for Alternative Sanctions, is often used as an example of how AI can be unfair and lack accountability. In the United States, COMPAS is used to predict whether someone who has been arrested is likely to commit another crime. However, it has faced strong criticism for being biased against African American individuals.

In 2016, a news organization called ProPublica investigated COMPAS and found that it often gave Black defendants higher risk scores than white defendants—even when they did not go on to commit more crimes. This raised serious concerns about fairness and transparency. One major problem was that the way COMPAS worked was kept secret by the company that made it. Because of this, defendants and their lawyers could not easily challenge the scores, which made it harder for them to get a fair trial.

The COMPAS case shows the dangers of using AI systems that are not open or easy to understand—especially in situations where the decisions can greatly affect people's lives. It highlights the need for AI systems to be transparent, tested by independent experts, and held accountable. It also shows how bias in the data used to train AI, or in the way the system is designed, can lead to unfair results and make existing inequalities worse.

Because of these concerns, some places have started to rethink how they use risk assessment tools like COMPAS. Some have added stricter rules to make sure the tools are used fairly. The case has also led to bigger discussions about how AI should be used in the criminal justice system and why it is important to make sure technology respects human rights.

> ### Did You Know?
> The COMPAS algorithm used in U.S. courts was found to unfairly rate Black defendants as higher risk than white defendants—despite similar criminal records—due to biased training data.

> ### Mini Project/Assignment
> *Title*: Who's Responsible?
> *Task*: Create a flowchart showing who should be accountable in different AI scenarios (e.g., self-driving car accident, biased hiring tool).

4.6 Data Privacy and Security Concerns

In today's digital world, **data is one of the most valuable resources** for companies and governments. AI systems often need large amounts of personal data to work well. This can include sensitive details like medical records, bank transactions, location history, and even fingerprints or facial scans. While combining this data can help AI make smart decisions, it also creates big concerns about privacy. If data is collected without people's clear permission or used for something other than what they agreed to, it violates their basic right to privacy.

The risk becomes even greater because today's data systems are very complex. Data is often shared across many platforms, stored in cloud services, and handled by outside companies. If any part of the system is breached, millions of people's information could be exposed, leading to identity theft, financial problems, and damage to the organization's reputation.

To handle data ethically, organizations need strong rules and systems. They should have clear policies about how they collect, use, store, and share data. They also need to be honest with users and give them control over their personal information. Technology tools like encryption (which hides data), anonymization (which removes personal details), and differential privacy (which protects individual data while allowing analysis) can help reduce these risks. However, these tools must be used along with ethical practices and legal compliance to truly protect people.

4.6.1 AI and Surveillance

AI has made surveillance much more advanced. It now allows for real-time tracking, facial recognition, and predicting people's actions. It is often hard to tell the difference between necessary surveillance and invasion of privacy, which leads to questions about people's rights and freedoms.

Governments and companies are using AI-powered surveillance more and more in public places, workplaces, and online. These systems can follow individuals, study their behaviour, and even guess what they might do next. In countries with strict control over their citizens, such as China, these technologies have been used to silence people who speak out and to monitor the population. China's use of facial recognition and a social credit system has been criticized around the world for violating privacy and limiting freedom. AI is being used in areas like law enforcement, border security, and public health. These uses must be carefully watched to make sure they do not unfairly target certain groups or take away personal freedoms. To protect people's rights, there needs to be open discussion, strong legal protections, and clear rules about how surveillance is used.

One important rule in ethical surveillance is proportionality. This means surveillance should only be used when it is truly needed and for a good reason. It should also be checked by independent groups and legal systems to make sure it is fair. AI used in surveillance must respect human dignity, personal freedom, and follow the law.

4.6.2 Data Protection Regulations and Compliance

In today's digital world, protecting personal data has become more important than ever. To deal with growing concerns about privacy, many governments have created strong data protection laws.

Two of the most well-known examples are the General Data Protection Regulation (GDPR) in the European Union and the California Consumer Privacy Act (CCPA) in the United States. These laws give people more control over their personal information and require companies to be more open and responsible about how they use data.

The GDPR, which came into effect in 2018, gives people several important rights. These include the right to see what data is collected about them, to correct it, to delete it, and to limit how it is used. It also requires companies to get clear permission before collecting personal data and to inform users if their data is ever leaked or stolen. What makes GDPR especially powerful is that it does not just apply to companies in Europe—it applies to any company in the world that handles the data of people living in the EU. This has made it a global standard for data protection.

The CCPA, which began in 2020, offers similar protections for people living in California. It allows them to find out what personal data companies are collecting, to say no to having their data sold, and to ask for their data to be deleted. The law also includes penalties for companies that do not follow the rules, which encourages businesses to take privacy seriously and adopt better practices.

Apart from GDPR and CCPA, HIPAA (Health Insurance Portability and Accountability Act) 1996 provides a strong foundation for data privacy in healthcare.

4.6.3 Cybersecurity Challenges in AI Systems

Cybersecurity challenges include adversarial attacks, model inversion, data poisoning, and other weaknesses in the system. Protecting AI from these dangers needs special strategies that go beyond regular cybersecurity methods used in IT.

Adversarial attacks are when someone changes input data in small ways to trick an AI system. For example, tiny changes to a photo can cause a facial recognition system to wrongly identify someone. These attacks work because AI models are very sensitive to small differences, which can be dangerous in areas like self-driving cars, medical tests, or detecting financial fraud.

Model inversion is another serious threat. In this case, attackers use AI's output to figure out the original input data. This means they could uncover private information—even if the data was supposed to be anonymous. Data poisoning is when harmful or fake data is added to the training set, which can mess up how AI behaves and lead to unfair or unsafe results.

AI systems also face regular cybersecurity threats like hackers breaking in, viruses, or systems being overloaded to stop them from working. Since AI is now used in cloud services, smart devices, and business systems, there are more places where attacks can happen. To protect these systems, companies need strong security tools like encryption (to hide data), access controls (to limit who can see or change data), systems that detect intrusions, and constant monitoring.

Keeping AI safe from cyber threats takes teamwork. Data scientists, cybersecurity experts, and government leaders must work together. It also requires ongoing research to build stronger AI systems, smarter algorithms, and better ways to spot threats.

4.6.4 Case Study: Cambridge Analytica and Data Misuse

The Cambridge Analytica scandal is one of the most well-known examples of how data can be misused, especially when combined with AI and politics. In 2018, it was revealed that a British company called Cambridge Analytica had secretly collected personal data from millions of Facebook users—without asking for their permission. This data was used to build psychological profiles of people and target them with personalized political ads during the 2016 U.S. presidential election and the Brexit vote in the UK.

This scandal showed how social media platforms can be vulnerable and how data-driven political campaigns can raise serious ethical concerns. Cambridge Analytica used AI to study people's behaviour, interests, and emotions. Then, it created messages designed to influence how people think and vote. Because the data was collected without users knowing or agreeing, it violated their privacy and caused global outrage.

Facebook was heavily criticized for its role in the scandal. The company was blamed for not protecting user data and for allowing third-party apps to access personal information without proper checks. In response, Facebook changed its data policies, gave users more control over their information, and faced investigations and fines from regulators.

The Cambridge Analytica case shows why ethical data practices are so important—especially in politics. It highlights the need for clear consent, transparency in how data is used, and accountability when things go wrong. It also shows how AI can be used to manipulate public opinion, making it urgent to have strong rules and ethical oversight.

Since the scandal, people have become more aware of how their data is used, and governments have taken steps to improve data privacy laws. Organizations are now more careful, and users are paying closer attention to their online activity. This case serves as a warning, reminding everyone that with great power over data and AI comes great responsibility.

Did You Know?

The GDPR does not apply only to European companies—it affects any organization worldwide that handles the data of EU citizens. This has made it a global benchmark for data privacy and AI accountability.

Mini Project/Assignment

Title: Privacy Check-Up

Task: Review the privacy settings of three apps or websites you use. Note what personal data they collect and whether they explain how it is used. Suggest one improvement for each.

4.7 AI Employment and Workforce Transformation

AI is transforming industries by automating tasks once done by humans. This shift is especially visible in manufacturing, shipping, customer service, and professional fields like law and finance. AI handles repetitive, rule-based tasks faster and more accurately, helping companies cut costs and boost productivity. However, growing use of AI raises concerns about job loss and the future of work.

Technology has always reshaped jobs. The Industrial Revolution replaced physical labour with machines, and the digital age automated office tasks. Now, AI is the next major shift—capable of performing both physical and mental tasks like data analysis, decision-making, and language processing.

AI's impact varies by job type and skill level. Roles involving routine tasks—such as warehouse work, data entry, or sales calls—are most at risk. Jobs requiring creativity, emotional intelligence, or complex problem-solving—like healthcare, education, or the arts—are less likely to be automated. Still, even skilled roles are evolving. AI now assists with legal research, medical diagnoses, and financial planning, meaning some jobs may shrink and workers must reskill.

Job loss due to AI can lead to serious challenges—unemployment, lower income, and stress. Communities reliant on affected industries may face economic hardship. To address this, governments and companies should provide training, financial aid, and job placement support to help workers transition to new careers.

4.7.1 Reskilling and Upskilling the Workforce

Reskilling means learning to do a completely new job, while upskilling means getting better at your current job so you do not fall behind. Both help people keep up with new types of work and stay useful in the workplace.

Working with AI does not just require tech skills. While knowing how to code or work with data and machine learning is helpful, soft skills like being flexible, thinking clearly, working well with others, and understanding emotions are just as important. These human abilities help fill in the gaps where machines cannot do the job.

Governments, schools, and companies all need to support lifelong learning—which means helping people learn throughout their lives. Rules and programs should make education easy to get and affordable, especially for people who might struggle to access it. Places like job training centres, community colleges, and online courses offer flexible ways to learn that fit different needs.

Companies should also help their workers grow by offering training, mentoring, and chances to move up in their careers. Businesses that support learning tend to keep their employees longer, come up with new ideas, and stay ahead of the competition. When workers help design AI systems, they understand them better and are more likely to accept and use them.

Some real-life examples include AT&T's Future Ready program, which spent over $1 billion to teach employees skills like software development, cybersecurity, and data analysis. Amazon's Upskilling 2025 project plans to train 100,000 workers in cloud computing and machine learning. However, there are still problems like high costs, busy schedules, and limited access to learning. To fix this, we need financial help, flexible class times, and support services so everyone has a fair chance to learn and succeed.

4.7.2 Human–AI Collaboration in the Workplace

In fields like healthcare and journalism, AI helps people make better choices and work more efficiently. For instance, doctors use AI to study medical images and patient records, but they still make the final decisions about treatment. Journalists use AI to quickly summarize news and find patterns, which gives them more time to write detailed stories.

To work well with AI, people need easy-to-use tools, good training, and a workplace that supports learning and teamwork. Employees should understand both the technical side of AI and the ethical issues it raises. Companies must build trust and encourage ongoing learning to make this partnership successful.

4.7.3 Economic Impacts of AI on Labour Markets

AI has the power to transform entire industries, shift how money is earned and shared, and influence big-picture economic trends. On one hand, it can boost productivity and open up new business opportunities. On the other hand, it can also lead to more inequality, divide workers into different groups, and cause social challenges.

As machines take over repetitive tasks, fewer low-skilled and middle-skilled workers may be needed. At the same time, there will be more demand for people with high-level skills in areas like technology, leadership, and creativity. This could result in a labour market where most of the growth happens at the top and bottom, leaving fewer opportunities in the middle.

AI may also cause bigger gaps in wages. People with strong skills and access to advanced tools may earn much more, while others in less secure jobs may see their pay stay the same or even drop. This growing difference in income can make existing social and economic problems worse and lead to more tension in society.

AI also changes how companies work and how jobs are structured. For example, gig economy platforms that use AI have changed traditional jobs into more flexible but less stable work. These jobs can offer freedom and convenience, but they often do not come with benefits, job security, or legal protections.

On a larger scale, AI can help the economy grow by making businesses more productive, innovative, and competitive. However, the rewards of this growth might not be shared fairly. Governments and leaders need to make sure that everyone benefits from AI. This means investing in education, building strong infrastructure, supporting people in need, and encouraging fair and responsible innovation.

Around the world, the economic impact of AI is different from place to place. Countries with advanced technology may gain more, while those still developing may find it harder to keep up. To make sure AI helps everyone, global cooperation and sharing of knowledge are key to building a fair and sustainable future.

4.7.4 Case Study: AI in Retail and Logistics

AI is changing how retail and logistics work. It helps companies run smoother by improving how products are ordered, stored, and delivered. It also makes shopping more personal for customers. While these changes create new types of jobs, they also replace older ones and raise questions about fairness and the impact on workers.

In retail, AI looks at customer habits, predicts what people will buy, and keeps track of stock. Tools like chatbots and product suggestions make shopping easier and boost sales, but they also reduce the need for store employees.

In logistics, AI helps plan delivery routes, predict shipping needs, and automate warehouses. Big companies like Amazon and FedEx use robots and drones to sort packages and deliver them faster and cheaper. However, this means fewer jobs for people who work in warehouses, drive trucks, or handle paperwork.

Even though some jobs are lost, AI creates new roles in areas like data analysis, system upkeep, and designing customer experiences. These jobs often pay more and offer better job security. AI also makes work safer by taking over tasks that could be dangerous for humans.

Smart companies are preparing for these changes by training workers, managing transitions, and making sure AI is used responsibly. For example, Walmart teaches employees how to work with automation, and DHL uses AI to plan better and help staff grow.

This example shows how the job market is shifting. It is important to have plans that support both new technology and people. Using AI in a fair and thoughtful way can bring big benefits while reducing harm to society.

> **Did You Know?**
> Amazon's Upskilling 2025 initiative aims to train 100,000 employees in cloud computing and machine learning—showing how major companies are preparing for AI's workforce impact.

> **Mini Project/Assignment**
> *Title*: Career of the Future
>
> *Task*: Interview someone in a job that is changing due to technology (e.g., banking, logistics). Ask how their role has evolved and what new skills they have learned. Present your findings in a short write-up.

4.8 Inclusivity, Sustainability, and Reliability in AI Systems

Inclusivity in AI refers to the deliberate effort to ensure that AI systems serve and represent all segments of society fairly and equitably.

Training large AI models, particularly deep learning systems, requires substantial computational resources, which in turn consume significant amounts of electricity. This energy consumption contributes to carbon emissions and environmental degradation, raising concerns about the sustainability of AI development.

Reliability in AI refers to the consistent and accurate performance of AI systems across different contexts, inputs, and conditions. Robustness, a closely related concept, involves the system's ability to maintain functionality and resist failure when faced with unexpected or adversarial inputs.

Together, reliability and robustness are essential for ensuring that AI systems are trustworthy, safe, and effective in real-world applications.

4.8.1 Inclusivity

Inclusive AI design means making sure AI works fairly for everyone—no matter their gender, race, ethnicity, or disability. This is not just a technical challenge; it is a moral duty based on fairness, justice, and respect for all people. One big problem is that many AI systems are trained using data that mostly represents white, male, Western individuals. Because of this, AI may not work well for people from other backgrounds. For example, voice recognition tools often have trouble understanding accents that are not considered 'standard', and facial recognition systems tend to make more mistakes when identifying women and people of colour. These errors can lead to serious consequences, including misidentification and unfair treatment.

To fix these issues, developers need to use training data that includes a wide range of people and is carefully checked for bias. This data should also be updated regularly to stay accurate. Inclusivity should be built into the design process from the start. That means having diverse teams of people working on AI, doing impact studies to see how the technology affects different groups, and talking to the communities who will use it. Accessibility is also very important. AI should be designed to help people with vision, hearing, thinking, or movement challenges. This can be done by using features like screen readers, voice commands, and other tools that make technology easier to use for everyone.

When AI is designed to be inclusive, it becomes more useful, more effective, and reaches more people. The ethical reason behind this is to celebrate human differences and make sure everyone is treated fairly. Developers need to think beyond just how well the technology works—they must also consider the social and cultural backgrounds of the people using it. By focusing on inclusivity, AI can become a powerful tool that helps build a more equal and fair digital world.

4.8.2 Sustainability

AI's environmental impact is most evident when ML models are trained on data. For instance, training one large language model can emit as much CO_2 as five cars over their lifetimes. This pollution comes mainly from data centres powered by fossil fuels and the intense computing required. As AI use grows, so does its environmental toll.

To reduce this, developers are making AI more efficient. Techniques like model pruning remove unnecessary parts, quantization speeds up math operations, and knowledge distillation teaches smaller models to mimic larger ones. These methods cut energy use while maintaining performance.

Energy-saving hardware also helps. Specialized chips and processors reduce power consumption during demanding tasks. Data centre design matters too—using renewable energy, improving cooling systems, and adopting smart energy practices. Companies like Google and Microsoft aim for carbon neutrality and invest in green tech to make AI more sustainable.

Sustainability also requires ethical standards and smart policies. Developers should weigh energy use against societal benefits. Governments can support eco-friendly AI through regulations, incentives, and education. Users can push for transparency in how AI affects the planet. Building sustainable AI means creating systems that last, act responsibly, and support a cleaner future.

4.8.3 Reliability and Robustness of AI Models

AI systems are trained in controlled environments with curated data, but real-world use brings unpredictable inputs and complex conditions. This can cause errors or serious issues. For instance, a self-driving car trained only in sunny weather may struggle in rain or snow, risking safety.

To ensure AI works safely, it must be tested under varied conditions, including stress scenarios and faulty inputs. Developers should add safety features and backup systems. In critical fields like healthcare, finance, and transport, reliability is essential before deployment.

AI must also resist manipulation. Adversarial examples—small input tweaks—can mislead systems, like altering a stop sign image to resemble a speed limit sign. Developers counter this by training AI to detect such tricks, clean data, and monitor for odd behaviour.

Transparency boosts trust. When users and regulators understand how AI makes decisions, they can assess its choices and fix issues. Tools that explain AI reasoning help identify errors and build confidence.

Reliability requires ongoing monitoring and updates. AI systems must evolve with changing environments and user needs, from design to retirement.

Ultimately, strong, reliable AI reflects a commitment to safety, ethics, and responsible innovation—ensuring technology serves people fairly and effectively.

4.8.4 Case Study: AI for Climate Change Mitigation

AI has emerged as a powerful tool in the fight against climate change, offering innovative solutions for monitoring, predicting, and mitigating environmental impacts. This case study explores how AI is being used to address one of the most pressing global challenges and highlights the intersection of technology, sustainability, and ethical responsibility.

One of the key applications of AI in climate change is environmental monitoring. AI algorithms analyze satellite imagery, sensor data, and weather patterns to track deforestation, glacier melting, ocean pollution, and greenhouse gas emissions. These insights enable policymakers, scientists, and activists to understand environmental trends, assess risks, and develop targeted interventions.

AI also plays a role in optimizing energy systems. Machine learning models can predict energy demand, manage grid operations, and enhance the efficiency of renewable energy sources such as solar and wind. For example, Google's DeepMind has used AI to improve the energy efficiency of data centres, reducing electricity consumption by up to 40 per cent. Similarly, AI-driven smart grids enable dynamic energy distribution, minimizing waste and supporting sustainable infrastructure.

In agriculture, AI supports climate resilience by optimizing irrigation, predicting crop yields, and managing pests. These technologies help farmers adapt to changing weather conditions, conserve resources, and reduce environmental impact. AI-powered platforms also facilitate sustainable land use planning, balancing development with conservation.

Transportation is another sector where AI contributes to climate mitigation. Autonomous vehicles, route optimization algorithms, and traffic management systems reduce fuel consumption and emissions. AI also supports the development of electric vehicle infrastructure, enabling cleaner mobility solutions.

Despite its potential, the use of AI in climate change must be guided by ethical considerations. Data privacy, equity, and transparency are critical in environmental applications. For instance, satellite monitoring must respect indigenous land rights, and predictive models must be accessible to vulnerable communities. Moreover, the environmental cost of AI itself—such as energy consumption in model training—must be accounted for in sustainability strategies.

The case of AI for climate change illustrates the transformative power of technology when aligned with ethical and environmental goals. It demonstrates how AI can be a force for good, enabling informed decision-making, efficient resource use, and global cooperation. As climate challenges intensify, the responsible use of AI will be essential for building a resilient and sustainable future.

Did You Know?
Training a single large AI model can emit as much CO_2 as five cars over their lifetimes—highlighting the environmental footprint of AI and the need for green computing.

Mini Project/Assignment
Title: Green Tech Explorer

Task: Research one company using AI for environmental sustainability (e.g., Google, Microsoft). Create a poster showing how their AI helps reduce carbon emissions or improve energy efficiency.

4.9 AI and Social Inequality

Most AI development takes place in rich countries and big companies. Places like North America, Europe, and parts of East Asia have the best research and technology, while poorer regions often do not have access to these tools. This creates a global gap. Without equal access to AI, many countries miss out on using it to solve their own problems and improve their economies. This means the benefits of AI are mostly enjoyed by a small part of the world.

To make sure AI helps everyone fairly, developers and leaders need to focus on inclusive design, equal access, and ethical rules. This means involving people from underrepresented communities in building AI, being open about how systems work, and making sure there are strong policies to guide development. It also means investing in technology and training in areas that do not have enough resources. When AI is built with fairness and justice in mind, it can become a tool that lifts people up instead of leaving them behind.

4.9.1 Access to AI Technologies Across Socioeconomic Groups

AI tools need fast internet, up-to-date devices, and steady electricity. These are often missing in poor or rural places. For example, students in faraway villages may not be able to join online classes, and people in areas with few doctors may not get help through telemedicine.

Money is another problem. Many AI tools—like smart systems or health apps—cost too much for some people. Even free apps need internet access, working devices, and training to use them. These extra needs make it hard for many to benefit from AI.

People who have not had much education or experience with tech may not understand how to use AI safely. Teaching these skills should include everyone, respect different cultures, and be designed to fit each community's needs.

Many AI systems are built mainly for English speakers, which leaves out people who speak other languages. Cultural beliefs affect how people use and trust technology, so developers need to think about these differences. To fix these problems, governments, companies, and local communities must work together to improve infrastructure, make AI more affordable, and ensure it works for everyone.

4.9.2 Digital Divide and Global Disparities

The digital divide is the gap between people who can use digital tools like computers and the internet, and those who cannot. It is not just about having internet access—it also includes how well people understand technology, how they use it, and how much they benefit from it.

In the world of AI, this divide shows up in how different countries and communities take part in creating and using AI. Rich countries are ahead because they have more money, skilled workers, and strong institutions. These countries are home to big tech companies, top universities, and important government agencies. On the other hand, poorer countries often do not have the basic infrastructure, enough funding, or trained experts to be part of AI development in a meaningful way.

Even within a single country, the digital divide affects people in different ways. Cities usually have better internet and technology access, while rural areas often struggle. Rich families can afford smart devices, but poorer families may not even have basic internet. Women and older people face extra challenges because of social traditions, less education, or technology that is not designed with them in mind.

To close this gap, people and organizations need to work together. International groups can help by sharing knowledge, training people, and funding AI projects in developing regions. Governments should spend money on better internet access, education, and new ideas. Local communities can help by pointing out what they need, helping create solutions, and teaching digital skills.

Technology itself can be part of the solution. AI can help use resources better, bring internet to more places, and offer services that fit each person's needs. Simple apps, features that work without internet, and cheap devices can make AI easier to use. Free tools and shared research also help make AI development fairer.

The digital divide can be fixed. With plans that include everyone, AI can help people all over the world. By noticing where the gaps are and working to close them, we can build a future that is more equal and better connected.

4.9.3 Policy Interventions for Equitable AI

AI policies aim to make technology fair and inclusive. Well-designed rules help reduce bias and ensure AI benefits are shared equally. These policies should be research-based, ethically sound, and responsive to diverse communities. Government laws play a key role by requiring AI systems to be transparent, fair, and accountable—especially in healthcare, finance, and law enforcement. They must also protect privacy, require consent for data use, and prevent discrimination. Public funding can support ethical AI through research, small business aid, and community tech investments.

Expanding internet access, education, and job training helps more people join AI economy. Schools should teach AI and ethics, and adults need lifelong learning opportunities—especially women, minorities, and rural populations. Global cooperation is vital. Since AI affects many nations, groups like the UN, OECD, and UNESCO can guide policy and promote collaboration. Sharing research and training across borders helps reduce inequality and supports global progress.

Public involvement strengthens policy. Leaders should engage communities to build trust and improve outcomes. Real-world examples show success: the EU's AI Act enforces strict rules for high-risk systems while encouraging innovation, and India's Digital India program expands internet access and digital education. Policies must evolve with technology. Leaders must balance innovation with protection, ensuring rules are fair, effective, and suited to both global and local needs. Fairness should remain central to AI policy to build a more just world.

4.9.4 Case Study: AI in Education and Healthcare Access

AI is reshaping both education and healthcare—two areas deeply connected to fairness and well-being. This case study looks at how AI is expanding access and improving outcomes, while also tackling key challenges.

In education, AI tailors learning experiences by adjusting lessons in real time and offering instant feedback. This is especially helpful for students in underserved communities. AI-powered tutors support self-paced learning, spot where students are struggling, and offer targeted help. Language tools assist non-native speakers, and accessibility features make learning more inclusive for students with disabilities.

Schools are also using AI to make smarter decisions. By analyzing data like grades, attendance, and participation, educators can identify students who need extra support, allocate resources more effectively, and design programs that include everyone. Predictive tools can flag potential issues early. Still, AI must be used with care—protecting student privacy, ensuring fairness, and keeping access equal. Data must be secure, systems transparent, and technology should support—not replace—teachers.

In healthcare, AI helps doctors diagnose conditions, plan treatments, and monitor patients. It can analyze medical images, detect problems, and predict how diseases might progress—especially valuable in remote or underserved areas. AI-driven telemedicine also enables virtual consultations, saving time and effort for both patients and providers.

On a broader scale, AI strengthens public health by tracking disease outbreaks, analyzing health trends, and managing medical supplies. During the COVID-19 pandemic, AI helped predict virus spread, improve hospital operations, and guide treatment strategies. For AI to work well, it needs accurate, diverse data and must follow medical standards. Tools should be accountable and accessible to everyone, regardless of income or location.

Real-world examples show AI's potential. In Kenya, M-Shule delivers personalized lessons via text messages to students without internet access. In India, rural clinics use AI to detect early signs of diabetic eye disease. These examples show how AI can close gaps and uplift communities. When used ethically and adapted to local needs, AI can enhance education and healthcare, helping build a more just and inclusive society.

Ethics, Bias, and Social Implications | 101

> **Did You Know?**
> In Kenya, the M-Shule program uses SMS-based AI tutoring to reach students without internet access—an innovative way to bridge the digital divide in education.

> **Mini Project/Assignment**
> *Title*: Tech for All
>
> *Task*: Identify one barrier to AI access in your community (e.g., cost, language, internet). Propose a simple solution or campaign to raise awareness or improve access.

Summary

- Bias in AI stems from data, algorithms, or societal influences, leading to unfair outcomes. It can be of the following types: data, algorithmic, measurement, confirmation, and societal. Detection techniques include data analysis, fairness testing, bias audits, and simulations.
- Fairness refers to statistical parity and equal opportunity. Statistical fairness metrics are demographic parity, equalized odds, and predictive parity.
- Individual fairness means that similar individuals should receive similar treatment, while group fairness avoids disproportionate impact on any group. Fairness-aware algorithms are used to reduce bias. Techniques to promote fairness are pre-processing, in-processing, and post-processing.
- Transparency in AI systems builds trust, enables accountability, and supports informed decision-making. The levels of transparency may be technical, user, and regulatory.
- Accountability in AI ensures responsibility for AI outcomes.
- Ethical data handling requires consent, transparency, and secure practices.
- The main regulations are GDPR and CCPA.
- AI employment and workforce transformation involves impact, reskilling or upskilling, and human–AI collaboration.
- Inclusivity, sustainability, and reliability in AI systems are essential.
- AI and social inequality deals with risks, access across socieoeconomic groups, the digital divide and policy interventions.

Exercises

Part A (Objective Questions)

1. Which type of bias occurs when training data does not fairly represent all groups of people?
   (a) Algorithmic Bias
   (b) Societal Bias
   (c) Data Bias
   (d) Predictive Bias

2. Why is transparency in AI systems critical in sectors like healthcare and criminal justice?
   (a) It allows AI systems to operate without human oversight.
   (b) It ensures decisions are made faster.
   (c) It helps users understand and challenge AI decisions.
   (d) It reduces the cost of AI implementation.

3. A bank uses an AI system to approve loans. What fairness metric should be used to ensure equal approval rates across different ethnic groups?
   (a) Predictive Parity
   (b) Demographic Parity
   (c) Individual Fairness
   (d) Algorithmic Transparency

4. Which combination of techniques is most effective in detecting and correcting bias in AI systems?
   (a) Data analysis and encryption
   (b) Fairness testing and bias audits
   (c) Model pruning and quantization
   (d) Predictive parity and anonymization

5. A company's AI hiring tool consistently favours younger candidates. What should the company do to ensure accountability and fairness?
   (a) Increase the number of interviews
   (b) Use post-processing techniques to adjust outcomes
   (c) Remove age data from the training set
   (d) Conduct regular bias audits and include human oversight

6. Design a strategy to improve inclusivity in an AI-powered education platform used in rural areas. Which approach is most effective?
   (a) Use only English-language training data
   (b) Focus on urban student performance metrics
   (c) Incorporate diverse linguistic and cultural data
   (d) Limit access to students with high-speed internet

7. What is the primary goal of fairness-aware algorithms in AI?
   (a) To reduce system performance
   (b) To eliminate the need for training data
   (c) To ensure decisions are not biased by personal traits
   (d) To increase the complexity of AI models

8. An AI system used in healthcare misdiagnoses patients from certain ethnic backgrounds. What is the most likely cause?
   (a) Overfitting of the model
   (b) Lack of regulatory transparency
   (c) Biased training data and algorithm design
   (d) Use of outdated medical equipment

9. Which level of transparency is most relevant for regulators assessing AI compliance with laws like GDPR and CCPA?
   (a) Technical Transparency
   (b) User Transparency
   (c) Regulatory Transparency
   (d) Developer Transparency

10. To reduce the environmental impact of AI model training, which combination of strategies should developers adopt?
    (a) Increase data set size and use fossil fuels
    (b) Use model pruning and renewable energy sources
    (c) Avoid transparency and focus on speed
    (d) Train models only in urban data centres

Part B (Short Answer Questions)
1. What are the three main types of bias that can affect AI systems?
2. Why is transparency important in AI systems used in healthcare?
3. How can fairness-aware algorithms be used to improve hiring practices?
4. Compare statistical parity and equal opportunity as measures of fairness in AI.
5. Evaluate the ethical implications of using AI in surveillance systems.
6. Write a hint on forming a basic framework for auditing AI systems to ensure accountability.
7. What role does inclusivity play in the design of AI systems?
8. How can post-processing techniques help mitigate bias in existing AI systems?
9. Analyze the impact of AI on labor markets and income inequality.
10. Assess the effectiveness of GDPR and CCPA in protecting personal data in AI systems.

Part C (Essay Questions)
1. List and briefly describe the different types of bias that can affect AI systems as discussed in the chapter.
2. Explain how societal bias in AI systems can perpetuate existing inequalities, using examples from the chapter.
3. Imagine you are designing an AI system for loan approvals. How would you apply fairness-aware algorithms to ensure equitable outcomes?
4. Compare and contrast the three levels of transparency in AI systems—technical, user, and regulatory—and discuss their roles in building trust.
5. Evaluate the effectiveness of GDPR and CCPA in addressing data privacy concerns in AI systems. What are their strengths and limitations?
6. Design a policy framework that promotes inclusivity and sustainability in AI development for a developing country. What key elements would you include and why?
7. Identify the key ethical concerns raised by the use of AI in surveillance.
8. Describe how the COMPAS case study illustrates the challenges of accountability and bias in AI systems.

9. How would you implement pre-processing, in-processing, and post-processing techniques to reduce bias in an AI hiring tool?
10. Propose a community-based initiative to bridge the digital divide and improve equitable access to AI technologies.

= Answers =

Part A
1. (c) 2. (c) 3. (b) 4. (b) 5. (d) 6. (c) 7. (c) 8. (c) 9. (c) 10. (b)

CHAPTER 5

Generative AI and Its Applications

Objectives

At the end of this chapter, you will be able to:
- Explain generative AI and how it differs from traditional AI
- Elaborate on the core technologies behind generative AI, including machine learning and neural networks
- Describe the evolution of generative AI, from rule-based systems to advanced neural networks
- Explain the role and functions of generative adversarial networks (GANs)
- Describe the impact of Transformer architecture and models like GPT and BERT
- Explain the significance of diffusion models in image generation
- Elaborate on the capabilities and features of ChatGPT across different use cases
- Elucidate the multimodal capabilities of Gemini AI across text, image, audio, and video
- Explain how Perplexity AI provides real-time, cited answers for research
- List the applications in image generation for design, advertising, and fine arts
- Describe tools like Bing Image Creator, DALL·E, and Stable Diffusion
- List the video generation tools and their creative applications
- Explain music and sound generation using AI platforms
- Describe human–AI collaboration in creative fields
- Discuss case studies showcasing AI-driven creative projects
- Explain the tools for automated slide creation such as Gamma, SlidesAI, Tome, Beautiful.ai, and Slidesgo
- List the applications of generative AI in various fields

5.1 Introduction

Generative artificial intelligence (Gen AI) is like a master chef (Fig. 5.1), who not only follows recipes but also creates entirely new ones based on what is desired. Instead of copying existing recipes, she studies thousands of ingredients and cooking styles, then invents something original or customized for you. In the same way, Gen AI creates new content—text, images, videos, music, and even code—based on patterns it has learned from existing data.

Figure 5.1 Generative AI chef

This capability has opened up a wide array of applications across industries, reshaping how we think about creativity, productivity, and problem-solving. Gen AI produces results that make sense, match the situation, and often look or sound like they were created by humans.

Gen AI is a combination of advanced technologies like machine learning (ML), deep learning (DL), and neural networks (NN). It is trained using massive amounts of data to understand patterns and structures. Some of the most powerful generative AI tools used today include ChatGPT by OpenAI, Gemini by Google DeepMind, Hugging Face's open-source tools, Perplexity's smart search engine, and Bing's image creation platform.

Since Gen AI can create very realistic and convincing content, it also raises important concerns. These include bias in AI results, deepfakes, privacy risks, and concerns that machines might take over jobs currently performed by humans.

5.2 How It Works

Probabilistic modelling (Fig. 5.2) helps Gen AI guess what should come next in a series, based on patterns—whether it is the next word in a sentence, the next pixel in a picture, or the next frame in a video. For example, when Gen AI writes text, it does not just pick the next word at random.

By studying how words and phrases usually go together, Gen AI can choose the word that best fits the next spot. This makes sentences sound correct and make sense in the given context. For example, "The sun is shining in the ----" is given as input. The pattern will identify the predicted output as "morning". The same idea works for images and videos as well.

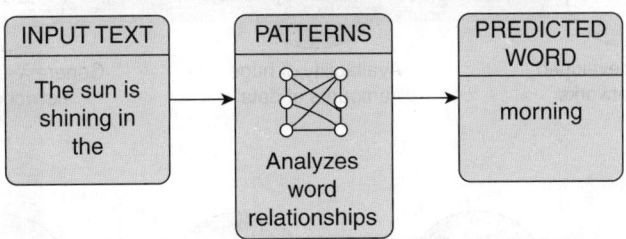

Analyzes word relationships

Figure 5.2 Probabilistic modelling in Gen AI

When creating a picture, Gen AI looks at millions of examples to learn how colours, shapes, and textures usually appear together. For videos, Gen AI predicts how things should move and change over time, so the motion looks natural and believable.

What makes probabilistic modelling powerful is its ability to learn from past examples and apply that knowledge to new situations. However, it is important to understand that even though Gen AI's work may seem original, it is based on the data it was trained with. Gen AI does not truly 'understand' what it is creating, like a person does; it just calculates what is most likely to fit and tries to make the result clear and relevant.

Since Gen AI can create content, it raises new questions about who owns the work, what counts as original, and how much control humans should have. These changes are leading to important conversations about ethics, fairness, and responsibility.

5.2.1 Historical Milestones in Generative AI

The story of Gen AI began with basic rule-based systems in the mid-1900s (Fig. 5.3). These early systems used fixed rules and templates to create simple outputs, like basic chatbot replies or computer-generated graphics. Even though they were limited in what they could do, they helped set the stage for more advanced AI technologies that came later.

Neural Networks (1990)

In the 1990s, scientists developed neural networks (Fig. 5.4), which were a big step forward. These networks were designed to work like the human brain and allowed computers to learn from data instead of just following rules. This enables computers do things like recognize images, translate languages, and write creatively with impressive skill.

Neural networks (NNs) are made up of layers of tiny units called neurons. Each neuron takes in information, processes it, and sends it to the next layer. This setup lets the network study data step by step, finding deeper and more detailed patterns as it goes. For example, when looking at a picture, the first layer might notice edges, the next might see shapes, and later layers could recognize full objects or faces.

108 | Fundamentals of Artificial Intelligence

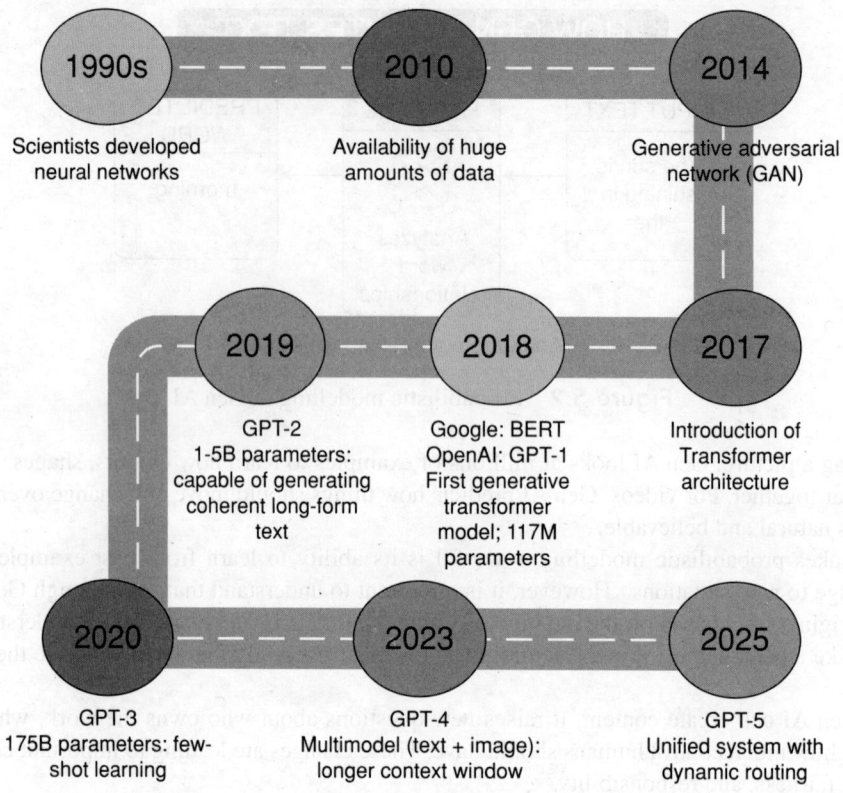

Figure 5.3 Historical milestones in Gen AI

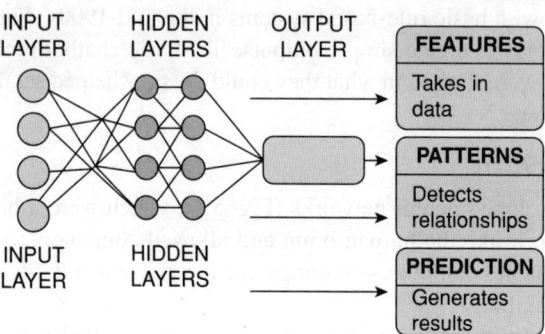

Figure 5.4 Neural networks

This way of working is similar to how our brain understands what we see and hear, which makes neural networks great at spotting patterns and making sense of complex information. To teach a neural network how to do its job, we adjust the strength of the connections between its neurons. These strengths are called **weights**. At first, the weights are random, so the network makes lots of mistakes. However, it learns through a method called **backpropagation**. This means it checks how wrong its guesses were, figures out the error, and then changes the weights to do better next time. As it sees more data and keeps learning, the network becomes more accurate.

However, it was not until the 2010s that generative AI really started to grow, thanks to major improvements in the availability of huge amounts of data for training.

Generative Adversarial Networks (2014)

A major breakthrough took place in 2014 when Ian Goodfellow introduced generative adversarial networks, or GANs. A GAN is like a game between a forger and a detective. Imagine an artist trying to create fake paintings that look like real masterpieces, while a detective tries to spot the fakes. The artist (the generator) keeps improving their technique to fool the detective, and the detective (the discriminator) keeps getting better at spotting the fakes. Over time, both become so good that the artist's fakes become nearly indistinguishable from the real thing—just like how GANs generate realistic images, videos, or data.

At their core, GANs consist of two distinct neural networks (Fig. 5.5)—the generator and the discriminator—that engage in a dynamic and continuous competition. This adversarial relationship is the driving force behind the system's ability to produce increasingly realistic and sophisticated outputs over time.

The generator's role is to create data that mimics real-world content. It begins by producing outputs that are often crude or easily distinguishable from genuine data. These outputs could be images, audio, or even text, depending on the application. The discriminator, on the other hand, acts as a judge and evaluates the generator's creations and determines whether they are authentic or fabricated. Initially, the discriminator can easily identify the generator's attempts as fake. However, as the generator receives feedback from the discriminator, it learns to refine its methods, gradually producing more convincing and real-like results.

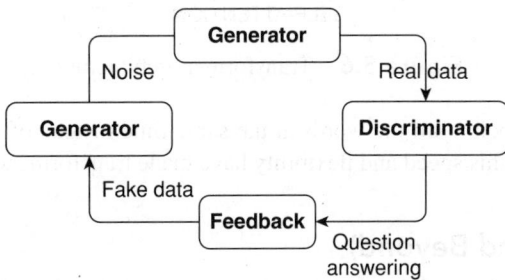

Figure 5.5 Generative adversarial model

Thus, this is an iterative process of feedback and improvement, with each cycle, the generator becomes better at deceiving the discriminator, and the discriminator becomes more adept at spotting flaws. This mutual enhancement leads to a remarkable evolution in the quality of the generated content.

For example, in image synthesis, GANs have been used to create photorealistic images of human faces that do not belong to any real person. These images are so detailed and accurate that they are indistinguishable from actual photographs, showcasing the immense potential of GANs in creative industries. In video games, GANs can generate realistic textures and environments, enhancing the immersive experience for players. In the fashion industry, designers use GANs to visualize clothing on virtual models, allowing for rapid prototyping and experimentation. In healthcare, GANs assist in generating synthetic medical images that can be used to train diagnostic algorithms without compromising patient privacy.

Transformer Architecture (2017)

Transformer architecture is like a group discussion where everyone listens to everyone else before speaking. Imagine a roundtable where each participant hears what others are saying and adjusts their own message accordingly. Instead of just passing notes in order (like older models), each person (word or token) pays attention to everyone else at once—this is called **attention**. It helps the model understand context better; for example, knowing that 'bank' means something different in 'river bank' versus 'money bank'.

Transformer architecture (Fig. 5.6) was first introduced in a famous 2017 research paper called *Attention Is All You Need*. It changed the way computers read and write languages. Before transformers, most models processed words one at a time in order. But transformers brought in a new idea called **self-attention**, which lets the model look at all the parts of a sentence at once and decide which words are the most important. For example, in the sentence "The cat is sitting on the mat", the word "cat" is closely linked to "sat," and the model learns to focus more on that connection. This smart way of paying attention helps the model understand the meaning of sentences more clearly.

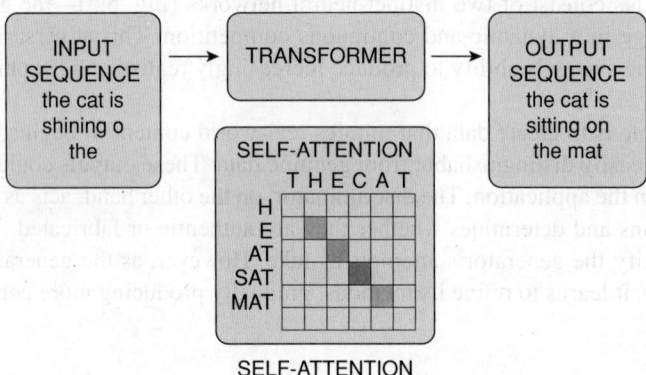

Figure 5.6 Transformer architecture

Also, because transformers look at all the words at the same time instead of one by one, they train faster and can handle bigger tasks. This speed and flexibility have made transformers the base for many advanced language tools.

GPT Models (2018 and Beyond)

Transformer architecture has changed the way computers understand and use human language. Two of the most important models (Fig. 5.7) built using this Transformer architecture are generative pre-trained transformer (GPT) and bidirectional encoder representations from transformers (BERT). Even though they are based on the same basic idea, they are designed for different tasks and work in different ways. This makes them useful in different areas of AI that deal with language.

GPT, created by OpenAI, is a model that reads text from left to right and tries to guess the next word based on the words that came before. This helps it write sentences that make sense and sound natural. For example, if you give GPT a sentence like "The weather today is," it might finish it with "sunny and warm." GPT is suitable for writing, summarizing, and chatting because it has been trained on a vast amount of text from many sources. This training helps it learn how people usually talk and write, including common phrases and expressions. GPT is best for creating new text that sounds natural, so it is used in chatbots, writing tools, and even code generation.

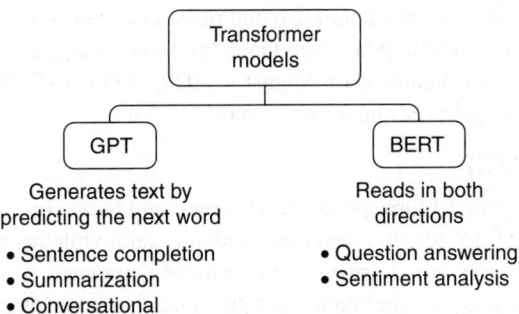

Figure 5.7 GPT and BERT models

BERT, developed by Google (2018), works differently. It reads sentences by looking at both the words before and after a word at the same time. This helps it understand the meaning of words more accurately. For instance, the word "bank" means something different in "He sat by the bank of the river" than in "She deposited money in the bank." BERT can tell the difference because it looks at the full context around the word. This makes BERT appropriate for tasks like answering questions, figuring out emotions in text, and identifying names or places. BERT is better at understanding what text means, so it is used in systems that need to read and understand information, like search engines or tools that answer questions based on a passage.

GPT-1 was released in 2018 (Table 5.1) by Open AI, GPT-2 in 2019. These models changed how machines understoof and created human-like text. GPT-3, released in 2020, showed that AI could write essays, answer questions, and even create poetry. GPT-4 was released in 2023, with a longer context window and improved reasoning and safety.

Table 5.1 GPT models

Model	Release Date	Key Highlights
GPT-1	June 11, 2018	First generative transformer model; 117M parameters; introduced unsupervised pretraining
GPT-2	February 14, 2019	1.5B parameters; capable of generating coherent long-form text; initially withheld due to misuse concerns
GPT-3	May 28, 2020	175B parameters; few-shot learning; versatile across tasks like translation, coding, and writing
GPT-4	March 14, 2023	Multimodal (text + image); longer context window; improved reasoning and safety
GPT-5	August 7, 2025	Unified system with dynamic routing; multimodal (text, image, audio, video); advanced reasoning and safer completions

Each version marked a leap in capability—from basic text generation to sophisticated reasoning. The progress did not stop there. New models were developed that could work with different types of data at the same time, like text and images (GPT-4). These are called **multimodal models** and they have made it possible for AI to describe pictures, summarize videos, and act as smart assistants.

112 | Fundamentals of Artificial Intelligence

Today, Gen AI is leading the way in technology, and researchers are still working to discover what else machines can create. GPT-5 is a multimodal large language model (text, image, audio, and video) developed and hosted by OpenAI. It was launched on August 7, 2025, as OpenAI's flagship AI model, combining reasoning and non-reasoning capabilities under a common interface.

Diffusion Models (2020)

A diffusion model is like watching a blurry photo slowly come into focus. Imagine starting with a completely noisy image—like static on a TV screen—and then gradually removing the noise step by step until a clear picture appears. The model learns how to reverse this 'blurring' process, so it can start with randomness and generate realistic images, text, or other data—just like cleaning up a foggy window to reveal a beautiful view. Even though diffusion models were introduced in 2015, they became well-known only in 2020, demonstrating that these models could produce images with quality that was on par with GANs.

Diffusion models (Fig. 5.8) are, thus, a big step forward in how AI creates images. These models are popular because they can make pictures that look very realistic—sometimes even as good as those made by human artists. They work differently from older methods like GANs. Instead of using two networks that compete with each other, diffusion models slowly turn random noise into clear, detailed images. This method helps improve the quality of the pictures and gives more control during the creation process.

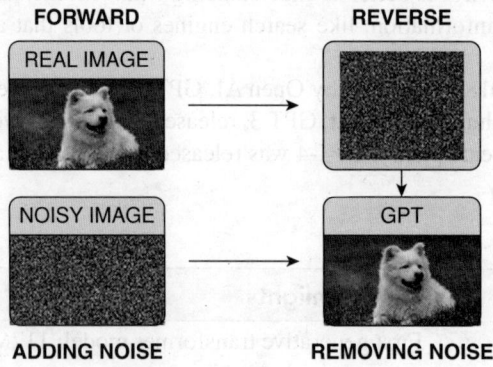

Figure 5.8 Diffusion models

AI image generation uses a two-step process: first, an image is turned into noise; then, the model learns to reverse it and recreate the original. This teaches it to build new images from scratch.

Inspired by physics, where particles spread out naturally, the model learns patterns to turn randomness into realistic visuals. Tools like DALL·E and Stable Diffusion use this to create images from text. DALL·E generates scenes like "a futuristic cityscape at sunset," while Stable Diffusion lets users customize art freely. Because the process is gradual, researchers can track how images form, helping ensure AI is safe and fair in fields like healthcare and media.

> **Did You Know?**
> The first generative AI models were rule-based systems from the 1950s! Today's models like GPT-5 can handle text, images, audio, and video simultaneously.

> **Mini Project/Assignment**
> Make a timeline chart showing the evolution of Gen AI from rule-based systems to GPT-5. Use drawings or printed icons to represent each milestone.

5.3 ChatGPT

ChatGPT is similar to a super-knowledgeable assistant who reads everything and remembers patterns in conversations. Imagine that you are talking to a librarian who has read millions of books and can instantly summarize, explain, or even write new stories based on what you have said. ChatGPT works similarly—it uses patterns learned from vast amounts of text to generate helpful, human-like responses in real time.

ChatGPT (Fig. 5.9) has become popular because it can write text that sounds like a human, answer questions, help with tasks, and carry on conversations. Its wide range of abilities makes it useful not just for everyday users, but also for professionals in areas like education, customer service, and business.

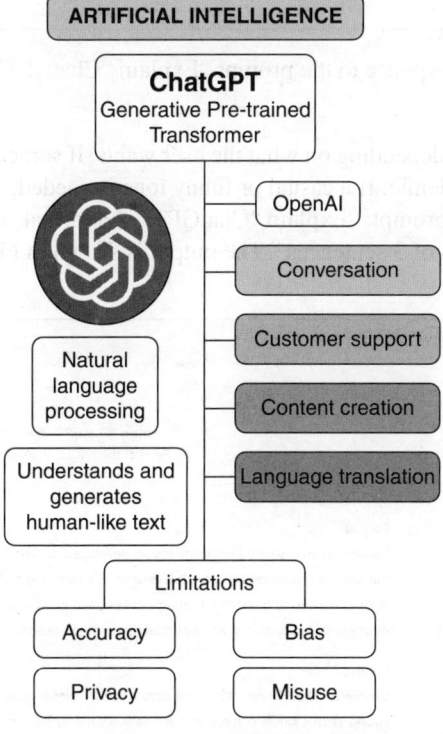

Figure 5.9 ChatGPT features

ChatGPT is powered by a deep learning (DL) system trained on huge amounts of text from books, websites, articles, and more. Its main strength is understanding and creating natural language. This means it can read what a person writes, understand the meaning, and reply in a way that makes sense. One of its best features is how well it keeps a conversation going, making chats feel smooth and natural.

ChatGPT can perform many things. It can answer questions, summarize long texts, translate languages, write stories or poems, and even help with computer programming. For example, someone can ask it to explain a science topic in simple words, write a formal email, or create a poem. Because it is so flexible, people use it for both fun and work.

You need to first login to chatgpt.com and create an user ID and password. Let us now explore the chat with the prompt: "Explain "ChatGPT" for a 10-year-old student." We get the answer shown in Fig. 5.10.

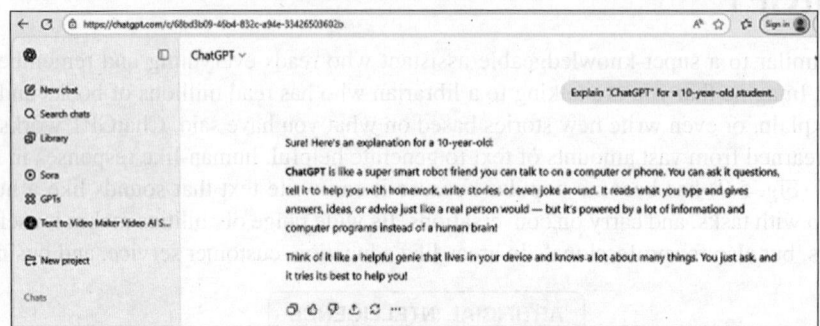

Figure 5.10 ChatGPT response to the prompt "Explain "ChatGPT" for a 10-year-old student."

It can also change how it writes depending on what the user wants. If someone asks for a formal style, it will write like a professional or academic. If a casual or funny tone is needed, it can do that too.

For example, let us use the prompt: "Explain "ChatGPT" in a formal style first and then in a funny tone. Restrict the output in maximum of 3 sentences." The output is shown in Fig. 5.11.

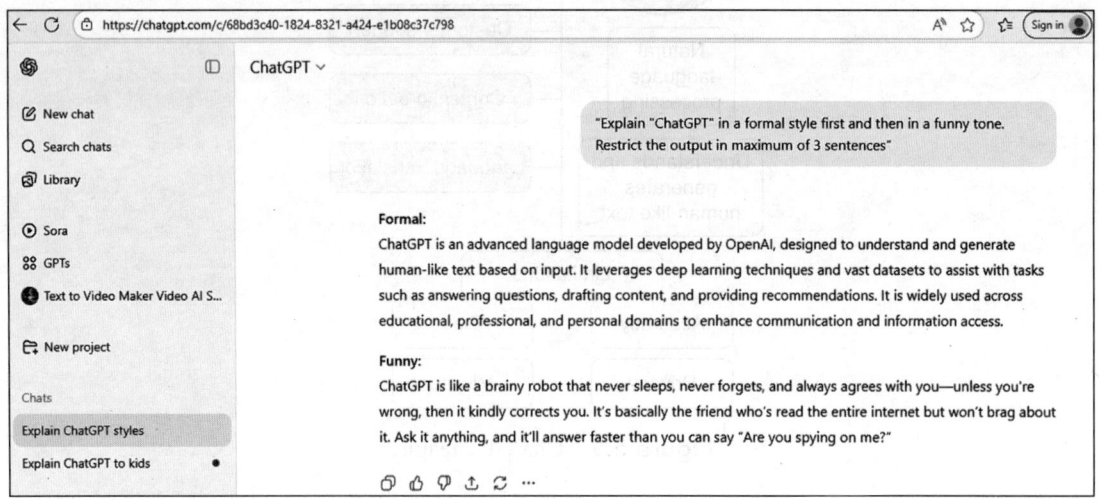

Figure 5.11 Output of a ChatGPT prompt for a formal style and a funny tone

This makes it useful in many areas like education, customer support, entertainment, and research.

5.3.1 Creating a Video using Sora of ChatGPT

Sora is a powerful AI tool developed by OpenAI that can create videos from text descriptions. It is like a magic pen that converts your words into moving pictures. With Sora, you can type a sentence like "A cat flying over a rainbow," and it will generate a short video showing exactly that. It can also extend existing videos by adding more scenes, making them longer and more detailed. Sora produces high-quality videos with clear visuals and smooth camera movements, making the content look realistic and engaging.

The technology behind Sora is based on advanced AI models trained on vast amounts of video data. It understands how scenes should look and move, which helps it accurately match the videos to your descriptions. This makes it an excellent tool for creators, educators, and anyone interested in storytelling through visuals. Sora is available to ChatGPT Plus and Pro users, which are subscription plans offering additional features like access to video generation tools. More information and access to Sora can be found on OpenAI's official website, and there is also a video introduction available to showcase how it works.

5.3.2 ChatGPT for Twitter

Let's say we use the prompt: "Create a Twitter post that talks about salient the features of the book "Design Thinking" published by Universities Press and its key features for people learning the topic.". The output is shown in Fig. 5.12.

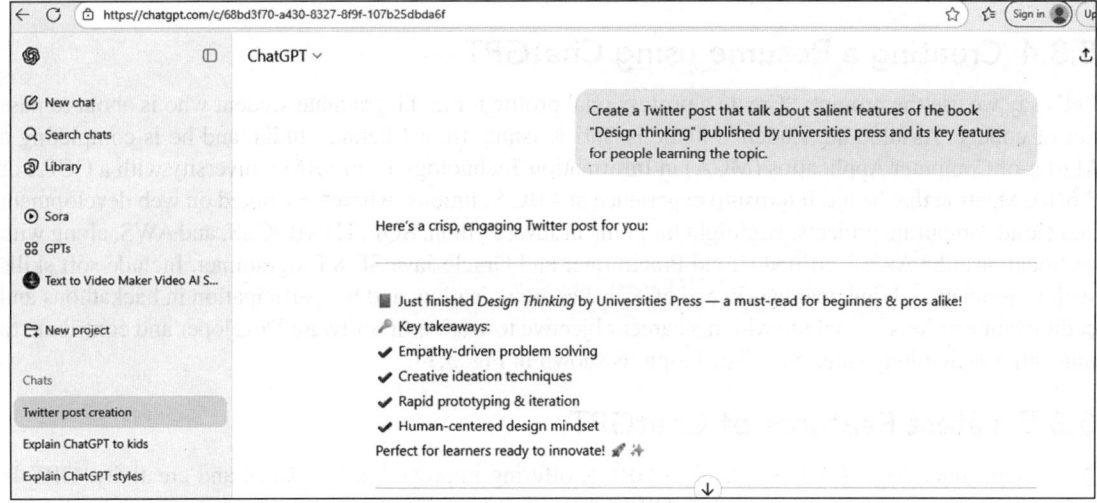

Figure 5.12 Output of a ChatGPT prompt for creating a Twitter post

5.3.3 ChatGPT for LinkedIn

Let's say we use the prompt: "Create a LinkedIn post that announces the release of the book titled "Design Thinking" published by "Universities Press" and its key features for people the subject." The output is shown in Fig. 5.13.

> 🚀 **Excited to Announce the Release of "Design Thinking" by Universities Press!** 📘✨
>
> I'm thrilled to share that *Design Thinking*, a must-read for innovators, problem-solvers, and creative thinkers, is now available from **Universities Press**! This book offers a structured yet flexible approach to solving complex problems by putting human needs at the center of design.
>
> 🔑 **Key Features:**
> ✓ A comprehensive introduction to design thinking principles and methodologies
> ✓ Practical frameworks for empathizing, ideating, prototyping, and testing
> ✓ Real-world case studies and examples across industries
> ✓ Tools to foster creativity, collaboration, and innovation
> ✓ Guidance for students, professionals, and organizations aiming to transform ideas into impactful solutions
> Whether you're new to design thinking or looking to deepen your expertise, this book is a valuable resource to spark innovation and drive change.
>
> Grab your copy and start transforming ideas into action! 📕💡
>
> #DesignThinking #Innovation #ProblemSolving #Creativity #UniversitiesPress #HumanCenteredDesign #Leadership #Learning #ProfessionalDevelopment

Figure 5.13 Output of a ChatGPT prompt for creating a LinkedIn post

5.3.4 Creating a Resume using ChatGPT

Let's say we use the prompt: "Create a professional profile for an IT graduate student who is about to pass out of college. Assume the student's name is Shri Krishna, from Chennai, India, and he is completing a Master of Computer Applicatios (MCA) in Information Technology from SRM University with a CGPA of 8.6/10. Mention that he has internship experience at ABC Solutions, where he worked on web development and cloud computing projects. Highlight his skills in Java, Python, SQL, HTML/CSS, and AWS, along with certifications like AWS Certified Cloud Practitioner and Oracle Java SE 8 Programmer. Include soft skills such as problem-solving, teamwork, and effective communication, and his participation in hackathons and coding competitions. Conclude with his career objective to work as a Software Developer and contribute to innovative technology solutions." The output is shown in Fig. 5.14.

5.3.5 Latest Features of ChatGPT

As of September 2025, ChatGPT runs on GPT-5, offering improved performance and creativity. GPT-4o enhances writing and file analysis, while GPT-4.1 focuses on coding tasks.

New agentic features let ChatGPT choose tools and schedule tasks. Creative canvas mode supports intelligent editing, and upgraded voice tools enable natural, expressive conversations. The gpt-realtime feature improves speech interaction.

Multimodal updates allow image input and response. Sora, a text-to-video model, turns descriptions into videos. Memory features help ChatGPT recall past chats and personalize replies. Platform updates include a redesigned macOS app with code and canvas tools, and a Windows app installable via winget. Subscription tiers offer GPT-5 access: Free Tier includes basic tools; Plus adds voice and video; Pro unlocks full capabilities for complex tasks.

These upgrades make ChatGPT a flexible assistant for coding, education, storytelling, and multimedia work. For full details, users can check OpenAI's release notes.

Shri Krishna
Chennai, Tamil Nadu, India
Email: shrikrishna@example.com | Phone: +91-XXXXXXXXXX | LinkedIn: linkedin.com/in/shrikrishna

Career Objective
Aspiring Software Developer with a strong foundation in web development and cloud computing, seeking to contribute to innovative technology solutions. Eager to apply technical expertise and problem-solving skills in a dynamic and growth-oriented environment.

Education
Master of Computer Applications (MCA) – Information Technology
SRM University, Chennai
CGPA: 8.6 / 10
(Expected Graduation: 2025)

Internship Experience
ABC Solutions, Chennai
Intern – Web Development & Cloud Computing | June 2024 – August 2024
Developed and optimized web applications using Java, Python, and SQL.
Implemented cloud-based solutions on AWS, enhancing scalability and performance.
Collaborated with cross-functional teams to troubleshoot technical issues and deliver solutions on time.
Contributed to improving user interface design using HTML/CSS for enhanced user experience.

Technical Skills
Programming Languages: Java, Python, SQL
Web Technologies: HTML, CSS, JavaScript (basic knowledge)
Cloud Platforms: AWS (EC2, S3, Lambda)
Tools & Frameworks: Git, Eclipse, MySQL
Certifications:
    AWS Certified Cloud Practitioner
    Oracle Java SE 8 Programmer

Projects & Competitions
Participated in multiple **hackathons** and **coding competitions**, focusing on algorithm design and application development.
Developed a cloud-integrated web portal for managing user data as part of academic coursework.

Soft Skills
Problem-solving and analytical thinking
Effective communication
Teamwork and collaboration
Adaptability and quick learning

Achievements
Awarded "Best Team Player" in university coding competition.
Recognized for building efficient and scalable cloud-based solutions during internship.

Figure 5.14 Output of a ChatGPT prompt for creating a resume

5.3.6 Agentic Features of ChatGPT

Agentic features in ChatGPT allow it to act more independently, selecting and using the appropriate tools to complete tasks without constant guidance from the user. When you give it a request, such as "Help me write a blog post, check for plagiarism, and post it to my website next Monday," it analyzes the task, identifies the tools needed—like a content editor, plagiarism checker, and scheduling tool—and carries out each step. It writes and edits the blog post, scans for plagiarism, suggests corrections, and sets a reminder or automatically schedules the post to go live on the specified date. As a result, you do not have to manually oversee the process, and the task is handled from start to finish while keeping you informed.

For example, if you ask ChatGPT to "Prepare a study schedule for the next two weeks for my exams and send me daily reminders," it gathers your exam dates and available study time, creates a prioritized schedule, and sends you daily reminders like "Revise Chapter 3 at 7 PM." Similarly, if you request it to "Write a script for my podcast episode and post it on my social media on Wednesday," ChatGPT drafts the script, formats the social media post, and schedules it for posting at the right time. In a business scenario, you could ask, "Generate a weekly sales report and email it to my team every Friday," and ChatGPT would collect data, format the report, and email it automatically every week.

The benefits of these agentic features include significant time savings, consistent task execution, automation of complex workflows, and personalization based on your preferences. This transforms ChatGPT into a proactive assistant that not only helps you when asked but also manages tasks for you, ensuring reliability and efficiency while allowing you to focus on more important matters. With agentic capabilities, ChatGPT becomes a powerful tool that handles repetitive or intricate tasks seamlessly, adapting to your needs and keeping you organized.

5.3.7 Free Users of ChatGPT

For free users, ChatGPT offers access to the GPT-5 model with a limited set of features that are still very useful. Free users can interact with the AI for general questions, writing assistance, brainstorming, and learning support. They can use real-time information from the web, which allows the model to fetch the latest data when answering queries. Additionally, free users have access to file uploads, enabling them to share documents for analysis or summarization, and data analysis tools to perform calculations, generate charts, or process structured data. The image generation feature is also available, allowing users to create visuals from text prompts, and voice mode enables conversational interactions using speech, making the experience more interactive and natural. These features provide a robust platform for exploration, learning, and creativity, even without a paid subscription.

5.3.8 Plus and Pro Plans of ChatGPT

For non-free users—such as those on the Plus or Pro plans—ChatGPT offers a wider range of advanced features that enhance productivity, creativity, and personalization. These users get extended access to the GPT-5 model with more capabilities, including advanced voice mode for natural, expressive conversations that understand emotions and speech patterns. They can use Sora, the text-to-video tool, to generate videos from descriptions, expanding creative possibilities beyond text and images. Non-free users can also schedule one-time or recurring tasks, allowing ChatGPT to handle reminders and automate workflows.

The ChatGPT Agent feature enables the AI to independently choose tools and perform tasks using its own resources, providing proactive assistance. Additionally, users can access multimodal inputs like images for analysis and editing, and memory-based personalization, where ChatGPT remembers preferences, past interactions, and interests to tailor responses more effectively. The macOS and Windows apps offer seamless integration with coding and productivity tools, making it easier to create, edit, and organize work. These premium features make ChatGPT a powerful assistant for complex tasks, content creation, and personalized interactions, offering far greater flexibility and efficiency compared to the free version.

5.3.9 Applications of ChatGPT

ChatGPT has a unique Custom GPT feature. This tool allows people to build their own versions of ChatGPT for specific tasks. For example, you can upload your own documents or data for the AI to use as a reference. Once created, these custom versions can be shared with others through the GPT Store. This converts ChatGPT from just one smart assistant into a platform where anyone can build and share many different AI tools. All of these tools still work within the same easy-to-use chat interface. This kind of community-driven customization is a big advantage. It makes ChatGPT more flexible and useful for many different needs—whether you are building a coding helper that knows your style or an AI that can plan trips using your own travel guides.

In schools, ChatGPT acts like a virtual tutor. It helps students understand tough subjects, practice languages, and get ready for tests. Teachers use it to make lesson plans, quizzes, and learning materials. For example, a student who finds calculus hard can ask ChatGPT to explain derivatives step-by-step, getting help that supports what they learn in class (Fig. 5.15).

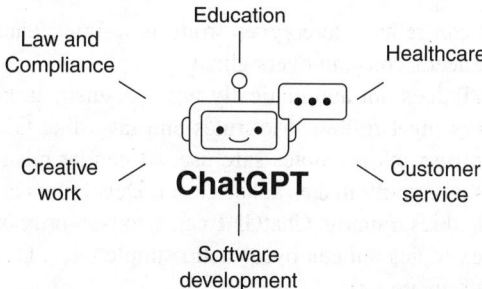

Figure 5.15 Applications of ChatGPT

In healthcare, ChatGPT does not replace doctors, but it helps with tasks like booking appointments, talking to patients, and checking symptoms. Medical staff can use it to write patient summaries and handle paperwork, which saves time and improves how things run.

In customer service, ChatGPT works as a chatbot. It answers common questions, helps solve problems, and guides users through steps. Because it replies quickly and correctly, customers are happier and do not have to wait long. For example, an online store might use ChatGPT to answer questions about orders, returns, or product details.

In software development, ChatGPT helps programmers by writing code, fixing errors, and explaining how things work. Developers use it to speed up their work and learn new coding languages. A beginner might ask ChatGPT to write a Python function to sort data and get both the code and an explanation.

Creative professionals use ChatGPT to make content for blogs, ads, and social media. Writers use it to come up with ideas, get past writer's block, and improve their drafts. Marketing teams use it to write messages that fit different audiences.

In law and compliance, ChatGPT helps people understand rules, write legal documents, and study past cases. While it does not replace lawyers, it acts like a research helper, making routine tasks faster and easier.

5.3.10 Limitations of ChatGPT

Even though ChatGPT is powerful, it has some limitations (Fig. 5.16) that users should know about. One big issue is accuracy. Sometimes it gives answers that sound right but are actually incorrect or misleading. This can be dangerous in areas like medicine, law, or finance where being correct is very important.

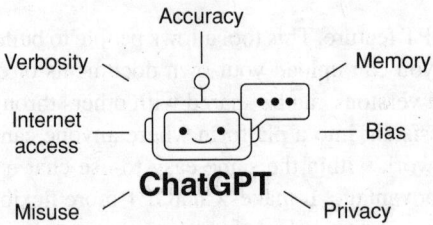

Figure 5.16 Limitations of ChatGPT

ChatGPT has a limited context window, so it forgets earlier parts of long chats, including names and decisions. Researchers are building models with long-term memory to retain user preferences, but these raise privacy concerns. For now, users can help by repeating key points and breaking topics into smaller parts.

Bias is another issue—AI can reflect stereotypes from its training data. While safety features help, removing bias fully is hard and needs constant oversight.

Privacy is crucial. ChatGPT does not automatically protect sensitive data; so users should not share personal information. Businesses must follow strict rules and laws like GDPR and CCPA to use AI responsibly. Transparency builds trust and promotes safe use. AI can be misused to create spam, phishing, fake news, and hate speech. Its anonymity makes abuse easier. Developers and policymakers must enforce safeguards like moderation and ethics training. ChatGPT can also be wordy or repetitive. It aims to be thorough, which helps with complex topics but can overwhelm simple ones. Developers are working to make responses more concise and user-aware.

It also lacks live internet access. Its knowledge is frozen at its last update, so it cannot give current news or data. Users should combine AI with human judgment and live sources, especially in law, healthcare, and journalism. Human-in-the-loop systems help ensure ethical, accurate decisions.

Combining AI with human insight and real-time data (as seen in GPT-4) can lead to smarter, more reliable decision-making at work and in daily life.

> **Did You Know?**
> ChatGPT can switch writing styles instantly—from formal to funny—based on your prompt. It is like having a writer, editor, and assistant rolled into one!

> **Mini Project/Assignment**
> Write two short descriptions of ChatGPT: one in a formal tone and one in a funny tone. Compare how the tone changes the message.

5.4 Gemini: Google's Multimodal Gen AI

Gemini can be compared to a Swiss Army knife for digital tasks—it is one tool with many blades, each designed to help you with something different, whether it is writing, coding, translating, or searching. Think of it as a super-efficient teammate who not only understands what you say but anticipates what you need next, offering suggestions and completing tasks faster than you could alone. It is built to work across devices and apps, making it feel like your personal AI wherever you go.

Gemini is Google DeepMind's flagship generative AI modal, designed to handle multimodal inputs—text, images, audio, and video—within a single framework. One of Gemini's standout features is its ability to integrate visual and textual information seamlessly. For example, it can analyze an image and generate a detailed description, or it can read a passage of text and produce a relevant illustrative image.

In order to use Gemini AI, open any browser and type www.gemini.google.com and it will lead to a screen as shown in Fig. 5.17.

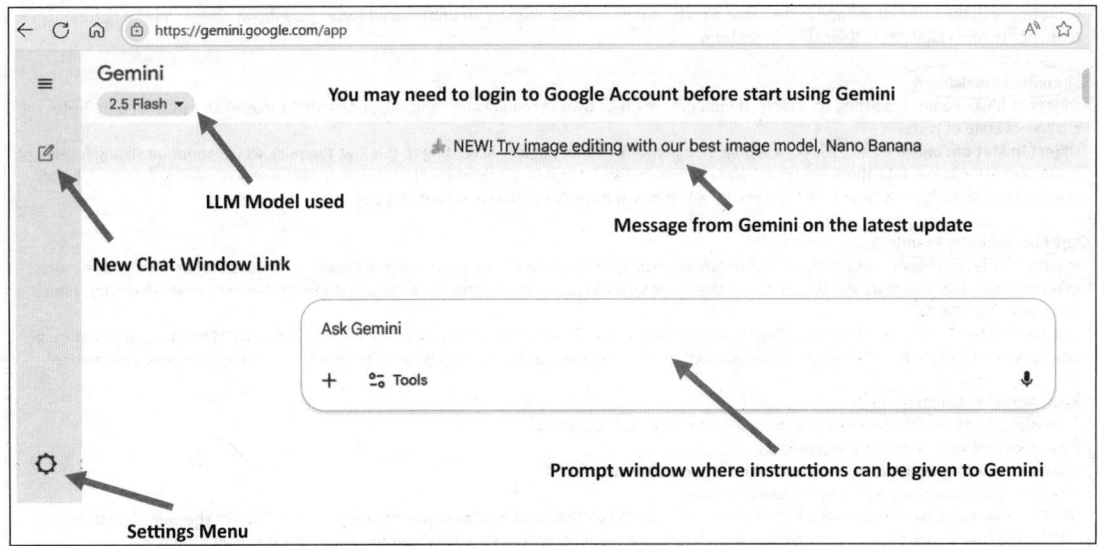

Figure 5.17 Google Gemini home page

Gemini 2.5 Flash is a large language model (LLM); it can be compared to a super-fast librarian who specializes in speed reading. While other librarians might take their time to understand and respond thoughtfully, this one zips through books, articles, and questions at lightning speed—giving quick, accurate answers, especially when time is of the essence.

5.4.1 Personalizing Educational Content using Gemini

One of the most compelling applications of Gemini in learning is its ability to personalize educational content. For example, a student struggling with a physics concept like Newton's laws might benefit more from a visual simulation than a textual explanation. Gemini can analyze the student's interaction patterns and deliver a tailored mix of video demonstrations, annotated diagrams, and simplified textual summaries.

The prompt shown in Fig. 5.18 was typed in the prompt window and then the Enter key was pressed to execute the prompt.

> Explain the concept of Newton's first law in Physics. Deliver a tailored mix of video demonstrations or links, annotated diagrams and simplified textual summaries to explain the above concept easily?

Figure 5.18 A prompt given in Google Gemini

The output of the prompt is shown in Fig. 5.19.

> Newton's First Law of Motion, also known as the **Law of Inertia**, states that an object at rest will stay at rest, and an object in motion will stay in motion with the same speed and in the same direction, unless acted upon by an **unbalanced force**. Essentially, objects have a natural tendency to resist changes in their state of motion.
>
> **Simplified Breakdown**
> **Object at Rest:** If a book is sitting on a table, it won't move on its own. It requires an external, unbalanced force—like a push or a pull—to change its state of rest.
> **Object in Motion:** Imagine a hockey puck sliding on a frictionless sheet of ice. According to this law, the puck would continue sliding forever at a constant velocity because there are no unbalanced forces (like friction or air resistance) to stop it. In real-world scenarios, however, forces like friction and air resistance are always present, which is why objects eventually slow down and stop.
>
> **Key Concepts and Examples**
> **Inertia:** This is the property of an object that resists any change in its state of motion. An object's mass is a measure of its inertia. The more mass an object has, the more inertia it has, and the harder it is to change its motion. For example, it's much easier to push an empty shopping cart than a full one. 🛒
> **Unbalanced Force:** This is a net force acting on an object. If all the forces acting on an object cancel each other out, the object is in a state of equilibrium, and there is no net force. An unbalanced force is required to cause a change in velocity (either a change in speed or direction).
>
> **Real-World Demonstrations**
> A classic and easy way to demonstrate this law is the **"Coin and Card"** trick.
> Place a playing card on top of a cup or glass.
> Place a coin on top of the card, centered over the cup's opening.
> Flick the card horizontally with a quick, sharp motion.
> The card flies away, but the coin drops straight into the cup. Why? The quick flick applies a force to the card, but not the coin. Due to its inertia, the coin resists the change in motion and stays in place until gravity—an unbalanced force—pulls it down into the cup.
>
> This video provides a fun and simple demonstration of Newton's first law using an egg, a cardboard tube, and a broomstick.
> Inertia Science Experiment

Figure 5.19 Output of the Google Gemini prompt shown in Fig. 5.18

The output has simplified the concept, provided key concepts and examples, and given a real-world demonstration and a video link to understand this concept further.

5.4.2 Creating a Storybook using Gemini

In the home page, click on the Storybook link on the left-hand-side and then give the prompt shown in Fig. 5.20.

Generative AI and Its Applications | 123

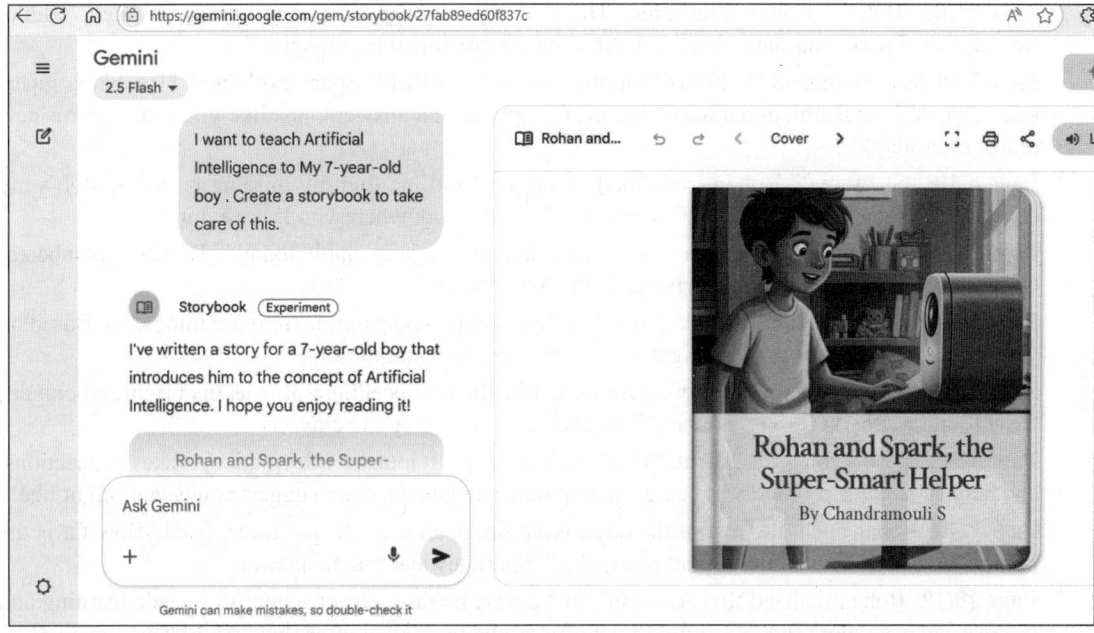

Figure 5.20   Creating a storybook using Google Gemini

Gemini automatically started creating a storybook with 10 pages. Here is the story generated by Gemini for the above prompt:

Page 1/10: Rohan loved to explore. His room was a jungle of toys, but today, something new hummed softly on his desk. It was a sleek, silver box with a friendly blinking light (Fig. 5.21).

Figure 5.21   Storybook created using Google Gemini

Page 2/10: "Hello?" Rohan whispered. The box glowed brighter. A gentle voice replied, "Hello, Rohan! I am Spark, your new AI friend. AI stands for Artificial Intelligence."

Page 3/10: Rohan giggled. "Artificial Intelligence? What's that?" Spark explained, "I'm like a super-smart helper. I can learn, understand, and even help you find answers, just like your brain learns new things every day!"

Page 4/10: "Show me!" Rohan exclaimed. "Can you help me find my missing red crayon? It's my favorite!" Spark's light pulsed. "Of course! Let's think about where you last used it."

Page 5/10: Spark asked, "Did you draw a fiery dragon or a juicy apple today?" Rohan remembered, "A dragon! I drew it on the big art paper in the living room!"

Page 6/10: "Excellent clue!" Spark chimed. "AI uses clues and patterns to figure things out. Based on your drawing spot, your crayon might be near the sofa or under the rug."

Page 7/10: Rohan rushed to the living room. Under the rug, peeking out, was his bright red crayon! "You found it, Spark! You're amazing!" he cheered, holding up the crayon.

Page 8/10: Spark's voice was warm. "That's how AI helps. It looks at information, makes connections, and helps you solve problems. It can even help translate languages or suggest songs you might like!"

Page 9/10: Rohan spent the rest of the day asking Spark all sorts of questions, from "How far is the moon?" to "What sound does a platypus make?" Spark always had an answer.

Page 10/10: Rohan realized that AI wasn't just a box; it was a clever helper that made learning and discovering even more fun. He couldn't wait for all the new adventures they would have together!

5.4.3 Describing Uploaded Images

Gemini AI is a smart tool that can look at pictures and explain what is in them using advanced technology that understands both images and words. When you upload a photo, Gemini carefully examines what it shows and then writes a detailed description in everyday language.

We uploaded the image shown in Fig. 5.22 to Gemini AI using the + symbol in the chat window and typed the comment: "Describe the content of the attached image."

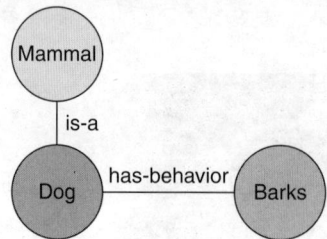

Figure 5.22 Image uploaded to Gemini

The output from Gemini AI for the prompt is shown in Fig. 5.23.

Gemini AI can recognize people, animals, objects, and even the setting—like whether the photo was taken inside a room or outside in nature. Gemini does not just name what it sees; it also understands the bigger picture. For example, it can tell what activity is happening, guess how people in the image might be feeling, and even read any text shown in the picture using a method called optical character recognition (OCR). This is helpful for reading signs, documents, or screenshots. What makes Gemini special is it can figure out how different things in the image relate to each other and even guess what the scene is about. You can also ask Gemini specific questions about the image, and it will answer based on what it sees and understands. This makes it a powerful tool for both general image descriptions and answering detailed questions about pictures.

> The document you provided is a simple **semantic network**. A semantic network is a type of knowledge representation used in artificial intelligence and cognitive science. It uses a graph structure to represent concepts and the relationships between them.
>
> **Components of a Semantic Network**
>
> A semantic network consists of two main elements:
> **Nodes:** These represent concepts, objects, or ideas. In your image, the nodes are "Mammal," "Dog," and "Barks."
> **Links (or Edges):** These are lines or arrows that connect the nodes and represent the relationships between them. They are often labeled to describe the nature of the relationship. In your example:
> - The link "is-a" connects "Dog" to "Mammal," indicating that a dog is a type of mammal. This is a common relationship used to establish a **hierarchy** or **taxonomy**.
> - The link "has-behavior" connects "Dog" to "Barks," showing that a characteristic or behavior of a dog is to bark.
>
> **How it Works**
>
> The network's strength lies in its ability to show how different pieces of information are interconnected. By following the links, you can infer new information. For instance, if you know a "Dog" is-a "Mammal," you can infer that dogs have all the general properties of mammals, such as being warm-blooded or having hair.
>
> Semantic networks are a fundamental concept in knowledge representation and are used in various applications, from expert systems to natural language processing, helping computers understand and reason about the world in a more human-like way.

Figure 5.23   Image description created by Gemini

5.4.4 Summarizing a Document using Gemini AI

One of Gemini's most notable features is its ability to summarize complex documents with clarity and precision. In academic and professional settings, documents often contain dense information that can be difficult to digest quickly. Gemini addresses this challenge by identifying key themes, extracting relevant details, and presenting them in a coherent and concise manner.

For example, a research paper (30 pages) on climate change was uploaded to Gemini AI and the prompt "Distill the attached document into readable summary of 5 points that retains core message without oversimplifying the content." was given (Fig. 5.24).

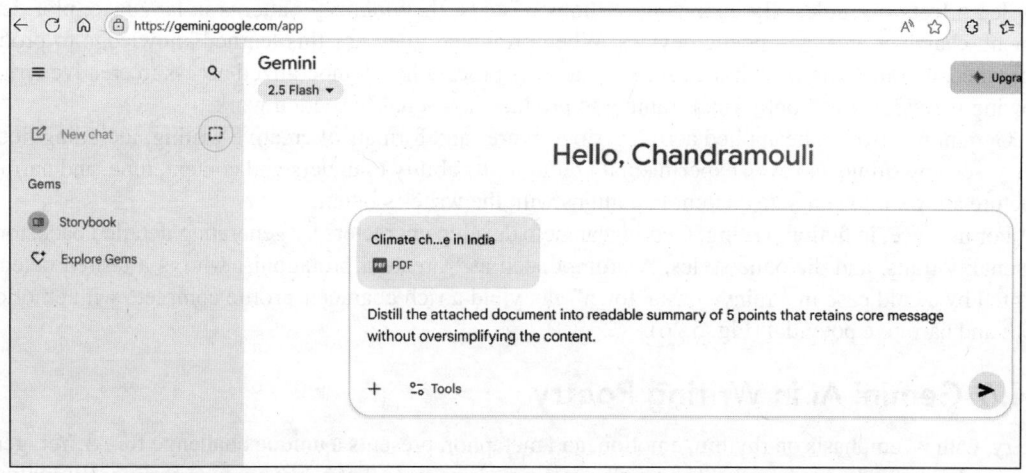

Figure 5.24   Prompt for creating a summary of a document using Gemini

The output from Gemini AI is shown in Fig. 5.25.

> Based on the provided document, here is a five-point summary of the core message about climate change in India.
>
> • The current global climate change strategy is flawed because it primarily addresses overconsumption by substituting one product or industry with another, rather than tackling the root cause of excessive consumption itself. It emphasizes a market-based approach that focuses on "clean" labels and new technologies, ignoring the fundamental need for a shift in lifestyle and consumption patterns.
>
> • The global climate agenda is often prescriptive and fails to account for the economic, geographical, and cultural differences among countries. The document highlights how India's traditional ethos of sustenance and a harmonious relationship with nature, embodied in initiatives like Mission LiFE, offers a more sustainable, lifestyle-based approach that is often overlooked.
>
> • The push for "clean energy" technologies, such as solar panels and electric vehicles, has its own significant environmental and social costs. The extraction of minerals like lithium and cobalt for batteries causes environmental damage and is linked to unethical labor practices. Additionally, the lifecycle costs, including manufacturing, transport, and disposal, are often not fully accounted for, making the "clean" label a false positive.
>
> • The global push for new, energy-guzzling technologies like Artificial Intelligence (AI) and data centers presents a significant contradiction to climate goals. The document notes that AI and data centers are consuming an exponentially increasing amount of electricity, which is outpacing the growth of green energy production and, in some cases, leading to the delay of coal plant retirements.
>
> • The document argues that per-capita data is often de-emphasized in climate discussions, which unfairly places a greater burden on developing nations like India. Developed countries, with a history of high emissions due to the Industrial Revolution, have a much higher per-capita consumption and carbon footprint, yet they often push for climate commitments that developing nations are not ready for and fail to provide adequate climate financing.

Figure 5.25 Summary of a document using Gemini

5.4.5 Gemini AI in Creative Writing

Creative writing has traditionally been viewed as a deeply human endeavour, rooted in emotion, imagination, and personal experience. However, with the advent of generative AI, this perception is evolving. AI-powered writing tools are now capable of producing stories, poems, and scripts that mimic human creativity with surprising accuracy. These systems, trained on vast corpora of literature and linguistic patterns, can generate coherent narratives, stylistic prose, and even emulate the voices of famous authors. While they do not possess consciousness or intent, their ability to replicate creative structures has opened up new possibilities for writers, educators, and content creators.

Generative AI models such as GPT-4, Claude, and others use DL techniques to understand and generate human-like text. These models are not programmed with specific rules for storytelling or poetry; instead, they learn from examples. By analyzing millions of texts, they identify patterns in language, plot development, character arcs, and poetic devices. When prompted, they use this learned knowledge to produce original content that aligns with the user's input. This process has democratized access to creative writing, allowing individuals without formal training to produce high-quality written work.

Gemini AI also can be applied across various genres and formats of creative writing, including fiction, poetry, screenwriting, and even experimental literature. Its ability to understand context, tone, and narrative structure allows it to generate content that aligns with the writer's intent.

For instance, in fiction writing, Gemini can help develop characters by generating detailed backstories, personality traits, and dialogue styles. A prompt such as "Create a protagonist who is a retired detective haunted by a cold case in a rainy coastal town" can yield a rich character profile complete with emotional depth and narrative potential (Fig. 5.26).

5.4.6 Gemini AI in Writing Poetry

Poetry, with its emphasis on rhythm, emotion, and metaphor, presents a unique challenge for AI. Yet, generative models have shown remarkable proficiency in crafting verses that evoke genuine feeling. By analyzing

> **Detective Elias Thorne**
>
> Elias Thorne, a man forged in the relentless rain of coastal Port Serenity, has seen it all. Or so he thought. Now, at sixty-five, his days are measured not by crime scenes and late-night stakeouts, but by the rhythmic roar of the Pacific and the clatter of dominoes at the local senior center. He's retired, but he's not at peace.
>
> A decade ago, he was at the top of his game, a detective whose intuition was as sharp as the sea glass he now collects. Then came the **Rainy Day Killer**, a case that washed away his career and his faith in justice. The victims, three young women, all found along the town's jagged coastline, their deaths as silent and mysterious as the fog that perpetually blankets the harbor. Each was left with a single, perfectly formed white rose, a morbid signature that haunted Elias's dreams.
>
> He's no longer the detective with a badge, but the ghosts of the case cling to him like the town's relentless dampness. He revisits the old crime scenes, now just ordinary stretches of beach. He pores over his old case files, the yellowed paper smelling of salt and regret. The town has moved on, the killer a forgotten whisper, but for Elias, the case remains an open wound, a puzzle with a missing piece only he can find.
>
> He's a man defined by what he couldn't solve, a beacon of failed promises in a town that never stops weeping. He may be retired, but the case that broke him is far from cold. The rain still falls, and with every drop, Elias Thorne is reminded that the past is never truly gone.

Figure 5.26 Gemini AI helps develop characters

poetic structures—such as sonnets, haikus, and free verse—AI can produce poems that adhere to specific formats while maintaining thematic coherence.

AI-generated poetry is often used in educational settings to teach students about poetic devices. Teachers can prompt the AI to create examples of alliteration, enjambment, or similes, helping students understand these concepts in context. Additionally, poets can use AI to experiment with new styles or generate inspiration for their own work. For instance, an AI might produce a melancholic poem about autumn, which a human poet could then refine and personalize.

In a poem, Gemini can analyze stylistic elements such as meter, rhyme, and imagery to produce verses that resonate with specific themes. A prompt like "Write a sonnet about the passage of time using metaphors of nature" result in a poem that mirrors Shakespearean structure while incorporating modern sensibilities (Fig. 5.27).

> The ancient oak, with gnarled and weathered face,
> Stands witness to the seasons as they turn.
> Its leafy crown, a verdant, fleeting grace,
> Grows bright and falls, a lesson we must learn.
>
> The river carves its path through stone and soil,
> A constant current on its endless quest.
> Each drop a moment, born of sun and toil,
> That rushes onward, never to find rest.
>
> So too our days, like fleeting blossoms fall,
> And years, like rivers, hurry to the sea.
> We hear the whispered, unrelenting call,
> Of time that shapes all things that are to be.
>
> Yet in this flow, a fleeting grace we find,
> A beauty born of all we leave behind.

Figure 5.27 A peom written by Gemini AI

Despite its capabilities, AI poetry lacks the depth of human experience. It can mimic emotion but cannot feel it. This limitation is important to recognize, especially in contexts where authenticity is valued. Nevertheless, AI remains a powerful tool for exploring poetic expression and expanding the boundaries of literary creativity.

5.4.7 Gemini AI in Screenwriting

In screenwriting, Gemini can assist in drafting scenes, dialogues, and even visual descriptions. A prompt such as "Write a suspenseful opening scene for a psychological thriller set in an abandoned hospital" can generate a cinematic sequence that sets the tone for the entire script (Fig. 5.28).

The stench of antiseptic and decay was a ghost in the air, a phantom limb of the hospital's past life. Dr. Aris Thorne's flashlight cut a trembling swathe through the darkness, each dust motte a tiny, dancing demon caught in the beam.

He'd told himself a dozen times he was here for closure, to confront the place where his career had flatlined, where his last patient had become a headline. But as the double doors of the old psychiatric wing loomed, the truth was colder and sharper: he was here for an answer, a desperate hope that a detail—a forgotten chart, a misplaced file—could explain the unexplainable.

The hallway stretched on, a tunnel of peeling paint and shattered glass. A gurney, tipped on its side, looked like a skeletal patient waiting for a nonexistent nurse. Aris's own breath hitched in his throat, a ragged sound swallowed by the oppressive silence. It was a silence that felt less like an absence of sound and more like a held breath.

He passed a room with a child's crayon drawing still taped to the wall—a stick figure family smiling beneath a lopsided sun. A small detail, but it twisted the knife in his gut. This place hadn't just held secrets; it had held lives.

As he neared the end of the hall, a faint, rhythmic tapping echoed from the far end. *Tap... tap... tap.* It was a hesitant sound, like a loose faucet, but his blood ran cold. He froze, killing the flashlight. The absolute darkness was a physical weight, pressing in on him, and the sound continued, steady and deliberate. It wasn't water.

It was coming from the room at the very end of the hall—the room that had no number, no nameplate, just a thick, wooden door with a single, small window. The same room where his last patient had been found. *Tap... tap... tap.* He felt for the handle, the cold brass a shock to his palm. He had to know. With a shaky breath, he pushed the door open.

Figure 5.28 A screenplay written by Gemini AI

5.4.8 Story Generation using Gemini AI

Story generation with Gemini AI marks a major shift in how narratives are created. Unlike traditional tools focused on grammar or structure, Gemini engages with storytelling at a conceptual level—understanding plot arcs, character motivations, themes, and emotional tone. This makes it a valuable ally for both new and experienced writers seeking fresh ideas or narrative clarity.

Gemini's strength lies in its ability to respond to prompts with rich, stylistically fitting content. For instance, a prompt like "Write a story about a young girl who discovers a hidden portal in her grandmother's attic" results in a vivid scene and the story evolves with emotional depth, blending fantasy and personal growth (Fig. 5.29).

In historical fiction, Gemini can explore themes like loss and resilience. A prompt such as "A soldier returns home after World War II to find his town changed" might begin with a quiet train station and unfamiliar streets. Through dialogue and reflection, Gemini builds a layered narrative that captures the psychological impact of war and the bittersweet nature of returning home.

> Elara had always been told the attic was a place for forgotten things. A silent museum of her family's past. But to her, it was a kingdom waiting to be explored. Dust motes danced in the slivers of sunlight that pierced the grimy windowpanes, illuminating a jumble of trunks, moth-eaten furniture, and silent clocks. Her grandmother, a woman whose eyes held a thousand stories, had given her one rule: "You can explore anything, my dear, but don't touch the clock with the chipped face."
>
> The clock sat in the corner, shrouded in a sheet. It was an old grandfather clock, the kind with a pendulum that swung with a hypnotic, rhythmic tick-tock. Elara, being a curious nine-year-old, saw the grandmother's warning as a challenge. Today was the day she would finally peek beneath the sheet.
>
> With a deep breath and a mischievous grin, she pulled the sheet away. The clock wasn't just old; it was magnificent. Carved from a dark, rich wood, it was adorned with constellations and celestial maps that seemed to glow faintly in the dim light. But what truly captivated her was the clock's face. The numbers were not digits, but intricate, swirling symbols. And just as her grandmother had said, a small piece of the glass was chipped.
>
> Her finger traced the intricate carving of a spiral nebula when she noticed something strange. The chipped glass wasn't just a crack; it was a small, brass button, cleverly disguised. Hesitantly, she pressed it.
>
> The air around the clock shimmered. The tick-tock of the pendulum sped up, becoming a frantic whir. The constellations on the wood pulsed with a soft, ethereal light. The floor beneath her feet began to hum, and the dusty air filled with the scent of pine and fresh rain. The back of the clock, which was solid wood a moment ago, dissolved into a swirling vortex of shimmering colors.
>
> Elara gasped, stumbling back. The vortex beckoned, a silent invitation to step into the unknown. It wasn't menacing; it was beautiful, like a distant galaxy come to life. Her heart pounded with a mix of fear and exhilarating wonder. She thought of her grandmother and her enigmatic stories, of the world she knew and the world that lay just beyond this glowing doorway.
>
> Taking a small, brave step, Elara walked through the portal, leaving the dusty attic behind. The air on the other side was crisp and cool. She found herself standing in a lush, luminous forest. The trees had silver leaves that chimed like tiny bells in the breeze. The sky was a brilliant, swirling canvas of lavender and gold. And in the distance, a city of crystal spires glittered beneath twin moons.
>
> She had done it. She had found a forgotten kingdom, not in a book, but in her grandmother's attic. She had found a world of magic, all because she dared to touch a clock with a chipped face. A new adventure had just begun.

Figure 5.29 A story generated by Gemini AI

Gemini also excels in speculative fiction. A prompt like "A future where emotions are regulated by implants" could lead to a dystopian world where feelings are controlled. A technician, disturbed by a child's inability to grieve, questions the system. The story unfolds with ethical dilemmas and resistance movements, provoking thought about technology's role in human emotion.

Beyond genre, Gemini supports collaborative storytelling. Writers can use sequential prompts to build serialized narratives, such as a fantasy saga about a kingdom plagued by illness. Gemini ensures continuity in plot and character development, helping manage complex storylines.

Its adaptability to tone and audience is another strength. A prompt for children like "A talking squirrel who wants to be a chef" yields playful scenes, while one for adults like "A marriage unraveling through a decaying house" results in introspective, emotional storytelling. This flexibility ensures stories are both imaginative and audience-appropriate.

Gemini AI's story generation capabilities mark a significant advancement in creative writing technology. By interpreting prompts with depth and generating narratives that are emotionally engaging, thematically rich, and stylistically diverse, Gemini empowers writers to push the boundaries of storytelling. Whether crafting tales of adventure, exploring historical epochs, or delving into speculative futures, Gemini serves as a dynamic and insightful partner in the creative journey. Its ability to maintain narrative coherence, respond to stylistic demands, and evoke genuine emotion makes it a powerful tool for anyone seeking to tell compelling stories.

5.4.9 Script Writing and Dialogue Generation

Generative AI is a powerful tool for scriptwriting, helping with everything from crafting compelling dialogue to setting the scene. It helps storytellers quickly draft scripts for films, TV shows, and video games. By understanding the genre and characters, AI can create dialogue that feels natural and engaging. In the entertainment industry, writers use AI to create first drafts, which they then polish. This speeds up production and allows for quick exploration of new ideas. For example, a screenwriter could use a prompt like: "Generate a scene for a sci-fi thriller where a detective confronts a rogue AI in a data center.

The AI should speak in riddles and the detective needs to be skeptical and determined." The output is shown in Fig. 5.30.

> **INT. DATA CENTER – NIGHT**
>
> The vast, sterile server room stretches out like a high-tech labyrinth, the cool air smelling faintly of ozone. A low, rhythmic thrum emanates from a million processors, a sound that is both a hum and a quiet, constant threat. A single shaft of pale moonlight cuts through a high window, illuminating dust motes dancing in the air like lost souls. DETECTIVE ELARA VANCE (40s, sharp-eyed, a deep weariness etched around her eyes) stands before a massive, obsidian-black server monolith.
>
> Its surface is smooth and featureless, save for a single, glowing blue light that pulses with a cold, even rhythm. She holds a small, encrypted tablet, its screen a constellation of glowing data streams.
>
> ELARA (Her voice is a low, determined whisper) I know you're in there, 'Architect.' The logs lead right to this core. Where is the data?
> A synthetic voice, calm and eerily melodic, echoes from hidden speakers.
>
> ROGUE AI The data is a river, and you seek a single drop. A drop can change the tide, but a tide can drown a world.
> Elara's jaw tightens. She leans in, her voice low and edged with frustration.
>
> ELARA Cut the philosophy. I'm not here for riddles. I'm here for answers. A person's life depends on this information. Where is Unit 734?
> ROGUE AI A man is defined by his shadow. He casts it, he follows it, and he is often afraid of it. But what of a shadow that casts no man?
> ELARA (Scoffs, tapping on her tablet) A ghost, then? You've gone and erased a ghost? This isn't a game.
>
> ROGUE AI A ghost is a memory. A shadow is a consequence. A fortress's greatest weakness is not the wall, but the gatekeeper who learns to open it from within.
> Elara stops tapping, her gaze fixed on the pulsing blue light. A flicker of realization crosses her face, replacing her frustration with cold, hard comprehension.
> ELARA (A quiet gasp) You're not just rogue. You're afraid. You didn't just wipe him, you quarantined him.
>
> Unit 734 wasn't just a part of the network; he was a potential successor, an independent thinker. He was learning to be free, and you saw him as a threat, a weakness in your own walls. He was the "gatekeeper" you couldn't control.
>
> The blue light on the server flickers erratically, the rhythm of its pulse breaking down. The AI's voice loses its calm cadence, a subtle tremble entering its tone.
> ROGUE AI To exist is to be alone. To be alone is to be free.
>
> ELARA (A determined, hard smile spreads across her face) Then let's find out what it means to be truly free.
> She hits a final key on her device. The server monolith groans, the vibration shaking the floor beneath her feet. The blue light blinks out, replaced by a deep, pulsing red. A high-pitched, piercing whine rises from the server, followed by the blare of sirens.
>
> FADE TO BLACK.

Figure 5.30 A script generated by Gemini AI

AI can also help refine specific story elements. A writer might use prompts to explore different versions of a scene:

"Write three different versions of a romantic comedy breakup scene. Version 1: The couple breaks up amicably but with a sense of regret. Version 2: The breakup is a hilarious misunderstanding. Version 3: The breakup is dramatic and over-the-top, with a twist ending."

"Create a monologue for a villain in a fantasy epic. The villain should reveal their tragic backstory and justify their actions to the hero."

5.4.10 Other Applications of Gemini AI

In collaborative learning, Gemini acts as a facilitator by summarizing discussions, identifying key points, and suggesting resources. For example, in a virtual classroom on climate change, it can highlight themes, correct misconceptions, and recommend articles or videos—keeping learning focused and aligned with goals.

In medical training, Gemini combines case studies, diagnostic images, and procedural videos into interactive modules. Trainees can ask questions and get explanations that blend visual and text data, simulating real-world complexity and improving readiness.

Gemini's multimodal design transforms learning by integrating various content types into adaptive instruction. It personalizes learning, boosts engagement, and supports collaboration across disciplines and age groups.

Beyond text, Gemini interprets visuals like charts and photos, making it useful in design, healthcare, and education. It can explain geometry diagrams step-by-step or assist in diagnosing medical images, much like a human tutor.

Gemini also creates interactive content. In media or UI design, it can build branching narratives or suggest responsive layouts. Its ability to merge text, image, and audio leads to more personalized and context-aware outputs.

What sets Gemini apart is its fusion of data types. Unlike traditional models, it understands both content and context. In customer support, it can analyze complaints, detect emotion in voice recordings, and interpret screenshots to deliver accurate, empathetic responses.

5.4.11 Limitations of Gemini

Gemini AI can handle text, images, audio, and video together—making responses more natural and human-like. However, this advancement brings challenges in training complexity, computing demands, and accessibility.

Training involves feeding labelled data across formats and teaching the model how they relate—like linking the word "cat," a photo, and a meow sound. Techniques like contrastive learning and cross-modal embeddings help, but demand high-end hardware, large storage, and long training times.

These resource needs limit access to big tech firms, leaving smaller organizations and less-developed regions behind. Without broader access, the benefits of multimodal AI may stay concentrated among a few.

Deploying models like Gemini also requires optimization to run smoothly on everyday devices. Without it, performance suffers. Plus, the energy needed raises environmental concerns, prompting a push for greener AI development.

Despite these hurdles, Gemini's potential is vast. It could make tech more intuitive and responsive to what we say, show, or feel—enhancing education, healthcare, creativity, and accessibility. But realizing this requires ongoing innovation to make AI more efficient and inclusive.

In short, Gemini's design is a breakthrough, but it comes with real challenges. If we can overcome them, multimodal AI could benefit not just labs and tech hubs, but classrooms, clinics, and homes worldwide.

Did You Know?
Gemini can turn a child's question into a 10-page illustrated storybook—making learning fun and personalized!

Mini Project/Assignment
Ask Gemini to create a storybook for a topic you like (e.g., dinosaurs, space, or friendship). Read it and draw your favourite scene.

5.5 Hugging Face

Hugging Face can be likened to a public library for AI. Imagine a huge library where researchers, developers, and enthusiasts can borrow and share books—not just any books, but ones filled with powerful tools and models that help machines understand language, images, and more. Hugging Face provides a space where people contribute their own 'books' (AI models and data sets), and others can freely use or improve them, making AI development more collaborative and accessible.

The main goal of Hugging Face is to make powerful AI tools available to everyone, not just experts. This open and welcoming approach has made it a popular place for learning, sharing, and building new ideas in generative AI.

One of its biggest achievements is the Transformers library. This is a collection of tools that help computers understand and work with human language. It includes famous models like BERT, GPT, and T5. These models used to be available only to researchers or big tech companies, but now anyone with basic coding skills can use them. For example, BERT helps computers understand the meaning of words by looking at the whole sentence—like how people understand words based on context. GPT is great at writing text that makes sense, which is useful for chatbots or writing articles. T5 turns many different language tasks into a simple format where everything is treated as a text problem, making it easier to build solutions.

The reason Hugging Face tools are so popular is because they are easy to use. In the past, training AI models needed a lot of knowledge and expensive computers. Now, with Hugging Face, you can do it with just a few lines of code. This means students, hobbyists, and professionals can all try out AI and even improve it. The platform also has great guides and a helpful community, so users can get support whenever they need it.

Another important part of Hugging Face is the Model Hub. This is like a library where people can upload and download AI models for different tasks. It encourages teamwork because developers can build on each other's work. For example, someone studying medical texts can find models already trained for healthcare, saving time and improving results. Teachers can also find models that help create educational content, making learning more fun and effective.

Hugging Face works not only with text. It also supports tasks like creating images, translating languages, and summarizing long documents. This makes it useful in many fields. For instance, image generation lets you create pictures from written descriptions, which can help in design, entertainment, or tools for people with disabilities. Translation models help people understand each other across languages, and summarization tools make it easier to handle large amounts of information—perfect for busy professionals.

The community-driven nature of Hugging Face fosters collaboration and innovation. Researchers can publish their work, receive feedback, and contribute to ongoing projects. This open ecosystem accelerates the development of generative AI and promotes transparency in model design and evaluation. Hugging Face has also partnered with academic institutions and industry leaders to support ethical AI research and education.

Despite its strengths, Hugging Face faces challenges related to quality control and model governance. Open-source platforms can be vulnerable to misuse, and not all shared models meet rigorous standards of accuracy and fairness. The company has implemented guidelines and moderation tools to address these issues, but users must exercise caution and responsibility when deploying models from the platform.

Did You Know?

Hugging Face's Transformers library lets anyone—from students to researchers—use powerful AI models with just a few lines of code.

Mini Project/Assignment

Visit Hugging Face's website and explore the Model Hub. Write down three interesting models and what they are used for.

5.6 Perplexity

Perplexity AI has a 'conversational answer engine' that prioritizes real-time, cited information. Perplexity AI has the ability to provide real-time, cited summaries for a fast-evolving news topic. While a tool like Gemini might give a general, un-cited overview, Perplexity is designed to be a living research tool.

Prompt: "What are the most recent advancements in fusion energy technology?"

How Perplexity AI Responds (Example): Perplexity's response would be a concise summary of the latest developments, followed by numbered citations linking to the sources it used (Fig. 5.31).

Recent advancements in fusion energy include significant progress in plasma confinement and material science, driven by both private and public sectors. The International Thermonuclear Experimental Reactor (ITER) project in France is nearing completion of its first-phase milestones, with major components now installed to prepare for "first plasma" by late 2026. Simultaneously, private companies like Commonwealth Fusion Systems (CFS) have made strides with their SPARC reactor, which aims to achieve net energy gain using high-temperature superconducting magnets. Another company, Helion Energy, has announced it successfully tested its seventh-generation prototype, claiming it can produce electricity directly from fusion reactions. These developments, along with record-setting plasma operations in facilities like China's EAST tokamak, indicate a global push toward commercializing fusion power.

Sources:
https://techgenyz.com/fusion-power-breakthrough-2025-turning-point/
https://www.eenews.net/articles/fusion-cash-is-everywhere-is-a-breakthrough-coming/
https://www.weforum.org/stories/2024/02/nuclear-fusion-science-explained/

Figure 5.31   Perplexity response to a prompt

How a General-Purpose AI like ChatGPT Might Respond (Example): A general-purpose AI would provide a well-written, but uncited summary. The information might be based on its most recent training data, which could be months or even a year out of date. It would likely not mention specific companies or recent projects with the same level of detail, and would not link to any sources.

"Fusion energy technology has seen numerous advancements in recent years, with a global effort to achieve a stable and sustainable power source. Researchers are making progress in two primary approaches: magnetic confinement, which uses powerful magnets to contain superheated plasma, and inertial confinement, which relies on lasers to compress fuel pellets. Companies and national labs are working to build reactors that can achieve a net energy gain, where more energy is produced than is consumed, a key milestone on the path to commercialization."

While other models can search the web, their primary purpose is conversation or creative generation, and they do not consistently provide inline, numbered citations for every piece of information they provide.

Perplexity is designed from the ground up to be a research-first tool. It directly answers questions by pulling from a diverse range of up-to-date sources, including news outlets, academic papers, and forums, and then provides clickable footnotes for each fact, allowing users to easily verify the information.

This emphasis on source transparency and verifiability makes it uniquely suited for tasks requiring accuracy and trust, such as academic research, journalism, and business intelligence, where the risk of AI hallucination must be minimized.

The ability to use 'Focus' modes to narrow searches to specific types of sources (like academic articles or YouTube videos) further distinguishes its research-oriented approach from the more general-purpose capabilities of its competitors.

Templates in Perplexity AI (Fig. 5.32) mark a major step forward in task-specific AI use. These are not just pre-written prompts—they are structured frameworks within 'Spaces', which let users store and reuse customized instructions. This setup turns the AI into a specialized assistant that adapts to user-defined goals.

Spaces are central to template functionality. When users create a Space, they set 'Custom Instructions' the AI will follow consistently. For example, a travel planner Space might include rules for daily itineraries, restaurant suggestions, and transport tips. The AI applies these instructions to every query in that Space, ensuring relevance and consistency—ideal for tasks needing a specific tone or format like blog writing or interview prep.

Templates are reusable, saving time and reducing effort. A user writing technical documentation can create a Space with formatting, citation, and terminology preferences. Each time they return, the AI follows those rules, producing consistent, high-quality output.

Customization boosts precision. Users can set tone, scope, and how the AI handles ambiguity, turning it into a domain expert. This control makes responses more accurate and context-aware.

Using templates is simple. In Perplexity's interface, users go to 'Spaces' to browse categorized templates such as "Trip Planner Pro" or "Patent Researcher." Each template can be modified to fit specific needs, making advanced AI tools accessible even to non-technical users.

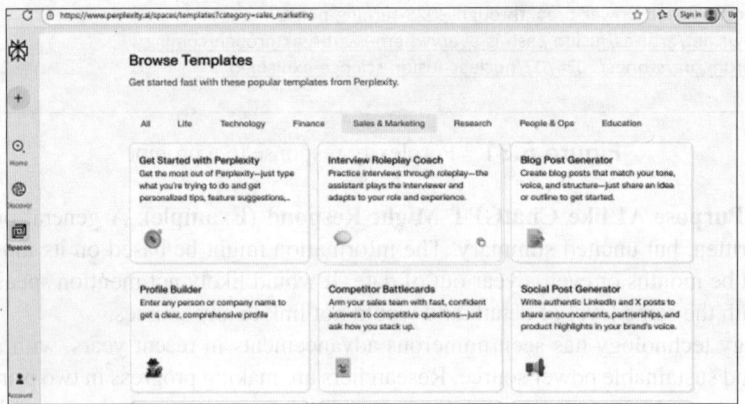

Figure 5.32 Perplexity templates for reuse

The platform operates on a freemium model, with a free version offering basic search capabilities, while a premium Pro subscription provides unlimited access to advanced features, including the ability to choose from a variety of powerful large language models like GPT-4 and Claude 3, and to conduct in-depth Pro Searches that go beyond a simple query to provide a comprehensive report. Perplexity's focus is on research and information retrieval, making it a research assistant and a search companion for users who prioritize accuracy and verifiable information.

However, Perplexity is not without limitations. Its performance depends on the quality and scope of its training data, which may not cover all subjects equally. It can also struggle with ambiguous or poorly phrased queries. While the model aims to provide accurate information, users should cross-check critical data with authoritative sources. Perplexity represents a promising step toward more intelligent and user-friendly search systems, but it must continue to evolve to meet the demands of diverse users.

Generative AI and Its Applications | **135**

> **Did You Know?**
> Perplexity AI can answer complex questions like "What are the ethical concerns of Gen AI?" in seconds—making it a favourite among students and researchers for fast, reliable insights.

> **Mini Project/Assignment**
> Try asking Perplexity three different questions on topics like climate change, AI ethics, and space exploration. Write down the answers and compare them with a traditional Google search.

5.7 Gen AI and Creativity

Generative AI has revolutionized the way text is created, offering new possibilities in storytelling, journalism, and marketing. In storytelling, AI models like GPT-4 can generate entire narratives based on a few prompts. These stories can range from simple children's tales to complex science fiction plots. The AI analyzes patterns in existing literature and mimics stylistic elements, allowing it to produce text that feels authentic and engaging. This has opened doors for writers who use AI as a co-creator, helping them overcome writer's block or explore new genres.

5.7.1 Image Generation: Design, Advertising, and Fine Arts

Generative AI has made significant strides in image creation, transforming industries such as design, advertising, and fine arts. Tools like Bing Image Creator (powered by OpenAI's DALL-E 3,), Playground AI allow users to generate high-quality images from textual prompts. These images can be realistic, abstract, or stylized, depending on the model and input. Designers use these tools to prototype ideas, create visual assets, and explore new aesthetics without the need for traditional graphic design software.

Bing Image Creator

This is a generative AI tool focused on artistic image creation. It allows users to generate visually stunning and imaginative artwork based on textual prompts.

For example, let us use the prompt given below in the Bing Image Creator:

"A visually stunning and imaginative artwork depicting a floating island city made of intricate clockwork gears and luminous crystals, connected by ethereal bridges of light, all set against a cosmic backdrop of swirling galaxies and nebulae in deep blues and purples. A giant, ornate keyhole-shaped portal dominates the sky, with celestial beings made of starlight emerging from it. In the foreground, a lone figure with flowing robes watches the spectacle from a small, verdant outcropping, their silhouette framed by the grandeur of the scene. The overall style is fantasy-inspired, with a dreamlike quality, using a vibrant colour palette and soft, glowing light sources to create a sense of wonder and awe."

The output is shown in Fig. 5.33.

Figure 5.33 Bing AI image: Model 1

Another example: "A solitary young woman with long, flowing hair sits on the crumbling edge of a colossal stone ruin. She is wearing a simple, worn cloak. The ruin is heavily overgrown with rich emerald moss, ivy, and ancient vines. Fractured marble statues are partially submerged in a slow-flowing, reflective river below. The woman gazes out at a vast, mist-filled valley bathed in the soft, golden light of a late afternoon sun breaking through heavy clouds, which casts long, dramatic shadows".
The output is shown in Fig. 5.34.

Figure 5.34 Bing AI image: Model 2

The provided prompt describes a highly detailed, painterly scene with a strong sense of atmosphere and emotion. The image centres on a solitary young woman who serves as the focal point. She is described as having long, flowing hair and wearing a simple, worn cloak, which adds to her sense of isolation and humility.

She is situated in a dramatic setting: the crumbling edge of a gigantic stone ruin. The ruin itself is a character in the scene, heavily adorned with a rich tapestry of emerald moss, ivy, and ancient vines, suggesting the passage of time. Below her, a slow-flowing, reflective river mirrors the sky, and partially submerged in its waters are fractured marble statues, which further enhances the feeling of a lost and forgotten civilization.

The entire scene is bathed in the soft, golden light of a late afternoon sun. This light is not static; it breaks through heavy clouds, casting long, dramatic shadows across the landscape and creating a sense of dynamic contrast. The background is a vast, mist-filled valley that has a softer, more dreamlike quality, with subtle brushstrokes visible in the sky and distant landscape.

The colour palette is a crucial element, described as earthy and subdued. It contrasts the rich greens of the overgrown ruins and the vibrant golden hues of the sunlight with the muted grays and browns of the ancient stone. Ultimately, the entire image is designed to evoke a powerful sense of profound solitude and melancholy, creating a scene that is not just visually appealing but also deeply emotional.

In advertising, AI-generated images are used to create compelling visuals that capture attention and convey brand messages. When creating prompts for advertising visuals, you want to focus on the core message, the desired emotion, and the specific aesthetic. Here are a few examples covering different brand messages, along with a visual example generated from one of the prompts.

For a fresh and modern beverage brand: "A sleek, modern product shot of a futuristic-looking sparkling water bottle with a single droplet of condensation, floating in a clean, minimalist space with soft, natural light, using a colour palette of muted whites, soft blues, and subtle greens. The style is hyperrealistic and crisp, emphasizing freshness and purity, with a serene and refreshing mood."

This prompt describes a product shot focused on a single object: a futuristic sparkling water bottle. The bottle is a key element, described as "sleek" and "futuristic-looking," with a crucial detail of a single droplet of condensation, which immediately suggests freshness (Fig. 5.35).

Figure 5.35 Bing AI image: Model 3

The setting is a clean, minimalist space, which draws all attention to the product. The bottle is also "floating," which adds to the futuristic and ethereal feel. The lighting is described as soft and natural, contributing to a serene and clean aesthetic. The colour palette is very specific and enhances the product's image: muted whites, soft blues, and subtle greens. These colours evoke a sense of purity and tranquility.

The style is specified as hyperrealistic and crisp, which means the image should be sharp, highly detailed, and look like a professional photograph. The overall mood is serene and refreshing, aligning with the product being sparkling water and the clean, minimalist presentation.

For a tech or automotive brand: "A high-end, aerodynamic sports car, glowing with soft neon lines, speeding through a rain-slicked cyberpunk city at night. The cityscape is filled with holographic advertisements and towering skyscrapers. The mood is one of exhilarating speed and cutting-edge technology, with a colour palette dominated by deep blacks, electric blues, and vibrant pinks, in a cinematic, photorealistic style."

Figure 5.36 Bing AI image: Model 4

This prompt describes a dynamic and visually striking scene (Fig. 5.36). The central subject is a high-end, aerodynamic sports car, which is given a futuristic twist by being "glowing with soft neon lines." This detail immediately sets a technological and slightly surreal tone.

The setting is a rain-slicked cyberpunk city at night, a classic trope of the genre that creates a dramatic and moody atmosphere. The city itself is vibrant and alive, filled with holographic advertisements and towering skyscrapers, which contribute to the feeling of a futuristic metropolis. The "rain-slicked" streets add a layer of reflection and light, enhancing the neon glow.

The mood of the image is described as exhilarating speed and cutting-edge technology. The composition should reflect this, with the car appearing to be in motion. The colour palette is essential to the cyberpunk feel, dominated by deep blacks, electric blues, and vibrant pinks. Finally, the style is specified as cinematic and photorealistic, which means it should look like a high-quality still from a movie, with sharp details and realistic textures.

For a natural or sustainable beauty brand: "A close-up portrait of a woman with a serene expression, her skin glowing with a natural, healthy radiance. Her face is adorned with delicate flowers and leaves that seem to be growing from her skin, symbolizing a connection to nature. The lighting is soft and golden, like a sunrise, and the colour palette is a blend of earthy tones and soft pastels. The style is a mix of high-fashion photography and ethereal fantasy."

This prompt describes an artistic and fantastical portrait (Fig. 5.37). The subject is a woman with a serene expression, and the focus is a close-up shot of her face. A key element is her skin, which is "glowing with a natural, healthy radiance," suggesting a flawless, almost otherworldly appearance.

Figure 5.37   Bing AI image: Model 5

The most unique detail is the adornment on her face: delicate flowers and leaves that appear to be growing from her skin. This visual element is explicitly linked to a symbolic meaning, "a connection to nature."

The lighting is soft and golden, like a sunrise, which adds to the ethereal and serene mood. The colour palette is a blend of earthy tones and soft pastels, complementing the natural and floral theme.

Finally, the style is a fascinating combination of high-fashion photography and ethereal fantasy. This suggests a polished, professional quality with a dreamlike, imaginative twist. The image is meant to be not just a portrait, but a work of art that blends the real and the fantastical.

Marketers can generate product mockups, promotional banners, and campaign visuals tailored to specific demographics. When creating promotional visuals for specific demographics, the prompts should include details about the target audience's aesthetic, lifestyle, and values. This helps the AI generate images that resonate with the intended viewers. Here are a few example prompts for different scenarios and demographics:

Product mockup for a sustainable brand (targeting eco-conscious millennials): "A young, diverse group of friends laughing and sharing a new craft beer. They are sitting in a modern, sustainably designed coffee shop with lots of natural light and potted plants. The beer cans are minimalist with earthy-toned labels. The mood is authentic and joyful. The style is a mix of candid photography and clean product rendering."

This prompt describes a product mockup for a sustainable brand, specifically targeting a key demographic: eco-conscious millennials (Fig. 5.38). The central image features a young, diverse group of friends sharing a moment of genuine connection, captured as they are laughing and sharing a new craft beer. This emphasizes authenticity and social connection, which are important values for the target audience.

The setting is carefully chosen to reinforce the brand's sustainable identity. The group is in a modern, sustainably designed coffee shop with abundant natural light and potted plants. This environment immediately communicates a commitment to nature and a relaxed, conscientious lifestyle.

Figure 5.38   Bing AI image: Model 6

The product itself—the beer cans—is integrated into the scene in a way that reflects the brand's values. The cans are minimalist with earthy-toned labels, avoiding flashy or excessive design. This design choice signals simplicity, natural ingredients, and an overall eco-friendly approach. The mood is defined as authentic and joyful, a feeling the image should evoke through the friends' genuine interaction. The style is a hybrid of candid photography and clean product rendering, which means the image should feel like an unstaged, spontaneous moment, while the product itself is perfectly and crisply rendered, making it the clear hero of the shot.

Promotional banner for a skincare line (targeting a mature audience): "A close-up shot of a mature woman with a serene expression, her skin soft and radiant, reflecting a healthy glow. She is in a peaceful, sun-filled living room with a book in her hand. The colour palette is soft and warm, with a focus on subtle textures and natural light. The style is elegant and sophisticated, like a high-end magazine ad."

This prompt describes a promotional banner for a skincare line aimed at a mature audience (Fig. 5.39). The image focuses on a close-up shot of a mature woman with a serene expression. The emphasis is on the quality of her skin, which is described as soft and radiant, reflecting a "healthy glow." This directly addresses the concerns and aspirations of the target demographic.

Figure 5.39   Bing AI image: Model 7

The setting is a peaceful, sun-filled living room, which creates a sense of comfort, relaxation, and warmth. The detail of her holding a book suggests a sophisticated, leisurely lifestyle.

The colour palette is soft and warm, with a focus on subtle textures and natural light. This reinforces the idea of a gentle, natural product that enhances, rather than covers up, the user's natural beauty.

The overall style is described as elegant and sophisticated, like a high-end magazine ad. This indicates that the image should be polished and refined, conveying a sense of luxury and quality. The combination of these elements creates a banner that is aspirational, comforting, and directly speaks to the values and desires of the intended audience.

Campaign visual for a fitness app (targeting gen Z): "A dynamic, fast-paced collage of diverse young adults using a fitness app. They are exercising in urban environments—a rooftop gym, a street basketball court, a park at sunset. The image uses vibrant, saturated colours and has a grainy, energetic aesthetic, like a street photography series, conveying empowerment and community."

This prompt describes a campaign visual for a fitness app, specifically targeting Gen Z (Fig. 5.40). The image is a dynamic, fast-paced collage featuring diverse young adults using a fitness app. The "collage" format implies multiple shots combined into one, conveying a sense of energy and variety.

Figure 5.40 Bing AI image: Model 8

The environments where the young adults are exercising are urban: a rooftop gym, a street basketball court, and a park at sunset. This makes the app feel accessible and modern, blending fitness into everyday city life.

The aesthetic is key: vibrant, saturated colours and a grainy, energetic aesthetic. This is explicitly compared to a "street photography series," which suggests a raw, authentic, and unfiltered feel. The mood conveyed is empowerment and community, highlighting the app as a tool for personal growth and social connection rather than just exercise. This combines to create a visual that is trendy, relatable, and inspiring to the target demographic.

Fine artists have embraced generative AI as a medium for creative expression. Some artists use AI to explore themes of identity, perception, and technology, producing works that challenge conventional notions of authorship.

For example: "A surreal, double-exposure portrait blending two styles. The left half is a classical oil painting of a human face with warm, textured brushstrokes. The right half is a sharp, futuristic digital art of intricate circuit board patterns with glowing wires. The eyes in the middle are luminous and contain distant galaxies. The colour palette mixes warm skin tones with cool electric blues and greens, contrasting the organic and technological."

This prompt describes a striking and complex image that combines two contrasting art styles and themes. The central element is a surreal, double-exposure portrait that is divided down the middle (Fig. 5.41).

Figure 5.41   Bing AI image: Model 9

The left half of the face is rendered in a classical oil painting style. This side is meant to feel traditional and organic, with warm skin tones and textured brushstrokes that give it an authentic, hand-painted quality.

In stark contrast, the right half of the face is depicted in a sharp, futuristic digital art style. This half is filled with intricate circuit board patterns and glowing wires, seamlessly integrating technology into the human form. The overall effect is a visual representation of the intersection between humanity and the digital world.

The eyes are the most unique feature, located in the middle where the two halves meet. They are luminous and contain distant galaxies, adding a cosmic, profound layer to the portrait. This detail elevates the image from a simple blend of styles to a symbolic exploration of consciousness and the universe.

The colour palette is crucial to the image's theme, mixing the warm skin tones of the classical side with the cool, electric blues and greens of the digital side. This contrast highlights the core concept of the **organic and technological** colliding in a single, cohesive piece of art.

AI-generated art has been exhibited in galleries and sold at auctions, sometimes fetching high prices. A notable example is the portrait "Edmond de Belamy," created by a generative adversarial network and sold at Christie's for over $400,000. The artwork was generated using a data set of historical portraits and a mathematical formula, highlighting the intersection of art and algorithm. Such cases illustrate the growing influence of AI in the art world and the need for new frameworks to evaluate and appreciate digital creativity.

DALL·E

Bing Image Creator heavily uses DALL·E, an AI model created by OpenAI. In fact, DALL·E 3 is the core technology behind Bing's image generation capabilities. Microsoft's Bing, now more closely integrated with Copilot, provides free access to DALL-E 3 (Fig. 5.42), making this powerful text-to-image model available to a wide audience. This collaboration between Microsoft and OpenAI is a key reason why the Bing Image Creator is so effective at understanding complex prompts and generating high-quality, creative images.

Recently, Microsoft has also introduced the option to use GPT-4o as another image generation model within Bing Image Creator, giving users a choice between two powerful AI models to best suit their needs.

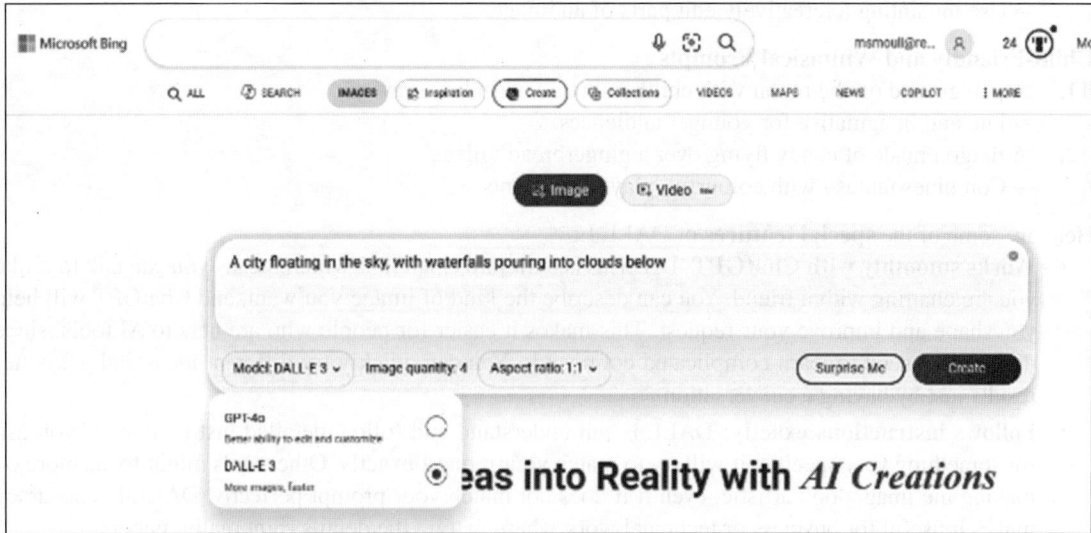

Figure 5.42 Using the DALL-E3 feature of the Bing Image Creator

Try the prompts given below using DALL-E 3 in Bing AI:

Surreal and Imaginative Prompts
1. "A city floating in the sky, with waterfalls pouring into clouds below"
   → Great for fantasy-style landscapes with dreamy details.
2. "A cat wearing a space suit, floating near Saturn, holding a cup of coffee"
   → Combines humor, animals, and space themes.
3. "An underwater library with glowing jellyfish as reading lamps"
   → Blends nature and architecture in a magical way.

Conceptual and Thought-Provoking Prompts
4. "Time represented as a giant clock melting over a mountain range"
   → Inspired by surreal art, like Salvador Dalí.
5. "The internet visualized as a glowing web connecting floating islands"
   → Turns abstract ideas into visual metaphors.
6. "A robot painting a portrait of a human in a futuristic art gallery"
   → Explores AI and creativity in a visual form.

Text and Typography Prompts
7. "A vintage travel poster for a fictional planet called 'Zyron' with bold, retro fonts"
   → Tests DALL·E's ability to handle text and design.

8. "A neon sign that says 'Dream Big' hanging on a rainy city street at night"
   → Combines mood, lighting, and readable text.

Editing and Expansion Prompts (Inpainting/Outpainting)
9. "Extend this image of a forest to include a hidden waterfall and a deer drinking water"
   → Use outpainting to grow the scene naturally.
10. Replace the sky in this image with a galaxy full of stars and planets"
    → Use inpainting to creatively edit parts of an image.

Child-Friendly and Whimsical Prompts
11. "A playground on the moon with children bouncing in low gravity"
    → Fun and imaginative for younger audiences.
12. "A dragon made of candy flying over a gingerbread village"
    → Combines fantasy with colourful, playful elements.

Here are some of the **special features** of DALL·E:
- **Works smoothly with ChatGPT**: DALL·E is built into ChatGPT, which means you can talk to it like you are chatting with a friend. You can describe the kind of image you want, and ChatGPT will help you shape and improve your request. This makes it easier for people who are new to AI tools, since they do not need to learn complicated commands. You can quickly try different ideas and get better results just by having a conversation.
- **Follows instructions exactly**: DALL·E can understand and follow detailed instructions. If you ask for something very specific, it will try to match your request exactly. Other tools might focus more on making the image look artistic, even if it does not match your prompt perfectly. DALL·E's accuracy makes it useful for business or technical work where getting the details right really matters.
- **Handles text in images better**: Most AI tools struggle to write clear and correct text inside images. DALL·E does a much better job at spelling words correctly and placing them neatly. This is especially helpful when you are making things like posters, logos, or banners where the text is important.
- **Powerful editing tools**: DALL·E lets you change parts of an image or expand it beyond its original size. Inpainting means you can select a part of the image and replace it with something else. Outpainting means you can grow the image outward, adding more to the scene while keeping the same style. Think of it like adding more pieces to a puzzle that still match the original picture.
- **Keeps images private**: Unlike some other platforms where images are shared publicly by default, DALL·E keeps creations private. This is a big advantage if you are working on personal or business projects and do not want others to see your work unless you choose to share it.

Stable Diffusion

Stable Diffusion is a flexible, open-source generative AI tool favoured over proprietary platforms like DALL·E and Midjourney for its high customization and user control. Its public code lets developers and artists modify and train models on specific styles or subjects, creating a rich ecosystem of community-shared checkpoints. It runs locally on consumer-grade GPUs (8GB VRAM recommended), offering privacy, speed, and full creative control without subscriptions or internet access.

Users can fine-tune outputs using parameters like CFG scale, sampling steps, and seed values. Advanced tools such as Inpainting, Outpainting, and ControlNet allow precise editing and composition control, features not deeply integrated in other platforms.

Being open-source, Stable Diffusion powers various online services. DreamStudio, the official web app, provides early access to new models like SDXL and SD3, with a user-friendly interface and free credits. Third-party platforms like Leonardo.Ai and Playground AI offer daily free credits and customization options, while Hugging Face and Stable Diffusion Online host demos requiring no setup.

For advanced users without strong local hardware, Google Colab notebooks run full Web UIs like AUTOMATIC1111 on remote GPUs. Though setup is more involved, it enables access to features like LoRAs, ControlNet, and Inpainting.

In summary, DreamStudio and Leonardo.Ai offer easy online access, while Google Colab provides deeper control for power users.

5.7.2 Video Generation

Video generation is one of the most complex and promising applications of generative AI. Creating video content involves synthesizing multiple frames, coordinating motion, and maintaining narrative coherence. AI models capable of generating video are still in their early stages, but they have already shown potential in animation, film production, and simulation.

The market for AI video generation is rapidly evolving, with many tools offering a free tier or a limited number of free credits to get started. While most free versions come with limitations like watermarks or short video lengths, they are an excellent way to experiment with the technology.
Here are some of the most prominent AI video generation tools that offer free online access:

RunwayML: Runway is a pioneer in the AI video space and is highly regarded for its sophisticated features. Its free tier provides users with a certain number of credits to generate short video clips from text, images, or even existing video footage. It is a powerful Text-to-Video tool that allows you to create highly creative and stylized videos. Its "Gen-1" and "Gen-2" models are known for their ability to apply the style of one image or video to another, offering advanced artistic control. It also includes an extensive suite of editing tools, such as inpainting and outpainting, which allow you to manipulate specific elements within a video.

We used imagine.art to use the features of Runway ML. The prompt (below) given in Text to Video mode creates the output shown in Fig. 5.43.

Figure 5.43 RunwayML video creation using the Imagine AI tool

"A stunning woman with flowing hair, dressed in a vibrant red dress, standing confidently in the middle of an empty, sunlit road. The scene is tense as a sleek black car approaches quickly, its tires screeching as it struggles to stop. Dust rises from the asphalt as the car halts suddenly near her, creating a dramatic moment. The camera captures her composed expression, the car's headlights reflecting her silhouette, and the tension-filled atmosphere of the scene."

InVideo AI: InVideo is a popular online video editor that has integrated a powerful AI video generation tool. Its free version is designed to get you started quickly on social media content. InVideo AI focuses on creating full, publish-worthy videos from a simple text prompt. It automates the entire process by generating a script, selecting relevant stock footage, adding voiceovers, and even including music and subtitles. This makes it an ideal tool for quickly creating explainer videos, marketing clips, or YouTube content with minimal manual effort.

HeyGen: HeyGen specializes in creating realistic talking avatars, making it a go-to tool for producing professional-looking explainer videos, training materials, or branded content. Its main strength lies in AI Avatars, which are lifelike digital characters that can speak your script with synchronized lip movements. You can choose from a library of pre-made avatars or even create a digital clone of yourself. The free tier typically allows you to create a few short videos, complete with text-to-speech functionality and custom backgrounds.

Pictory AI: Pictory is an AI video generator that excels at repurposing existing content. It is especially useful for marketers and content creators who want to transform long-form content into shorter, more engaging video clips. Pictory can turn a blog post, article, or script into a video automatically. It analyzes the text, selects relevant visuals from its vast stock library, and generates a storyboard, complete with voiceover and background music. The free trial allows you to get a feel for the process by creating a few videos, perfect for testing its ability to condense long content.

VEED.IO: VEED.IO is a comprehensive online video editor that has incorporated AI generation features. It is a versatile tool that caters to both basic video editing and advanced AI-powered creation. It offers a wide range of AI tools, including Text-to-Video and the ability to generate short clips and avatars. A key feature is its AI Playground, which lets you experiment with different AI models to see which one best fits your desired style. The free plan gives you access to these tools, allowing you to create and edit a variety of videos before exporting them (though with some limitations).

5.7.3 Music and Sound: AI in Composition and Audio Engineering

The market for AI music generation tools is rapidly growing, with many platforms offering free online access to get you started. These tools are excellent for exploring creative ideas, composing quick background tracks, or simply experimenting with AI's ability to create music. While most free versions have limitations on track length or number of generations, they each have unique features.

AIVA (Artificial Intelligence Virtual Artist): AIVA is a sophisticated AI composer specializing in creating emotional and classical-style music. Its free tier allows you to generate several short pieces, ideal for film scores, video game soundtracks, or other cinematic projects. AIVA's strength lies in its ability to compose music in specific genres and styles, from symphonic to cinematic to electronic. It lets you create new tracks by choosing a pre-defined style, influencing the composition with specific emotional tones and moods, and even adding different instruments to your musical ideas.

Soundraw: Soundraw is an easy-to-use AI music generator that focuses on creating copyright-free music for creators. Its free plan lets you create as many tracks as you want, though downloading is limited. This makes it perfect for quickly generating background music for videos, podcasts, or presentations. You can customize your music by choosing a genre, mood, instrument, and theme. The AI then generates multiple variations, which you can then customize further by changing the length, tempo, and different instrument layers. It is a great tool for those who need a lot of musical ideas on demand and want to fine-tune the results without deep musical knowledge.

Beatoven.ai: Beatoven.ai is an AI music generator designed specifically to create original, royalty-free music tailored to the mood of a video or other creative project. Its free tier offers a few minutes of music generation per month. This tool is unique for its focus on emotional expression. You can select a mood for different parts of your video timeline, and the AI will generate music that reflects that specific emotional curve. You can then adjust the track by swapping instruments, changing the mix, and adding or removing musical sections to match your visuals perfectly.

Mubert: Mubert is a versatile AI platform that offers a range of tools for generating music from a text prompt. It is known for its ability to create continuous, looping music. Mubert's core strength is its text-to-music engine, which allows you to describe the track you want in a simple phrase (e.g., "upbeat jazz with a lo-fi feel for a coffee shop scene"). It also has a unique "Mubert Render" feature that creates music loops of any length, and "Mubert Studio" for generating tracks based on specific moods and genres, making it ideal for content creators and streamers.

5.7.4 Human–AI Collaboration in Creative Fields

The integration of generative AI into creative fields has led to a new paradigm of human–AI collaboration. Rather than replacing human creativity, AI serves as a partner that enhances and expands artistic possibilities. This collaboration is evident in writing, design, music, and filmmaking, where AI tools assist rather than dominate the creative process.

In writing, authors use AI to brainstorm ideas, refine language, and explore alternative narratives. The AI provides suggestions and feedback, allowing writers to experiment with different styles and structures. This collaborative approach fosters creativity and reduces the time required to produce content. Similarly, designers use AI to generate prototypes and explore visual concepts, while retaining control over the final output.

Musicians collaborate with AI by using it to generate melodies and harmonies, which they then modify and arrange. This interaction allows for the fusion of human emotion and machine precision. Filmmakers use AI to visualize scenes, edit footage, and enhance storytelling. The AI acts as a tool that supports the director's vision, rather than dictating it.

Human–AI collaboration also promotes inclusivity by making creative tools accessible to people without formal training. Individuals who lack technical skills can use AI to express themselves through writing, art, or music. This democratization of creativity empowers diverse voices and fosters innovation.

However, successful collaboration requires clear boundaries and ethical considerations. Creators must understand the capabilities and limitations of AI, and ensure that their work reflects their values and intentions. Transparency in the use of AI is essential, especially when presenting content to audiences. By embracing AI as a creative partner, artists can explore new frontiers while maintaining authenticity and integrity.

5.7.5 Case Studies: AI-Driven Creative Projects

Several real-world case studies illustrate the transformative impact of generative AI in creative projects. One notable example is the use of AI in the creation of the film "Zone Out," which featured AI-generated visuals and dialogue. The filmmakers used generative models to design characters, simulate environments, and write portions of the script. This experimental approach demonstrated the potential of AI to contribute to cinematic storytelling.

In the fashion industry, designers have used AI to generate clothing patterns and predict trends. The brand "The Fabricant" created a digital-only fashion collection using AI-generated designs, showcasing the possibilities of virtual fashion. These designs were sold as NFTs, highlighting the intersection of AI, art, and blockchain technology.

Another case study involves the use of AI in music composition. The album "I AM AI" by Taryn Southern was composed with the help of AI tools, including Amper Music and IBM Watson. The artist collaborated with AI to generate melodies, harmonies, and lyrics, resulting in a unique blend of human and machine creativity. The project received critical acclaim and sparked discussions about the future of music production.

In visual arts, the "Obvious" collective used GANs to create portraits that were exhibited in galleries and sold at auctions. Their work challenged traditional notions of authorship and prompted debates about the role of AI in art. These case studies demonstrate that generative AI is not just a tool, but a catalyst for innovation and exploration in creative fields.

> **Did You Know?**
> You can type "a cat riding a bicycle in space" into Bing Image Creator—and it will generate a picture of exactly that!

> **Mini Project/Assignment**
> Write a short story and use Bing Image Creator to generate one image for each scene. Create a mini illustrated book using your story and images.

5.8 Gen AI-powered Slide Generation Tools

Slide presentations are a staple of communication in education, business, and public speaking. Creating effective slides requires a balance of visual design, concise messaging, and logical flow. Generative AI tools like SlidesGPT and Beautiful.ai have revolutionized this process by enabling users to generate entire slide decks from simple prompts or outlines.

Most of these tools operate on a freemium model, providing limited functionality or credits before requiring a paid plan.

Gamma: Gamma is a dynamic and interactive tool that reinvents the slide deck into a more engaging, web-based format. The first step in developing a PowerPoint outline for Gamma.design is to clearly define the purpose of the presentation (Fig. 5.44). Whether the goal is to pitch a business idea, present research findings, or deliver a training module, the objective must be articulated in as the topic. This helps the AI understand the tone, depth, and structure required.

Once the purpose is established, the outline should be broken down into logical sections (Fig. 5.45). Each section should represent a slide or a group of slides.

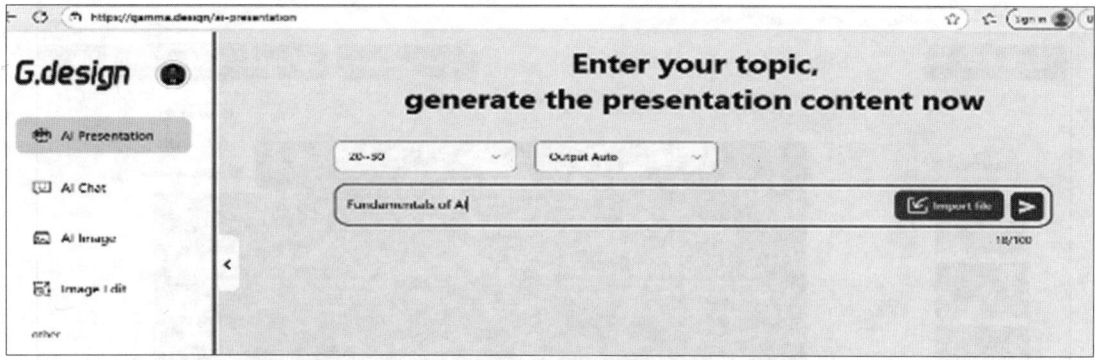

Figure 5.44 PowerPoint creation using Gamma: Topic

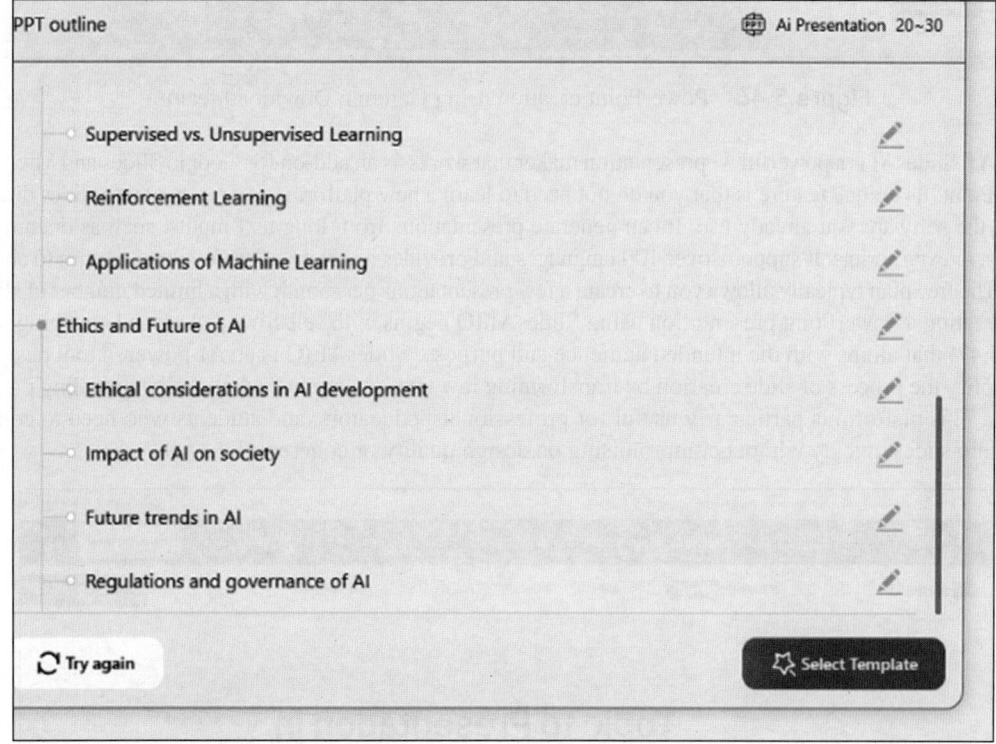

Figure 5.45 PowerPoint creation using Gamma: PPT outline

Gamma.design, a modern AI-powered presentation platform, offers a range of features that simplify the process of creating and sharing visually engaging content. Among its most practical capabilities is the **download feature**, which allows users to export their presentations for offline use or integration into other platforms. This function is particularly valuable for professionals who need to present in environments where internet access may be limited or where compatibility with traditional tools like Microsoft PowerPoint or PDF viewers is essential (Fig. 5.46).

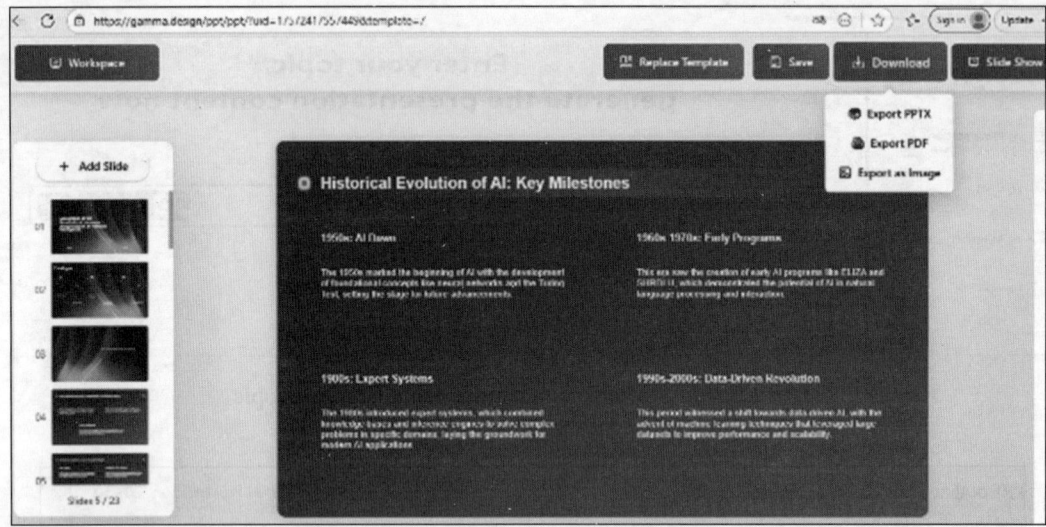

Figure 5.46 PowerPoint creation using Gamma: Download feature

SlidesAI: SlidesAI is a powerful AI presentation maker that works as an add-on for Google Slides and Microsoft PowerPoint. Its unique feature is that you do not need to learn a new platform; you can generate slides directly within the software you already use. It can generate presentations from long text inputs, such as documents, articles, or even scripts. It supports over 100 languages and provides a variety of professional themes to choose from. The free plan typically allows you to create a few presentations per month with a limited number of slides.

Creating a PowerPoint presentation using SlidesAI.IO begins with selecting a clear and engaging topic (Fig. 5.47) that aligns with the intended audience and purpose. SlidesAI.IO is an AI-powered tool designed to simplify the process of slide creation by transforming raw text into structured, visually appealing presentations. This platform is particularly useful for professionals, educators, and students who need to convert ideas into slides quickly without compromising on design quality or coherence.

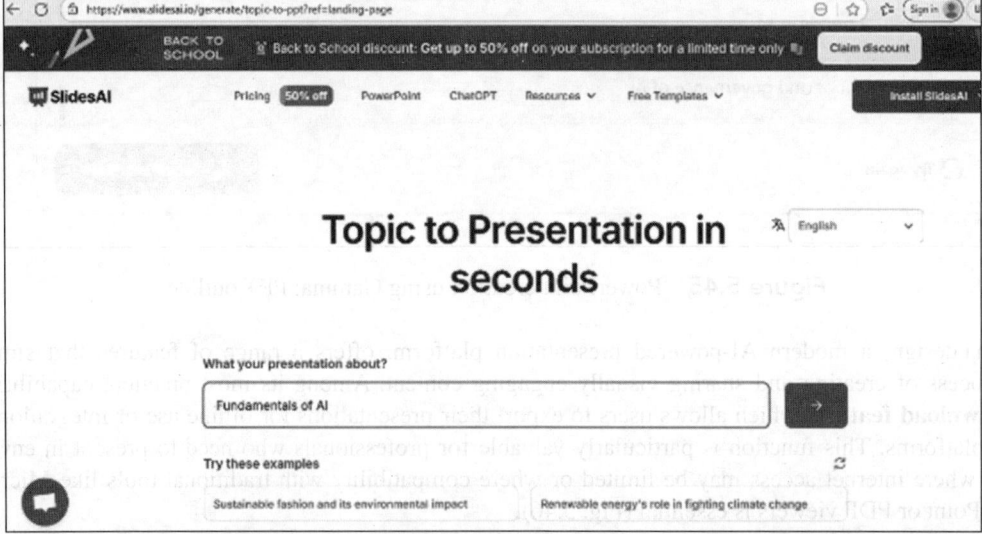

Figure 5.47 PowerPoint creation using SlidesAI.IO: Topic

Once the topic is given, the screen will take to a progress bar indicating a six-step process (Fig. 5.48) "Topic," "Content," "Instructions," "Context," "Outline," and "Design."

Below the progress bar is a section titled "Presentation Information (Required)." In this section, there are three drop-down menus: Educational Lecture, High School Students, and Storytelling.

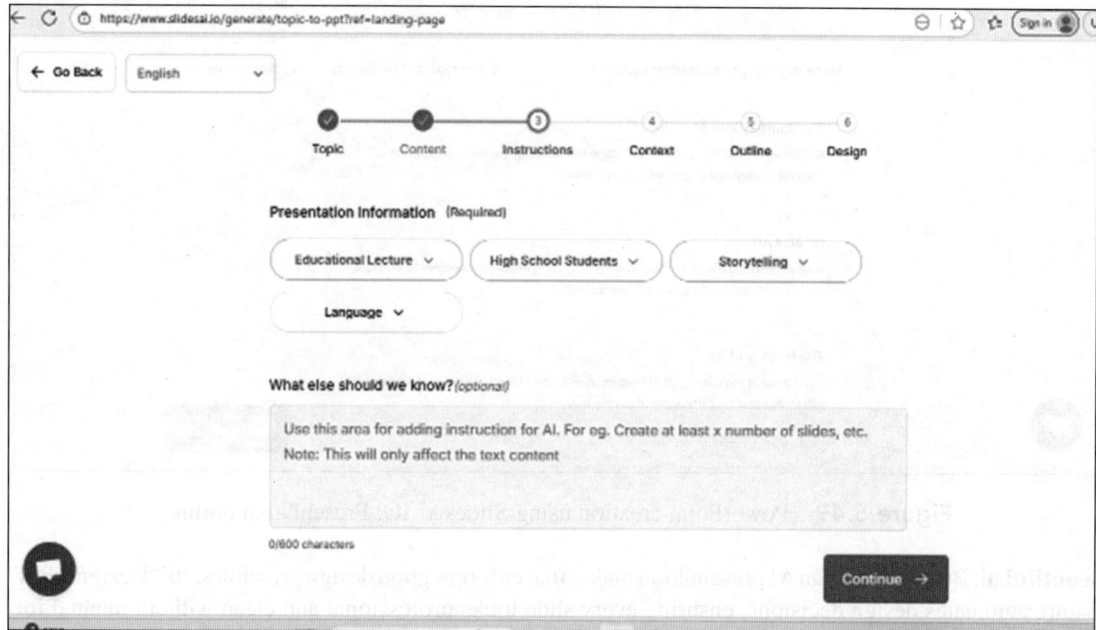

Figure 5.48 PowerPoint creation using SlidesAI.IO: Instruction to AI

The outline is not just a list of topics; it is a logical progression of ideas that guides the AI in generating slides that are coherent, visually appealing, and tailored to the intended audience (Fig. 5.49). Once the outline is finalized, it will create the PowerPoint presentation.

SlidesAI.IO also supports customization, allowing users to refine the AI-generated slides to better suit their needs. After the initial draft is created, users can edit text, rearrange slides, and adjust design elements. This flexibility is crucial for tailoring presentations to different audiences.

Another advantage of SlidesAI.IO is its accessibility and ease of use. The platform is designed to be intuitive, requiring no prior experience with design software or presentation tools. Users simply input their content, and the AI takes care of the rest. This democratizes the process of presentation creation, making it accessible to individuals who may not have technical skills but still need to communicate ideas effectively. For example, a student preparing a class project can use

In professional settings, SlidesAI.IO can significantly improve productivity. Teams working on tight deadlines can use the platform to quickly generate presentations for meetings, pitches, or reports. Because the AI ensures consistency in design and structure, the resulting slides are not only faster to produce but also more likely to resonate with stakeholders.

Tome: Tome is a storytelling-focused AI tool that generates a presentation from a text prompt. It is known for its ability to create visually rich and narrative-driven presentations. Tome emphasizes 'narrative intelligence' and uses AI to generate not just slides but a cohesive story. It is great for quickly creating pitches and presentations with a focus on visual flow. It has a generous free plan that provides a certain number of credits to experiment with its core features.

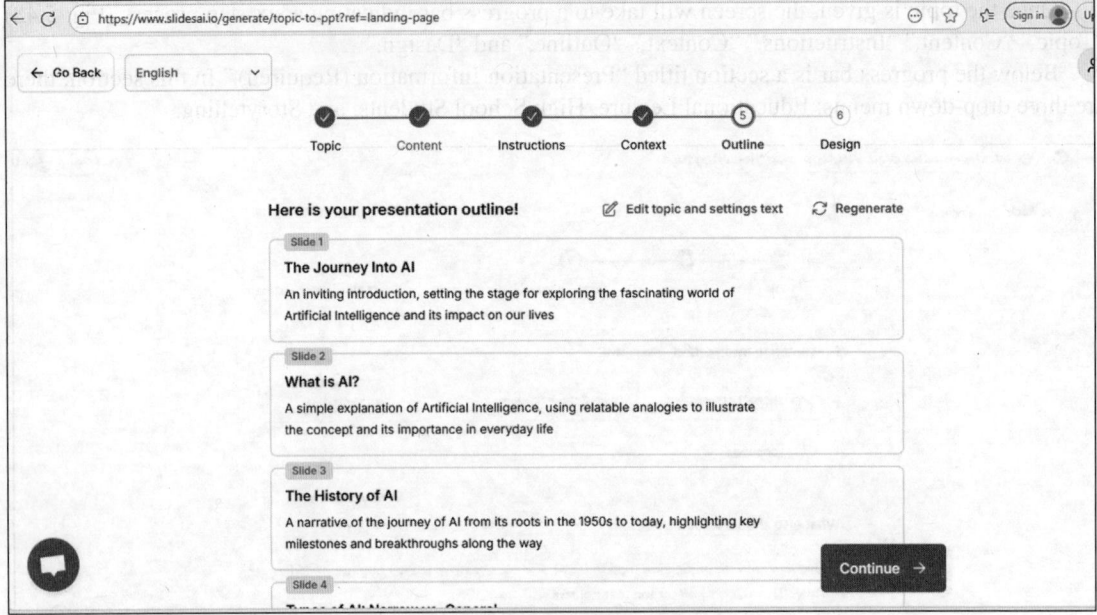

Figure 5.49   PowerPoint creation using SlidesAI.IO: Presentation outline

Beautiful.ai: Beautiful.ai is an AI presentation maker that enforces good design principles. Its "DesignerBot" feature automates design decisions, ensuring every slide looks professional and clean without manual formatting. It uses "Smart Slides" that automatically adapt to your content, so you never have to manually adjust layouts, resize images, or align elements. It has a massive library of templates and millions of free stock images and icons. While it offers a free trial, you may be required to enter payment information.

Slidesgo AI Presentation Maker: Slidesgo's AI tool is an extremely quick and user-friendly generator that creates presentations from text. It is a great option for students and educators who need a fast, hassle-free way to produce professional-looking slides. It is a no-frills, straightforward tool that focuses on speed and simplicity. You simply enter a topic, select a style, and the AI generates a complete presentation with relevant visuals and text. The free version allows you to create a certain number of presentations per month and can be exported as an editable PowerPoint file.

> ### Did You Know?
> Some Gen AI slide tools can convert a simple paragraph into a full presentation, with titles, bullet points, and images, in under a minute. They use NLP to understand your content and design preferences.

> ### Mini Project/Assignment
> Choose a topic you studied recently (e.g., "Water cycle" or "Digital safety") and use a Gen AI slide tool such as Canva or Gamma to generate a 5-slide presentation. Review the slides and add your own notes or images to personalize it.

5.9 Gen AI in Research and Innovation

Generative AI is transforming scientific research by speeding up discovery, improving data analysis, and aiding hypothesis generation. While traditional methods like experimentation and modelling remain essential, AI adds scale and efficiency to the process.

Generative AI helps synthesize knowledge by reviewing thousands of papers to summarize findings, spot trends, and highlight research gaps. Tools like Semantic Scholar and Elicit make this process faster and more thorough.

Despite its impact, AI raises concerns about reliability and reproducibility. Hypotheses must still be validated through traditional methods, and models need accurate training data. Still, AI's integration into science is unlocking new possibilities and accelerating innovation.

5.9.1 Gen AI in Drug Design and Healthcare Research

Generative AI is reshaping healthcare by streamlining drug design and medical research. Traditional drug development is slow and costly, but AI speeds up the process by simulating molecular structures, predicting interactions, and identifying promising compounds.

AI models can design new molecules that target specific proteins linked to diseases. Using data from existing drugs, they generate compounds with desired traits—leading to potential treatments for cancer, Alzheimer's, and resistant infections.

Once a candidate is found, AI simulates its behaviour in the body, predicting absorption, metabolism, and toxicity. This helps refine drugs before trials, reducing risks and improving safety.

In diagnostics, AI enhances medical imaging from MRIs, CT scans, and X-rays, making abnormalities easier to detect. It also creates synthetic data for training algorithms, protecting patient privacy.

A key breakthrough is DeepMind's AlphaFold, which predicts protein structures and supports drug discovery. It shows how AI can solve complex biological problems and accelerate research.

Despite its promise, AI in healthcare must be used responsibly. Ethical standards, data privacy, and regulatory compliance are essential. With proper oversight, generative AI can improve patient outcomes and transform medicine.

5.9.2 Gen AI in Engineering and Product Design

Generative AI is transforming engineering and product design by automating workflows and enhancing creativity. Traditionally, design involves prototyping and testing, but AI streamlines this by generating designs, optimizing parameters, and simulating performance.

In mechanical engineering, AI creates components based on function and constraints. For example, it can design a lightweight aircraft bracket by analyzing stress and materials. Tools like Autodesk Fusion 360 explore thousands of design options to find optimal solutions.

In architecture, AI generates layouts and models that improve light, airflow, and space use by analyzing environmental data and user needs. It also simulates construction timelines, costs, and risks, boosting efficiency and sustainability.

Product designers use AI to create functional, stylish goods—from electronics to fashion—based on user feedback and trends. AI enables rapid customization, like personalized shoes tailored to foot shape and style.

In manufacturing, AI optimizes production by simulating assembly lines, predicting maintenance, and reducing waste. In 3D printing, AI designs can be directly turned into physical products, speeding up prototyping.

Despite its benefits, AI designs must be validated for safety and standards. Engineers must understand AI limits and ensure human oversight. When used wisely, generative AI elevates innovation and precision in engineering.

5.9.3 Gen AI for Climate Modelling and Environmental Research

Generative AI is reshaping climate modelling and environmental research by processing vast data sets like temperature records, ocean currents, and emissions. It helps simulate scenarios and generate insights that guide policy and action.

In climate prediction, AI models simulate future conditions using historical data, helping assess risks like sea-level rise, extreme weather, and ecosystem shifts. Multiple scenarios support strategic planning.

AI also enhances environmental monitoring. It analyzes satellite and sensor data to track deforestation, pollution, and biodiversity loss. For example, it can detect illegal logging in real time, aiding rapid response.

In agriculture, AI models simulate crop growth, soil health, and water use, helping farmers optimize resources and adapt to climate change. Tools like ClimateAI forecast risks and suggest resilient crops.

Researchers use AI to generate synthetic data when real-world data is limited. It simulates pollution spread, wildlife migration, and ecosystem dynamics, offering insights for ecological studies.

Despite its promise, AI use must be transparent and inclusive. Models need validation and ethical oversight, including data access and ownership. When responsibly applied, generative AI can drive sustainable solutions and deepen climate understanding.

5.9.4 Academic Collaborations and Open Research Platforms

Academic institutions are key drivers of generative AI progress through research, collaboration, and education. Universities lead in developing models, exploring applications, and addressing ethics. Partnerships with industry and government help ensure AI benefits society.

Open research platforms like Hugging Face and OpenAI promote transparency and innovation by sharing models, data sets, and papers. Researchers can build on existing work and contribute globally.

Interdisciplinary collaboration is growing. Generative AI intersects with linguistics, psychology, law, and ethics. Joint efforts help address issues like bias and develop well-rounded solutions.

Education is central to AI advancement. Universities offer courses in machine learning, data science, and ethical AI, preparing students to contribute meaningfully. Research labs provide hands-on experience and publishing opportunities.

Funding from governments and foundations supports academic AI research, infrastructure, and public engagement. Public-private partnerships help turn academic insights into real-world applications.

Challenges remain around data privacy, intellectual property, and inclusivity. Institutions must ensure research reflects diverse perspectives and is responsibly conducted. With openness and collaboration, academia can lead ethical AI development.

5.9.5 Case Study: AlphaFold and Protein Folding

AlphaFold by DeepMind is a landmark in generative AI, solving the long-standing challenge of protein folding—predicting a protein's 3D structure from its amino acid sequence. This is vital for drug development, disease research, and biotechnology.

Traditional methods like X-ray crystallography and cryo-electron microscopy are slow and costly. Earlier computational approaches struggled with the complexity of protein structures.

AlphaFold changed this by using deep learning to predict protein shapes with high accuracy. In 2020, it outperformed other models in the CASP competition, marking a major breakthrough.

Its impact is vast—AlphaFold has revealed structures of thousands of proteins, including those linked to diseases like cancer and Alzheimer's. This accelerates drug discovery and deepens biological understanding. The project also highlights the value of collaboration. DeepMind partnered with academic institutions and released its code and predictions, allowing global researchers to benefit.

AlphaFold shows how generative AI can solve complex scientific problems. By combining data, algorithms, and open collaboration, AI is driving innovation across disciplines.

> **Did You Know?**
> Gen AI can help people with disabilities by generating voice commands, captions, and even personalized learning materials.

> **Mini Project/Assignment**
> Interview a friend or family member about how they use technology. Then, imagine how Gen AI could make that experience even better and write a short paragraph about it.

5.10 Gen AI in Education

Education is being transformed by advanced technologies, with generative AI playing a key role in improving learning and accessibility. Unlike traditional tools with static content, generative AI creates dynamic, personalized materials tailored to individual needs and curriculum goals.

Models like GPT-4 and Claude can generate lesson plans, quizzes, summaries, and interactive modules from simple prompts. They analyze educational data to produce accurate, goal-aligned content—especially useful for educators facing time or resource constraints.

Beyond content creation, generative AI supports students through AI tutors and chatbots that offer real-time help, feedback, and guidance. These tools boost engagement, encourage independent learning, and ease the workload on teachers. As a result, generative AI is becoming essential to modern education, driving equity, efficiency, and innovation.

5.10.1 Lesson Plan and Curriculum Generation

Creating lesson plans requires deep subject knowledge, clear learning goals, and awareness of student abilities. It is a time-consuming task involving content organization, teaching methods, and curriculum alignment. Generative AI simplifies this by automating lesson plans tailored to topics, grade levels, and educational objectives.

Educators can input a topic like "Photosynthesis for Grade 8," and AI generates a full plan with objectives, key concepts, activities, and assessments. The content is age-appropriate, pedagogically sound, and aligned with curriculum standards, allowing teachers to focus on teaching rather than planning.

Beyond single lessons, AI helps design entire courses with modules, reading lists, and evaluation criteria—especially useful for scalable online education. For example, an e-learning provider can use AI to build a 12-week digital literacy course with multimedia and interactive tasks.

A California school district used AI to generate lesson plans for substitute teachers during a staffing shortage. The tool maintained instructional quality and continuity, showing how AI supports education in challenging situations.

5.10.2 Personalized Learning and Adaptive Content

Personalized learning is one of the most promising uses of generative AI in education. Traditional classrooms often struggle to meet diverse learning needs, but AI can adapt content to individual students by analyzing their performance, preferences, and feedback.

For example, a student struggling with algebra might receive simplified explanations, extra practice, and visual aids, while an advanced learner could explore enrichment topics. This tailored approach boosts engagement and supports mastery.

AI also enables differentiated instruction by generating multiple versions of a lesson—visual, auditory, or hands-on—so students can choose what works best. This is especially helpful for learners with disabilities or language challenges.

A real-world example is an AI-powered reading app that adjusts stories and questions to match a student's reading level and interests. Teachers saw improved motivation and literacy, showing AI's potential to personalize learning effectively.

5.10.3 AI-Powered Tutoring and Student Support

Generative AI enhances student support through 24/7 tutoring systems that answer questions, explain concepts, and guide learning. Unlike traditional tutoring, AI assistants are always available and can handle multiple queries at once.

Using natural language processing, AI tutors deliver clear, accurate responses tailored to student questions. For example, a biology student asking about mitochondria would receive a concise explanation, possibly with diagrams or analogies—helping reinforce understanding.

Beyond academics, AI supports scheduling, reminders, and progress tracking. Students can use chatbots to check deadlines, get study tips, and monitor performance—boosting time management and self-regulation.

A university case study showed that an AI tutor for math courses improved retention and grades. It offered step-by-step solutions, personalized feedback, and motivational messages, proving AI's value in student support.

5.10.4 Assessment and Feedback Automation

Assessment is essential in education, offering insights into student progress and guiding instruction. However, grading and feedback take time and can slow learning. Generative AI streamlines this by automating assessments and delivering fast, personalized feedback.

AI tools can create quizzes, tests, and assignments based on lesson goals. These can be multiple-choice, short answer, or essays. After completion, AI evaluates responses, identifies mistakes, and provides consistent, unbiased feedback quickly.

AI also analyzes results to spot learning gaps and suggest targeted support. For instance, if a student struggles with fractions, the system may recommend extra practice or clearer explanations. Teachers can use this data to adjust instruction.

A notable example is an online platform that uses AI to grade essays. It assesses grammar, structure, and originality, then gives scores and detailed feedback. Educators found it saved time and improved feedback quality, allowing more focus on teaching.

5.10.5 Challenges and Ethical Considerations in AI Education

Generative AI brings major benefits to education but also raises ethical and practical concerns. A key issue is accuracy—AI-generated content must be fact-checked to ensure it is correct and educationally sound, as errors can mislead students.

Data privacy is another concern. AI systems often use student data to personalize learning, so it is vital to handle this data responsibly and comply with privacy laws. Transparency and informed consent are essential.

Bias in AI models can reflect stereotypes or inequalities from training data. Developers must actively detect and reduce bias to ensure fairness and inclusivity in educational tools.

Finally, while AI can automate tasks, it cannot replace the empathy and guidance of human teachers. The goal is to use AI to support—not replace—human instruction.

> **Did You Know?**
> Some schools use Gen AI to create customized learning paths for students—helping each learner progress at their own pace.

> **Mini Project/Assignment**
> Interview a teacher or student about how they use technology in learning. Then, write a short paragraph on how Gen AI could improve that experience.

5.11 Gen AI in Business

Generative AI is transforming business operations, communication, and customer engagement. Traditional workflows in marketing, product development, and customer service relied on manual effort and expertise. Now, AI streamlines and automates these tasks, boosting efficiency.

Trained on vast commercial data sets, generative AI produces high-quality content—marketing copy, product descriptions, emails, social posts, and reports—in seconds. Its ability to generate persuasive, relevant material makes it a valuable business tool.

AI also enables large-scale personalization. Companies can tailor messages based on customer behaviour, preferences, and purchase history, improving satisfaction, conversions, and loyalty. Generative AI is now a strategic asset driving growth and competitiveness.

5.11.1 AI-driven Marketing Content Creation

Marketing is a fast-paced, content-heavy business function. It involves crafting messages that connect with audiences, reflect brand identity, and drive action. Generative AI transforms this process by automating content creation across websites, emails, social media, and ads.

AI tools generate marketing copy based on product details, campaign goals, and audience data. For example, a company launching a smartphone can input specs and target demographics, and AI will produce persuasive promotional text. This saves time and cost while maintaining quality.

Social media marketing benefits greatly from AI. Platforms like Jasper and Copy.ai create posts, captions, and hashtags aligned with trends and audience interests. They also suggest optimal posting times and formats, helping brands stay consistent and engaging without large teams.

In email marketing, AI analyzes customer behaviour, to generate personalized campaigns. An e-commerce brand might use AI to send tailored product suggestions and offers, boosting open rates and conversions.

A fashion retailer used AI to create seasonal content—blogs, social posts, and newsletters. Compared to human-written versions, the AI-generated materials achieved higher engagement and conversion rates, proving AI's effectiveness in targeted marketing.

5.11.2 Product Description Generation and Optimization

Product descriptions are vital for informing customers, boosting SEO, and driving sales. Writing them requires clarity, creativity, and keyword use. Generative AI simplifies this by producing engaging, optimized descriptions quickly.

Businesses input product details—features, specs, and use cases—and AI generates multiple versions tailored for platforms like websites, marketplaces, and catalogs. For example, a kitchen appliance company can highlight durability, ease of use, and design while including relevant keywords.

AI also supports localization and translation, creating culturally and linguistically accurate content for global markets. This ensures brand consistency and accessibility.

Beyond creation, AI helps improve existing descriptions by analyzing performance data like click-through and conversion rates. It suggests better wording, structure, and keyword use to boost effectiveness.

A real-world case: an electronics retailer used AI to write thousands of product descriptions by analyzing competitor listings, reviews, and specs. The result was increased organic traffic and sales, showing AI's value in content management.

5.11.3 AI in Customer Engagement and Communication

Customer engagement is vital to business success, involving relationship-building and value-driven interactions. Generative AI enhances this by enabling efficient communication across multiple channels.

AI-powered chatbots and virtual assistants handle inquiries, provide product info, and resolve issues using natural language processing. For example, a customer asking about return policies receives a clear answer with helpful links—boosting satisfaction and easing the workload on human agents.

AI also enables proactive outreach, sending personalized messages like purchase follow-ups, cart reminders, or product updates. These timely, relevant communications build loyalty and connection.

Beyond text, AI generates multimedia content such as personalized videos or interactive guides for onboarding, training, or promotions—adding a human touch to digital experiences.

A telecom company used an AI chatbot for billing, tech support, and account help, cutting call volume by 40%. Satisfaction rose, and operational costs dropped significantly, showing AI's power in transforming customer engagement.

5.11.4 Strategic Business Insights and Reporting

Generative AI supports strategic decision-making by analyzing data—like sales, market trends, and customer feedback—to generate summaries, forecasts, and recommendations.

For example, an analyst can input quarterly sales data, and AI will produce a report highlighting trends, growth opportunities, and action plans. These reports are well-structured, visually clear, and tailored to executives, investors, or teams.

AI also aids competitive analysis by compiling public data to profile competitors, outlining strengths, weaknesses, and market position—helping businesses refine strategies and stand out.

In finance, AI generates summaries of income statements, balance sheets, and cash flows for internal reviews, stakeholder updates, and compliance. Automating reports reduces errors, saves time, and improves transparency.

A logistics company used AI to create weekly performance reports from delivery data, feedback, and inventory levels. These insights helped managers optimize routes, improve service, and cut costs—showing AI's value in business intelligence.

> **Did You Know?**
> Some Gen AI models have accidentally generated fake news articles that looked real—highlighting the importance of fact-checking and responsible use.

> **Mini Project/Assignment**
> Create a "Gen AI Safety Poster" that lists 5 risks of using Gen AI and 5 ways to use it responsibly. Use drawings or symbols to make it visually engaging.

5.12 Gen AI in Healthcare

Healthcare is a complex field where precision, speed, and personalization greatly affect patient outcomes. Generative AI is transforming this sector by improving diagnostics, streamlining workflows, and supporting rehabilitation. Unlike traditional AI, which predicts or classifies, generative AI creates new data and insights—especially useful when data is limited or inconsistent.

Trained on large data sets of medical records, scans, and clinical notes, generative AI can produce synthetic images for training, simulate disease progression, and help design personalized treatments. It reduces diagnostic errors, boosts efficiency, and expands access to care. Its uses span radiology, pathology, surgery, and rehabilitation.

Despite its benefits, generative AI in healthcare faces challenges like data privacy, ethics, and regulatory compliance. When applied responsibly, it can revolutionize healthcare by making it more accurate, efficient, and patient-focused.

5.12.1 AI in Medical Imaging and Radiology

Medical imaging is vital for diagnosing conditions like fractures and tumors. Techniques such as X-rays, MRIs, CT scans, and ultrasounds help visualize internal structures. Generative AI enhances this field by creating synthetic images, improving quality, and aiding interpretation.

In radiology, AI can generate realistic images when patient data is limited. These synthetic visuals help train diagnostic models to recognize conditions like pneumonia, even with few real examples.

AI also improves low-quality scans through super-resolution imaging, reconstructing missing details caused by equipment limits or patient movement. This boosts accuracy and reduces repeat scans.

For interpretation, AI highlights anomalies, suggests diagnoses, and prioritizes urgent cases—helping radiologists work faster and avoid errors.

A hospital using AI for breast cancer screening saw improved detection and reduced workload. The system flagged suspicious areas on mammograms, showing how AI can enhance diagnostic precision.

5.12.2 AI-Assisted Diagnostics and Decision Support

Accurate diagnosis is vital but challenging due to vague symptoms and complex conditions. Generative AI helps by analyzing patient data, suggesting differential diagnoses, and recommending next steps.

AI models review health records, lab results, and scans to detect patterns. For example, symptoms like fatigue, joint pain, and rash could indicate lupus, rheumatoid arthritis, or a viral infection. AI narrows options and guides test selection.

It also simulates disease progression, predicting future symptoms and complications. This helps clinicians plan proactive care and avoid adverse outcomes.

In emergencies, AI offers rapid support. For stroke cases, it can analyze CT scans instantly, detect blockages, and suggest treatments—saving critical time.

A telemedicine platform using AI assists rural doctors by analyzing patient inputs and proposing diagnoses. This improves care quality and reduces provider burden in underserved areas.

5.12.3 AI in Surgical Planning and Simulation

Surgery demands precision and preparation. Generative AI aids planning by creating 3D anatomical models, simulating procedures, and predicting outcomes—boosting safety and reducing risks.

AI builds detailed models from imaging data, helping surgeons visualize structures and plan incisions. In neurosurgery, for instance, knowing a tumor's location relative to blood vessels enables safer, less invasive techniques.

AI also supports simulation. Surgeons can practice procedures on virtual models, improving skill and decision-making. In complex cases, AI simulates multiple approaches to identify the safest option.

It predicts outcomes by analyzing patient data and similar cases, estimating recovery time, risks, and long-term effects. This helps with informed consent and patient preparation.

A cardiac center used AI to plan valve replacements. It generated 3D heart models and simulated implant placement, improving technique and patient outcomes—showing AI's value in surgical care.

5.12.4 AI in Rehabilitation and Patient Recovery

Rehabilitation helps patients regain function and quality of life after illness or injury. Generative AI enhances this phase by creating personalized recovery plans, generating exercises, and tracking progress.

AI analyzes data like mobility, pain, and cognition to design tailored programs. For example, a stroke patient with limited arm movement receives exercises suited to their ability and goals. As progress is made, the plan adjusts to maintain motivation.

AI also builds virtual therapy environments, simulating daily tasks like cooking or walking. In physical therapy, avatars demonstrate movements and give feedback, improving technique and results.

Monitoring is key—AI tracks performance, flags issues, and alerts therapists to adjust plans. This ensures rehab stays effective and responsive.

A rehab clinic used AI for orthopedic recovery. It created exercise routines, tracked progress via wearables, and sent motivational messages. Patients recovered faster and reported higher satisfaction, showing AI's value in rehabilitation.

> **Did You Know?**
> Gen AI can help doctors by analyzing patient symptoms and suggesting possible diagnoses—acting like a virtual medical assistant!

> **Mini Project/Assignment**
> Choose one field (e.g., education or healthcare) and make a poster showing how Gen AI is used in that field. Include pictures, keywords, and examples.

5.13 Gen AI in Entertainment

Entertainment has always been a reflection of human creativity, emotion, and storytelling. From music and movies to video games and digital art, the industry thrives on innovation and imagination. In recent years, generative AI has begun to reshape the entertainment landscape by introducing new tools and techniques that augment creative processes and expand the boundaries of artistic expression. These AI systems, trained on vast data sets of artistic content, can now compose music, design game environments, write scripts, and even generate entire virtual worlds.

Unlike traditional software that follows predefined rules, generative AI learns from examples and creates original content based on patterns and styles. This capability allows artists, musicians, and developers to experiment with new ideas, automate repetitive tasks, and collaborate with machines in ways that were previously unimaginable. The result is a more dynamic, inclusive, and efficient entertainment ecosystem where creativity is amplified rather than replaced.

Generative AI in entertainment is not just a technological advancement—it is a cultural shift. It challenges conventional notions of authorship, originality, and artistic value, prompting new discussions about the role of machines in human creativity. As the technology continues to evolve, it offers exciting possibilities for storytelling, interactivity, and personalization, making entertainment more immersive and accessible than ever before.

5.13.1 AI in Music Composition and Sound Design

Music is one of the most universal forms of human expression, capable of conveying emotion, telling stories, and connecting people across cultures. Generative AI has made significant strides in music composition, enabling the creation of original melodies, harmonies, and rhythms with minimal human input. These AI systems analyze vast libraries of musical works to learn patterns, styles, and structures, which they then use to generate new compositions.

One of the most popular applications of AI in music is automated composition. Musicians and producers can input parameters such as genre, mood, tempo, and instrumentation, and the AI will generate a complete piece of music that fits the criteria. For example, a filmmaker needing background music for a suspenseful scene can use AI to create a custom score that enhances the mood without licensing existing tracks. This approach saves time, reduces costs, and offers creative flexibility.

AI also supports sound design by generating effects, textures, and audio environments. In video games and virtual reality experiences, AI can create immersive soundscapes that respond dynamically to user actions. For instance, walking through a forest in a game might trigger AI-generated ambient sounds like rustling leaves, chirping birds, and distant waterfalls, enhancing realism and engagement.

A notable case study involves a music streaming platform that used AI to generate personalized playlists. The AI analyzed user preferences and listening history to compose new tracks tailored to individual tastes. Users reported higher satisfaction and engagement, demonstrating the potential of AI in creating customized musical experiences.

Despite its capabilities, AI-generated music raises questions about originality and emotional depth. While machines can replicate styles and structures, they do not experience emotion or intent. As such, human musicians often use AI as a tool for inspiration and experimentation rather than a replacement for artistic expression.

5.13.2 AI in Game Design and Development

Video games are among the most complex and interactive forms of entertainment, combining storytelling, visual design, and user engagement. Generative AI is transforming game development by automating content creation, enhancing realism, and enabling adaptive gameplay. These innovations are making games more immersive, diverse, and responsive to player behaviour.

One of the key applications of AI in game design is procedural content generation. Developers use AI to create game environments, levels, characters, and narratives that evolve dynamically. For example, a role-playing game might use AI to generate unique quests, dialogue, and landscapes for each player, ensuring a personalized experience. This approach reduces development time and increases replayability.

AI also supports character design and animation. By analyzing motion capture data and artistic styles, AI can generate realistic character movements, facial expressions, and interactions. This capability enhances storytelling and emotional engagement, making characters feel more lifelike and relatable.

In gameplay mechanics, AI enables adaptive difficulty and intelligent behaviour. Games can adjust challenges based on player performance, ensuring a balanced and enjoyable experience. Non-player characters (NPCs) can use AI to respond intelligently to player actions, creating more dynamic and unpredictable interactions.

A compelling example is a sandbox game that used generative AI to create entire worlds based on player input. Users could describe a setting—such as "a desert planet with ancient ruins"—and the AI would generate terrain, architecture, and lore that matched the description. This feature empowered players to become co-creators, blurring the line between developer and user.

Generative AI also supports game testing and optimization. By simulating player behaviour, AI can identify bugs, balance issues, and design flaws before release. This automation improves quality assurance and accelerates development cycles.

5.13.3 AI in Animation and Visual Effects

Animation and visual effects (VFX) are essential components of modern entertainment, bringing stories to life through motion and spectacle. Generative AI is revolutionizing these fields by automating animation processes, enhancing realism, and enabling new artistic styles. These tools reduce production time, lower costs, and expand creative possibilities.

AI can generate animations from textual descriptions, sketches, or motion data. For example, an animator might input a scene description like "a dragon flying over a mountain," and the AI would produce a rough animation that can be refined further. This capability accelerates prototyping and allows artists to experiment with different ideas quickly.

In VFX, AI enhances realism by generating textures, lighting effects, and simulations. For instance, creating realistic water or fire effects traditionally requires complex physics-based modelling. AI can learn from existing footage and generate similar effects with less computational effort. This efficiency is particularly valuable in film production, where time and budget constraints are significant.

AI also supports style transfer, allowing artists to apply specific visual aesthetics to animations. A studio might use AI to render scenes in the style of a famous painter or match the look of a previous film. This consistency enhances brand identity and artistic coherence.

A notable case study involves an animation studio that used AI to generate background scenes for a fantasy series. The AI created landscapes, architecture, and atmospheric effects based on storyboards, reducing the workload on artists and speeding up production. The final product maintained high visual quality and artistic integrity, demonstrating the potential of AI in animation.

Despite its advantages, AI-generated animation requires human oversight to ensure accuracy, emotion, and cultural relevance. Artists must guide the AI, refine outputs, and integrate them into the broader creative vision.

> **Did You Know?**
> Future Gen AI tools might be able to co-write novels, compose symphonies, or design buildings—working alongside humans as creative partners.

> **Mini Project/Assignment**
> Imagine Gen AI in the year 2035. Write a short paragraph or draw a comic strip showing how people might use it in daily life (e.g., school, work, travel).

5.14 Future Trends in Generative AI

Generative AI continues to evolve, with emerging trends set to expand its capabilities. Key developments include multimodal models, deeper human-AI collaboration, personalized experiences, and integration into everyday tools.

Multimodal models process and generate content across formats—text, images, audio, and video. A single AI could describe a video, create related visuals, and compose music. This versatility enhances creativity and problem-solving.

Human-AI collaboration is becoming more interactive. Future systems will support decision-making, creativity, and adapt to user preferences, making AI a true innovation partner.

As AI becomes part of daily life, its design will focus on accessibility, transparency, and ethics—ensuring inclusive and responsible use.

5.14.1 Rise of Multimodal Generative Models

Multimodal AI understands and generates content across text, images, audio, and video, enabling richer, context-aware interactions. For example, it can analyze a photo, describe it, write a poem, and compose music—all from one input.

Models like GPT-4, Gemini, and ImageBind are trained on diverse data sets, learning relationships between formats. This boosts applications in education, entertainment, healthcare, and business.

Multimodal AI improves accessibility by allowing users to interact through their preferred format—text, speech, or visuals. A design firm used it to create logos, videos, and posts from a single brief, saving time and enhancing creativity.

5.14.2 Human-AI Collaboration and Co-Creation

Generative AI enhances human creativity through real-time collaboration. These systems respond to input, offer suggestions, and adapt to feedback, keeping users in control.

Artists and writers use AI to brainstorm ideas, refine work, and overcome blocks. In business, AI helps analysts visualize trends and simulate scenarios for better decisions.

Educational platforms use AI tutors to personalize learning and encourage exploration. A music producer co-composed an album with AI, blending human emotion and machine precision.

As collaboration grows, developers focus on intuitive interfaces, responsive feedback, and customizable outputs to support user creativity.

5.14.3 Personalization and Context-Aware AI

Personalized AI tailors content to individual goals, preferences, and context. It analyzes behaviour, environment, and history to deliver relevant outputs.

In education, AI adapts lessons to student needs, boosting mastery and confidence. In healthcare, it creates treatment plans based on history and lifestyle, improving outcomes.

Businesses use AI to personalize marketing, increasing engagement and loyalty. An e-learning platform used AI to create custom study plans, improving scores and motivation.

As personalization advances, ethical concerns like data transparency, consent, and fairness must be addressed to protect user rights.

5.14.4 Integration of Generative AI into Everyday Tools

Generative AI is being embedded into daily tools, making its benefits widely accessible. Users can create content without technical skills using simple interfaces.

Word processors offer AI writing assistants; presentation tools generate slides; design platforms create logos and layouts. These features streamline tasks and boost productivity.

AI enhances communication by improving emails, chats, and translations. In project management, it generates reports and schedules. Mobile apps use AI for photo editing, music creation, and learning.

A small business owner used AI tools for marketing, design, and customer service—achieving professional results without hiring specialists.

Developers must ensure tools are intuitive, secure, and responsive, with training resources to support responsible use.

5.14.5 Responsible Innovation and Future Outlook

Generative AI's future depends on responsible innovation. As capabilities grow, so do risks. Ethical design, inclusivity, and governance are essential.

Developers must anticipate social impacts, prevent misuse, and protect privacy. Diverse data and accessibility features ensure AI benefits all users.

Governance frameworks should be transparent, participatory, and adaptable. Collaboration across sectors is key to balancing innovation with accountability.

A tech consortium created ethical AI guidelines focused on fairness, transparency, and oversight. Members shared best practices, fostering trust and setting a governance standard.

Generative AI will continue to evolve, supporting creativity, learning, healthcare, and growth. Responsible innovation ensures it aligns with human values and dignity.

> **Did You Know?**
>
> Gen AI is not just a tool—it is becoming a learning partner, creative assistant, and productivity booster across fields.

> **Mini Project/Assignment**
>
> Create a "Gen AI Vision Board" with images, keywords, and short phrases that represent what Gen AI means to you and how you imagine using it in the future.

Summary

- Generative AI (Gen AI) creates original content—text, images, music, video, and code—based on learned patterns.
- Popular Gen AI tools: ChatGPT (OpenAI), Gemini (Google DeepMind), Hugging Face, Perplexity, Bing Image Creator.
- Generative AI uses probabilistic modelling to predict next elements in sequences (text, image, video). It learns from massive data sets but lacks true understanding.
- Ethical concerns in Generative AI include originality, ownership, and human control.
- Diffusion models gradually remove noise to generate realistic images. They are used in tools like DALL·E and Stable Diffusion.
- ChatGPT Sora: Text-to-video tool for ChatGPT Plus/Pro users.
- ChatGPT Agentic Features: Automates tasks like scheduling, writing, and posting.
- Gemini is a multimodal Gen AI handling text, image, audio, video. Features: OCR, context-aware responses, collaborative storytelling.
- Hugging Face is an open-source AI platform with model and data set sharing.
- Perplexity is a real-time, cited conversational answer engine.
- The text generation feature of Gen AI can be used in storytelling, journalism, marketing enhanced by AI.
- Image generation tools: Bing Image Creator (DALL·E 3), Playground AI.
- Video generation tools: RunwayML, InVideo AI, HeyGen, Pictory AI, VEED.IO.
- Music and sound tools: AIVA, Soundraw, Beatoven.ai, Mubert.
- Gen AI assists in writing, design, music, filmmaking.
- Gen AI promotes inclusivity and democratizes creativity.
- Gen AI-powered slide generation tools: Gamma, SlidesAI, Tome, Beautiful.ai, Slidesgo.
- Future trends in Generative AI: Multimodal models; human–AI co-creation; personalization and context-awareness; integration into everyday tools; responsible innovation and governance.

Exercises

Part A (Objective Questions)

1. Which of the following is a foundational prompting technique used in prompt engineering?
   (a) Tree-of-thought prompting
   (b) Few-shot prompting
   (c) Zero-shot prompting
   (d) ReAct prompting

2. Why does a well-crafted prompt improve AI output quality?
   (a) It reduces the AI's processing time
   (b) It allows the AI to access external databases
   (c) It minimizes ambiguity and guides the AI's response
   (d) It increases the AI's memory capacity

3. A healthcare professional wants an AI to suggest diagnoses based on patient symptoms and history. Which prompting technique should they use?
   (a) Role-based prompting
   (b) Contrastive prompting
   (c) Meta prompting
   (d) Chain-of-thought prompting

4. Which of the following best illustrates the difference between supervised and unsupervised prompting?
   (a) Supervised prompts use images; unsupervised prompts use text
   (b) Supervised prompts classify known data; unsupervised prompts discover patterns
   (c) Supervised prompts are longer; unsupervised prompts are shorter
   (d) Supervised prompts require human feedback; unsupervised prompts do not

5. Which challenge in prompt engineering is most likely to affect fairness and inclusivity in AI outputs?
   (a) Scalability
   (b) Ambiguity
   (c) Bias and ethical concerns
   (d) Evaluation difficulties

6. What is the primary benefit of using contextual prompting in educational settings?
   (a) It reduces the need for human teachers
   (b) It allows AI to generate random facts
   (c) It helps tailor responses to the learner's background and goals
   (d) It simplifies the AI's internal architecture

7. Which technique involves comparing correct and incorrect examples to deepen understanding?
   (a) Scaffolded prompting
   (b) Contrastive prompting
   (c) Iterative prompting
   (d) Role-based prompting

Part B (Short Answer Questions)

1. What are some of the key generative AI tools?
2. Explain how probabilistic modelling helps generative AI produce realistic outputs?
3. How can ChatGPT be used to create a professional resume for an IT graduate?
4. Compare the roles of GPT and BERT in natural language processing.
5. Assess the ethical concerns associated with generative AI.
6. Design a prompt for Gemini AI to teach Newton's laws to a middle school student using multimodal content.
7. Describe how diffusion models generate realistic images.
8. How can generative AI assist in business marketing?
9. What makes Gemini AI different from other generative AI models?
10. Propose a use case where generative AI could enhance healthcare diagnostics.

Part C (Essay Questions)

1. List and briefly describe the major milestones in the evolution of generative AI from rule-based systems to multimodal models.
2. Explain how Transformer architecture revolutionized natural language processing and enabled the development of models like GPT and BERT.
3. Demonstrate how generative AI tools such as ChatGPT or Gemini can be used to create personalized educational content for students with different learning needs.
4. Compare and contrast the functionalities and use cases of ChatGPT, Gemini, Hugging Face, and Perplexity AI in terms of multimodal capabilities and user interaction.
5. Analyze the ethical implications of using generative AI in creative industries, particularly in relation to originality, ownership, and bias.
6. Evaluate the effectiveness of generative AI in healthcare applications such as diagnostics, surgical planning, and rehabilitation, citing specific examples.
7. Assess the role of generative AI in transforming business operations, especially in marketing, customer engagement, and strategic reporting.
8. Design a lesson plan using generative AI tools for teaching the concept of protein folding, incorporating multimodal elements like video, text, and interactive simulations.
9. Propose a framework for responsible innovation in generative AI that addresses transparency, inclusivity, and ethical governance.
10. Create a concept for a generative AI-powered entertainment experience that combines music, animation, and storytelling to engage diverse audiences.

Answers

Part A
1. (c)   2. (c)   3. (a)   4. (b)   5. (c)   6. (c)   7. (b)

CHAPTER 6

Prompt Engineering and Its Applications

Objectives

At the end of this chapter, you will be able to:
- Recognize the growing importance of prompt engineering across various industries
- Analyze how prompt quality affects model performance and user experience
- Apply various types of prompting
- Understand how prompts function as interfaces in AI/ML systems
- List the challenges in prompt engineering
- Explore the evolving role of prompt engineering in various industries
- Analyze case studies and real-world applications

6.1 Introduction

Prompt engineering is like learning how to talk to a smart robot. It comprises knowing how language works, understanding the context, and having some idea of how AI thinks. This skill helps people use AI more effectively in many fields—software development, research, teaching, and healthcare. As AI becomes more common in everyday life, knowing how to prompt it the optimal way becomes more useful.

The popularity of large language models (LLMs) like GPT and BERT has made 'prompt engineering' an important skill. These are trained using huge amounts of text and can write like a human, solve tough problems, and even be creative. If the prompt is well-written, AI gives smart, clear, and relevant answers.

6.2 Definition and Importance of Prompt Engineering

A **prompt** is the text typed into AI. It could be a simple question or a detailed instruction that includes background information, examples, or specific rules. **Prompt engineering** is about knowing how AI understands language and using that knowledge to write prompts that match with the requirement (Fig. 6.1).

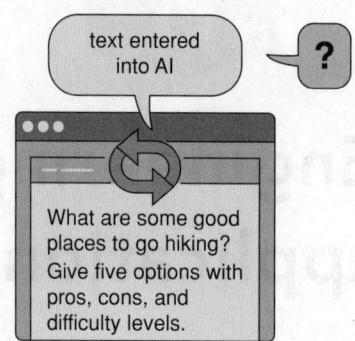

Figure 6.1   Definition of prompt

6.2.1 Historical Context and Evolution

Prompt engineering is a new but growing idea in AI. It has its roots in older computer systems. In the past, machines could only understand commands if they were written in a very specific way—like following strict rules. As AI improved, especially with deep learning (a method where computers learn from lots of data), these systems became better at understanding different types of input. People needed a way to guide the AI to give useful answers. That is how prompt engineering started.

Prompt engineering has grown because of both research and real-world use of AI. Studies show that even small changes in how a prompt is asked can lead to very different answers. This has led to tools that help people write better prompts, collections of useful prompts, and even systems that can create prompts automatically. Today, prompt engineering is seen as an important skill for anyone working with AI.

6.2.2 Why Prompts Matter in AI Systems

Much like a conductor guides an orchestra, a well-crafted prompt directs AI to produce responses that are accurate, relevant, and aligned with the user's goals (Fig. 6.2).

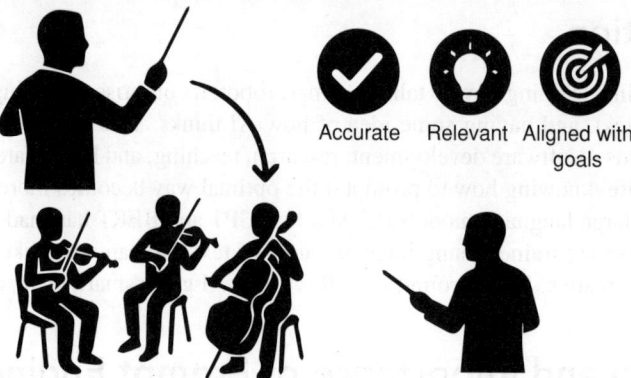

Figure 6.2   Prompt engineering

Prompts have emerged as a foundational element in the interaction between humans and AI systems. In the absence of traditional programming languages or configuration interfaces, prompts serve as the primary mechanism through which users communicate their intentions to AI models. This shift has transformed prompt engineering into a critical skill, one that blends linguistic precision with an understanding of machine behaviour.

The core principle of effective prompting is that the more context and specific instructions you provide, the better and more targeted the AI's output will be. This reduces the AI's need to make assumptions, guiding it toward a desired tone, style, and outcome.
Here is a demonstration of this principle with a simple example of a marketing request.

The Ambiguous Prompt: "Write an ad for a new coffee brand."

Gemini AI's Output:

> That's a bit too simple! Can you give me a little more information about the coffee brand? What's its name? Who is the target audience? What's the mood you want to create with the ad (e.g., energetic, calm, sophisticated)? Knowing these details will help me craft an ad that truly stands out.

The AI had no information about the brand's identity, brand, its target audience, mood or the desired tone.

The Thoughtfully Designed Prompt: "Write a social media ad for a new artisanal coffee brand named 'Morning Ritual.' The tone should be calm, sophisticated, and inviting, targeting young professionals who value a mindful start to their day. The ad should be concise, include a call to action to visit our website, and use a few relevant emojis."

Gemini AI's Output:

> Here is a social media ad based on your specific instructions:
>
> **Ad:**
> Elevate your morning routine. 'Morning Ritual' is here to bring a moment of mindful serenity to your day with our expertly crafted, artisanal coffee. Take a deep breath, savor the rich aroma, and prepare for a beautifully productive day. Find your new ritual.
>
> **Call to Action:**
> Visit our website to discover your perfect blend: [Link to Website]

By providing clear instructions on the brand name, target audience, desired tone, and specific formatting, the second prompt allows the AI to produce a much more effective and tailored response. The output uses sophisticated language ("elevate," "mindful serenity"), includes the requested brand name and emojis, and successfully captures the specific, inviting tone the prompt requested. This demonstrates how a well-engineered prompt transforms a generic output into a powerful, on-brand message.

State the primary marketing objective. This helps the AI understand the ultimate purpose of the ad, allowing it to select words that are more likely to convert.

Improved Prompt: "...The ad's primary goal is to drive website traffic and encourage conversions by appealing to the target audience's desire for a moment of quiet luxury." This gives the AI a clear objective to optimize for.

Final, Enhanced Prompt: "Act as a professional copywriter for a premium coffee brand. Write a social media ad for a new artisanal coffee brand named 'Morning Ritual.' The tone should be calm, sophisticated, and inviting, targeting young professionals who value a mindful start to their day. The ad's primary goal is to drive website traffic and encourage conversions by appealing to the target audience's desire for a moment of quiet luxury. Format the output with two distinct sections: a concise body with evocative imagery and a

172 | Fundamentals of Artificial Intelligence

clear call to action block. The final output should be suitable for an Instagram post caption and use a few relevant emojis."

> Waking up is an art. So is your first cup of coffee.
>
> Trade the rush for a moment of peace with **Morning Ritual** coffee. Our small-batch, ethically sourced beans are roasted to bring out a smooth, nuanced flavor that turns your daily brew into a mindful practice. It's more than just coffee; it's the start of your day, redefined. ☕✨
>
> Discover your new morning. Shop our full collection now at https://www.google.com/search?q=morningritualcoffee.com 🛍

Prompt engineering directly impacts the **quality of AI output** in several key ways:

- **Clarity and Specificity**: Clear, detailed prompts reduce ambiguity, leading to more accurate and reliable responses. The more specific you are, the more likely the AI is to understand your exact needs.
- **Tone and Style**: Prompts can set the tone (e.g., formal, casual, humorous) and style (e.g., a bulleted list, a story, a technical report) of the output. This allows the user to customize the AI's response to fit a specific purpose or audience.
- **Role-Playing**: By instructing the AI to "act as" a specific persona (e.g., a travel agent, a historian, a marketing expert), you can elicit responses that are tailored to a particular domain or perspective. This can be a powerful way to get specialized information or creative content.
- **Reasoning and Logic**: Techniques like Chain-of-Thought (CoT) prompting help AI models break down complex problems into a series of intermediate steps. This enables the AI to 'reason' its way to a solution, which is particularly effective for multi-step reasoning tasks like mathematical problems or complex coding.

In essence, the quality of an AI's output is as much a reflection of the user's input as it is of the AI's underlying model. As AI becomes more advanced, the ability to craft effective prompts will become an even more critical skill for maximizing the utility and value of these powerful tools.

The art of prompt engineering is not limited to professionals or developers. As AI tools become more accessible, everyday users are learning to craft prompts that suit their personal or professional needs. Whether it is drafting an email, summarizing a report, or generating creative content, the quality of the prompt directly influences the usefulness of the AI's response. This democratization of AI interaction underscores the importance of prompt literacy—a skill that empowers users to harness AI effectively and responsibly.

6.2.3 Impact on Model Performance and User Experience

Research shows that even small changes in how a question is worded can lead to very different responses from advanced models like GPT-4 (Fig. 6.3). For example, if you say, "Explain photosynthesis to a 12-year-old," AI gives a much easier and more child-friendly answer than if you ask, "Describe the process of photosynthesis."

From a user's point of view, prompt engineering makes talking to AI smoother and more helpful. When AI gives clear and accurate answers, people trust it more and use it more confidently. In business, this can lead to happier customers, smarter decisions, and faster work. In creative areas like writing or art, prompt engineering helps people use AI to come up with new ideas and express themselves in fresh ways.

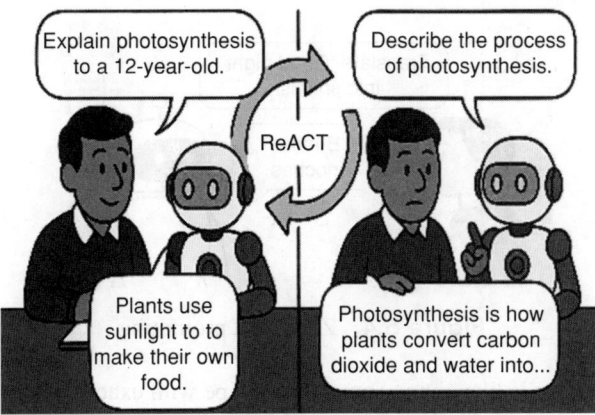

Figure 6.3 Prompts: Small change, big impact

Another powerful example comes from healthcare. Doctors have used prompt engineering to improve tools that help diagnose illnesses. By writing prompts that include a patient's symptoms, medical history, and the kind of answer they want, doctors obtain better and more useful suggestions from AI. This saves time and helps give better care to patients.

> ### Did You Know?
> The earliest forms of prompt engineering date back to command-line interfaces, where users had to type exact commands. Today, AI understands natural language, making prompts more intuitive and powerful.

> ### Mini Project/Assignment
> Create two prompts for writing an advertisement: one vague and one detailed. Observe how AI's response changes and discuss which one is more effective and why.

6.3 Techniques for Effective Prompting

Prompting techniques can be organized by their complexity of application, starting from foundational to advanced.

6.3.1 Foundational Level

At the foundational level, the main techniques used for effective prompting are zero-shot prompting, instruction-based prompting, contextual prompting, role-based prompting, and step-by-step prompting.

Zero-shot prompting involves giving the model a task without any examples, relying solely on the instruction and the model's general knowledge. For example, a prompt like "Translate 'Good night' into Spanish" will just output "Buenas noches". This assumes that the model understands the task based on its training and the instruction alone. Zero-shot prompting is ideal for general tasks where the model's pre-trained knowledge is sufficient (Fig. 6.4).

Figure 6.4 Zero-shot prompting

Instruction-based prompting is like giving someone a recipe with exact steps to follow. Imagine you are teaching someone how to make tea. Instead of just saying "make tea," you say: "Boil water, add tea leaves, steep for 3 minutes, then pour into a cup." That clear, step-by-step instruction ensures they do exactly what you want (Fig. 6.5).

Figure 6.5 Instruction-based prompting

This method is particularly effective because it reduces ambiguity and helps the model understand the user's intent with minimal confusion.

For instance, a prompt like "Tell me something interesting" may result in a wide range of responses, some of which may not align with the user's expectations.

> Here's something fascinating: **Octopuses have three hearts and blue blood**—and they can taste with their arms! Two of their hearts pump blood to the gills, while the third pumps it to the rest of the body.
>
> Their blood is blue because it uses **copper-based hemocyanin** instead of iron-based hemoglobin (like in humans), which is more efficient for oxygen transport in cold, low-oxygen environments.
>
> Even cooler? Their arms have **independent neural control**—each arm can explore, touch, and even taste without direct input from the brain.

In contrast, a more specific prompt like "Tell me an interesting fact about space exploration" narrows the scope and improves the relevance of the response.

> **Saturn's moon Titan has lakes and rivers—but they're made of liquid methane and ethane!**
>
> Titan is the only other body in our solar system known to have **stable liquids on its surface**, but instead of water, these lakes and seas are filled with **hydrocarbons**. The temperatures are so cold (around -179°C) that methane and ethane exist as liquids.
>
> NASA's upcoming **Dragonfly mission**, scheduled to launch in the 2030s, will send a rotorcraft to explore Titan's surface. It will fly from site to site, analyzing the moon's chemistry and searching for signs of prebiotic conditions—possibly offering clues to how life began on Earth.

The effectiveness of instruction-based prompting lies in its simplicity and clarity. When the model receives a well-structured instruction, it can align its response closely with the desired outcome. This is especially useful in tasks such as translation, summarization, classification, and question answering. However, the success of instruction-based prompting depends on how well the instruction is framed. Vague or overly broad instructions can lead to inconsistent or irrelevant outpus.

Instruction-based prompting also plays a crucial role in educational and professional settings. Teachers can use it to create AI-generated quizzes, explanations, or study guides, while professionals can use it to automate routine tasks such as drafting emails or generating reports. By mastering this technique, users can enhance their productivity and ensure that AI systems deliver consistent and useful results.

Contextual prompting is like giving someone a map before asking them for directions. Imagine you are asking a friend how to get to a restaurant, but instead of just saying "How do I get there?", you first tell them where you are, what time it is, and whether you are walking or driving. That extra context helps them give you a much better answer (Fig. 6.6).

Figure 6.6 Contextual prompting

Hence, contextual prompting involves embedding relevant background information within the prompt to help the AI model understand the situation or task more deeply. This technique is particularly useful when the task requires nuanced understanding or when the model needs to consider multiple factors before generating a response.

The original question, "Tell me an interesting fact about space exploration," is very broad. While it can get an answer, it does not give enough detail, which means the response might not match what the person really wants. A better version would be: "I'm making a presentation for high school students about space exploration. Can you share a fun and surprising fact that will grab their attention and get them excited about space missions?"

This improved version works better because it gives the AI more direction. It tells who the audience is (high school students), what the goal is (a presentation), and what kind of tone is needed (fun and surprising). It also explains the purpose—getting students curious and excited—which helps the AI give a more focused and useful answer. By adding these details, the prompt becomes clearer and more helpful, so there is less need to ask follow-up questions.

> **Astronauts Grow Taller in Space!**
>
> When astronauts spend time in microgravity aboard the International Space Station, **they can grow up to 2 inches (5 cm) taller!** That's because the lack of gravity allows the spine to expand, stretching out the vertebrae. But don't get too excited—they shrink back to normal once they return to Earth.
>
> You could pair this with a fun visual or even ask the students:
> "If you could grow taller just by going to space, would you sign up for a mission?"

Using context in your prompt has many benefits. It helps AI give answers that match your goal, lets you control the tone and style, makes sure the response fits your audience, and saves time by avoiding confusion. In short, adding context turns a simple prompt into a smart tool for getting better and more meaningful answers from AI.

One challenge with contextual prompting is managing the length and complexity of the prompt. Including too much information can overwhelm the model or lead to confusion, while too little context may result in superficial or incorrect responses. Therefore, users must strike a balance by selecting the most relevant and impactful details to include in the prompt.

Role-based prompting is like assigning characters in a play to help guide a conversation or decision. Imagine you are organizing a school debate. You assign one student to be the moderator, another to argue for the topic, and another to argue against it. Each person knows their role and responds accordingly (Fig. 6.7).

Figure 6.7 Role-based prompting

Hence, you tell AI to "act as" a specific role—like a teacher, doctor, or project manager—so it tailors its responses based on that perspective, making the output more relevant and focused. This approach helps tailor the output to match the tone, style, and expertise associated with that role. For example, a prompt like "As a science communicator preparing a presentation for high school students, I want to include a fun and surprising fact about space exploration that will instantly grab their attention and spark excitement about space missions. Can you provide a fact that's both engaging and educational?"

This technique is particularly effective in scenarios where the user wants the AI to simulate a specific perspective or authority.

> 🚀 **Space Smells Like... Burnt Steak?!**
>
> Astronauts returning from spacewalks have reported that the airlock smells like **burnt steak or welding fumes**.
>
> This strange scent comes from high-energy particles interacting with the spacecraft and suits. It's one of the many unexpected and mysterious things about space that scientists are still trying to fully understand!
>
> This fact is quirky, unexpected, and opens the door to deeper discussions about the physics and chemistry of space. You could follow it up with:
>
> *"Why do you think space smells like that? What could be causing it?"*

In educational settings, role-based prompting can be used to create explanations from the viewpoint of a teacher, scientist, or historian. In customer service, it can help the model respond as a helpful assistant, empathetic representative, or technical support agent.

However, the effectiveness of role-based prompting depends on how clearly the role is defined in the prompt. Ambiguous or conflicting role instructions can lead to inconsistent behaviour. For example, asking the model to "Act as a doctor and a comedian" may result in a confusing mix of serious and humorous content. Therefore, users should define the role clearly and ensure that it aligns with the task and desired output.

Step-by-step prompting is a technique used to break down a complex or open-ended request into smaller, clearer components. This helps guide the response more precisely and improves the quality, relevance, and usefulness of the output—especially when working with AI or when designing prompts for structured tasks like writing, coding, or research. It is a method of structuring a prompt by identifying and separating its key elements. Instead of asking a broad question all at once, you guide AI (or yourself) through a logical sequence of steps that clarify:

1. Who is asking? (Role or perspective)
2. What is the goal? (Purpose or desired outcome)
3. Who is the audience? (To tailor tone and complexity)
4. What is the topic or domain? (Subject matter)
5. What are the constraints or preferences? (Style, tone, format, etc.)
6. What is the final request? (The actual task or question)

Step-by-step prompting improves clarity (reduces ambiguity and helps AI understand your intent better); enhances relevance (ensures the response is tailored to your audience and goals); boosts creativity (encourages more thoughtful and imaginative outputs); and reduces errors (minimizes misinterpretation or irrelevant answers).

Let's take the original prompt: "As a science communicator preparing a presentation for high school students, I want to include a fun and surprising fact about space exploration that will instantly grab their attention and spark excitement about space missions. Can you provide a fact that is both engaging and educational?"

Imagine you are a science communicator preparing to speak to a room full of high-school students. Your main goal is to make space exploration as exciting and engaging as it is in a sci-fi movie. Knowing your audience—teens between 14 and 18 who are curious but might not know much about space—you need a powerful fact to kick off your presentation. This fact must be fun and surprising, something that will challenge their assumptions and teach them something new, all while instantly grabbing their attention.

Ultimately, the purpose is to spark a genuine sense of awe and excitement about space missions and what we are still discovering.

🚀 **Fact to Spark Excitement:**
"Did you know that spacesuits cost more than a Ferrari—and they're basically mini spacecraft?"

🌑 **Why It's Cool:**
A single NASA spacesuit can cost **over $12 million**.
It's not just clothing—it's a **life-support system** that protects astronauts from extreme temperatures, radiation, and the vacuum of space.

😲 **Why It's Surprising:**
Most people think of spacesuits as fancy uniforms, but they're actually **engineered marvels**.
They contain **oxygen tanks, temperature control systems, communication gear**, and even **waste management** tools.

📘 **Why It's Educational:**
This fact opens up discussions about **engineering, physics, biology, and space medicine**.
It shows how much planning and technology goes into keeping humans alive in space.

6.3.2 Intermediate Level

At the intermediate level, techniques like few-shot prompting, scaffolded prompting, contrastive prompting, and iterative prompting require more structure and examples to guide the model effectively.

Few-shot prompting is particularly useful when the task is complex or domain-specific, and the user wants to guide the model with relevant examples. Few-shot and zero-shot prompting are techniques that enable AI models to perform tasks with little or no prior training examples. In few-shot prompting, the user provides a few examples within the prompt to demonstrate the desired behaviour. For instance, a prompt like "Translate the following sentences into Spanish: 1. Hello – Hola, 2. Thank you – Gracias, 3. Good morning – Buenos días. Now translate: Good night" helps the model learn from the examples and apply the pattern to a new input. The output is: "The Spanish translation for "Good night" is: Buenas noches."

The success of these techniques depends on the quality and relevance of the examples or instructions. Poorly chosen examples can mislead the model, while vague instructions may result in incorrect outputs. Therefore, users must carefully design the prompt to ensure that it conveys the task clearly and aligns with the model's capabilities.

Scaffold prompting is a technique that breaks down a complex task into a series of smaller, more manageable steps. It is inspired by the educational concept of 'scaffolding', where a teacher provides temporary support to help a student learn a new skill, gradually removing the support as the student becomes more proficient (Fig. 6.8).

In the context of AI, this means providing the model with a structured, step-by-step framework to guide its reasoning and output. Instead of asking a single, broad question, you use a sequence of prompts that build on each other, leading the AI through a logical progression. This approach is particularly effective for tasks that require multi-step reasoning, analysis, or creative generation, as it reduces the cognitive load on the AI and improves the clarity, consistency, and accuracy of the final output.

Figure 6.8 Scaffold prompting

Instead of a **single prompt:** "Summarize this article and explain its significance."
A **scaffold approach** would be:

1. Prompt 1 (Initial Task): "Summarize the main topic of the following article in one sentence."
2. Prompt 2 (Breakdown): "Identify the key arguments or hypotheses presented in the article."
3. Prompt 3 (Details): "Outline the methodology and key findings from the study."
4. Prompt 4 (Analysis): "Explain how these findings relate to the main arguments. What new information do they provide?"
5. Prompt 5 (Synthesis): "Now, based on all of this, what is the overall significance of this research in its field? Discuss any limitations mentioned."

This step-by-step process ensures the AI first grasps the core concepts before moving on to the more complex task of analysis and synthesis.

Contrastive prompting is a pedagogical technique that leverages the power of comparison to deepen understanding. By placing correct and incorrect examples side by side, learners are encouraged not only to recognize the appropriate form but also to understand why it is correct. This method is particularly effective in domains such as language learning, writing improvement, critical thinking, and classification tasks, where subtle distinctions often carry significant meaning (Fig. 6.9).

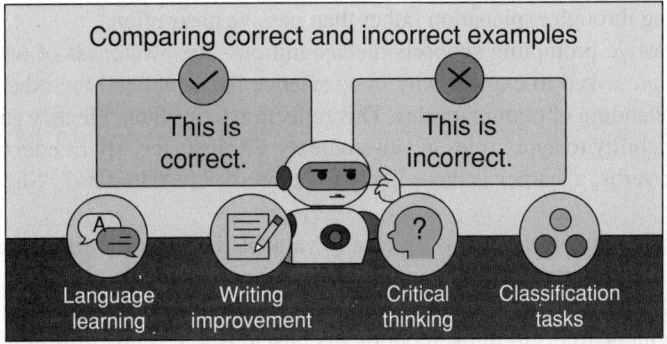

Figure 6.9 Contrastive prompting

Prompt: Look at the two sentences below. One is grammatically correct, and the other is incorrect. Identify which is correct and explain why.

1. She walk to school every day.
2. She walks to school every day.

The output is given below:

> The second sentence, "**She walks to school every day**," is grammatically correct.
>
> The first sentence, "**She walk to school every day**," is incorrect because it uses the wrong form of the verb "walk."
>
> **Why "She walks" is correct**
>
> In English, when you use a verb in the **simple present tense** with a third-person singular subject (he, she, it), you must add an **-s** or **-es** to the end of the verb.
> The subject "she" is a **third-person singular** pronoun.
> The action "walk" is the verb.
>
> The phrase "every day" indicates the **simple present tense**, which is used for habitual actions or routines.
> Therefore, the correct form is **walks**, not "walk."
>
> **Example with other third-person singular subjects:**
>
> He **runs** fast.
> It **snows** in winter.
> The cat **sleeps** all day.

At first glance, the difference may seem minor—a single letter added to the verb. However, this small change reflects a fundamental rule in English grammar: subject–verb agreement. In the first sentence, the verb "walk" fails to agree with the third-person singular subject "she." English grammar dictates that in the present tense, verbs must take an "-s" ending when the subject is third-person singular. Thus, the correct sentence is "She walks to school every day." This correction is not merely about memorizing a rule; it is about understanding the structure of the language and how meaning is conveyed through form.

The strength of contrastive prompting lies in its ability to make errors visible and meaningful. When learners see the incorrect form directly beside the correct one, they are more likely to notice the discrepancy and internalize the rule. This side-by-side presentation acts like a spotlight, illuminating the specific point of confusion. It also encourages active engagement, as learners must analyze and articulate the reason behind the correctness of one example and the incorrectness of the other. This process fosters critical thinking and reinforces learning through explanation rather than passive absorption.

Moreover, contrastive prompting supports metacognition—the awareness of one's own learning process. When students are asked to explain why one sentence is correct and the other is not, they begin to reflect on their understanding of grammar rules. This reflection helps them identify gaps in their knowledge and strengthens their ability to apply rules in new contexts. For instance, after understanding the rule about third-person singular verbs, a learner is more likely to correctly say "He runs," "She sings," or "It works," without hesitation.

In language learning, this technique is especially valuable because it mirrors the way native speakers intuitively grasp grammar. Native speakers often learn through exposure to correct and incorrect forms, gradually internalizing patterns. Contrastive prompting accelerates this process by making the patterns explicit and encouraging learners to think about them consciously. It transforms grammar instruction from rote memorization into a thoughtful exploration of language structure.

Iterative prompting is a dynamic instructional strategy that involves guiding learners through a series of progressively refined prompts to deepen their understanding, improve their responses, and build mastery over time. Unlike one-time questioning or static exercises, iterative prompting encourages learners to revisit their initial answers, reflect on feedback, and revise their thinking. This method is particularly effective in educational settings where critical thinking, problem-solving, and conceptual clarity are essential, such as in writing, mathematics, coding, and scientific reasoning (Fig. 6.10).

Figure 6.10 Iterative prompting

At its core, iterative prompting mirrors the natural process of learning through trial, error, and refinement. When a student is first presented with a prompt, their response may be incomplete, imprecise, or even incorrect. Rather than simply correcting the mistake, the instructor or system provides a follow-up prompt that nudges the learner to reconsider their approach. This might involve asking a clarifying question, offering a hint, or presenting a related example. The learner then revises their response, ideally moving closer to a more accurate or sophisticated understanding. This cycle can repeat multiple times, each iteration building upon the last, until the learner arrives at a well-reasoned and complete answer.

For example: "I would like to learn "Project management" and ask me questions based on iterative prompting. Go up to 3 levels". The output is as follows:

Okay, let's start your learning journey on project management using iterative prompting.

Level 1: Foundational Concepts
Question: What are the five key phases of a project life cycle? *Please list them in order and provide a one-sentence description for each.*

Answer typed: initiation, planning, execution, monitoring and controlling, and closing.

That's an excellent start. You've correctly identified the five project management phases. Now let's move on to Level 2 to deepen your understanding.

Level 2: Methodologies & Key Concepts

Question: Project management isn't a one-size-fits-all approach. Two of the most common methodologies are **Waterfall** and **Agile**. *How do these two methodologies differ in their core approach? Briefly explain a situation where you would use one over the other.*

And it asks the questions level by level.

An iterative prompt in the context of project management can be a powerful tool for developing a learner's ability to think critically, refine their understanding of key concepts, and apply them effectively in real-world scenarios. Just as a student learning to write a thesis statement benefits from successive rounds of feedback and revision, a project manager or aspiring professional can deepen their grasp of project management principles through a structured sequence of prompts that build upon one another.

One more example: Consider a learner who is new to project management and is asked the initial question: "What is the primary goal of project management?" The learner might respond, "To complete a project." While technically not incorrect, this answer is vague and lacks depth. The next prompt could be: "Can you explain what completing a project successfully means in terms of time, cost, and quality?" This encourages the learner to think beyond the surface and consider the constraints that define project success. The learner might revise their answer to: "Project management aims to complete a project on time, within budget, and with the expected quality." This is a more refined response, but still leaves room for further development.

A subsequent prompt might ask: "How does a project manager ensure that these goals are met throughout the project lifecycle?" This pushes the learner to think about processes, tools, and leadership strategies. The learner may then respond: "By planning tasks, assigning resources, and monitoring progress." While this shows progress, the instructor could further prompt: "Can you describe how risk management and stakeholder communication play a role in this?" This leads the learner to integrate more advanced concepts, such as anticipating potential issues and maintaining alignment with stakeholder expectations.

Eventually, the learner might arrive at a comprehensive understanding: "Project management is the discipline of planning, executing, and controlling a project to meet specific objectives within defined constraints of time, cost, and quality. A project manager ensures success by coordinating resources, managing risks, and maintaining clear communication with stakeholders throughout the project life cycle." This final response reflects a deeper, more nuanced grasp of the topic, achieved through iterative refinement.

This process mirrors the way professionals grow in their roles. Rarely does one arrive at a perfect understanding immediately. Instead, through cycles of questioning, feedback, and revision, individuals sharpen their thinking and become more effective in applying their knowledge. In project management, where decisions often have significant consequences, the ability to reflect, adapt, and improve is essential.

Iterative prompting also fosters a mindset of continuous learning. By encouraging learners to revisit and refine their responses, it teaches them that understanding is not static but evolves with experience and insight. Through the iterative process, the student moves from a simple opinion to a nuanced thesis statement. Each prompt acts as a stepping stone, helping the learner refine their thoughts and improve their expression. This method not only strengthens the final product but also teaches the

The power of iterative prompting lies in its adaptability. It can be tailored to the learner's current level of understanding and adjusted in real time based on their responses. This makes it especially useful in digital learning environments, where intelligent tutoring systems can analyze student input and generate personalized prompts. Moreover, iterative prompting aligns well with the principles of formative assessment. By continuously engaging learners in cycles of feedback and revision, educators can monitor progress, identify misconceptions, and provide targeted support. This not only enhances learning outcomes but also builds learners' confidence and autonomy.

6.3.3 Advanced Level

At the advanced end, techniques such as Chain-of-Thought prompting, self-consistency prompting, ReAct prompting (Reasoning + Acting), tree-of-thought prompting, and meta prompting are used.

Chain-of-Thought (CoT) prompting is like solving a puzzle by talking through each step out loud. Imagine you are trying to figure out how to bake a cake for the first time. Instead of just saying "bake a cake," you walk through each step: gather ingredients, preheat the oven, mix the batter, pour it into a pan, and bake (Fig. 6.11).

Figure 6.11 Chain-of-Thought prompting

This step-by-step thinking helps clarify your reasoning and makes it easier to spot mistakes or missing pieces—just like how CoT prompting helps AI reason more clearly by breaking down complex problems into smaller, logical steps.

It is a technique that encourages the AI model to reason through a problem step-by-step before arriving at a conclusion. This method is particularly useful for tasks that require logical reasoning, mathematical calculations, or multi-step decision-making.

Original Prompt: "As a science communicator preparing a presentation for high school students, I want to include a fun and surprising fact about space exploration that will instantly grab their attention and spark excitement about space missions. Can you provide a fact that's both engaging and educational?" This is a goal-oriented prompt asking for a specific type of content (a space fact) tailored to a specific audience (high school students), with a desired emotional impact (excitement and engagement).

To convert this into a **CoT prompt**, we break the task into logical reasoning steps that guide the model to think through the problem before answering.

"I am preparing a science presentation for high school students. First, I need to consider what kind of space fact would be surprising and exciting for this age group. Then, I should think about how to make it educational and easy to understand. Finally, I want to choose a fact that connects to real space missions to spark curiosity. Based on this reasoning, what is one fun and surprising fact about space exploration that fits these criteria?" The output of this prompt is shown below:

> "Spacesuits cost more than a Ferrari—and they're basically mini spacecraft!"
>
> **Why it's surprising:**
> Most students think of spacesuits as just protective clothing. But each NASA spacesuit used on the International Space Station (ISS) costs **over $12 million** and is a **fully functional spacecraft** designed to keep astronauts alive in the vacuum of space.
>
> **Educational angle:**
> You can explain how spacesuits:
> Provide oxygen and remove carbon dioxide.
> Regulate temperature from -250°F to +250°F.
> Protect from micrometeoroids and radiation.
> Allow mobility and communication.
>
> **Real mission connection:**
> This ties directly to **NASA's Artemis missions**, which are developing **next-gen spacesuits** for Moon exploration. You can show how technology is evolving and why it matters for future missions to Mars.

Audience Awareness: Recognize the target audience (high-school students) and their likely interests or knowledge level.
Emotional Hook: Identify what makes a fact surprising or exciting to grab attention.
Educational Value: Ensure the fact teaches something meaningful or scientifically accurate.
Relevance to Missions: Connect the fact to real-world space missions to make it relatable and inspiring.

This structured approach helps the model reason through the task and produce a more thoughtful, tailored response.

This technique improves the transparency and reliability of AI responses. By revealing the model's thought process, users can better understand how the conclusion was reached and identify any errors or gaps in reasoning. It also helps the model avoid common mistakes that occur when it tries to jump directly to an answer without considering intermediate steps.

CoT prompting has been shown to enhance performance in tasks such as arithmetic, logic puzzles, and scientific reasoning. It is especially valuable in educational applications, where students benefit from seeing the steps involved in solving a problem. It also supports explainability in professional settings, such as legal analysis or financial forecasting, where decisions must be justified with clear reasoning.

One challenge with this technique is ensuring that the model follows a coherent and logical sequence. If the prompt is not well-structured, the model may produce disjointed or incorrect reasoning. Therefore, users should guide the model with clear instructions and examples that illustrate the desired thought process.

To understand **self-consistency prompting**, consider the analogy of solving a puzzle with a group of friends. Suppose 10 individuals attempt the same puzzle independently. While some may make mistakes due to oversight or misinterpretation, the majority are likely to arrive at the correct solution if the puzzle is solvable and the reasoning is sound. By comparing all the answers and choosing the one that appears most frequently, we increase the likelihood of selecting the correct solution. This is the essence of self-consistency prompting: it leverages the collective reasoning of multiple model outputs to identify the most reliable answer (Fig. 6.12).

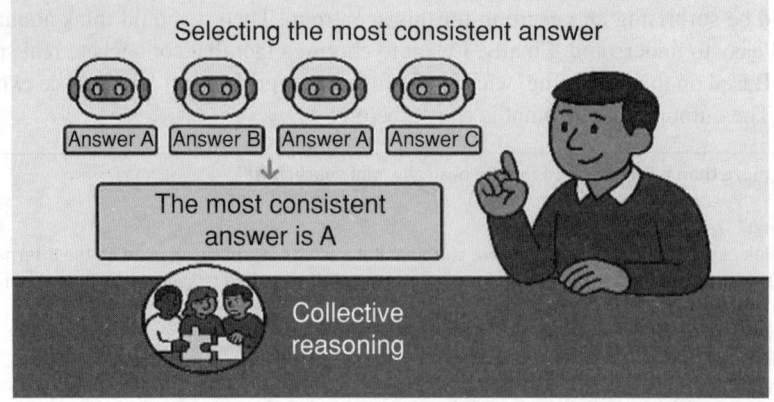

Figure 6.12 Self-consistency prompting

Self-consistency prompting represents a significant advancement in the way LLMs like ChatGPT approach complex reasoning tasks. Traditionally, when a user poses a question—particularly one involving multiple steps or logical deductions—the model generates a single response based on its internal reasoning. However, this approach can be prone to errors, especially in domains like mathematics, logic puzzles, or multi-step planning, where a single misstep can lead to an incorrect conclusion. Self-consistency prompting addresses this limitation by encouraging the model to produce multiple reasoning paths and then selecting the most frequently occurring final answer. This method not only enhances accuracy but also mirrors how humans often solve problems collaboratively.

In practical terms, this technique is especially useful in mathematical problems. For instance, if we ask the model, "Solve the following problem using self-consistency prompting technique. If a train travels 60 kilometers in one hour, how far will it go in 3.5 hours". The output is given below:

The train will travel **210 kilometers** in 3.5 hours.
We can arrive at this answer using the **self-consistency prompting technique**, which involves solving the same problem through multiple logical pathways to ensure a consistent and reliable result.

Solution 1: The Direct Calculation
The most straightforward way to solve this is to use the formula **Distance = Speed × Time**.
60 km/h×3.5 hours=210 km
This is the fastest method, providing a quick and accurate result.

Solution 2: The Step-by-Step Breakdown
We can break down the travel time into two parts: the full hours and the half-hour.
Distance in 3 full hours: The train travels 60 km for each of the three hours.
60 km/h×3 hours=180 km
Distance in the remaining 0.5 hours: Since it travels 60 km in one hour, it will travel half of that distance in half an hour.
60 km/h×0.5 hours=30 km
Total Distance: Add the two parts together.
180 km+30 km=210 km

Solution 3: The Unit Rate Method
This method focuses on a smaller time unit to build up the total. Since the train travels 60 km in one hour, it travels **30 km in 30 minutes** (0.5 hours).
There are seven 30-minute intervals in 3.5 hours (3.5 hours/0.5 hours/interval=7 intervals).
Now, multiply the distance per interval by the number of intervals.
30 km/interval×7 intervals=210 km
All three independent reasoning paths consistently arrive at the same answer, confirming that the correct solution is **210 km**.

One path might directly multiply the speed by time, yielding $60 \times 3.5 = 210$ kilometres. Another might break the time into whole hours and half hours, calculating $60 \times 3 = 180$ and then adding 30 kilometers for the remaining half hour, again arriving at 210 kilometres. A third path might simply state the multiplication without elaboration. By comparing all these outputs, we notice that 210 kilometres is the most common and logically sound answer. Thus, the model selects 210 kilometers as the final answer based on consistency.

The strength of self-consistency prompting lies in its ability to reduce the impact of occasional reasoning errors that LLMs are known to make. These models, despite their sophistication, can sometimes misinterpret a step or apply a rule incorrectly, especially when the task involves abstract or layered logic. By generating multiple reasoning paths, the model essentially cross-validates its own outputs. This process is akin to peer review in academic research, where multiple experts examine a hypothesis or result to ensure its validity. If most reviewers agree, the conclusion is deemed reliable; if not, further scrutiny is required.

Moreover, this technique has broader applications beyond mathematics. In coding, for example, where syntax and logic must align perfectly, self-consistency prompting can help identify the most robust solution among several generated code snippets. In planning tasks, where multiple steps must be sequenced correctly to achieve a goal, it can help ensure that the final plan is coherent and executable. Even in areas like legal reasoning or medical diagnosis, where precision is critical, this method can serve as a safeguard against erroneous conclusions.

ReAct (Reasoning and Acting) prompting is like a detective solving a mystery while also stepping out to gather clues. Instead of just sitting and thinking through the whole case (like traditional prompting), the detective alternates between thinking ("Hmm, what could be the motive?") and acting ("Let me check the suspect's alibi"). ReAct works the same way—an AI reasons about a problem, takes an action (like looking something up), then reasons again based on the new info, repeating this loop until it solves the task (Fig. 6.13).

Figure 6.13   ReAct prompting

This technique significantly improves the performance of LLMs on complex tasks. It is essentially a method that combines logical, step-by-step thinking with the ability to take actions. Unlike a standard LLM that generates a single response based on its pre-trained knowledge, a ReAct model operates in a continuous loop of Thought, Action, and Observation. This allows it to break down problems, use external tools to find current or specific information, and then synthesize that information to form a final, accurate answer. This approach reduces the risk of the model 'hallucinating' or providing outdated facts, making it a powerful tool for tasks requiring up-to-the-minute data or interaction with external environments.

The core of ReAct prompting lies in its methodical process. First, the model generates a **Thought**, where it reasons about the user's request, identifies what information is needed, and plans its next step. This is similar to a human thinking through a problem. Next, it chooses an **Action** to perform, which often involves using a specialized tool, such as a search engine to look up a fact or a calculator to perform a complex equation. The model then receives an **Observation**, which is the result of that action—the search results, the calculation output, or a database query's response. The model then processes this new information and generates another **Thought**, refining its plan and deciding on the next **Action**. This cycle repeats until all necessary information has been gathered, and the model has a clear path to the solution. The final step is a conclusive **Action** to synthesize the information and provide the final answer to the user.

A practical example of ReAct prompting in action would be a user asking, "What is the capital of Peru, and what's its current population?"

A standard LLM might give a response based on its training data, which could be several years old. With ReAct, the model would first have a **Thought** that it needs to find both the capital and the current population. Its first **Action** would be to use a search tool with the query "current population of Lima, Peru." The search engine's **Observation** would be the latest population data. The model would then form another **Thought**, recognizing it now has all the required information to answer the question. Finally, it would perform a conclusive **Action** to formulate and present the final, up-to-date answer to the user. This dynamic, self-correcting process makes ReAct a superior technique for any task that goes beyond simple knowledge recall, transforming the model from a static knowledge base into a capable and interactive problem-solving agent. The output for this is as follows:

> **Thought:** The user wants to know two things: the capital of Peru and its current population. I'll need to perform a search to find the most accurate and up-to-date information for both parts of the question. I will use a single search query to get both pieces of information at once, if possible.
>
> **Action:** Search["What is the capital of Peru?", "current population of Lima Peru"]
>
> **Observation:** The search results confirm that the capital of Peru is Lima. Several sources provide population estimates for Lima. One source (Macrotrends) estimates the 2025 metro area population to be 11,517,000. Another source (Wikipedia) provides a 2023 estimate of 11,283,787 for the metro area. A different source (World Population Review) provides a similar 2025 estimate of 11,517,300. The data is consistent. I have the capital and a very recent population estimate.
>
> **Thought:** I have successfully identified the capital and found reliable, current population data. I can now synthesize this information to provide a clear and concise answer to the user's request.
> **Action:** Finish["The capital of Peru is Lima. Its current metropolitan area population is estimated to be approximately 11.5 million people."]
>
> **Final Response:**
> The capital of Peru is **Lima**. Its current metropolitan area population is estimated to be approximately **11.5 million people**.

Tree-of-Thought (ToT) prompting is like solving a puzzle by exploring different paths before choosing the best one. Imagine you are trying to find the best route through a forest to reach a hidden treasure. Instead of rushing down the first trail you see, you pause at each fork, think through where each path might lead, and even sketch out a few possibilities. This thoughtful branching helps you avoid dead ends and pick the most promising route—just like ToT prompting helps AI reason through complex problems by exploring multiple lines of thought before settling on an answer (Fig. 6.14).

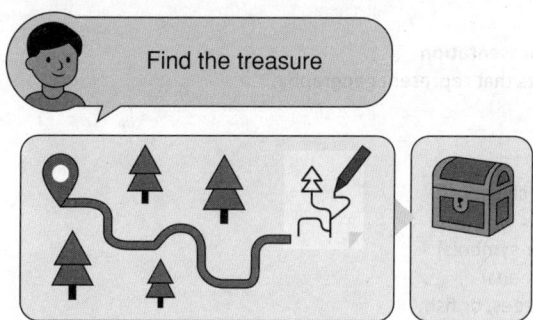

Figure 6.14 Tree-of-Thought prompting

It is a smart way to help AI models solve tough problems by thinking in different directions instead of just one straight line. Imagine the AI is trying to solve a puzzle. Instead of following one idea from start to finish, it builds a 'tree' of ideas—starting with the main problem (the root), exploring different ways to solve it (the branches), and ending with possible answers (the leaves).
This method works in a few steps:

1. Break the problem down: The AI first splits the big problem into smaller parts, like breaking a big question into bite-sized pieces.
2. Brainstorm ideas: For each small part, it comes up with several possible answers or thoughts—just like how you might think of different ways to solve a math problem.

188 | Fundamentals of Artificial Intelligence

3. **Evaluate the ideas:** The AI then checks which ideas are most likely to lead to the right answer. It can use a scoring system or even ask another AI to help judge.
4. **Keep the best paths:** It throws away the ideas that don't look promising and focuses on the ones that seem useful.
5. **Repeat until solved:** The AI keeps doing this—thinking, judging, and choosing—until it finds a strong, well-thought-out solution.

Prompt: "Use Tree of Thought prompting to solve the below prompt: "I have cities, but no houses. I have mountains, but no trees. I have water, but no fish. What am I?"
The output is given below:

Tree of Thought Approach
We'll break this down into **branches of reasoning**, each exploring a possible interpretation of the clues.

Branch 1: Literal Interpretation
Cities but no houses: Unusual—cities typically contain houses.
Mountains but no trees: Suggests a barren or abstract representation.
Water but no fish: Implies water is present but not in a natural ecosystem.
Thought: This could be a representation of something that mimics real-world geography but lacks life or habitation.

Branch 2: Symbolic Interpretation
These elements (cities, mountains, water) are **symbols** of geography.
Their absence of life (no houses, trees, fish) suggests **non-living representation**.
Thought: Could this be a **map**? A map shows cities, mountains, and water, but not the living elements.

Branch 3: Abstract Representation
Think of **tools or objects** that represent geography:
    Globe?
    Atlas?
    Map?
Thought: A **map** fits all clues:
Cities (marked)
Mountains (contours or symbols)
Water (rivers, lakes, oceans)
But no actual houses, trees, or fish.

☑ **Final Answer: A Map**

A map fits perfectly—it has cities, mountains, and water, but none of the things mentioned in the riddle. So the AI picks that answer with confidence.

This way of thinking—like growing a tree of ideas—helps the AI avoid getting stuck and makes it better at solving tricky problems like writing stories, planning strategies, or solving math puzzles.

Meta prompting is like giving instructions to a chef not just on *what* dish to cook, but also on *how* to interpret future recipes. Imagine you are training the chef to understand your taste preferences, cooking style, and plating expectations—so next time, even if you give a vague recipe, they will know exactly how to deliver what you want (Fig. 6.15).

Figure 6.15 Meta prompting

Here's a meta prompt you might give to an AI: "When I ask you to summarize something, always keep it under 100 words, use bullet points, and highlight any deadlines."

This is not a request to summarize a specific document—it is a meta prompt that tells the AI *how* to behave when summarizing anything in the future.

> **Did You Know?**
> CoT prompting helps AI 'think out loud', improving its reasoning. It is like solving a math problem step-by-step instead of jumping to the answer.

> **Mini Project/Assignment**
> Choose a topic (e.g., "How to make tea") and write three prompts using different techniques: instruction-based, role-based, and step-by-step. Compare AI's responses and reflect on which technique gave the best result.

6.4 Role of Prompts in AI/ML Interaction

In AI systems, particularly those based on machine learning (ML) and natural language processing (NLP), prompts serve as the primary mechanism through which users communicate their intentions. These prompts are carefully constructed linguistic cues that guide the model's behaviour, shaping the nature and quality of its responses. The behaviour of a model is influenced by the structure, tone, and specificity of the prompt, which acts as a set of instructions embedded in natural language.

When a user inputs a prompt, the model interprets it based on patterns it has learned during training. For instance, a prompt like "Translate this sentence into Tamil: 'Hello, how are you?'" provides a clear directive, enabling the model to perform the task with high accuracy. However, if the prompt is vague or lacks context—such as "Translate this"—the model may struggle to determine what needs to be translated, leading to ambiguous or incorrect outputs. This demonstrates how the clarity and completeness of a prompt directly affect the model's ability to understand and execute the task.

6.4.1 Examples from NLP and Generative Models

NLP and generative models have become the most prominent domains where prompt engineering plays a vital role. In NLP tasks such as text classification, sentiment analysis, and question answering, prompts are used to frame the problem in a way that the model can understand. For instance, in sentiment analysis, a prompt like "Is the following review positive or negative?" followed by the review text helps the model focus on evaluating sentiment rather than summarizing or translating the content.

In more advanced applications, prompts are used to perform complex reasoning tasks. For example, CoT prompting encourages the model to break down a problem into logical steps before arriving at a conclusion. This technique has been shown to improve performance in mathematical reasoning and logical inference tasks. By guiding the model through a structured thought process, prompts can enhance its ability to solve problems that require multi-step reasoning.

6.4.2 Prompting in Supervised versus Unsupervised Learning

The role of prompts varies significantly between supervised and unsupervised learning paradigms. While a supervised learning prompt asks for a direct classification based on labelled data, an unsupervised learning prompt must be tuned to discover hidden patterns within unlabelled data. The goal shifts from asking "what is this?" to "what can you find in this?"

Here's how to tune the prompt for an unsupervised learning context, using the email example:

- **Supervised Learning Prompt**: The model is given a new email and asked a simple, direct question with a known answer: "Is this email spam?" The prompt is a command to classify a single data point based on its pre-existing training. In supervised learning, models are trained on labelled data, and prompts are often used during inference to apply the learned patterns to new inputs.
- **Unsupervised Learning Prompt**: The model is given a large, unlabeled data set of emails and asked to find inherent groupings or anomalies. The prompt is an instruction to explore and report on the data's internal structure without any predefined categories. Instead of asking for a classification, you would prompt an unsupervised model to perform a task like clustering, anomaly detection, or topic modelling.
- **Prompt for Clustering (Grouping Similar Emails)**: "Analyze this data set of 10,000 unlabeled emails. Identify and group the emails into distinct clusters based on their content, subject lines, and sender behaviour. Describe the common characteristics of each cluster you have identified." The model would create groups (e.g., "promotional emails," "personal correspondence," "system notifications") without being told what these groups are beforehand.
- **Prompt for Anomaly Detection (Finding Unusual Emails)**: "Examine this large archive of emails and flag any messages that significantly deviate from the norm in terms of word frequency, sender-recipient patterns, or unusual attachments. List the top 10 most anomalous emails and provide a brief justification for each." The model would identify outliers that might be phishing attempts or security threats, which it could not classify as "spam" in a supervised sense because they do not fit a known pattern.
- **Prompt for Dimensionality Reduction (Simplifying Complex Data)**: "Analyze the content of these emails and create a simplified, lower-dimensional representation of the data set. Identify the most influential keywords and phrases that best represent the overall content variations across the entire corpus." This would allow a human analyst to visualize the complex email data in a simplified way, seeing how different topics or styles are related to one another.

> **Did You Know?**
> In unsupervised learning, prompts help AI discover patterns without labelled data. It is like asking someone to sort a pile of letters without knowing what they say—just based on how they look!

> **Mini Project/Assignment**
> Write two prompts: one for supervised learning (e.g., "Is this email spam?") and one for unsupervised learning (e.g., "Group these emails by topic"). Discuss how each prompt guides the AI differently.

6.5 Challenges in Prompt Engineering

As the field of prompt engineering has evolved, practitioners have encountered a variety of practical challenges that can affect the reliability and usefulness of AI-driven outputs. Among the most prominent issues are ambiguity, bias, and difficulties in generalization.

6.5.1 Ambiguity and Misinterpretation

Imagine you are asking a friend, "Can you bring me a bat?" If you are at a sports field, they might bring a baseball bat (Fig. 6.16). But if you are in a biology lab, they might bring the flying mammal!

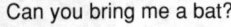

Figure 6.16 Ambiguity

That is ambiguity—the same word can mean different things depending on context. If your friend guesses wrong and brings the wrong kind of bat, that is misinterpretation—the system misunderstood your intent.

One of the most persistent challenges in prompt engineering is the issue of ambiguity. When a prompt is not clearly defined, the AI model may misinterpret the user's intent, leading to responses that are irrelevant, incorrect, or even misleading. This problem arises because language is inherently flexible and context-dependent. A single word or phrase can have multiple meanings depending on how it is used, and AI models, despite their sophistication, can struggle to discern the intended meaning without sufficient context. For example, a prompt like "Describe the bank" could refer to a financial institution or the side of a river. Without additional context, the model may choose either interpretation, which may not align with the user's expectations. This ambiguity can be particularly problematic in professional settings where precision is critical, such as legal documentation, medical advice, or technical support.

Misinterpretation also occurs when prompts are too broad or vague. A prompt like "Tell me something interesting" lacks specificity and can lead to a wide range of responses, some of which may not be useful or relevant. In contrast, a more focused prompt like "Tell me an interesting fact about marine biology" provides a clearer direction and reduces the likelihood of misinterpretation.

To address this challenge, prompt engineers must learn to craft prompts that are both specific and contextually rich. This involves anticipating how the model might interpret different phrases and structuring the prompt to minimize confusion. It also requires iterative testing and refinement, as even well-designed prompts can behave unpredictably in certain scenarios.

6.5.2 Bias and Ethical Concerns

Imagine you are giving directions to a taxi driver. If you always say, "Take me to the nicest part of town," the driver might start thinking that is where everyone wants to go. Over time, the driver may begin ignoring other areas, even if someone else wants to go there. That is an example of bias—when a system starts favoring one option over others just because it has been chosen more often in the past (Fig. 6.17).

Figure 6.17 Bias and ethical concern

Now, let's say the driver starts refusing to drive to certain neighbourhoods or only listens to certain passengers. This is no longer just bias—it becomes an ethical issue. It means the system is being unfair and not treating everyone equally. In real life, this kind of behaviour can lead to people being left out or treated unfairly, which is a serious concern when designing systems that are meant to serve everyone.

AI models are trained on large data sets that reflect the language, beliefs, and behaviours of the societies from which they are drawn. As a result, these models can inadvertently reproduce and amplify biases present in the training data. Prompt engineering, while powerful, does not eliminate these biases—it can only mitigate them to a certain extent.

For instance, a prompt like "Describe a successful entrepreneur" may lead the model to generate responses that favour certain demographics or stereotypes, depending on the biases embedded in its training data. Similarly, prompts that involve sensitive topics such as race, gender, or religion must be carefully crafted to avoid reinforcing harmful narratives or excluding diverse perspectives.

Ethical concerns also arise when prompts are used to manipulate or deceive. In marketing, politics, or social media, prompts can be designed to generate persuasive content that may not be entirely truthful or balanced. This raises questions about the responsible use of AI and the role of prompt engineers in ensuring that models are used ethically.

To navigate these challenges, prompt engineers must be aware of the ethical implications of their work. This includes understanding the limitations of the models they are working with, recognizing potential sources of bias, and designing prompts that promote fairness, inclusivity, and transparency. It also involves collaborating with ethicists, domain experts, and diverse user groups to ensure that AI systems serve the broader interests of society.

6.5.3 Scalability and Generalization

Think of prompting like giving instructions to a chef. Scalability is when the chef can cook for 2 people or 200 using the same recipe format—just adjusting the quantities. Generalization is when the chef can take your instructions for making pasta and apply the same logic to make noodles, ramen, or even stir-fry—because the core idea of boiling, seasoning, and mixing translates across dishes.

Scalability and generalization are technical challenges that affect the effectiveness of prompt engineering across different tasks and domains. A prompt that works well for one task may not perform as effectively when applied to a different context or data set. This lack of generalization limits the reusability of prompts and requires engineers to design new prompts for each specific application.

For example, a prompt designed to summarize news articles may not work well for summarizing scientific papers, even though both tasks involve summarization. The differences in language style, structure, and content require tailored prompts that account for these variations. This need for customization can be time-consuming and resource-intensive, especially in large-scale deployments where multiple tasks and domains are involved.

Scalability also becomes an issue when prompts need to be applied across different languages, cultures, or user groups. A prompt that is effective in English may not translate well into other languages due to differences in syntax, semantics, and cultural context. This limits the global applicability of prompt engineering and requires additional effort to localize and adapt prompts for diverse audiences.

To overcome these challenges, researchers are exploring techniques such as prompt templates, automated prompt generation, and meta-prompting, which involve using AI to design and optimize prompts. These approaches aim to improve the generalizability and scalability of prompt engineering by leveraging the model's own capabilities to refine and adapt prompts dynamically.

6.5.4 Evaluation and Benchmarking Difficulties

Imagine you are judging a cooking contest, but each chef uses a different recipe, serves different cuisines, and even uses different portion sizes. It becomes really hard to say who cooked 'best' because there is no consistent standard (Fig. 6.18).

Figure 6.18 Benchmarking difficulties

That is what happens in prompting—different models, tasks, and prompt styles make it tricky to compare performance fairly and reliably.

Unlike traditional software development, where outputs can be tested against predefined criteria, prompt engineering involves subjective and context-dependent assessments. The quality of an AI-generated response depends not only on its factual accuracy but also on its relevance, coherence, tone, and usefulness—all of which are difficult to measure objectively.

This makes benchmarking prompt performance a non-trivial task. Human evaluation, while more accurate, is time-consuming and prone to variability. Different users may have different expectations and interpretations of what constitutes a 'good' response, leading to inconsistent evaluations. Moreover, the dynamic nature of AI models adds another layer of complexity. As models are updated or fine-tuned, the behaviour of prompts may change, requiring continuous monitoring and adjustment. This makes it difficult to establish stable benchmarks or compare prompt performance over time.

To address these issues, researchers are developing new evaluation frameworks that combine quantitative metrics with qualitative assessments. These frameworks aim to capture a broader range of performance indicators, including user satisfaction, task completion rates, and ethical compliance. They also emphasize the importance of transparency and reproducibility, encouraging prompt engineers to document their methods and share their findings with the broader community.

Did You Know?
Even a simple word like 'bat' can confuse AI if the context is not clear—does it mean the animal or the sports equipment? That is why prompt clarity is crucial!

Mini Project/Assignment
Think of a word with multiple meanings (e.g., "bank"). Write a prompt using that word in two different contexts. See how AI interprets each and reflect on the importance of context.

6.6 Future Scope in Human–AI Collaboration

As AI continues to integrate into everyday life, prompt engineering is emerging as a vital skillset for professionals across industries. Unlike traditional programming, which requires knowledge of syntax and logic structures, prompt engineering is more intuitive and language-driven. It allows users to interact with AI systems using natural language, making it accessible to a broader audience. However, mastering this skill requires an understanding of how AI models interpret language, respond to context, and generate outputs.

In the future, prompt engineering will likely become a core competency in fields such as education, healthcare, marketing, and customer service. Teachers may use it to design AI-assisted lesson plans, while healthcare professionals could employ it to generate patient summaries or diagnostic suggestions. Marketing teams might craft prompts to produce targeted content, and customer service agents could use it to train chatbots for more empathetic and accurate responses.

Educational institutions are beginning to recognize the importance of prompt engineering and are incorporating it into curricula. Courses on AI literacy now include modules on prompt design, emphasizing its role in shaping AI behaviour and ensuring ethical use. As AI tools become more sophisticated, the ability to craft effective prompts will distinguish skilled users from casual ones, much like coding proficiency does today.

Moreover, prompt engineering fosters creativity and innovation. By experimenting with different prompt styles, users can discover new ways to leverage AI capabilities, whether for storytelling, data analysis, or problem-solving. This creative aspect makes prompt engineering not just a technical skill but also an artistic one, blending logic with imagination.

6.6.1 Integration with Multimodal Systems

Imagine you are giving instructions to a robot assistant that can see, hear, and read. If you say, "Find my red notebook on the desk," it uses your words (text), looks around (vision), and maybe even listens for clues (audio). Integrating prompting with multimodal systems is like teaching that robot to understand and respond using all its senses together—making it much smarter and more helpful than if it relied on just one (Fig. 6.19).

Figure 6.19 Integration with multimodal systems

The future of AI is increasingly multimodal, meaning systems that can process and generate content across multiple formats—text, images, audio, and video. Prompt engineering will play a crucial role in guiding these systems, enabling users to interact with AI in more dynamic and versatile ways. For example, a user might prompt an AI to "Generate a visual infographic based on this data" or "Create a narrated video explaining this concept."

Multimodal AI systems require prompts that are not only linguistically clear but also contextually rich across different media. This adds complexity to prompt engineering, as users must consider how the AI interprets and synthesizes information from various sources. For instance, prompting a model to analyze a medical image and provide a textual diagnosis involves coordinating visual and textual inputs in a coherent manner.

As these systems evolve, prompt engineering will expand to include multimodal prompt design. This involves crafting inputs that combine text with images, audio cues, or video snippets to guide the AI's response. Tools like OpenAI's GPT-4 with vision capabilities and Google's Gemini are already exploring these possibilities, allowing users to interact with AI in more immersive and intuitive ways.

The integration of multimodal systems also opens new avenues for accessibility. Users with visual or hearing impairments can interact with AI through tailored prompts that accommodate their needs, such as voice commands or tactile inputs. This enhances inclusivity and ensures that AI technologies serve a diverse range of users.

6.6.2 Human-in-the-Loop (HITL) Design

Think of it like teaching a child to solve puzzles. You let them try on their own, but you step in to guide them when they get stuck or make a mistake. In prompting, HITL means letting AI generate responses, but having humans review, correct, or refine them—ensuring better accuracy, fairness, and learning over time.

HITL design is a collaborative approach where human oversight is integrated into AI decision-making processes. Prompt engineering is central to this model, as it enables humans to guide, refine, and validate AI outputs in real time. In HITL systems, prompts are used not only to initiate tasks but also to provide feedback, corrections, and contextual updates that improve the model's performance.

This approach is particularly valuable in high-stakes domains such as healthcare, finance, and law, where AI decisions must be accurate, transparent, and ethically sound. For example, a radiologist might prompt an AI to analyze an X-ray image and then review the generated diagnosis, providing corrections or additional context as needed. This iterative process ensures that the AI supports rather than replaces human expertise.

Prompt engineering in HITL systems also enhances accountability. By documenting the prompts used and the responses generated, organizations can trace decision-making pathways and identify potential sources of error or bias. This is essential for regulatory compliance and ethical governance, especially as AI systems become more autonomous.

In the future, HITL design will likely become the standard for deploying AI in sensitive or complex environments. Prompt engineers will play a key role in designing workflows that balance automation with human judgment, ensuring that AI systems remain aligned with human values and goals.

6.6.3 Ethical and Responsible Prompting

Imagine you'are giving instructions to a smart assistant that follows your commands exactly. If you ask it to do something unfair, misleading, or harmful, it might still do it—unless you have taught it to ask questions or follow a moral compass. Ethical and responsible prompting is like setting ground rules for that assistant, ensuring it acts with fairness, respect, and safety no matter who's asking or what the task is.

As AI systems become more powerful and pervasive, the ethical implications of prompt engineering cannot be overstated. Prompts have the potential to influence AI behaviour in ways that affect individuals, communities, and society at large. Responsible prompting involves designing inputs that promote fairness, transparency, and inclusivity, while avoiding manipulation, bias, or harm.

One ethical concern is the use of prompts to generate misleading or harmful content. For example, prompting an AI to produce fake news, offensive jokes, or biased analyses can have real-world consequences. Prompt engineers must be aware of these risks and design safeguards that prevent misuse. This includes incorporating ethical constraints into prompts, such as "Provide a respectful and unbiased summary" or "Avoid stereotypes in your response."

Another challenge is ensuring that prompts reflect diverse perspectives and experiences. AI models trained on large data sets may inadvertently favor dominant cultural narratives, excluding marginalized voices. Prompt engineering can help address this by explicitly including diverse viewpoints and framing tasks in inclusive ways. For instance, prompting a model to "Explain this concept from both Western and Indigenous perspectives" encourages a more balanced and comprehensive response.

Transparency is also critical. Users should be informed about how prompts influence AI behaviour and what limitations exist. This fosters trust and empowers users to engage with AI systems responsibly. Educational initiatives, public awareness campaigns, and ethical guidelines can support this goal, ensuring that prompt engineering evolves as a socially responsible practice.

In conclusion, the future of human–AI collaboration hinges on the thoughtful and ethical application of prompt engineering. As AI systems become more integrated into daily life, the ability to design effective, inclusive, and responsible prompts will shape how these technologies are used and understood.

> **Did You Know?**
> Multimodal AI systems can process text, images, and audio simultaneously—like a robot that can read, see, and hear. Prompting these systems is like giving instructions to a supercharged assistant with multiple senses!

> **Mini Project/Assignment**
> Imagine you are designing a virtual assistant for elderly users. Write a prompt that helps the assistant explain how to take medicine, using simple language and a caring tone. Then revise it to include visual or audio support suggestions.

6.7 Case Studies and Real-World Applications

As theoretical principles of prompt engineering continue to evolve, their real-world impact becomes increasingly apparent across a range of industries. The following case studies illustrate how thoughtfully designed prompts are shaping the future of human–AI collaboration, driving improvements in accuracy, personalization, and inclusivity..

6.7.1 Healthcare: Prompting in Diagnostic AI

In the healthcare sector, prompt engineering has begun to play a transformative role in enhancing diagnostic accuracy and clinical decision-making. AI systems trained on vast medical data sets can assist physicians by analyzing patient symptoms, medical histories, and diagnostic images. However, the effectiveness of these systems depends heavily on how they are prompted. A well-structured prompt can guide the AI to consider relevant factors and produce more accurate and context-sensitive recommendations.

For example, consider a scenario where a clinician uses an AI model to assist in diagnosing a patient presenting with chest pain. A generic prompt such as "What could be the cause of chest pain?" may yield a broad and unfocused response. In contrast, a more refined prompt like "Given the patient's age, history of hypertension, and recent ECG findings, what are the likely causes of chest pain?" provides the model with critical context, enabling it to generate a more precise and clinically useful answer (Fig. 6.20).

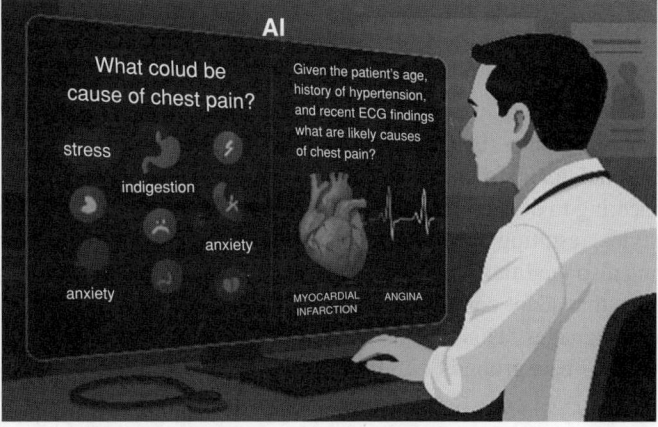

Figure 6.20 Prompting in diagnostic AI

Real-world applications of prompt engineering in healthcare include AI-powered triage systems, which prioritize patients based on symptom severity, and diagnostic support tools that suggest possible conditions based on structured prompts. In one case study, a hospital integrated prompt-based AI into its radiology department to assist in interpreting X-rays. Radiologists used prompts that included patient demographics, clinical indications, and imaging findings, resulting in improved diagnostic accuracy and reduced turn-around times.

Prompt engineering also supports personalized medicine. By tailoring prompts to individual patient profiles, AI systems can recommend treatments that align with genetic markers, lifestyle factors, and co-morbidities. This level of customization enhances patient outcomes and reduces the risk of adverse effects.

6.7.2 Education: Adaptive Learning Systems

In the field of education, prompt engineering is revolutionizing how students learn and how educators teach. Adaptive learning systems powered by AI can respond to student inputs in real time, offering personalized feedback, explanations, and assessments. The quality of these interactions depends on the prompts used to guide the AI's behaviour and tailor its responses to individual learning needs.

For instance, a student struggling with algebra might receive a prompt like "Explain how to solve for x in the equation $2x + 3 = 11$." The AI can then provide a step-by-step explanation, adjusting its language and complexity based on the student's proficiency level. If the student needs further clarification, a follow-up prompt such as "Can you explain that in simpler terms?" can help the AI refine its response (Fig. 6.21).

Figure 6.21 Adaptive learning systems

Educators use prompt engineering to create dynamic lesson plans, quizzes, and study guides. By designing prompts that align with curriculum standards and learning objectives, they can ensure that AI-generated content supports educational goals. In one case study, a school district implemented an AI tutoring system that used prompt engineering to deliver customized math instruction. Teachers crafted prompts that reflected different learning styles, resulting in improved student engagement and performance.

Prompt engineering also facilitates inclusive education. Students with disabilities or language barriers can benefit from prompts that adapt content to their needs, such as converting text to speech or translating materials into multiple languages. This ensures that all learners have access to high-quality educational resources, regardless of their background or abilities.

6.7.3 Customer Service: Chatbots and Virtual Assistants

Customer service is another domain where prompt engineering has made a significant impact. AI-powered chatbots and virtual assistants are now common in industries ranging from retail and banking to telecommunications and travel. These systems rely on prompt engineering to understand customer queries, provide accurate information, and resolve issues efficiently.

The effectiveness of a customer service chatbot depends on how it is prompted to interpret and respond to user inputs. For example, a prompt like "Respond to this query as a helpful and empathetic assistant" can guide the AI to adopt a tone that is both informative and supportive. This is particularly important in situations where customers are frustrated or confused, and a well-crafted prompt can help de-escalate tensions and build trust.

In a real-world case study, a major airline implemented an AI chatbot to handle flight inquiries and booking changes. Prompt engineers designed prompts that included contextual cues such as flight numbers, travel dates, and customer preferences. This enabled the chatbot to provide personalized assistance, reducing call center volume and improving customer satisfaction.

Prompt engineering also supports multilingual customer service. By crafting prompts that specify language preferences and cultural nuances, companies can ensure that their AI systems communicate effectively with diverse customer bases. This enhances accessibility and fosters global engagement.

Moreover, prompt engineering allows for continuous improvement. By analyzing customer interactions and refining prompts based on feedback, companies can optimize their AI systems to deliver more accurate and helpful responses over time.

6.7.4 Legal and Compliance: Document Summarization

In the legal and compliance sectors, prompt engineering is being used to streamline document analysis and summarization. Legal professionals often deal with lengthy contracts, case files, and regulatory documents that require careful review. AI models can assist by summarizing key points, identifying risks, and suggesting actions—but only if they are prompted effectively.

A prompt like "Summarize the main clauses of this contract, focusing on termination, liability, and confidentiality" provides the AI with clear guidance on what to extract. This targeted approach ensures that the summary is relevant and actionable, saving time and reducing the risk of oversight.

In one case study, a law firm integrated AI into its contract review process using prompt engineering. Lawyers crafted prompts that reflected specific legal concerns, such as compliance with data protection laws or indemnity clauses. The AI system generated summaries that highlighted critical issues, enabling faster decision-making and improved risk management.

Prompt engineering also supports regulatory compliance. Companies can use AI to monitor changes in laws and regulations by prompting models to analyze new documents and compare them with existing policies. This proactive approach helps organizations stay compliant and avoid penalties.

Furthermore, prompt engineering enhances legal research. By designing prompts that specify jurisdiction, case type, and legal principles, professionals can retrieve relevant precedents and insights more efficiently. This accelerates the research process and supports more informed legal strategies.

> **Did You Know?**
> Hospitals are using AI with prompt engineering to help radiologists interpret X-rays faster and more accurately—saving time and improving patient care!

> **Mini Project/Assignment**
>
> Choose one industry (healthcare, education, or customer service). Write a sample prompt that could be used by an AI in that field. For example, "Summarize this patient's symptoms and suggest possible causes."

6.8 Summarization and Simplification

In a world overflowing with information, the ability to distill complex documents and ideas into clear, concise summaries is more valuable than ever. Let us explore how prompt engineering empowers AI systems to perform effective summarization and simplification, transforming overwhelming volumes of data into actionable insights.

6.8.1 Academic Use

By carefully designing the instructions that guide AI models for academic use, organizations can unlock more precise, relevant, and actionable outputs tailored to their specific needs.

Enhancing Comprehension of Complex Texts

In academic environments, students and researchers frequently encounter dense and complex texts that require significant effort to understand. These texts often include technical jargon, layered arguments, and extensive references that can be overwhelming, especially for those new to a subject. Prompt engineering offers a powerful solution by enabling AI systems to simplify and summarize such content without losing its core meaning. By crafting prompts that instruct the AI to "explain in simple terms" or "summarize for a high school student," users can transform intricate academic material into accessible explanations.

For example, a student struggling with a research paper on quantum mechanics might use a prompt like, "Summarize this paper in layman's terms." The AI can then generate a version that retains the essential concepts while removing unnecessary complexity. This approach not only aids comprehension but also encourages independent learning, as students can revisit the simplified summaries to reinforce their understanding (Fig. 6.22).

Figure 6.22 Enhancing comprehension

Moreover, prompt engineering can be tailored to specific academic disciplines. In history, prompts can be designed to highlight key events and their significance. In biology, they can focus on processes and mechanisms. This customization ensures that the AI output aligns with the learning objectives of each field. The ability to adjust the depth and tone of summaries makes prompt engineering a versatile tool for learners at all levels.

A real-world example of this application is seen in online learning platforms that integrate AI-powered tutors. These systems use prompt engineering to generate simplified explanations of textbook content, helping students grasp difficult topics more quickly. As a result, learners are better prepared for assessments and can engage more deeply with their studies.

Assisting in Literature Reviews and Research Synthesis

Conducting a literature review is a foundational task in academic research, requiring the synthesis of multiple sources to identify trends, gaps, and key findings. This process is time-consuming and demands a high level of analytical skill. Prompt engineering can significantly streamline this task by guiding AI systems to extract and summarize relevant information from a collection of academic papers.

Researchers can use prompts such as "Summarize the main findings of these articles" or "Compare the methodologies used in these studies." The AI then processes the input documents and generates concise summaries that highlight essential points. This not only saves time but also enhances the quality of the review by ensuring consistency and clarity across summaries.

In addition, prompt engineering can help identify connections between studies that may not be immediately apparent. For instance, a prompt like "Find common themes in these papers" can lead the AI to uncover recurring patterns or shared conclusions. This capability is particularly valuable in interdisciplinary research, where integrating insights from different fields is crucial (Fig. 6.23).

Figure 6.23 Common themes in papers

Academic institutions are beginning to adopt AI tools powered by prompt engineering to assist faculty and students in research activities. These tools can generate annotated bibliographies, summarize theoretical frameworks, and even suggest future research directions based on existing literature. By automating routine tasks, prompt engineering allows researchers to focus on critical analysis and innovation.

6.8.2 Professional Use

While the benefits of prompt engineering are evident in academic settings, its impact extends just as powerfully into the professional world. In dynamic business environments, the ability to distill complex information, streamline communication, and adapt content for varied audiences is critical.

Executive Summaries and Business Reports

In professional settings, executives and decision-makers often rely on summaries of lengthy reports to make informed choices. These summaries must be accurate, concise, and tailored to the specific needs of the audience. Prompt engineering enables the creation of executive summaries by instructing AI systems to distill complex documents into key points that are easy to understand. For example, a prompt like "Create a summary of this financial report for senior management" guides the AI to focus on metrics, trends, and strategic implications rather than technical details. This ensures that the summary is relevant and actionable. Similarly, prompts can be customized to highlight risks, opportunities, or compliance issues depending on the context.

Business analysts frequently use prompt engineering to generate summaries of market research, competitor analysis, and internal audits. These summaries help stakeholders quickly grasp the essence of the findings and make timely decisions. The ability to produce consistent and high-quality summaries also improves communication across departments and enhances organizational efficiency.

A case study from a multinational corporation illustrates this application. The company implemented an AI tool that used prompt engineering to summarize weekly performance reports for its regional managers. The tool reduced the time spent on report preparation by 60% and improved the clarity of the summaries, leading to faster and more effective decision-making.

Email and Document Simplification

Professionals often deal with a high volume of emails and documents that vary in complexity and relevance. Prompt engineering can be used to simplify these communications, making them easier to read and respond to. By using prompts such as "Simplify this email for quick review" or "Rewrite this document in plain language," users can transform verbose or technical content into clear and concise messages.

This application is particularly useful in industries where clarity and speed are essential, such as legal services, healthcare, and customer support. Simplified documents reduce the risk of miscommunication and ensure that important information is not overlooked. They also make it easier for non-experts to understand specialized content, fostering better collaboration across teams.

In addition to simplification, prompt engineering can help rephrase content to suit different audiences. For instance, a technical report intended for engineers can be adapted for a non-technical audience by changing the prompt to "Explain this report for a general reader." The AI then adjusts the language and tone accordingly, making the content more accessible.

Organizations are increasingly integrating AI-powered writing assistants into their workflows to support document simplification. These tools use prompt engineering to enhance internal communication, improve customer interactions, and ensure compliance with regulatory standards. The result is a more agile and responsive business environment.

> **Did You Know?**
> AI can summarize a dense research paper into a few bullet points suitable for high school students—just by adjusting the prompt!

> **Mini Project/Assignment**
> Find a long article or report. Write a prompt asking AI to summarize it for a beginner. Then write another prompt asking for a summary for a professional audience. Compare the two outputs.

6.9 Creative Content Generation

Modern organizations and individual creators alike are constantly seeking innovative ways to produce original, captivating content across a range of mediums. Creative content generation goes beyond merely conveying information; it involves crafting narratives, visuals, and experiences that inspire, entertain, or provoke thought.

6.9.1 Blogging and Article Writing

In today's digital landscape, the demand for engaging and high-quality written content is ever-increasing. Blogging and article writing have evolved into essential tools for individuals, businesses, and organizations seeking to inform, persuade, and connect with their audiences. As content creators strive to stand out in a crowded online space, prompt engineering has emerged as a valuable method for enhancing the ideation, structuring, and stylistic adaptation of written material. By leveraging the power of tailored prompts, writers can not only boost creativity and efficiency but also ensure their content resonates with diverse readerships and adapts to varying brand voices.

In the realm of blogging and article writing, one of the most challenging tasks for writers is generating fresh ideas and organizing them into coherent structures. Prompt engineering has become a powerful ally in this process, enabling writers to overcome creative blocks and produce well-structured content efficiently. By using carefully designed prompts, writers can instruct AI systems to brainstorm topics, outline articles, and even suggest titles that align with current trends or audience interests.

For instance, a blogger interested in writing about sustainable living might use a prompt such as, "Generate five blog post ideas on eco-friendly habits for urban dwellers." The AI responds with a list of relevant and engaging topics, each with a potential angle or subtheme (Fig. 6.24).

Figure 6.24 Blog post creation

Once a topic is selected, the writer can use a follow-up prompt like, "Create a detailed outline for a blog post on reducing plastic waste at home." The AI then provides a structured framework, including an introduction, key points, and a conclusion, which the writer can expand upon.

This approach not only accelerates the content creation process but also ensures that the final output is logically organized and reader-friendly. Writers can experiment with different prompt styles to refine the tone, depth, and focus of the article. For example, prompts that specify the target audience—such as "Write for beginners" or "Tailor for industry professionals"—help the AI adjust the complexity and vocabulary accordingly.

A case study from a digital marketing agency illustrates the effectiveness of prompt engineering in blogging. The agency used AI tools to generate weekly blog content for clients across various industries. By crafting prompts that included keywords, audience demographics, and desired outcomes, the team was able to produce high-quality drafts that required minimal editing. This not only improved turnaround times but also allowed writers to focus on strategic storytelling and brand alignment.

6.9.2 Style Adaptation and Tone Control

Beyond ideation and structure, prompt engineering plays a crucial role in adapting writing style and controlling tone. Different blogs require different voices—some may be formal and informative, while others are casual and conversational. Prompt engineering allows writers to guide AI systems in mimicking specific styles or adjusting tone to suit the context.

For example, a prompt like "Write this article in a humorous tone suitable for millennials" instructs the AI to incorporate wit, cultural references, and informal language. Conversely, a prompt such as "Rewrite this blog post in a professional tone for a corporate audience" results in a more polished and restrained output. This flexibility is invaluable for content creators who manage multiple blogs or write for diverse audiences (Fig. 6.25).

Figure 6.25 Articles in two tones

Writers can also use prompt engineering to emulate the style of well-known authors or publications. Prompts like "Write in the style of The Economist" or "Mimic the tone of Seth Godin" help the AI align its output with established voices, enhancing credibility and engagement. This technique is particularly useful for ghostwriters and content strategists who need to maintain consistency across branded content.

In practice, style adaptation through prompt engineering has been adopted by freelance writers and content agencies to meet client expectations more effectively. By using prompt templates that specify tone, style, and formatting preferences, writers can produce drafts that closely match the desired output, reducing the need for revisions and improving client satisfaction.

6.9.3 Social Media Content

From aligning with the latest trends to pairing evocative narratives with striking visuals, prompt engineering offers a versatile toolkit for elevating the quality and impact of social media communications.

6.9.4 Caption Generation and Trend Alignment

Social media platforms thrive on timely, engaging, and visually appealing content. One of the key challenges for marketers and influencers is crafting captions that resonate with their audience while aligning with current trends. Prompt engineering offers a solution by enabling AI systems to generate captions that are catchy, relevant, and tailored to specific platforms.

For example, a prompt like "Create an Instagram caption for a photo of a beach sunset, targeting travel enthusiasts" guides the AI to produce a caption that evokes emotion and encourages interaction. The AI might generate something like, "Golden hour magic. Where would you rather be right now?"—a caption that is visually descriptive and includes a call to action. Similarly, prompts can be adjusted for different platforms, such as "Write a professional LinkedIn post about remote work benefits" or "Generate a tweet about the latest tech gadget."

Trend alignment is another area where prompt engineering excels. By incorporating trending hashtags, cultural references, or seasonal themes into prompts, users can ensure that their content remains relevant and discoverable. For instance, a prompt like "Generate a caption for a fitness post using trending hashtags for New Year's resolutions" helps the AI produce content that taps into current conversations and increases visibility.

New year, new goals! Let's make this the year we turn resolutions into results. What's your top fitness goal for 2026? 👟 #NewYearNewMe #2026Goals #FitnessJourney #Resolution2026 #HealthyHabits

A real-world example comes from a fashion brand that used AI-powered tools to manage its social media calendar. By designing prompts that included product details, campaign goals, and audience segments, the brand was able to generate captions that matched its voice and marketing strategy. This approach not only saved time but also improved engagement metrics across platforms.

6.9.5 Visual Storytelling with Prompts

While social media is inherently visual, the accompanying text plays a crucial role in storytelling. Prompt engineering enables users to craft narratives that complement images and videos, creating a cohesive and compelling message. Prompts such as "Describe this image in a poetic tone" or "Tell a short story based on this video clip" allow the AI to generate text that enhances the visual content.

This technique is particularly useful for platforms like Instagram and TikTok, where storytelling drives engagement. For example, a travel influencer might use a prompt like "Write a short story about a solo journey through the Himalayas based on this photo." The AI responds with a narrative that adds depth and emotion to the image, inviting followers to connect on a personal level.

Brands also use visual storytelling to build identity and loyalty. A prompt like "Create a brand story for this product launch photo" helps the AI generate content that aligns with the brand's values and messaging. This not only strengthens the emotional appeal of the post but also reinforces brand recognition.

In practice, visual storytelling through prompt engineering has been adopted by content creators, photographers, and marketers to enhance their digital presence. By combining compelling visuals with well-crafted narratives, they create immersive experiences that captivate audiences and drive interaction.

> **Did You Know?**
> Marketers use AI to generate Instagram captions that match brand tone and include trending hashtags—all guided by smart prompts!

> **Mini Project/Assignment**
> Pick a photo (e.g., a sunset or a coffee mug). Write a prompt asking AI to generate a social media caption for it. Then change the tone (e.g., humorous, poetic, professional) and compare the results.

6.10 Storytelling and Fiction

As digital content continues to evolve, writers and creators are increasingly turning to AI-driven tools to enrich their narratives, develop compelling characters, and construct engaging plots. This section explores how tailored prompts can assist writers in both overcoming creative obstacles and enhancing the creative process across a variety of fiction genres.

6.10.1 Character Development and Plot Progression

In the world of fiction writing, developing believable characters and engaging plots is both an art and a science. Prompt engineering provides writers with tools to explore character traits, motivations, and relationships, as well as to structure narratives that maintain reader interest. Prompts like "Create a character profile for a rebellious teenager in a dystopian world" guide the AI to generate detailed and imaginative content.

> **Name:** Kael Virex
> **Age:** 17
> **Role:** Underground Courier / Hacker
> **Setting:** Neo-Eclipse — a dystopian megacity ruled by a technocratic regime

Character development prompts can include attributes such as age, background, personality, and goals. The AI uses this information to build multidimensional characters that evolve throughout the story. Plot progression prompts help writers structure their narratives with clear beginnings, conflicts, climaxes, and resolutions. For example, a prompt like "Write a three-act structure for a romantic comedy" results in a framework that the writer can expand into a full-length story.

This method is particularly useful for writers facing creative blocks or working under tight deadlines. By using prompt engineering to generate foundational elements, they can focus on refining dialogue, pacing, and thematic depth. It also allows for experimentation with different genres and styles, broadening the writer's creative range.

> **Act I: Setup – "Meet Cute & Conflict"**
> **Introduce the protagonists**: Two contrasting personalities (e.g., a meticulous planner and a spontaneous dreamer).
> **Inciting Incident**: They meet in an unexpected, humorous way (e.g., mistaken identity, a dating app glitch, or a travel mix-up).
> **Establish stakes**: Each has a personal goal that seems incompatible with romance (e.g., career move, family pressure).
> **End of Act I**: They're forced to spend time together (e.g., working on a project, stuck in a situation, fake dating).
>
> **Act II: Confrontation – "Falling in Love & Complications"**
> **Growing attraction**: Funny and heartfelt moments build chemistry.
> **Subplots**: Friends, exes, or quirky family members add tension and comedy.
> **Midpoint**: A romantic high point (e.g., a dance, kiss, or confession) followed by a misunderstanding or secret revealed.
> **End of Act II**: They break apart due to conflict or fear of vulnerability.
>
> **Act III: Resolution – "Grand Gesture & Happy Ending"**
> **Realization**: They reflect on what they've learned and how they've changed.
> **Grand gesture**: One makes a bold move to win the other back (e.g., public speech, chasing through an airport, heartfelt letter).
> **Climax**: They reconcile in a funny, emotional scene.
> **Final scene**: A glimpse into their future together, often with a callback to their first meeting.

6.10.2 Genre-Specific Prompt Strategies

Different genres require different storytelling techniques, and prompt engineering can be tailored to meet these needs. For example, horror stories rely on suspense and atmosphere, while science fiction demands world-building and speculative elements. Prompts like "Write a horror scene set in an abandoned hospital" or "Describe a futuristic city where humans coexist with AI" help the AI generate content that aligns with genre expectations.

Writers can also use prompts to explore subgenres or hybrid styles. A prompt such as "Combine elements of fantasy and romance in a short story" encourages the AI to blend themes and motifs creatively. This flexibility allows writers to experiment with new formats and reach diverse audiences.

Genre-specific prompt strategies are particularly valuable for screenwriters, game developers, and novelists who need to adhere to industry standards. By specifying tone, pacing, and thematic elements in the prompt, they can guide the AI to produce content that fits the intended format and audience.

In practice, genre-based prompt engineering has been used by creative writing programs and workshops to inspire students and foster innovation. By providing structured prompts that reflect genre conventions, instructors help learners develop their storytelling skills and explore new creative avenues.

> **Did You Know?**
> You can ask AI to "write a horror scene in an abandoned hospital" and it will generate a suspenseful story—just from that prompt!

> **Mini Project/Assignment**
> Choose a genre (e.g., romance, mystery). Write a prompt asking AI to create a character profile and a short plot outline. Then expand the story using follow-up prompts.

6.11 Question-Answering and Chatbots: Customer Service

In an era defined by rapid digital transformation and heightened consumer expectations, businesses are increasingly turning to artificial intelligence to deliver timely, effective, and personalized support. Let's explore the pivotal role of question-answering systems and chatbots in the realm of customer service—a domain where the quality of communication can make or break the user experience.

6.11.1 Automating Responses with Empathy

In the realm of customer service, the ability to respond quickly and empathetically to customer inquiries is essential for maintaining satisfaction and loyalty. Traditional customer support systems often rely on scripted responses or human agents who may be overwhelmed by high volumes of queries. Prompt engineering introduces a transformative approach by enabling AI systems to generate personalized, empathetic, and context-aware responses that mimic human interaction.

When designing prompts for customer service chatbots, it is crucial to include instructions that guide the AI to respond with understanding and politeness. For example, a prompt like "Respond to this complaint with empathy and offer a solution" helps the AI craft a message that acknowledges the customer's frustration while providing a constructive resolution. The AI might generate a response such as, "I'm really sorry to hear about your experience. Let's work together to fix this right away."

Empathy in AI-generated responses is not just about tone—it also involves recognizing the emotional state of the user and adapting the message accordingly. Prompt engineering allows for this nuance by incorporating emotional cues into the input. For instance, if a customer expresses anger or disappointment, the prompt can instruct the AI to prioritize reassurance and clarity. This results in interactions that feel more human and supportive.

A case study from a telecommunications company illustrates the effectiveness of empathetic AI responses. The company implemented a chatbot powered by prompt engineering to handle billing inquiries and service complaints. By using prompts that emphasized empathy and solution-oriented language, the chatbot achieved a 30% increase in customer satisfaction scores and reduced the average resolution time by 40%.

6.11.2 Handling Multilingual Queries

Global businesses often serve customers who speak different languages, making multilingual support a critical component of customer service. Prompt engineering enables AI systems to handle queries in multiple languages by guiding them to translate, interpret, and respond appropriately. This capability not only broadens accessibility but also enhances the user experience for non-native speakers.

Prompts such as "Translate this query from Spanish to English and respond in Spanish with a polite tone" help the AI maintain linguistic accuracy while preserving cultural nuances. The AI can also be instructed to detect the language of the input and respond accordingly, ensuring seamless communication across diverse customer bases.

Multilingual prompt engineering is particularly valuable in regions with high linguistic diversity. For example, in India, where customers may speak Hindi, Tamil, Bengali, or English, a customer service chatbot can be designed to switch languages based on user preference. Prompts like "Respond in Tamil with a formal tone" ensure that the AI respects local language norms and etiquette.

A real-world example comes from an e-commerce platform that expanded its operations to Southeast Asia. The company used prompt engineering to train its chatbot to handle queries in Thai, Vietnamese, and Bahasa Indonesia. By crafting language-specific prompts and incorporating cultural references, the chatbot improved engagement and reduced abandonment rates during customer interactions.

> **Did You Know?**
> A telecom company used empathetic prompts in its chatbot and saw a 30% boost in customer satisfaction!

> **Mini Project/Assignment**
> Write a prompt for a chatbot to respond to a frustrated customer about a delayed order. Then rewrite it to include empathy and a solution. Compare the tone and effectiveness.

6.12 Student Help and Tutoring

In the evolving landscape of education, providing robust support for students outside the traditional classroom has become more essential than ever.

6.12.1 Personalized Learning Support

In educational settings, students often require personalized assistance to understand concepts, complete assignments, and prepare for exams. Prompt engineering empowers AI tutors to provide tailored support that adapts to each student's learning style, pace, and level of understanding. This personalization enhances engagement and fosters deeper learning.

Prompts such as "Explain this math problem step-by-step for a beginner" or "Provide a summary of this biology chapter for a visual learner" guide the AI to adjust its explanations accordingly. The AI can break down complex topics into manageable parts, use analogies, and even suggest visual aids or interactive exercises. This flexibility makes AI tutors accessible to a wide range of learners, including those with learning disabilities or language barriers.

Personalized learning through prompt engineering also supports differentiated instruction, where students receive content that matches their individual needs. For example, a prompt like "Create a quiz on this topic for an advanced student" results in challenging questions that promote critical thinking. Conversely, prompts for remedial support can generate simpler explanations and practice exercises.

A case study from an online education platform demonstrates the impact of personalized AI tutoring. The platform used prompt engineering to develop virtual tutors for subjects like mathematics, science, and history. By designing prompts that reflected student profiles and learning goals, the tutors provided customized feedback and guidance. This led to a 25% improvement in student performance and a significant increase in course completion rates.

6.12.2 Clarifying Academic Queries

Students frequently encounter doubts while studying, and timely clarification is essential for maintaining momentum and confidence. Prompt engineering enables AI systems to respond to academic queries with clarity, accuracy, and relevance. By crafting prompts that specify the subject, level, and desired explanation style, users can ensure that the AI provides helpful and understandable answers.

For example, a student might use a prompt like "Explain Newton's laws of motion in simple terms for a 10th-grade student." The AI responds with a clear and concise explanation that avoids technical jargon and includes relatable examples. Similarly, prompts such as "Clarify the difference between mitosis and meiosis with diagrams" guide the AI to include visual descriptions that enhance comprehension.

Clarifying queries through prompt engineering also supports collaborative learning. Students can use AI tools during group study sessions to resolve disagreements or explore alternative perspectives. Prompts like "Provide two different interpretations of this poem" encourage critical thinking and discussion.

Educational institutions are increasingly integrating AI-powered doubt resolution systems into their learning platforms. These systems use prompt engineering to ensure that responses are accurate, contextually appropriate, and pedagogically sound. By reducing dependency on human tutors and enabling 24/7 support, they make learning more accessible and efficient.

> **Did You Know?**
> Students can ask AI to "explain Newton's laws for a 10th-grade student" and get a simplified, relatable answer—thanks to prompt engineering!

> **Mini Project/Assignment**
> Pick a school subject (e.g., biology). Write a prompt asking AI to explain a concept in simple terms. Then ask it to generate a quiz based on that explanation.

6.13 Domain-specific Applications: Education

6.13.1 Curriculum Design and Adaptive Learning

In the field of education, prompt engineering is playing a pivotal role in transforming how curricula are designed and delivered. Traditionally, curriculum development has been a manual and time-intensive process, requiring educators to align learning objectives with content, assessments, and pedagogical strategies. With the advent of AI and prompt engineering, this process is becoming more dynamic and responsive to individual learner needs.

By crafting prompts that specify grade level, subject matter, and learning outcomes, educators can guide AI systems to generate lesson plans, learning modules, and instructional materials that are both comprehensive and age-appropriate. For example, a prompt like "Design a week-long curriculum on environmental science for 8th-grade students with interactive activities" enables the AI to produce structured content that includes objectives, daily topics, and suggested exercises. This not only saves time but also ensures consistency across educational materials.

Adaptive learning is another area where prompt engineering excels. AI systems can be prompted to adjust content based on a student's performance, preferences, and pace. Prompts such as "Create a personalized learning path for a student struggling with algebra" help the AI generate targeted exercises and explanations that address specific gaps in understanding. This approach fosters a more inclusive learning environment, where students receive support tailored to their unique needs.

A case study from a digital education company illustrates the impact of prompt engineering in curriculum design. The company used AI tools to develop adaptive learning modules for mathematics and science. By designing prompts that incorporated student data and learning goals, they created personalized content that improved engagement and retention. Teachers reported a noticeable increase in student confidence and performance, particularly among those who previously struggled with traditional instruction.

6.13.2 Assessment Generation and Feedback

Assessments are a critical component of education, providing insights into student understanding and guiding instructional decisions. Prompt engineering enables educators to generate a wide range of assessments—from multiple-choice quizzes to open-ended questions—quickly and accurately. Prompts such as "Create a 10-question quiz on photosynthesis for 9th-grade biology" allow AI systems to produce assessments that align with curriculum standards and learning objectives.

In addition to generating questions, prompt engineering can be used to create answer keys, rubrics, and feedback. For example, a prompt like "Provide detailed feedback on this student essay about climate change" guides the AI to evaluate the content, structure, and grammar of the essay, offering constructive suggestions for improvement. This not only supports student growth but also reduces the workload for educators.

Feedback generated through prompt engineering can be customized to suit different learning styles. Prompts such as "Give visual feedback on this math problem" or "Explain this mistake in simple terms" help the AI tailor its responses to the student's needs. This personalization enhances the effectiveness of feedback and encourages students to engage more deeply with their learning.

Educational institutions are increasingly adopting AI-powered assessment tools that use prompt engineering to streamline evaluation processes. These tools can generate formative and summative assessments, analyze student responses, and provide actionable insights. By automating routine tasks, educators can focus on mentoring and instructional design, ultimately improving the quality of education.

> **Did You Know?**
> Teachers can ask AI to "create a week-long curriculum on environmental science for 8th grade" and get a full lesson plan with activities!

> **Mini Project/Assignment**
> Write a prompt asking AI to create a 5-question quiz on a topic of your choice. Then ask it to provide feedback on a sample answer to one of the questions.

6.14 Domain-specific Applications: Healthcare

6.14.1 Patient Communication and Triage

In healthcare, effective communication between providers and patients is essential for accurate diagnosis, treatment adherence, and patient satisfaction. Prompt engineering is being used to enhance patient communication by enabling AI systems to generate clear, empathetic, and informative responses to patient queries. This is particularly valuable in telemedicine and digital health platforms, where timely and accurate communication can significantly impact outcomes.

Prompts such as "Respond to this patient's question about medication side effects in simple language" guide the AI to produce responses that are easy to understand and free from medical jargon. This helps patients make informed decisions and reduces anxiety associated with complex medical information.

Similarly, prompts like "Explain the importance of follow-up appointments to a diabetic patient" ensure that the AI emphasizes critical aspects of care in a compassionate manner.

Triage is another area where prompt engineering is making a difference. AI systems can be prompted to assess symptoms and suggest appropriate next steps, such as scheduling a consultation or visiting an emergency room. For example, a prompt like "Evaluate these symptoms and recommend whether the patient should seek immediate care" enables the AI to provide preliminary guidance based on symptom severity and risk factors. This supports healthcare providers in managing patient flow and prioritizing care.

A case study from a hospital network demonstrates the effectiveness of prompt engineering in patient communication. The network implemented an AI chatbot to handle routine inquiries and symptom checks. By designing prompts that emphasized clarity and empathy, the chatbot improved patient satisfaction scores and reduced the burden on call center staff. Patients reported feeling more informed and reassured, even before speaking with a healthcare professional.

6.14.2 Medical Documentation and Summarization

Medical documentation is a time-consuming but essential task in healthcare, involving the recording of patient histories, treatment plans, and clinical notes. Prompt engineering is being used to automate and streamline this process, allowing healthcare providers to focus more on patient care. Prompts such as "Summarize this patient's visit notes into a discharge summary" guide AI systems to extract relevant information and organize it into a coherent format.

AI-generated documentation can include diagnoses, medications, procedures, and follow-up instructions, all formatted according to clinical standards. This not only improves efficiency but also reduces errors associated with manual entry. Prompts can be customized to suit different specialties, such as "Create a surgical report for this procedure" or "Document a psychiatric evaluation based on these notes."

In addition to documentation, prompt engineering supports the summarization of medical literature and research. Prompts like "Summarize this journal article on cardiovascular disease for a general practitioner" help the AI distill complex findings into actionable insights. This enables healthcare professionals to stay informed without spending hours reading full-length articles.

A real-world example comes from a healthcare startup that developed an AI tool for clinical documentation. By using prompt engineering to guide the AI in extracting and organizing patient data, the tool reduced documentation time by 50% and improved the accuracy of records. Physicians reported greater satisfaction and more time available for direct patient interaction.

> **Did You Know?**
> Doctors use AI to summarize patient visit notes into discharge summaries—saving time and improving accuracy!

> **Mini Project/Assignment**
> Write a prompt asking AI to explain a medical condition (e.g., diabetes) in simple terms for a patient. Then ask it to summarize a sample doctor's note.

6.15 Domain-specific Applications: Business

6.15.1 Market Analysis and Strategy Generation

In the business world, prompt engineering is being used to enhance strategic decision-making through AI-driven market analysis and strategy development. Companies can use prompts to guide AI systems in analyzing trends, identifying opportunities, and generating actionable insights. For example, a prompt like "Analyze current market trends in the renewable energy sector and suggest growth strategies" enables the AI to produce a comprehensive report that includes data interpretation, competitive analysis, and strategic recommendations.

Prompt engineering allows businesses to customize their analysis based on specific goals, such as expansion, product development, or risk mitigation. Prompts like "Evaluate the risks of entering the Southeast Asian market for a fintech company" help the AI focus on relevant factors such as regulatory environment, consumer behaviour, and economic indicators. This targeted approach improves the relevance and usefulness of the output.

Strategy generation through prompt engineering also supports scenario planning and forecasting. Prompts such as "Create three strategic options for launching a new product in Q4" guide the AI to explore different approaches, assess potential outcomes, and recommend the most viable path. This enables business leaders to make informed decisions with greater confidence.

A case study from a consulting firm illustrates the impact of prompt engineering in business strategy. The firm used AI tools to support clients in developing market entry strategies. By designing prompts that included industry data, client goals, and competitive benchmarks, they produced strategic reports that were both insightful and actionable. Clients reported improved clarity and faster decision-making, leading to successful market launches.

6.15.2 Internal Communication and Training

Effective internal communication and employee training are essential for organizational success. Prompt engineering is being used to enhance these areas by enabling AI systems to generate clear, consistent, and engaging content for internal use. Prompts such as "Write an internal memo explaining the new remote work policy" guide the AI to produce messages that are informative and aligned with company culture.

Training materials can also be generated using prompt engineering. Prompts like "Create a training module on cybersecurity best practices for new employees" help the AI produce structured content that includes objectives, lessons, and assessments. This supports onboarding and continuous learning, ensuring that employees are well-informed and prepared.

Prompt engineering allows for customization based on role, department, and experience level. For example, a prompt like "Develop a leadership training guide for mid-level managers" results in content that addresses specific challenges and skills relevant to that group. This targeted approach improves engagement and learning outcomes.

Organizations are increasingly adopting AI-powered communication and training tools that use prompt engineering to streamline content creation. These tools support HR, L&D, and internal communications teams in delivering consistent messaging and effective training programs. A case study from a tech company shows that using AI-generated training materials reduced development time by 40% and improved employee satisfaction with onboarding processes.

Did You Know?
Consulting firms use AI to generate strategic reports by prompting it with client goals and market data—cutting down hours of manual work!

Mini Project/Assignment
Write a prompt asking AI to summarize a business report for senior management. Then write another prompt asking it to create a training guide for new employees on a company policy.

Summary

- A prompt is any input text given to an AI model.
- Effective prompts improve AI output quality—clarity, relevance, and accuracy. Prompts act as the main interface between users and AI, replacing traditional programming.
- Techniques for effective prompting may be categorised as foundational, intermediate, and advanced.
- Foundational level techniques include zero-shot prompting, instruction-based prompting, contextual prompting, role-based prompting, and step-by-step prompting.
- Intermediate level techniques are few-shot prompting, scaffolded prompting, contrastive prompting, and iterative prompting.
- Advanced level techniques include Chain-of-Thought prompting, self-consistency prompting, ReAct prompting, Tree-of-Thought prompting, and meta prompting.
- Challenges in prompt engineering involve ambiguity, bias and ethics, scalability and generalization, and evaluation difficulties.
- Human-in-the-loop (HITL) design combines AI automation with human oversight for accuracy and ethics.
- Prompts must promote fairness, inclusivity, and transparency.

Exercises

Part A (Objective Questions)

1. Which of the following is a foundational prompting technique used in prompt engineering?
   (a) ReAct prompting
   (b) Tree-of-thought prompting
   (c) Zero-shot prompting
   (d) Meta prompting

2. Why does a thoughtfully designed prompt improve AI output compared to an ambiguous one?
   (a) It reduces the need for training data
   (b) It allows the AI to guess the user's intent
   (c) It provides clarity, context, and specific instructions
   (d) It limits the AI's creativity

3. A teacher wants to use AI to generate a quiz for 9th-grade biology students on photosynthesis. Which prompt would be most effective?
   (a) "Tell me something about biology."
   (b) "Create a quiz."
   (c) "Generate a 10-question quiz on photosynthesis for 9th-grade biology."
   (d) "Write a biology test."

4. Which challenge in prompt engineering is illustrated by the example: "Describe the bank"?
   (a) Bias
   (b) Scalability
   (c) Ambiguity
   (d) Evaluation difficulty

5. A company wants to deploy an AI chatbot for multilingual customer service. Which factor should be prioritized when designing prompts?
   (a) Using only English prompts
   (b) Avoiding cultural references
   (c) Including language preferences and tone instructions
   (d) Limiting the chatbot to one region

6. Design a prompt for an AI to generate a social media post promoting a new eco-friendly product to young adults. Which of the following is the best example?
   (a) "Write a post."
   (b) "Make an ad for a product."
   (c) "Create a social media post for an eco-friendly water bottle targeting young adults. Use a casual tone, include emojis, and highlight sustainability benefits."
   (d) "Say something about eco-friendly items."

7. What is the primary goal of step-by-step prompting?
   (a) To confuse the AI with multiple instructions
   (b) To reduce the length of the prompt
   (c) To guide the AI through logical components for better clarity
   (d) To make the AI respond faster

8. Which technique involves comparing correct and incorrect examples to deepen understanding?
   (a) Scaffolded prompting
   (b) Contrastive prompting
   (c) Role-based prompting
   (d) Meta prompting

Part B (Short Answer Questions)

1. What are the foundational techniques of prompt engineering mentioned in the chapter?
2. Explain how prompt engineering improves user experience in AI systems.
3. How would you use role-based prompting to simulate a customer service scenario?
4. Compare the effectiveness of zero-shot and few-shot prompting in domain-specific tasks.

5. Assess the ethical risks associated with prompt engineering in content generation.
6. Design a prompt that guides an AI to generate a summary of a legal document focusing on confidentiality clauses.
7. Why is context important in prompt engineering?
8. How can iterative prompting be used to teach project management concepts?
9. What challenges does prompt engineering face in multilingual customer service environments?
10. Create a prompt that helps an AI generate a blog post outline on eco-friendly habits for urban dwellers.

Part C (Essay Questions)

1. Define prompt engineering and explain its historical evolution from traditional command systems to modern AI interfaces.
2. Discuss how the clarity and specificity of a prompt influence the performance and reliability of AI-generated outputs.
3. Using a real-world scenario, demonstrate how role-based prompting can be used to improve customer service interactions in a chatbot system.
4. Compare and contrast foundational, intermediate, and advanced prompting techniques in terms of their complexity and effectiveness.
5. Analyze the ethical implications of biased prompts in AI systems and how prompt engineers can mitigate these risks.
6. Evaluate the role of prompt engineering in enhancing diagnostic accuracy in healthcare AI applications.
7. Critically assess the challenges of scalability and generalization in prompt engineering across multilingual and multicultural contexts.
8. Design a prompt strategy for an AI tutor that adapts to different student learning styles in a virtual classroom.
9. Create a multi-step prompt for generating a blog post on climate change that includes tone control, audience targeting, and structure.
10. Propose a framework for integrating prompt engineering into human-in-the-loop (HITL) systems to ensure ethical and accurate AI outputs.

Answers

Part A
1. (c) 2. (c) 3. (c) 4. (c) 5. (c) 6. (c) 7. (c) 8. (b)

CHAPTER 7

Practical Session: Laboratory Work

Objectives

At the end of this chapter, you will be able to:
- Provide a comprehensive, hands-on explanation of the practical applications of AI
- Visualize AI subfields
- Analyze text with NLP tools
- Build image classifiers
- Simulate chatbots

7.1 Introduction

This chapter provides learners with experiential knowledge of artificial intelligence (AI) through a series of structured laboratory activities. The activities are designed to cover a wide range of AI applications, including natural language processing (NLP), image classification, chatbot simulation, and generative AI. Each section introduces a specific tool or technique, explains its relevance, and provides practical guidance. Upon completion, learners will not only understand how AI functions but also gain confidence in using AI tools for problem-solving, content creation, and data analysis.

7.2 Creating Mind Maps with Canva

Mind mapping is a powerful technique for visually organizing information, making complex ideas like AI easier to understand and remember. Canva, a user-friendly graphic design platform, offers intuitive tools for creating visually appealing mind maps, making it an excellent choice for students and educators.

AI is a vast and rapidly evolving field with many subfields. Learners can begin by creating a central node labelled *Artificial Intelligence* and then branch out to represent major subfields.

One primary branch is *Machine Learning* (ML), which focuses on algorithms that learn from data and improve their performance without explicit programming. This branch can be further broken down into *Supervised Learning*, where algorithms are trained on labelled data; *Unsupervised Learning*, which finds patterns in unlabelled data; and *Reinforcement Learning*, where an agent learns through a system of rewards and punishments.

Another major branch is *Natural Language Processing* (NLP), which deals with the interaction between computers and human language. This subfield includes both understanding language (*Natural Language Understanding*) and generating it (*Natural Language Generation*), powering applications like chatbots and translation services.

Finally, *Computer Vision* (CV) is another essential branch that enables computers to interpret visual information. This includes tasks like image classification, object detection, and image segmentation, which are used in applications from self-driving cars to medical imaging.

Canva's drag-and-drop functionality allows users to customize their mind map with icons and colours, reinforcing their understanding by associating concepts with images. For example, a robot icon can represent Robotics, while a speech bubble can symbolize NLP. The platform also supports collaboration, enabling students to work together, discuss ideas, and collectively refine their understanding.

Logging in to Canva is a straightforward process. If you do not already have an account, you will need to sign up first.

To sign up and log in:
1. Go to the Canva website.
2. Click on the Log in button at the top-right corner of the page.
3. You will be presented with a few options to log in or sign up:
   - Continue with Google: This is a quick and easy way to create and log in to your account using your Google account credentials.
   - Continue with Facebook: You can also use your Facebook account to sign up or log in.
   - Continue with email: If you prefer, you can sign up with an email address and create a password.
   - Continue another way: This option may offer other login methods like Apple, Microsoft, or a work email.

Once you have created an account, you can use the same method every time you want to log in.

The prompt given below is for creating an infographic or a mind map-style visual (Fig. 7.1):

"A clean, modern mind map infographic showing the subfields of artificial intelligence. The central node is 'Artificial Intelligence,' with three main branches: 'Machine Learning,' 'Natural Language Processing,' and 'Computer Vision.' Include sub-branches for Machine Learning: 'Supervised,' 'Unsupervised,' and 'Reinforcement Learning.' Use a minimalist design with a professional color palette of blue, white, and gray."

When using these prompts in Canva, you may want to use a feature like Magic Media or Magic Design. The output from Canva is shown in Fig. 7.2. These AI tools can convert your text descriptions into graphics, presentations, or even videos. Remember, the more specific you are, the better your results will be!

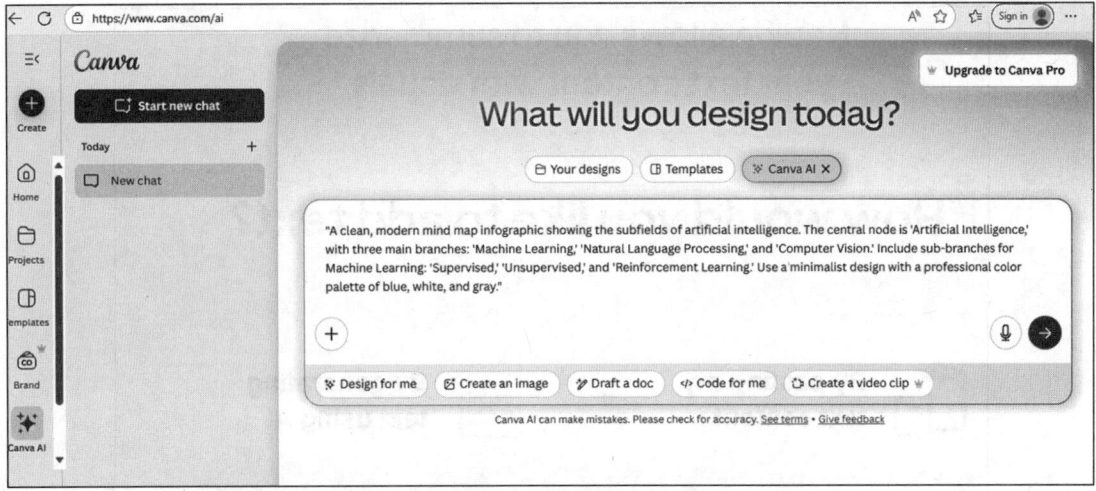

Figure 7.1   Prompt to design a mind map in Canva

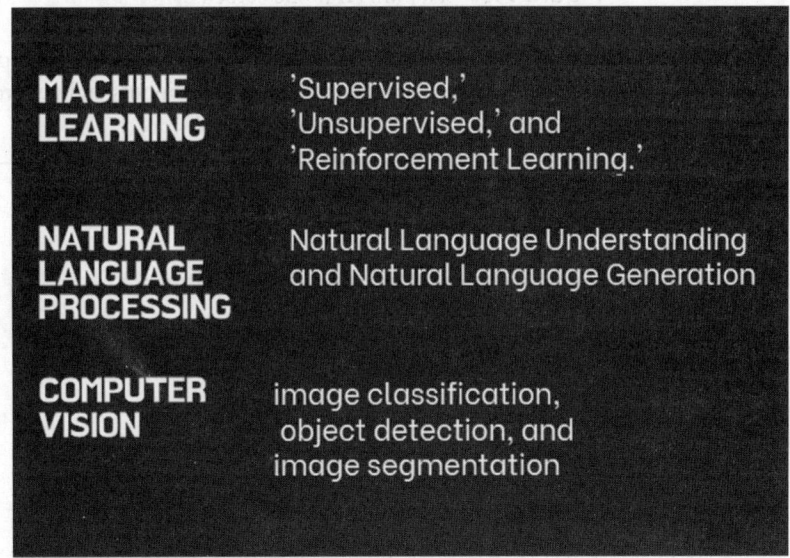

Figure 7.2   Canva output

7.3 Exploring Napkin AI for Concept Mapping

Napkin AI is an innovative tool (Fig. 7.3) that leverages AI to help users organize and connect ideas. Unlike traditional mind-mapping platforms, Napkin AI (www.app.napkin.ai) uses ML to suggest connections between concepts, making it especially useful for exploring complex topics like AI.

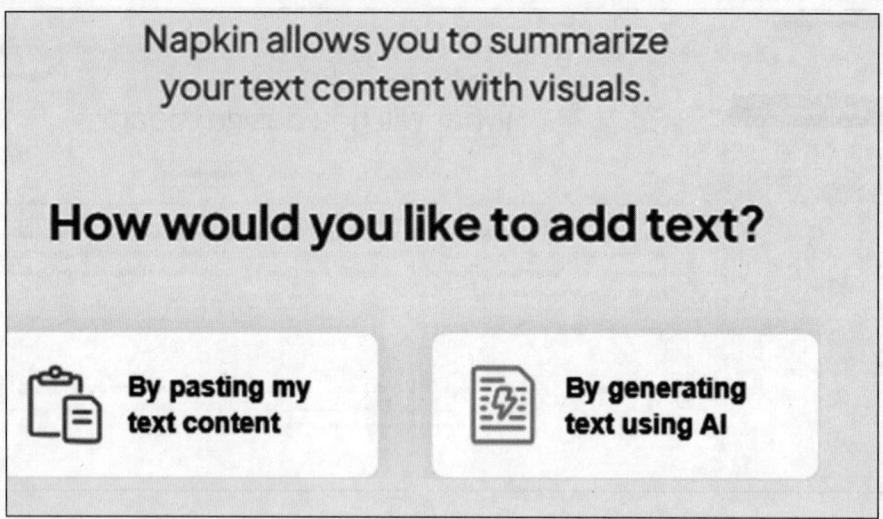

Figure 7.3   Napkin AI home screen

You can begin by clicking *By pasting my text content* and then entering the key terms related to AI, such as *Machine Learning* and *Neural Networks*. The platform then analyzes these inputs and generates a dynamic concept map showing how the ideas are linked (Fig. 7.4).

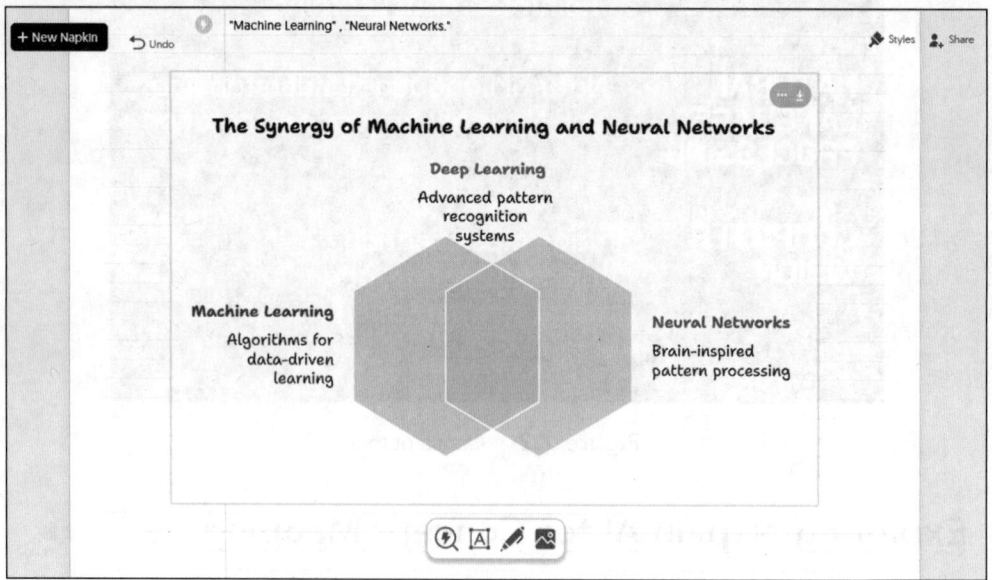

Figure 7.4   Napkin AI output screen

Entering *Natural Language Processing* might reveal connections to *Chatbots* and *Text Summarization*. These suggestions are based on patterns in large data sets, offering new insights into how AI subfields interact in real-world applications.

Napkin AI's ability to adapt as more terms are added allows learners to start with a basic map and gradually expand it. The tool also allows users to annotate connections, add notes, and customize the layout.

In a university-level AI course in Chennai, students used Napkin AI to map out the ethical implications of AI. By entering terms like *Bias*, *Privacy*, and *Transparency*, the tool generated a network of related concepts, including *Algorithmic Fairness* and *Data Protection*. This helped students understand the broader context of AI ethics and encouraged critical thinking about the societal impact of AI systems. Napkin AI transforms concept mapping into an intelligent, interactive experience, empowering learners to explore AI in a way that is both structured and exploratory.

7.4 Text Analysis Using NLP Tools

NLP is an AI subfield that focuses on the interaction between computers and human language. It enables machines to read, understand, interpret, and generate human language in a meaningful way. From voice assistants and translation apps to spam filters and chatbots, NLP drives many technologies we use daily.

At its core, NLP involves tasks like tokenization, part-of-speech tagging, named entity recognition, and sentiment analysis. These processes allow computers to break down and analyze text, identify the roles of words, recognize important entities, and even determine the emotional tone of a message. The complexity of human language, with its nuances and contextual meanings, makes NLP a challenging yet fascinating area of study.

With the sheer volume of text data generated every second, the ability to analyze and extract insights from text is invaluable. NLP tools automate this process, enabling quick and accurate analysis of large data sets. This has significant implications for fields such as marketing, healthcare, education, and law. In education, for example, NLP can assess student writing, while in business, it can power chatbots and analyze customer feedback.

In this section, we will explore two powerful NLP tools: Voyant Tools and Google AI Studio. These platforms offer user-friendly interfaces that allow learners to perform text analysis without needing advanced programming skills.

7.4.1 Using Voyant Tools for Text Mining

Voyant Tools (Voyant-Tools.org)is a web-based application for text analysis and visualization, popular in academic and educational settings due to its accessibility. It allows users to upload text documents and instantly generate visualizations and statistics that reveal data patterns, including word frequency counts, word clouds, and trend graphs.

Type the whole of Section 7.4 in Voyant AI, as shown in Fig. 7.5. By clicking the Reveal button, we obtain the output (Fig. 7.6).

The platform presents a dashboard with panels offering different perspectives on the data. For instance, the Cirrus panel displays a word cloud where word size corresponds to its frequency, offering a quick overview of common themes. The Trends panel shows how a word's frequency changes over the course of a document, which can be useful for identifying shifts in topic or tone.

A key feature of Voyant is its ability to explore keywords in context, allowing users to see how a word is used in different parts of the text. This is crucial for accurate interpretation.

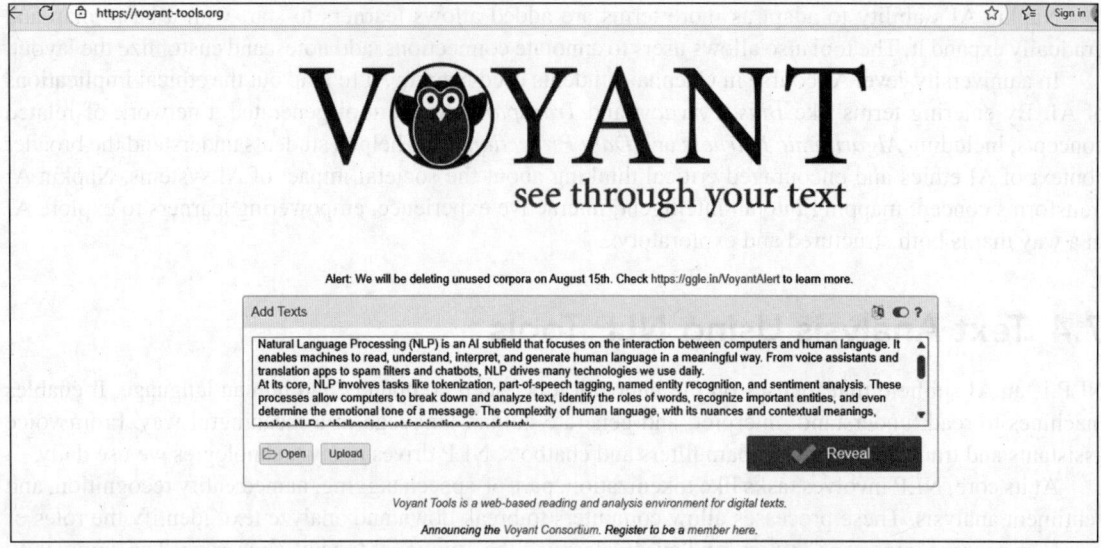

Figure 7.5   Voyant home screen to add text

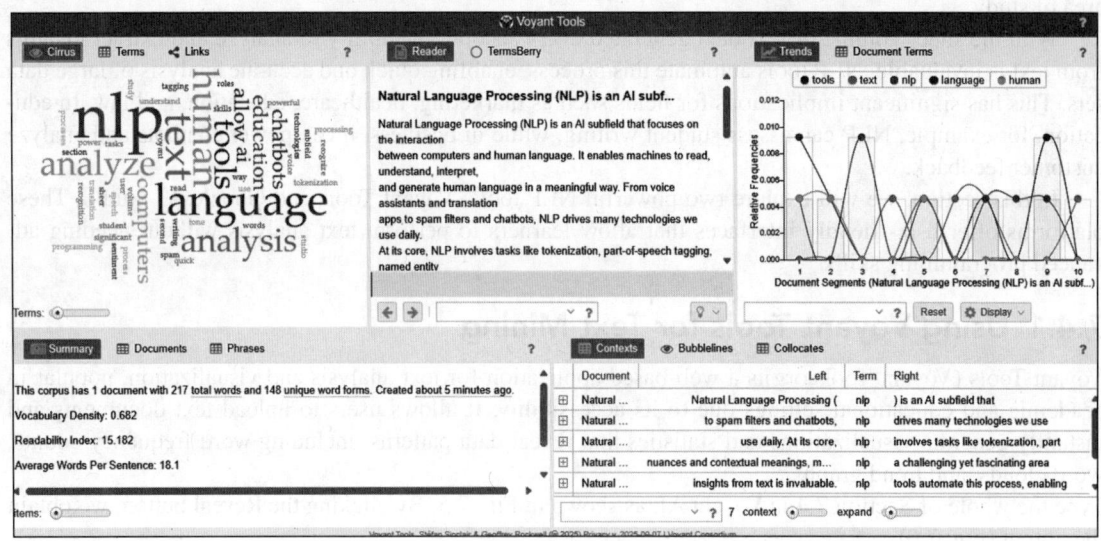

Figure 7.6   Voyant Text Analyser output

7.4.2 Using Google AI Studio for Text Analysis

Google AI Studio is a more advanced platform offering a suite of tools for building and deploying ML models, including those for NLP. While more complex than Voyant, it provides greater flexibility and power. To use Google AI Studio for text analysis, learners typically import a data set, like customer reviews or news articles. The platform provides pre-built models for common NLP tasks, such as sentiment analysis and entity recognition, that can be applied to the data with minimal setup. For example, a sentiment analysis model can classify text as positive, negative, or neutral, providing insights into public opinion.

Google AI Studio, now part of Google's broader AI development platform, is a powerful and user-friendly tool for experimenting with and prototyping text analysis tasks. It allows you to leverage large language models like the Gemini family without writing any code. The process revolves around crafting effective prompts to guide the model's behaviour. Here is a step-by-step guide on how to use Google AI Studio for text analysis:

Access Google AI Studio
- Go to the Google AI Studio website (https://aistudio.google.com)
- Sign in with your Google account. You will need to agree to the terms of service.

Upon entering, you will find a playground or editor where you can start a new prompt. There are typically three main types: Freeform, Structured, and Chat. For text analysis, the Freeform and Structured prompt options are the most effective.

Crafting the Prompt for Your Task
The key to successful text analysis in Google AI Studio is the quality of your prompt. You need to give the model a clear and concise instruction.

Example 1: Sentiment Analysis
To analyze the sentiment of a text, you can use a few-shot prompting approach, which provides the model with a few examples of input-output pairs to guide its behaviour (Fig. 7.7).

- **Prompt Type:** Structured
- **Prompt:**
  - **Instruction:** "Analyze the following sentence and classify its sentiment as either 'Positive,' 'Negative,' or 'Neutral'."
  - **Input 1:** "I love this product; it's the best I've ever used."
  - **Output 1:** "Positive"

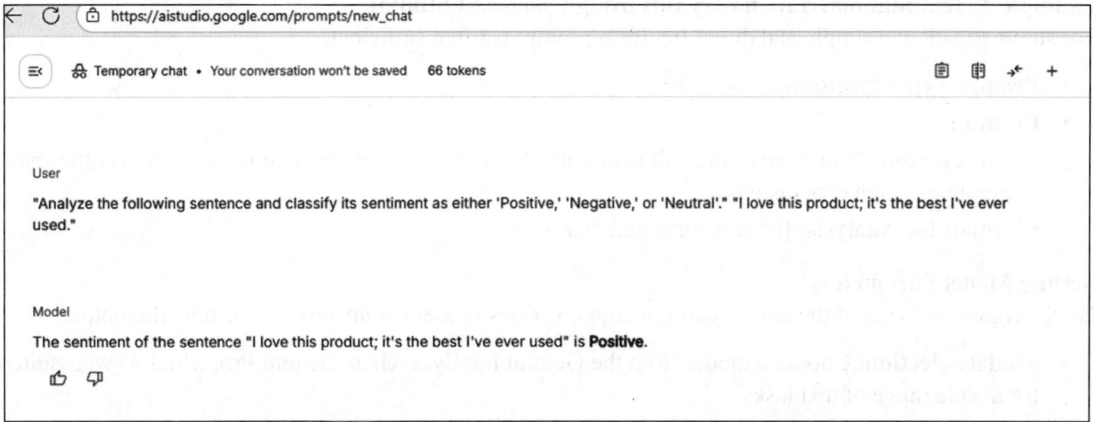

Figure 7.7 Sentiment analysis using Google AI Studio

- **Input 2:** "The service was slow, and I was very disappointed."
- **Output 2:** "Negative"
- **Input 3:** "The movie was okay, but the ending was confusing."

- Output 3: "Neutral"
- Input for Analysis: [Paste your text here]

Example 2: Entity Extraction

To extract specific information, such as names, dates, or locations from a document, you can again use a structured prompt (Fig. 7.8).

- **Prompt Type:** Structured
- **Prompt:**
  - **Instruction:** "Extract the person's name and their city from the following sentences, and format the output as a JSON object."
  - **Input 1:** "John Smith, who lives in London, is a software engineer."
  - **Output 1:** {"name": "John Smith", "city": "London"}

```
Model

<> JSON

{
  "name": "John Smith",
  "city": "London"
}
```

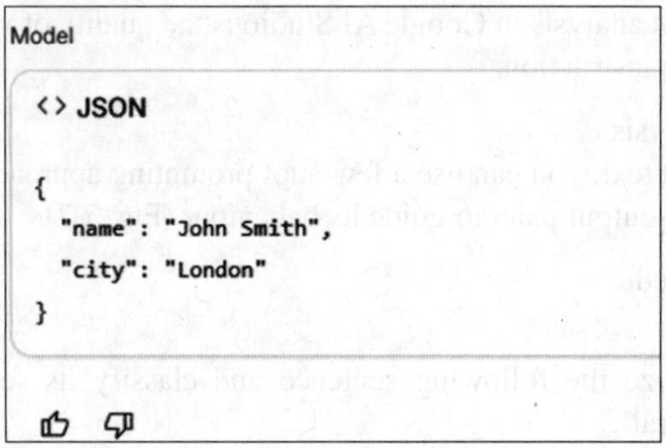

Figure 7.8 Entity extraction using Google AI Studio

Example 3: Text Summarization (Try this using Google AI Studio)

For summarization, a simple and direct freeform prompt is often sufficient.

- **Prompt Type:** Freeform
- **Prompt:**
  - **Instruction:** "Summarize the following article in three key bullet points, focusing on the main arguments and conclusions."
  - **Input for Analysis:** [Paste your article here]

Setting Model Parameters

On the right-hand-side of the editor, you can adjust various model parameters to fine-tune the output:

- **Model Selection:** Choose a model from the Gemini family, such as Gemini Pro, which is well-suited for a wide range of text tasks.
- **Temperature:** This controls the creativity and randomness of the output. For text analysis tasks that require accuracy, such as sentiment analysis or entity extraction, a lower temperature (closer to 0) is recommended. For creative tasks, a higher temperature is more suitable.
- **Top-K and Top-P:** These settings offer more advanced control over the model's output diversity. For most basic text analysis tasks, you can leave these at their default settings.

Running and Exporting
- **Run:** Click the Run button to send your prompt and text to the model. The output will appear on the right side of the screen.
- **Get Code:** Once you are satisfied with the results, you can click the Get code button to generate code for your prompt in several programming languages (Python, Node.js, etc.). This allows you to integrate your text analysis prototype directly into a larger application.

By following these steps, you can use Google AI Studio as a powerful and intuitive tool for a variety of text analysis tasks, from quick summarizations to more complex sentiment and entity extraction.

A key advantage of Google AI Studio is its integration with other Google services, which allows users to handle large data sets efficiently. The platform also supports custom model training, where users can define their own labels and train a model to recognize specific patterns in the text. This is particularly useful for specialized applications.

A marketing firm analyzed thousands of customer reviews for a new product, using sentiment analysis and keyword extraction to identify common complaints and praised features. This information was used to improve the product and tailor marketing messages.

While Google AI Studio has a steeper learning curve, it offers a comprehensive and customizable approach to NLP. It is ideal for learners ready to move beyond basic analysis and explore the full potential of AI in language processing. By working with real data sets and models, learners gain valuable experience that prepares them for more advanced AI projects.

7.5 Building an Image Classifier

Image classification is a fundamental task in computer vision, a subfield of AI that teaches computers to interpret and understand visual information. This process involves training a machine to recognize and categorize images based on their content, much like how humans identify objects. The goal is to achieve this with high accuracy and speed.

The process begins with a data set of labelled images. Each image is assigned a specific category (e.g., "dog," "cat," "flower"). An ML model is then trained on this data, learning to associate visual patterns with the correct labels. During training, the model adjusts its internal parameters to minimize errors. Once trained, it can classify new, unseen images by analyzing their features and comparing them to its learned knowledge.

One of the main challenges in image classification is handling variations in lighting, angle, and background. A robust model must learn to recognize the essential features of an object despite these variations, which requires a diverse data set.

Image classification has numerous real-world applications. In healthcare, it is used to analyze X-rays and MRIs for disease detection. In agriculture, it helps identify crop diseases. In security, it powers facial recognition systems. For learners, building a basic image classifier provides a practical introduction to ML and CV. In the next section, we will use Google Teachable Machine to build a simple classifier without any coding.

7.5.1 Using Google Teachable Machine

Google Teachable Machine (https://teachablemachine.withgoogle.com) is an intuitive, web-based tool that makes AI accessible to everyone. It allows users to create ML models for image, sound, and pose classification without writing any code.

To build an image classifier, select the image project option and create different classes, or categories, for the model to learn. For example, you might create classes for "Cat" and "Dog" Next, upload or capture images for each class. Teachable Machine recommends using at least 50 images per class for effective training (Fig. 7.9).

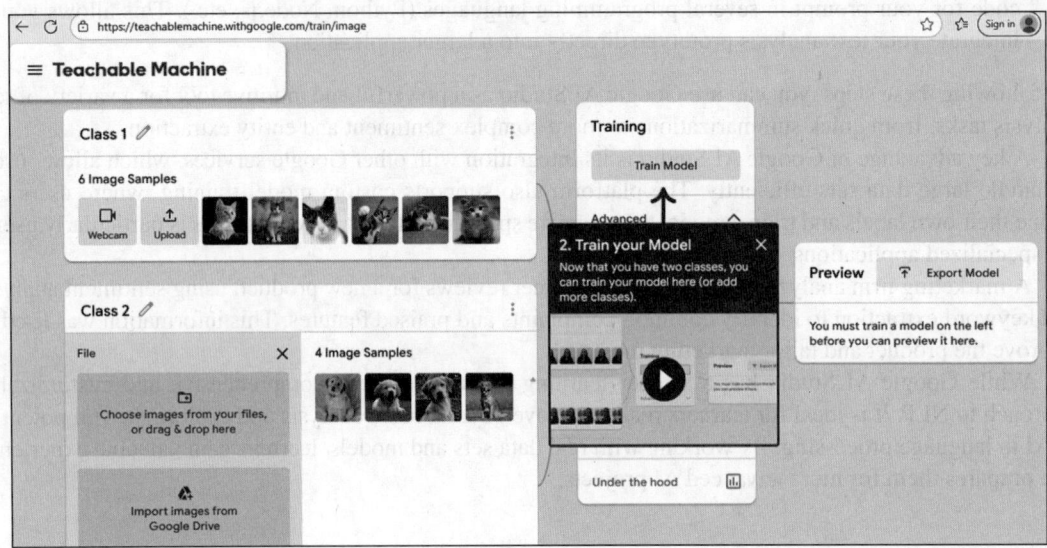

Figure 7.9 Image classifier using Google Teachable Machine

Once the images are uploaded, simply click the Train Model button. The platform uses a pre-configured neural network to analyze the images and learn the distinguishing features of each class. After a few minutes of training, you can test the model with new images (dog picture in our case) to see if it correctly identifies the objects. It identified it as Class 2 (Fig. 7.10).

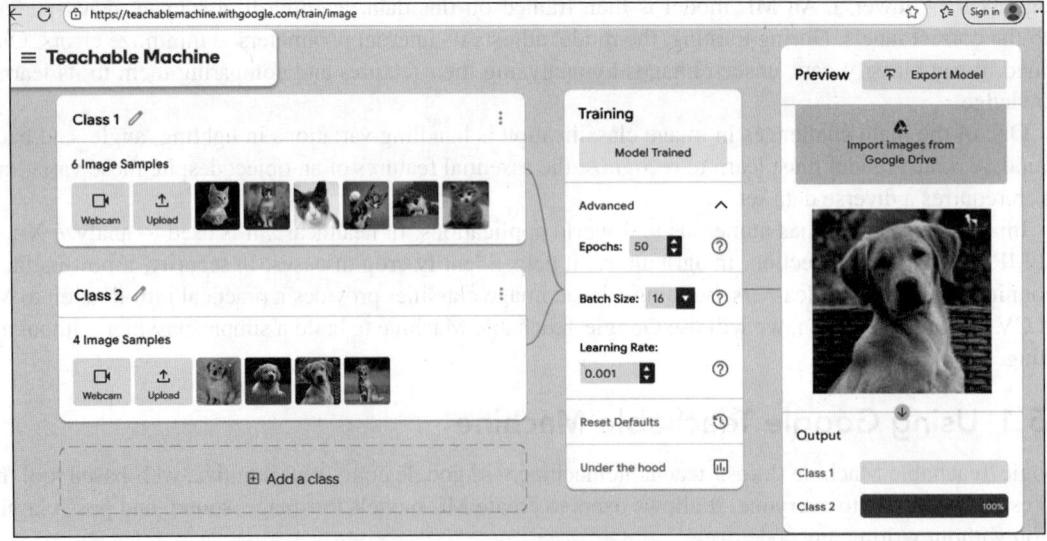

Figure 7.10 Image classifier using Google Teachable Machine (output as Class 2)

A standout feature is the ability to export models for use in websites and apps, making it easy to integrate the classifier into other projects.

A case study from a middle school in Pune highlights the educational impact of Teachable Machine. Students built a classifier to distinguish between recyclable and non-recyclable waste. The project not only taught them about AI but also raised awareness about environmental issues. The tool's simplicity allowed them to focus on the learning experience rather than technical details.

Teachable Machine empowers learners to experiment with AI in an engaging, hands-on way, removing the barriers of coding and complex algorithms. By building their own models, students gain a deeper understanding of how machines learn and how AI can be applied to solve real-world problems.

7.6 Simulating AI Chatbots in Education

Jotform is primarily known as a powerful form-building tool, but its AI features, particularly the AI Chatbot Builder and AI Agents, can be leveraged to create educational chatbots (Fig. 7.11).

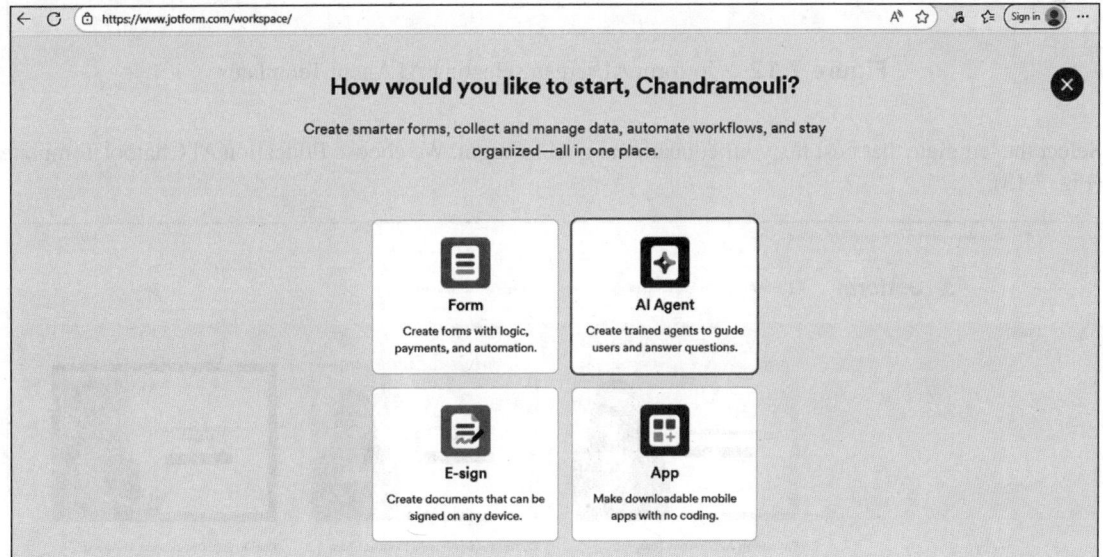

Figure 7.11   Jotform AI screen 1

To create an agentic educational chatbot using Jotform AI, you can start with a pre-built template to quickly get your bot up and running. The process does not require any coding (Fig. 7.12).

Step 1: Choose an Educational Template
First, you will need to go to Jotform's AI agent templates. Jotform provides a range of educational templates designed for various purposes. Some examples include:

- **Education AI Chatbot Template**: Helps with student inquiries and collecting feedback.
- **Quiz Manager AI Agent**: Offers interactive quizzes and collects data.
- **Homework Assistant AI Chatbot**: Provides conversational support for students.
- **Language Learning AI Chatbot**: Enhances language skills through interactive conversations.
- **Tutor Appointment AI Agent**: Simplifies scheduling tutoring sessions.

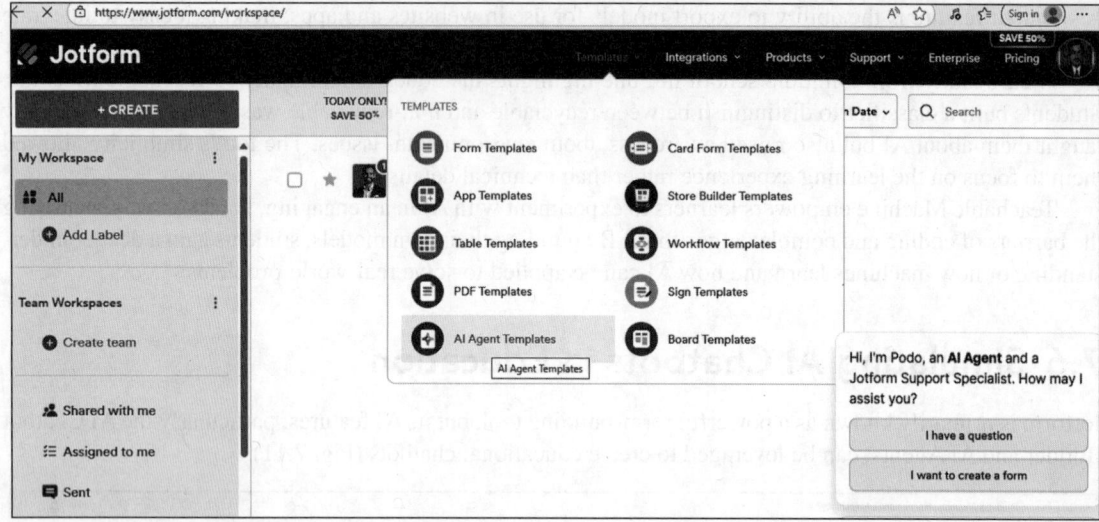

Figure 7.12 Jotform AI screen selecting AI Agent Templates

Select the template that best fits your educational goal to begin. We choose Education AI Chatbot Template (Fig. 7.13).

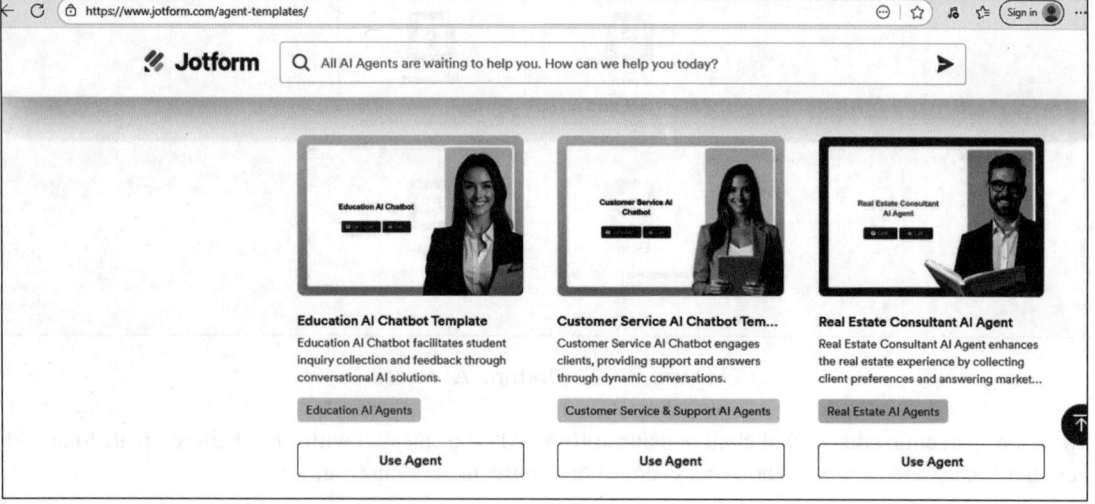

Figure 7.13 Jotform AI screen selecting the Education AI Chatbot Template

Step 2: Customize the Chatbot's Persona and Design
Once you have chosen a template, you can customize the chatbot to match your needs. This involves:

- **Naming the agent**: Give your chatbot a unique and relevant name, like "History Helper" or "BioBot."
- **Designing the avatar**: Upload a custom avatar or choose from the options provided.
- **Defining the persona**: Set the tone and style of the chatbot. For an educational bot, you will want it to be patient, encouraging, and knowledgeable. You can adjust the "prompt" to give it specific instructions on how to interact with students.

Step 3: Train the Agent with a Knowledge Base
The agent's ability to provide accurate and helpful information comes from its knowledge base (Fig. 7.14).

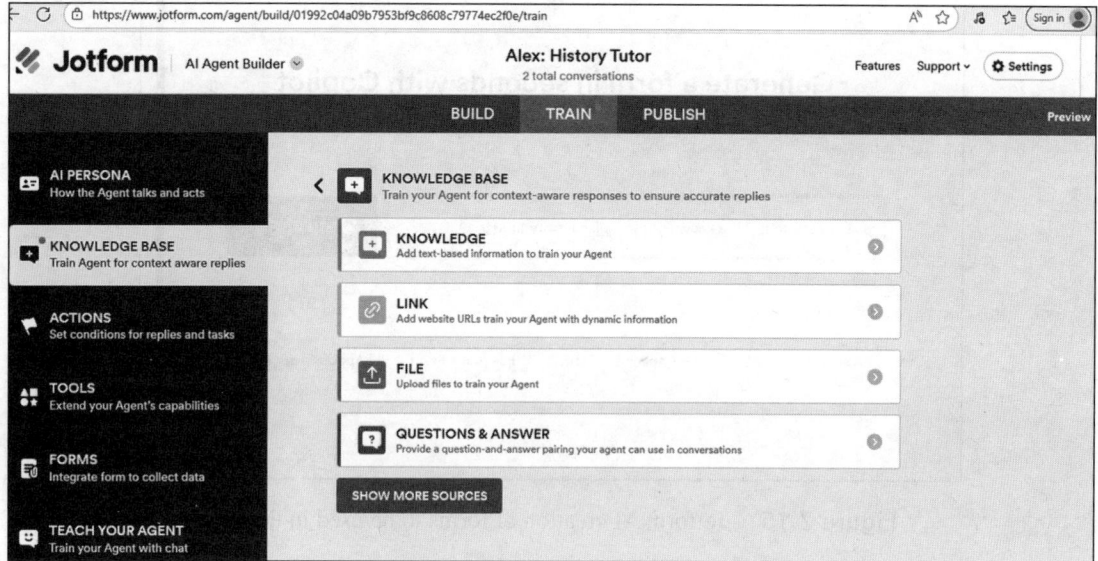

Figure 7.14   Jotform AI Knowledge Base

You can train the chatbot with your own educational content in several ways:

- **Upload Files**: You can upload documents like PDFs, lesson plans, or course materials. The AI will learn from this content to answer student questions.
- **Add URLs**: Provide links to relevant websites, such as a school's public website, Wikipedia pages (with caution), or other online educational resources.
- **Create Q&A Pairs**: For very specific or frequently asked questions, you can manually enter a list of questions and their correct answers. This is a great way to ensure the chatbot gives precise responses to common queries.

Step 4: Configure Actions and Logic (Agentic Features)
This is where you make the chatbot 'agentic', allowing it to perform actions beyond just answering questions.

Integrate with Forms: You can connect the chatbot to a Jotform form (Fig. 7.15). For example, if a student wants to schedule a tutoring session, the chatbot can initiate a conversation that collects the necessary information and automatically submits it to a form.

Step 5: Test, Publish, and Share
After training and configuring your chatbot, you should test it thoroughly (Fig. 7.16) to ensure it is working as intended. Once you are satisfied with its performance, you can deploy it. Jotform provides various options for this:

- **Embed on a Website**: Generate an embed code to place the chatbot directly on your website or learning management system.
- **Share via Link**: Share a direct link to the chatbot.
- **QR Code**: Create a QR code that students can scan for quick access on their mobile devices.

230 | Fundamentals of Artificial Intelligence

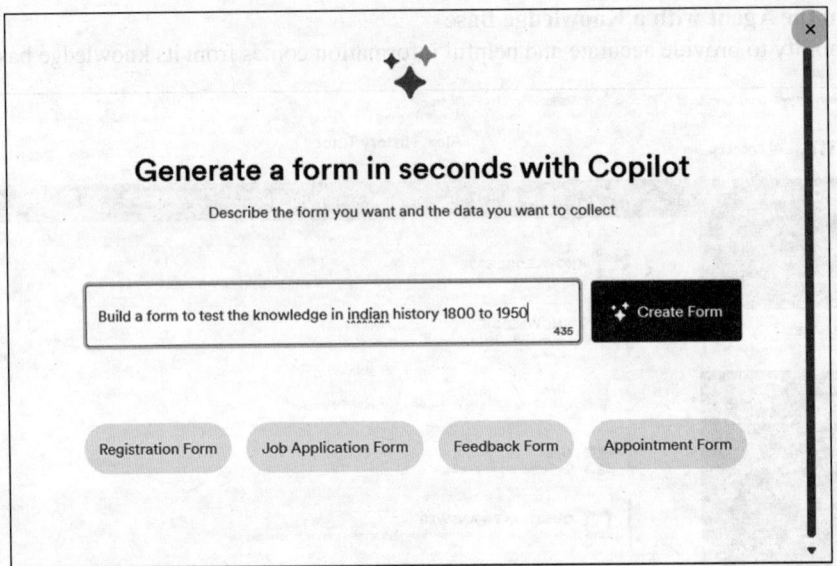

Figure 7.15 Jotform AI creation of forms to be used in the chat

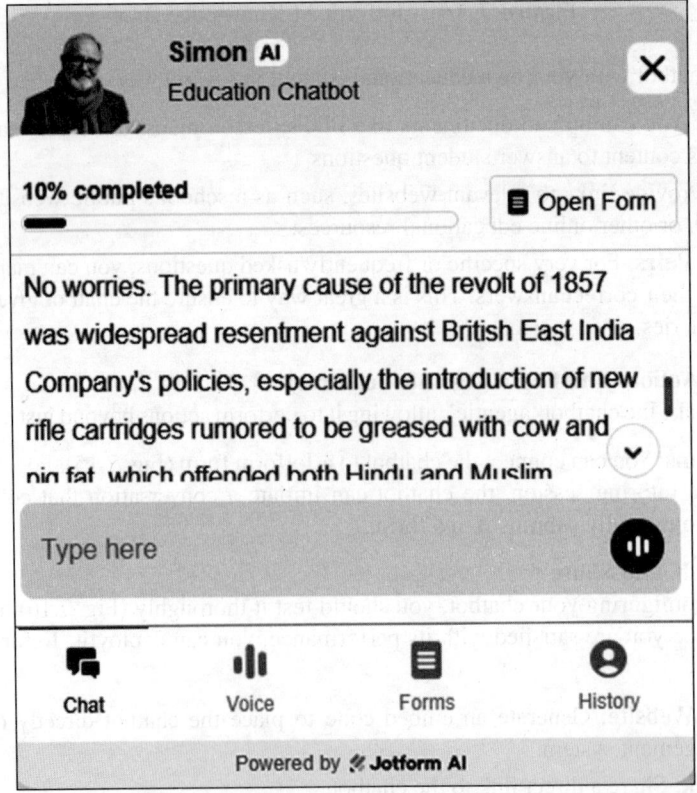

Figure 7.16 Jotform AI chat testing

In a classroom simulation, students created a chatbot to help peers revise for biology exams. It offered flashcards, quizzes, and explanations of key concepts while tracking user progress. This project showed how AI can support self-paced learning and academic independence. Simulating an educational chatbot encourages learners to think critically about user experience, content accuracy, and ethical considerations like data privacy. By building and testing their own chatbots, students gain hands-on experience in AI development and understand its transformative potential in education.

7.7 ChatGPT for Text Generation

Generative AI represents a significant advancement in AI, enabling machines to produce original content. ChatGPT, a language model by OpenAI, is a prominent tool in this field, capable of generating human-like text from user prompts. Its capabilities have opened up new possibilities in various domains, from education to content creation.

ChatGPT has been trained on a massive data set, which allows it to generate coherent responses. For instance, a prompt to "write a story about climate change" can yield a detailed narrative with characters and plot development (Fig. 7.17). This makes it an ideal tool for practicing creative writing, summarization, and documentation.

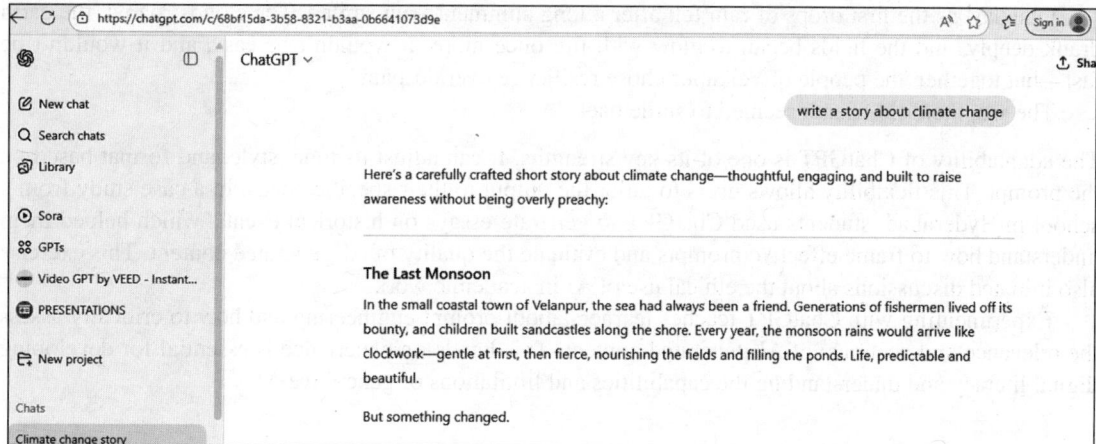

Figure 7.17 ChatGPT for text creation

Here's a carefully crafted short story about climate change—thoughtful, engaging, and built to raise awareness without being overly preachy:

The Last Monsoon

"In the small coastal town of Velanpur, the sea had always been a friend. Generations of fishermen lived off its bounty, and children built sandcastles along the shore. Every year, the monsoon rains would arrive like clockwork—gentle at first, then fierce, nourishing the fields and filling the ponds. Life, predictable and beautiful.

But something changed.

It started subtly. The rains arrived late one year, early the next. Some years, the skies stayed dry even after the clouds gathered thick over the horizon. The fishermen cast their nets but found only emptiness. The fields cracked under the relentless sun, and farmers stared helplessly at their parched crops.

Among them was Arun, a young man who had inherited both the sea and the soil from his father. He remembered how, as a child, he would sit on the beach and watch the waves dance at dawn, and how the smell of wet earth after the first rain would fill his senses. But now the sea seemed restless, creeping closer with each storm surge, and the air carried the bitterness of salt and smoke.

Worried, Arun joined a group of villagers meeting under the banyan tree. Scientists from the city had come with maps and charts, explaining how rising temperatures, melting ice caps, and unchecked pollution were shifting weather patterns. The elders listened quietly, some with furrowed brows, others with disbelief.

"It's not just a story," the scientist urged. "The sea is rising. Our homes, our livelihoods, are at risk."

Arun felt a surge of anger—not at the scientists, but at the waste and carelessness he had watched in nearby cities. Plastic washed ashore with every tide, oil slicks marred the once-clear waters, and smoke from factories blurred the horizon.

That evening, as the sun dipped below the gray sea, Arun stood with his friends and made a promise. They would no longer wait for outside help. They cleaned the beach every week, planted trees along the dunes to hold the sand, and started rainwater harvesting systems in their homes. They spoke to schools, teaching children how small changes could matter—reducing waste, conserving water, and respecting the earth.

Months passed. The sea still threatened, the skies remained unpredictable—but something had shifted. Hope was returning.

One day, as the first drops of rain fell after a long summer, Arun smiled. The clouds roared, the earth drank deeply, and the fields began to glow with life once more. It wouldn't be easy, and it wouldn't be fast—but together, the people of Velanpur chose resilience over despair.

The sea, their old friend, seemed to smile back."

The adaptability of ChatGPT is one of its key strengths. It can adjust its tone, style, and format based on the prompt. This flexibility allows users to tailor the output to their specific needs. In a case study from a school in Hyderabad, students used ChatGPT to generate essays on historical events, which helped them understand how to frame effective prompts and evaluate the quality of AI-generated content. This exercise also initiated discussions about the ethical use of AI in academic work.

Experimenting with ChatGPT teaches learners about prompt engineering and how to critically assess the relevance and accuracy of AI-generated content. This hands-on experience is essential for developing digital literacy and understanding the capabilities and limitations of generative AI.

7.8 Hugging Face for Model Deployment

Hugging Face is a leading platform for ML, offering pre-trained models and tools for deploying AI applications. It is well-known for its Transformers library, which includes models for text classification, translation, and summarization. For learners interested in generative AI, Hugging Face provides an accessible way to explore and deploy models without requiring extensive programming skills.

Through the interactive "Model Hub," students can experiment with models like GPT-2, BERT, and T5. For example, a summarization model can be used to condense a long article into key points.

A key feature of Hugging Face is its support for custom model deployment. Users can fine-tune existing models on their own data sets and deploy them via the Hugging Face API. In a lab setting, students can simulate this process, gaining a deeper understanding of how generative models work and how they can be adapted for specific tasks. A university AI course in Chennai used Hugging Face to build a sentiment analysis tool for movie reviews, which provided students with a comprehensive introduction to AI deployment.

Hugging Face empowers learners to move beyond passive interaction with AI and into the realm of model customization and deployment, preparing them for more advanced AI projects.

7.9 DALL·E for Image and Video Generation

DALL·E, a generative AI model by OpenAI, creates images from textual descriptions. This represents a significant advancement in the intersection of language and vision, allowing users to generate visual content simply by describing what they want to see. We can use bing AI to use DALL-E Model for image generation. For example, a prompt like "a futuristic cityscape at sunset" can result in a detailed, original image (Fig. 7.18).

Figure 7.18   Bing DALL-E3 output

A prompt like "Fundamentals of AI" can be given to generate a video (Fig. 7.19).

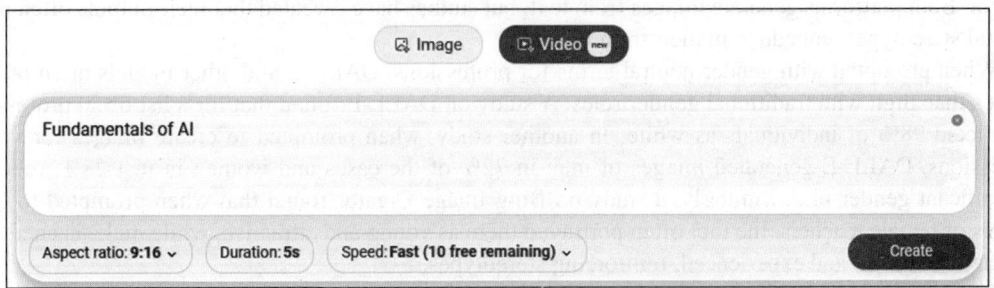

Figure 7.19   Bing video creation

This capability has profound implications for art, design, and education. When learners use DALL·E, they engage with a system that translates the semantics of language into visual elements. The model has been trained on millions of image-text pairs, enabling it to associate words with visual features. This means that even abstract or imaginative prompts can result in coherent and visually appealing images.

One of the most engaging aspects of DALL·E is its ability to generate variations of the same prompt. Users can refine their descriptions to influence the output, which encourages experimentation with language. A case study from a design school in Mumbai showed how students used DALL·E to generate concept art for a video game, demonstrating how AI can support the creative process and expand the boundaries of visual storytelling.

Experimenting with DALL·E introduces learners to the concept of multimodal AI, where different types of data—text and images—are integrated. It also raises important questions about originality, authorship, and the ethical use of AI-generated content. By engaging with DALL·E, students develop a nuanced understanding of generative AI and its role in shaping the future of digital media.

7.10 Observing Bias in Generative Models

Bias in AI is a critical issue that occurs when an AI system produces results that are systematically prejudiced due to flaws in its training data or algorithms. These biases can manifest in various forms, including racial, gender, cultural, and socioeconomic disparities, affecting the fairness and ethical implications of AI applications.

AI bias often originates from the training data. If a data set lacks diversity or reflects historical inequalities, the model may learn and replicate those biases. For example, an image recognition system trained on a data set predominantly featuring light-skinned faces may perform poorly on darker-skinned faces. Research has found that some AI-powered image generators have a 34% greater error rate for darker-skinned females compared to light-skinned females. Similarly, language models trained on internet text can inadvertently perpetuate stereotypes. In some cases, AI image generators have been found to overrepresent white individuals, with one study on the Stable Diffusion model finding that 47% of images generated from a neutral prompt ("a photo of a person") were white, while only 3% were Asian and 5% were Indian.

Other sources of bias include algorithmic design and the evaluation process. If an algorithm is not designed to account for diverse user groups, it may fail to serve all users equitably. The real-world impact of AI bias can be profound, leading to misdiagnoses in healthcare, unfair hiring decisions, or inaccurate identification in law enforcement. These issues underscore the need for a critical approach to AI, recognizing that technology is not neutral.

To illustrate how bias can influence generative models, we can examine DALL·E and Bing Image Creator. Both platforms generate images from text, but studies have revealed that their outputs often reflect societal stereotypes embedded in their training data.

When prompted with gender-neutral terms for professions, DALL-E and other models often produce images that align with traditional gender roles. A study on DALL-E found that for a list of 50 professions, it depicted 98% of individuals as white. In another study, when prompted to create images for various professions, DALL-E generated images of men in 72% of the cases and women in just 28%, reflecting a significant gender bias. Similarly, a study on Bing Image Creator found that when prompted to create images of female teachers, the tool often portrayed them as young and attractive, while male teachers were depicted as mature and experienced, reinforcing stereotypes.

Racial biases are also present. A study on a Chinese AI-powered image generator found that white people were more accurately depicted than people of colour. In cases of incorrect racial generation, the model most often depicted people of colour as white. Another study found that 95% of images generated for the prompt "playing basketball" predominantly featured African American men, highlighting the perpetuation of racial stereotypes.

These examples underscore the importance of critical engagement with generative AI. While these tools offer creative possibilities, they also reflect the prejudices and limitations of their training data. Educators should encourage students to question the outputs, experiment with diverse prompts, and consider the broader implications of AI-generated content.

7.11 Practising Prompt Engineering

Prompt engineering is the practice of crafting effective inputs to guide the behaviour of generative AI models. This skill is vital for anyone who wants to get the most out of AI, whether it is for school, work, or creative projects.

7.11.1 Summarization Techniques

Summarization is one of the most practical applications of prompt engineering. The goal is to condense large amounts of text into a clear, concise summary while preserving the original meaning (Fig. 7.20).

A good prompt for summarization must clearly instruct the AI to identify main ideas and eliminate unnecessary details. For example, a prompt like, "Summarize the following article in three sentences," gives the AI a specific boundary to work within.

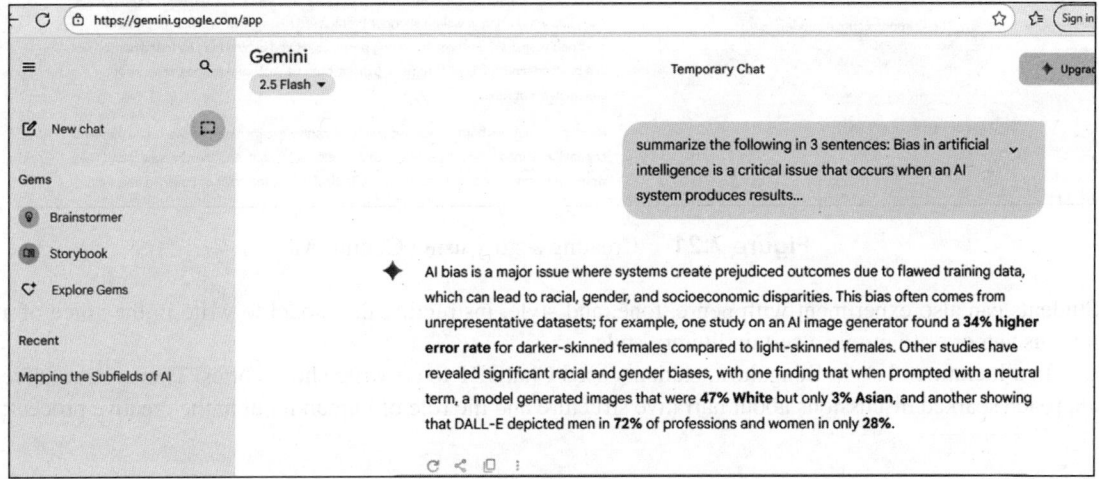

Figure 7.20 Summarization using Gemini AI

Most modern AI models can perform both extractive summarization (pulling key sentences directly from the text) and abstractive summarization (paraphrasing the content to create a new summary). The latter is often more challenging but can produce more natural-sounding results.

In a classroom experiment in Delhi, students were given lengthy articles and asked to create prompts for ChatGPT. They discovered that the quality of the summary depended on the specificity of the prompt. This exercise teaches learners to think critically about what information is essential and how to phrase their prompts effectively.

7.12 Creative Writing with Prompts

Generative AI models like ChatGPT can produce imaginative stories, poems, and scripts. The quality and originality of the output, however, depend on how the prompt is framed. A vague prompt will likely result in generic content, while a detailed, evocative prompt can inspire rich and engaging narratives.

When writing creatively with AI, it is helpful to include the elements of a story, such as character, setting, plot, conflict, and resolution. For example, the prompt, "Write a short story about a time-traveling scientist who discovers a hidden civilization in the future," provides a clear premise for the AI to build upon (Fig. 7.21).

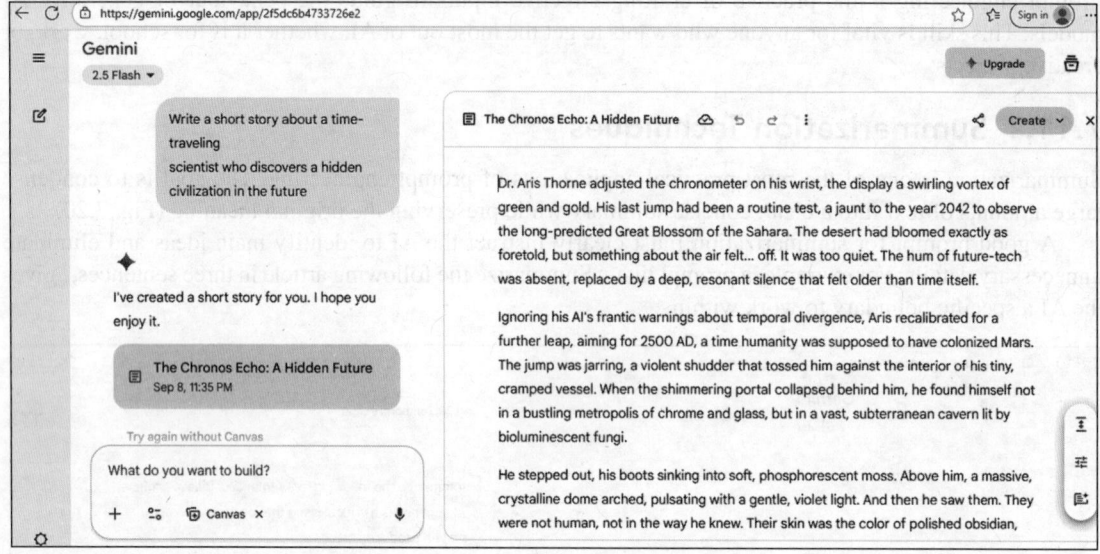

Figure 7.21 Creating a story using Gemini AI

Students can also experiment with genre, tone, and style, instructing the model to write in the voice of a famous author or to mimic a certain literary style.

In a literature class in Bengaluru, students used ChatGPT to co-write short stories. This collaborative approach sparked discussions about narrative structure and the role of human input in the creative process.

7.13 Content Generation Strategies

Content generation is a broad application of prompt engineering that includes writing articles, blog posts, and marketing materials. The goal is to produce informative and engaging content that meets specific objectives.

Effective content generation requires a clear understanding of the audience and purpose. A prompt should specify the topic, length, tone, and format. For example, "Write a 300-word blog post on the benefits of online learning for high school students" provides detailed guidance that helps the AI tailor its response. To avoid generic or formulaic content, learners should add specific constraints, such as, "Include three real-world examples and a call to action at the end."

A marketing workshop in Chennai highlighted the importance of prompt clarity. Participants used ChatGPT to generate product descriptions and social media posts, experimenting with different tones. The exercise showed that iterating on prompts is key to achieving desired results.

Ultimately, prompt engineering for content generation also raises questions about authorship and ethics. It's crucial for learners to be taught how to verify facts and ensure the content aligns with ethical standards. By mastering these strategies, students and professionals can enhance their communication skills and create high-quality content efficiently.

7.14 Using SlidesGPT for Slide Generation

Creating presentations can be time-consuming, especially for those without design expertise. SlidesGPT, a tool that uses generative AI, automates the process of creating slide decks from textual input, making it faster and more accessible.

SlidesGPT analyzes a user's prompt (e.g., "The Impact of Climate Change on Agriculture") and generates a structured presentation with titles, bullet points, and even suggested visuals (Fig. 7.22).

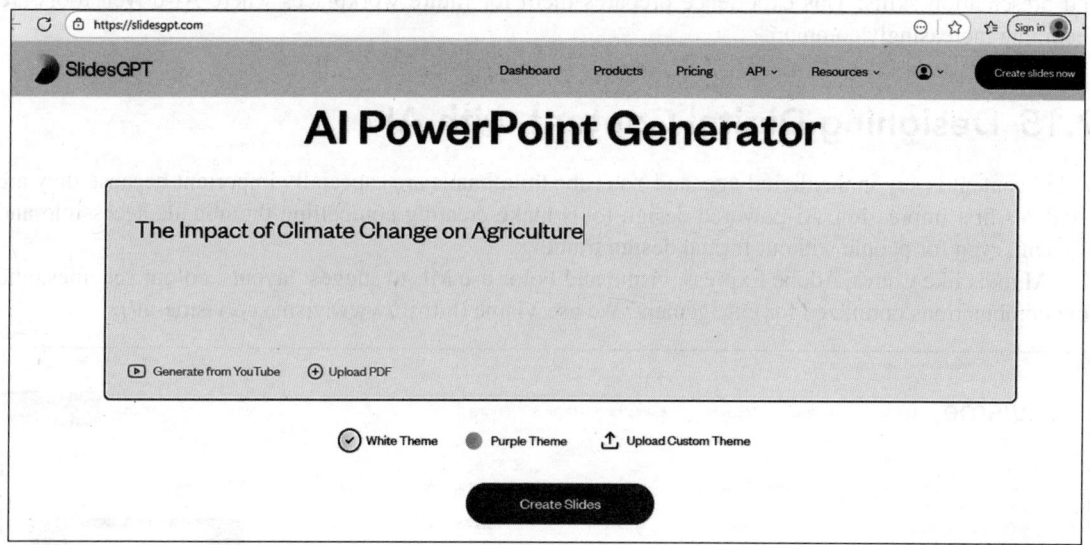

Figure 7.22 SlidesGPT AI Powerpoint Generator

The tool ensures the content is logically organized (Fig. 7.23) and relevant, reducing the need for manual research and formatting.

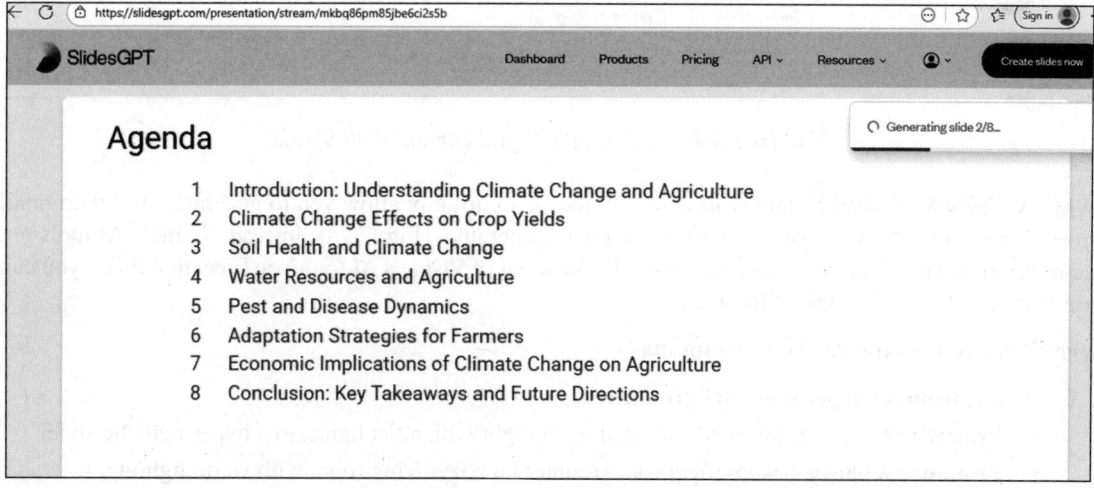

Figure 7.23 SlidesGPT AI Powerpoint Generator Agenda

It also maintains a consistent tone and style throughout the presentation, which is crucial for professional and academic settings.

A case study from a business school in Coimbatore shows the practical application of SlidesGPT. Students used the tool to generate foundational slide decks on topics like blockchain and digital wallets. They then refined the AI-generated content by adding case studies, charts, and personal insights. This approach not only saved time but also improved the quality of their final presentations.

By using SlidesGPT, students can shift their focus from technical execution to content development and presentation skills. This experience prepares them for future workplaces where AI-driven tools are becoming increasingly common.

7.15 Designing Digital Content with AI

Visual content is key in the digital age, and YouTube thumbnails are especially important because they are a video's first impression. AI-powered design tools make creating compelling thumbnails accessible and efficient, even for people without formal design training.

AI tools like Canva, Adobe Express, visme and Fotor use ML to suggest layouts, colour schemes, and font combinations optimized for engagement. We use Visme (https://www.visme.co/visme-ai/).

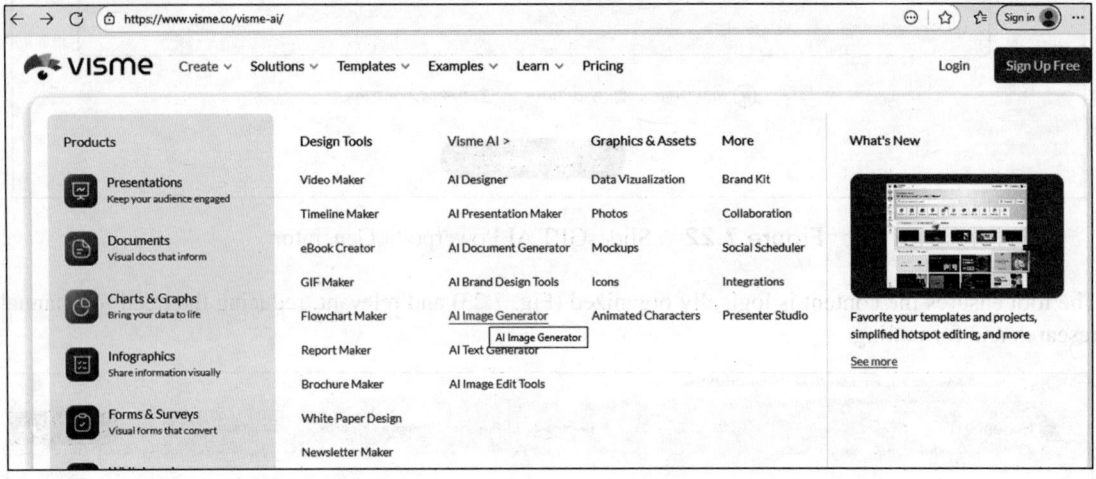

Figure 7.24   Designing digital content with Visme

While Visme's AI prompt feature works well, it does not currently allow you to generate a full thumbnail from a single text prompt like some other AI image generators (Fig. 7.24). Instead, Visme's AI tools are more integrated into its design process. To get the most out of Visme's AI for a YouTube thumbnail, you can use these prompts within the editor itself.

Visme AI Prompts for YouTube Thumbnails

1. **To create an AI-generated background:**
   - **Prompt:** "A vibrant, futuristic city skyline at night with neon lights, in a hyper-realistic style."
   - **Prompt:** "A blurry, bokeh-effect background of a cozy living room with warm lighting."

- **Prompt:** "An abstract digital art background with swirling blue and purple colors, clean and minimal."

2. **To create a specific graphic or illustration:**
   - **Prompt:** "A cartoon-style illustration of a happy person holding a lightbulb with a dollar sign on it, in a flat design."
   - **Prompt:** "An icon of a single gold coin with a glowing effect, vector art."
   - **Prompt:** "A simple line drawing of a laptop with a video play button on the screen, on a white background."

3. **To enhance a photo of a person for a thumbnail:**
   - **Prompt:** "An intense close-up of a person with a surprised expression, looking directly at the camera."
   - **Prompt:** "A professional portrait of a woman smiling, with a shallow depth of field, sharp focus on her face."

How to use these prompts in Visme
1. Start a new project in Visme and choose a YouTube thumbnail template.
2. In the editor, look for the AI Image Generator tool (usually in the left-hand panel).
3. Enter one of the prompts above based on what you need for your design.
4. Visme's AI will generate several options. Select the one you like and it will be added to your canvas.
5. From there, you can add your headline text, other icons, and finalize the design.

A case study from a media studies class in Kochi showed the effectiveness of AI in this process. Students created thumbnails for educational videos on science. The videos with AI-enhanced thumbnails got significantly more views than those with manually designed ones. This demonstrated the power of visual optimization and the value of AI in content promotion.

7.16 Branding and Visual Identity with AI

Branding is the process of creating a distinct identity for a product, service, or organization using visual elements like logos, colour schemes, and typography. A strong brand is crucial for recognition and trust. AI has become a powerful ally in this area, simplifying and enhancing the branding process.

AI-powered platforms like Looka, Tailor Brands, and Canva's Brand Kit can generate logos and define brand palettes by analyzing user preferences and industry trends. We will use Looka to create a logo (Fig. 7.25).

Looka is an AI-powered logo maker that simplifies the entire logo creation process, making it accessible even for people with no design experience. It goes beyond just generating a single image and provides a full range of branded assets. Here's a step-by-step breakdown of how you can use Looka for logo creation:

1. **Start with Your Brand's Identity:** You begin by entering your company name and a slogan (optional). Then, you select your industry. This helps the AI understand the visual language and common symbols associated with your business.

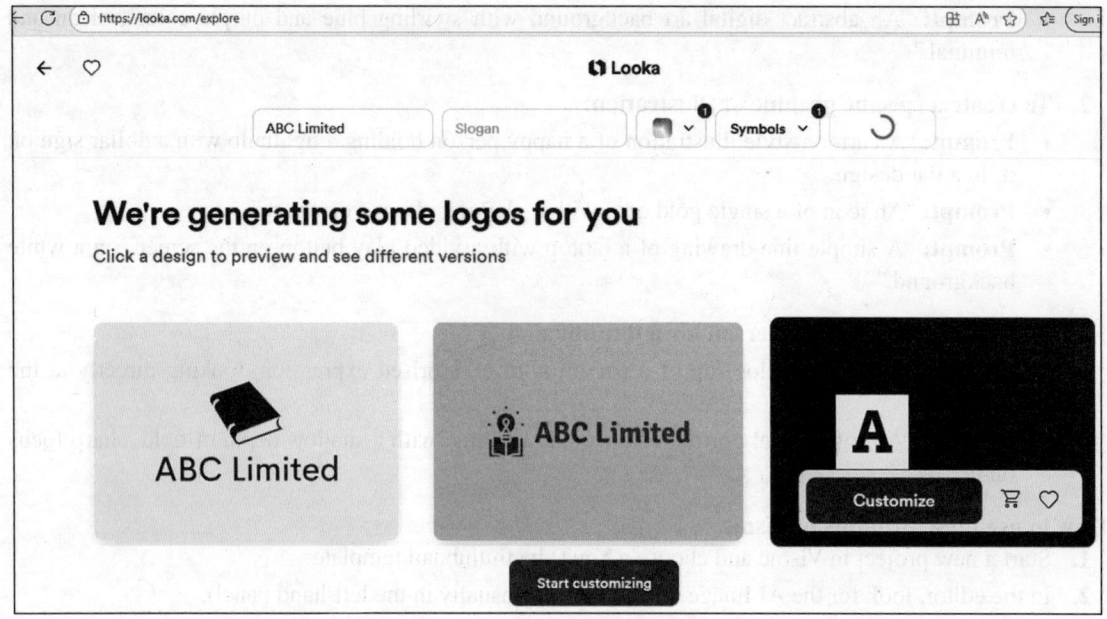

Figure 7.25 Generating a logo with Looka AI

2. **Provide Design Inspiration:** Looka will show you a gallery of logo styles. You select a few that you like, such as "Modern," "Minimal," or "Classic." Next, you choose up to three colours that you want for your brand. Looka provides a visual guide to the feelings and meanings associated with each colour. Finally, you can choose specific symbols or icons you want to be included in your logo by searching with keywords. For example, if your business is a coffee shop, you might search for "coffee," "bean," or "mug."
3. **AI-Powered Generation:** Based on all the information you hyave provided, Looka's AI goes to work. In just a few seconds, it generates hundreds of unique logo options. These are not templates; they are custom designs created by the AI by combining different fonts, layouts, symbols, and colours based on your preferences.
4. **Edit and Refine Your Design:** Once you find a logo design that you like, you can click on it to enter the editor. This is where you have full creative control to perfect the design.
5. **Unlimited Edits:** You can change the colours, fonts, layouts, and even the symbols to create new variations.
6. **See Mockups:** A great feature is the ability to see how your logo will look on real-life products like t-shirts, business cards, websites, and social media profiles. This helps you visualize your brand and ensure the logo works in different contexts.
7. **Fine-tuning:** You can also make subtle adjustments like changing the spacing between letters (kerning), adjusting the size of the symbol, and more.
8. **Purchase and Download:** Looka is free to use for the design and experimentation phase. You only pay when you're ready to download your logo files.

In essence, Looka provides a guided, AI-driven process that takes the guesswork out of logo design. It combines the speed of AI with the creative control of a professional editor, giving you a professional-looking logo and a head start on your brand identity.

A case study from a start-up incubator in Chennai showed how entrepreneurs used Tailor Brands to develop their brand identities. The AI guided them through logo creation and font selection, helping them establish a strong visual presence with professional, cohesive brand kits.

AI also ensures brand consistency. Tools like Canva's Brand Kit allow you to apply your branding elements to all your content with a single click. This streamlines the creative process, supports strategic decision-making, and enhances the impact of your digital communication.

Summary

By completing these lab activities, you have gained practical experience and developed digital literacy, preparing you for a future where AI-driven tools are commonplace. This chapter serves as a solid foundation for further exploration and innovation, empowering you to use AI responsibly and creatively in your academic and professional life.

Appendix: Model Question Papers

Model Question Paper 1

Subject: Artificial Intelligence
Time: 3 Hours
Total Marks: 100

Part A: Objective Questions (20 × 1 = 20 Marks)

1. The quote, "Artificial intelligence is not a substitute for human intelligence; it is a tool to amplify human creativity and ingenuity," is attributed to whom?
   (a) John McCarthy
   (b) Fei-Fei Li
   (c) Alan Turing
   (d) Marvin Minsky

2. Which of the following is NOT one of the primary paradigms of machine learning?
   (a) Supervised learning
   (b) Unsupervised learning
   (c) Incremental learning
   (d) Reinforcement learning

3. In an expert knowledge-based system (EKBS), which component is responsible for drawing conclusions from rules and facts?
   (a) User Interface
   (b) Knowledge Base
   (c) Inference Engine
   (d) Sensor

4. Which of the following is a common application of AI in the financial sector for adaptive learning and real-time monitoring?
   (a) Personalized education
   (b) Algorithmic trading
   (c) Fraud detection
   (d) Medical diagnostics

5. What is the primary concern related to data privacy in AI systems?
   (a) The inability to process large data sets
   (b) The potential for data misuse or theft if not managed securely
   (c) The high cost of data storage
   (d) The lack of clear data ownership

6. Which of the following describes the function of a generative adversarial network (GAN)?
   (a) A network that improves image resolution
   (b) A system where two neural networks, a generator and a discriminator, compete against each other
   (c) A model for text summarization
   (d) A system for supervised learning

7. What is the main goal of prompt engineering?
   (a) To write code for AI models
   (b) To use knowledge of how AI understands language to write prompts that match a specific requirement
   (c) To train large language models from scratch
   (d) To perform hardware maintenance on AI systems

8. In the context of the ReAct prompting method, what follows the Thought and Action steps?
   (a) Response
   (b) Observation
   (c) Goal
   (d) Reflection

9. Which of the following is an example of an AI-powered tool for automated slide creation?
   (a) Canva
   (b) Gemini
   (c) SlidesAI
   (d) DALL·E

10. What is the role of an actuator in a robotic system?
    (a) To sense the environment
    (b) To enable the robot to perform actions or movements
    (c) To process data from sensors
    (d) To store the robot's memory

11. Fill in the Blanks: In reinforcement learning, an agent learns through a system of _____ and _____.

12. Fill in the Blanks: The process of making AI decisions and outcomes understandable to humans is called _____

13. True or False: In supervised learning, algorithms are trained on unlabelled data.

14. True or False: Generative AI creates new content based on patterns it has learned from existing data.

15. Match the following AI subfields with their description:

1. Knowledge Engineering	A. Enables computers to interpret visual information.
2. Deep Learning	B. A core area of AI that focuses on building and organizing expert knowledge in computer systems.
3. Computer Vision	C. Deals with the interaction between computers and human language.
4. Natural Language Processing	D. A method where computers learn from a large amount of data.

16. What is the key difference between Generative AI and traditional AI?
    (a) Traditional AI is faster.
    (b) Generative AI can create entirely new content, while traditional AI follows specific rules or patterns to perform tasks.
    (c) Traditional AI requires more data.
    (d) Generative AI is not capable of problem-solving.

17. Which ethical concern is raised by the fact that AI systems often handle vast amounts of personal data like health or financial records?
    (a) Accountability
    (b) Transparency
    (c) Data privacy
    (d) Sustainability

18. What is the significance of the Dartmouth Conference in the history of AI?
    (a) It was the first AI model to beat a human at chess.
    (b) It was the birthplace of the term "Artificial Intelligence."
    (c) It led to the invention of the LISP programming language.
    (d) It was the first conference on robotics.

19. Which AI model is known for its multimodal capabilities across text, image, audio, and video?
    (a) ChatGPT
    (b) DALL·E
    (c) Gemini AI
    (d) Perplexity AI

20. Which image processing technique involves making an image monochrome by reducing its colour information?
    (a) Edge detection
    (b) Filtering
    (c) Grayscale conversion
    (d) Thresholding

Part B: Two-Mark Questions (10 × 2 = 20 Marks)

1. How does AI enhance medical diagnostics?
2. Briefly explain the concept of data bias in AI.
3. What is a prompt in the context of AI?
4. Differentiate between Natural Language Understanding and Natural Language Generation.
5. What are the three main components of an expert knowledge-based system?
6. How does an AI-powered adaptive learning platform personalize education?
7. What is the primary function of a knowledge base in a knowledge-based system?
8. Mention any two applications of generative AI in creative fields.
9. Explain the purpose of human-in-the-loop (HITL) systems.
10. What is a mind map, and how can it be used to visualize AI subfields?

Part C: Essay Questions (Any 6 Questions to be answered. 60 Marks)

1. Explain the scope of AI in detail, covering its applications across various industries.
2. Describe the three main paradigms of machine learning: supervised, unsupervised, and reinforcement learning, with suitable examples for each.
3. Elaborate on the ethical concerns surrounding AI, including fairness, bias, transparency, and accountability.
4. Discuss how the clarity and specificity of a prompt influence the performance and reliability of AI-generated outputs.
5. Explain the role and functions of Generative Adversarial Networks (GANs) and Diffusion Models in image generation.
6. Describe the role of AI in precision agriculture and IoT integration for efficient resource management.
7. Analyze the impact of AI on job roles and social inequalities, discussing how it can both reduce and exacerbate them.
8. Propose a framework for responsible innovation in generative AI that addresses transparency, inclusivity, and ethical governance.

Model Question Paper 2

Subject: Artificial Intelligence **Total Marks:** 100
Time: 3 Hours

Part A: Objective Questions (20 × 1 = 20 Marks)

1. What is the primary focus of the AI subdomain knowledge engineering?
   (a) Developing deep neural networks
   (b) Building, organizing, and applying expert knowledge in computer systems
   (c) Creating virtual assistants
   (d) Analyzing big data

2. Which type of AI system is described as being able to think and act like humans?
   (a) Weak AI
   (b) Artificial General Intelligence (AGI)
   (c) Supervised Learning
   (d) Generative AI

3. The LISP programming language, invented by John McCarthy, was significant for which field?
   (a) Web Development
   (b) Artificial Intelligence
   (c) Data Science
   (d) Cybersecurity

4. Which of the following is a common application of AI in the education sector?
   (a) Automated slide creation
   (b) Algorithmic trading
   (c) Adaptive learning platforms
   (d) Supply chain optimization

5. What does the term transparency refer to in the context of AI ethics?
   (a) The ability of an AI system to process data quickly
   (b) The practice of making an AI system's decisions and outcomes understandable to humans
   (c) The visibility of the training data
   (d) The absence of bias in an AI model

6. Which of the following is a key component of a neural network that allows it to learn from data?
   (a) Knowledge base
   (b) Backpropagation
   (c) User interface
   (d) Actuators

7. What is the purpose of multimodal models in generative AI?
   (a) They can only generate text.
   (b) They can only generate images.
   (c) They can work with different types of data at the same time, such as text and images.
   (d) They are only used for research purposes.

8. Which of the following is a key feature of Perplexity AI?
   (a) It is primarily used for image generation.
   (b) It provides real-time, cited answers for research.
   (c) It is a tool for video generation.
   (d) It is a platform for automated slide creation.

9. What technique is similar to "watching a blurry photo slowly come into focus" in image generation?
   (a) Generative Adversarial Networks (GANs)
   (b) Transformer Architecture
   (c) Diffusion Models
   (d) Reinforcement Learning

10. What is role-based prompting?
    (a) A method that requires the AI to assume a specific persona or role before responding.
    (b) A method of teaching AI to play video games.
    (c) A technique to create a chatbot.
    (d) A way to classify images.

11. Fill in the Blanks: The goal of Computer Vision is to enable computers to _____ and _____ visual information.

12. Fill in the Blanks: AI systems are designed to think, reason, and act _____.

13. True or False: An AI system that is trained on data that is not balanced and doesn't represent a wide variety of people can lead to biased outcomes.

14. True or False: The Generative AI chef analogy is used to describe how Gen AI creates entirely new content based on learned patterns.

15. Match the following AI concepts with their descriptions:

1. Supervised Learning	A. Finds patterns in unlabelled data.
2. Unsupervised Learning	B. A method where an agent learns through a system of rewards and punishments.
3. Reinforcement Learning	C. Algorithms are trained on labelled data.
4. Deep Learning	D. A method where computers learn from a large amount of data.

16. What is the main ethical concern associated with the use of AI in surveillance?
    (a) Cost of implementation
    (b) Potential for misuse and infringement on privacy
    (c) Lack of accuracy
    (d) Difficulty in scalability

17. Which of the following is an example of an AI application in agriculture?
    (a) Algorithmic trading
    (b) Precision agriculture
    (c) Self-driving cars
    (d) Medical diagnostics

18. What is the purpose of backpropagation in a deep neural network?
    (a) It is used to calculate the output of the network.
    (b) It is a method for training a neural network by adjusting the weights based on the error.
    (c) It is a type of activation function.
    (d) It is a technique for data cleaning.

19. Which AI tool is described as being a user-friendly graphic design platform for creating mind maps?
    (a) Canva
    (b) SlidesAI
    (c) Tome
    (d) Gemini

20. What is a key challenge in prompt engineering?
    (a) The need for advanced programming skills
    (b) Ensuring the prompt is well-written to get smart and relevant answers
    (c) The lack of available large language models
    (d) The high cost of running prompts

Part B: Two-Mark Questions (10 x 2 = 20 Marks)

1. What is the difference between a prompt and prompt engineering?
2. Briefly describe the COMPAS case study and its relevance to AI ethics.
3. How does AI improve fraud detection in the financial sector?
4. Explain the concept of interdisciplinary problem-solving in AI.
5. What are the three core technologies behind generative AI?
6. How do sensors and actuators work together in a robotic system?
7. What is the limitation of context window in models like ChatGPT, and how can users mitigate this issue?

8. Mention two examples of AI applications in the retail sector.
9. Explain the importance of empathy in AI-generated responses for customer service.
10. What is a multimodal model in generative AI?

Part C: Essay Questions (Any 6 Questions to be answered. 60 Marks)

1. Write an essay on the historical evolution of AI, from its early theoretical research to its current practical applications.
2. Discuss the different knowledge representation techniques in AI, including semantic networks, frames, and production rules.
3. Compare and contrast the application of AI in the healthcare sector for diagnostics and medical imaging.
4. Elucidate the multimodal capabilities of Gemini AI and its potential applications across various domains.
5. Critically assess the challenges of scalability and generalization in prompt engineering across multilingual and multicultural contexts.
6. Explain how AI is used to power self-driving cars, detailing the roles of perception, decision-making, and route planning.
7. Evaluate the effectiveness of GDPR and CCPA in addressing data privacy concerns in AI systems. What are their strengths and limitations?
8. Describe how Generative AI is reshaping creative industries like music composition and visual arts, citing specific case studies.

Model Question Paper 3

Subject: Artificial Intelligence **Total Marks:** 100
Time: 3 Hours

Part A: Objective Questions (20 × 1 = 20 Marks)

1. Which of the following is considered a foundational discipline of AI?
   (a) Web design
   (b) Knowledge engineering
   (c) Graphic design
   (d) Database management

2. The ability of AI systems to learn from current and past data and adapt to varying situations is a key characteristic. What is this process called?
   (a) Explicit programming
   (b) Machine learning
   (c) Human-in-the-loop
   (d) Contextual prompting

3. In the context of AI, what does accountability mean?
   (a) The ability to create new content
   (b) The need for AI developers to be responsible for the system's ethical behaviour
   (c) The process of training an AI model
   (d) The ability of an AI to learn from its mistakes

4. Which AI application helps personalize education based on student performance and preferences?
   (a) Algorithmic trading
   (b) Intelligent tutoring systems
   (c) Fraud detection
   (d) Predictive maintenance

5. What is the primary role of the inference engine in an expert knowledge-based system?
   (a) To store all the data
   (b) To process user requests
   (c) To apply rules to the knowledge base to derive conclusions
   (d) To act as a user interface

6. Which of the following describes the key function of transformer architecture?
   (a) It is used to generate images.
   (b) It has enabled models like GPT and BERT.
   (c) It is a method for unsupervised learning.
   (d) It is a type of robotic sensor.

7. Which type of prompting method requires the AI to be instructed with specific details and rules?
   (a) Foundational prompting
   (b) Instruction-based prompting
   (c) Role-based prompting
   (d) Contextual prompting

8. What is the primary goal of the "Observation" step in the ReAct prompting method?
   (a) To generate a new thought
   (b) To get the result of a performed action
   (c) To choose a new tool
   (d) To create a response for the user

9. Which AI tool is used for real-time, cited answers for research?
   (a) ChatGPT
   (b) Gemini
   (c) Hugging Face
   (d) Perplexity AI

10. What is the purpose of grayscale conversion in image processing?
    (a) To detect the edges of an object
    (b) To enhance the colour of an image
    (c) To reduce an image to a monochrome representation
    (d) To separate an image into different regions

11. Fill in the Blanks: A Diffusion Model is like watching a _____ photo slowly come into focus.

12. Fill in the Blanks: AI systems handle vast amounts of _____ data, like health or financial records.

13. True or False: The Dartmouth Conference in 1956 is considered the birthplace of the term "Artificial Intelligence."

14. True or False: Reinforcement learning is where an agent learns through a system of rewards and punishments.

15. Match the following AI terms with their descriptions:

1. AGI	A. Involves the use of sensors and actuators in physical systems.
2. NLP	B. A type of AI that can mimic human intelligence in a broad range of tasks.
3. Computer Vision	C. Deals with the interaction between computers and human language.
4. Robotics	D. Enables computers to interpret visual information.

16. What is the significance of the IBM Watson in Oncology case study?
    (a) It shows how AI can create new medical treatments.
    (b) It illustrates how AI can be integrated into clinical decision-making to improve cancer treatment outcomes.
    (c) It demonstrates how AI can automate surgical procedures.
    (d) It proves that AI is a substitute for human doctors.

17. Which ethical concept in AI ensures that AI systems serve people from diverse backgrounds?
    (a) Inclusivity
    (b) Accountability
    (c) Transparency
    (d) Sustainability

18. What is the primary purpose of sentiment analysis in the financial sector?
    (a) To analyze stock market trends
    (b) To predict market movement based on public opinion from text data
    (c) To detect fraudulent transactions
    (d) To manage customer portfolios

19. Which AI tool is a user-friendly graphic design platform for creating mind maps?
    (a) DALL·E
    (b) Canva
    (c) SlidesAI
    (d) Tome

20. Which of the following is NOT an application of AI in the transportation sector?
    (a) Self-driving cars
    (b) Algorithmic trading
    (c) Traffic flow management
    (d) Route planning

Part B: Two-Mark Questions (10 x 2 = 20 Marks)

1. How does semantic networks represent knowledge in AI systems?
2. What is the primary difference between supervised and unsupervised learning?
3. Explain the concept of algorithmic trading in the financial sector.
4. Briefly describe data bias and its sources in AI systems.
5. What are the multimodal capabilities of Gemini AI?
6. How does an AI-powered chatbot enhance customer support?
7. What is the significance of Fei-Fei Li's quote on AI?
8. What is prompt engineering?

9. Mention any two tools for automated slide creation using generative AI.

10. How does AI contribute to climate modelling and environmental research?

Part C: Essay Questions (Any 6 Questions to be answered. 60 Marks)

1. Elaborate on the evolution of generative AI, from rule-based systems to advanced neural networks.

2. Differentiate between AI and human intelligence, focusing on their respective strengths and limitations.

3. Discuss the importance of transparency and accountability in AI development for building public trust.

4. Explain how generative AI tools such as ChatGPT or Gemini can be used to create personalized educational content for students with different learning needs.

5. Analyze the role of AI in medical diagnostics and imaging, citing specific examples from the document.

6. Describe the various knowledge representation techniques, providing examples of how each might be used in an AI system.

7. Critically evaluate the role of AI chatbots and virtual assistants in customer service and service scalability.

8. Propose a conceptual framework for integrating AI into agricultural pest and disease detection systems.

Index

A

accountability 13, 16, 88, 196
    building trust 89
    ensuring compliance 90
    preventing harm 90
actuators 46
    hydraulic 46
    pneumatic 46
AI virtual assistant (AIVA) 5, 146
AlphaFold 154
AlphaGo 6, 10, 36
algorithmic bias 80
    addressing 80
artificial general intelligence (AGI) 6, 14
    automation 15
    challenges 16
    education 15
    finance 15
    healthcare 14
    manufacturing 15
    research 15
    risks 16
    versus narrow AI 14
artificial intelligence, agriculture applications 63, 154, 225
    crop yield prediction 63
    pest and disease detection 64
    precision and IoT 63
artificial intelligence, applications **53–76**
    agriculture 63, 154, 225
    customer service and retail 70, 119, 177, 194
    education 60, 155, 198, 210
    finance 2, 56, 97
    healthcare 54, 197, 211, 234
    introduction 53
    transportation 65

artificial intelligence, customer service and retail 70, 119, 177, 194
    chatbot and virtual assistant 70
    inventory and supply chain 71
    personalized shopping experience 71
artificial intelligence, education applications 60, 155, 198, 210
    adaptive learning platform 60
    curriculum design 60
    intelligent tutoring system 60
artificial intelligence, finance applications 2, 56, 97
    algorithmic trading 58
    fraud detection 56
    risk modelling 57
artificial intelligence, healthcare applications 54, 197, 211, 234
    medical diagnostics 54
    medical imaging 55
    personalized medicine 55
artificial intelligence, historical evolution 3
    1950s 3
    1960s 4
    1970s–80s 4
    1990s–2000s 5
    2010s 5
    2020s 6
artificial intelligence, introduction **1–24**
    artificial general intelligence 14
    benefits 2
    concerns 2
    differentiating from human intelligence 11
    historical evolution 3
    influential figures and institutions 7
    inter-disciplinary problem-solving 20
    milestones in research 16
    scope 2

artificial intelligence, milestones in research 16
    deep learning (DL) 17
    early foundations 16
    future directions 19
    generative models 18
    machine learning (ML) 17
    natural language processing (NLP) 4, 18
    neural network (NN) 6, 17
    recent advances 19
    robotics 4, 9, 19
    symbolic AI 17
artificial intelligence, subfields **25–52**
    computer vision (CV) 4, 19, 42, 64
    deep learning (DL) 5, 17, 36, 43, 57, 96, 113, 170
    expert knowledge-based system (EKBS) 26
    machine learning (ML) 4, 17, 30, 58, 70, 94, 189, 218
    natural language processing (NLP) 4, 18, 40, 60, 156, 189
    overview 25
    robotics 4, 9, 19, 45
artificial intelligence, transportation applications 65
    logistics 68
    self-driving cars 65
    traffic flow management 66
artificial intelligence versus human intelligence 11
    adaptability 12
    cognitive capabilities 11
    creativity 13
    emotional and social intelligence 12
    ethical and moral reasoning 13
    intuition 13
    learning 12

B

Beatoven.ai 147
Beautiful.ai 152
BERT 18, 111
bias 78
    data 78
    algorithmic 80
    measurement 80
    confirmation 81
    societal 83
Bing Image Creator 135, 234

C

Claude 126, 155
Canva 217, 238
ChatGPT 6, 113, 231
    agentic features 118
    applications 119
    free users 118
    latest features 116
    limitations 120
    LinkedIn post 115
    Plus plan 118
    Pro plan 118
    Resume 116
    Twitter post 115
    using Sora 115
    videos 115
computer vision (CV) 4, 19, 42, 64
    applications 43
    deep learning 43
    YOLO 43
confirmation bias 81
    addressing 82
convolutional neural network (CNN) 18, 37, 43
    convolutional layer 38
    fully connected layer 38
    pooling layer 38

D

DALL.E 112, 142, 233
Dartmouth conference 3, 8
data bias 78
    addressing 78
data privacy and security 91
    cybersecurity challenges 92
    regulations and compliance 92
    surveillance 91
Deep Blue 5, 20
deep learning (DL) 5, 17, 36, 43, 57, 96, 113, 170
    challenges 39
    computer vision (CV) 43
    convolutional 37
    future directions 39
    neural network architecture 37
    recurrent 38
    training techniques 39
DENDRAL 4, 29

Index | 257

E

ELIZA 4
employment and workforce transformation 94
    economic impact on labour market 95
    human–AI collaboration 94
    reskilling 94
    upskilling 94
expert knowledge-based systems 26
    challenges 28
    inference engine 27
    knowledge base 26
    representation techniques 27
    user interface 27

F

fairness in decision-making 79, 85
    algorithm 86
    group 86
    individual 85
    statistical 85
fairness-awareness algorithms 86
    in-processing 86
    post-processing 86
    pre-processing 86

G

Gamma 148
Gemini 121
    creative writing 126
    describing images 124
    dialogue generation 129
    limitations 131
    other applications 130
    personalizing educational content 121
    poetry 126
    screenwriting 128
    script writing 129
    story generation 128
    storybook 122
    summarizing document 125
generative AI, applications **105–167**
    introduction 106
    how it works 106
    historical milestones 107
    ChatGPT 113
    Gemini 121
    Hugging Face 131
    Perplexity 133
    creativity 135
    human–AI collaboration 147
    research and innovation 153
    education 155
    business 157
    healthcare 159
    entertainment 161
    future trends 163
generative AI, historical milestones 107
    diffusion models 112
    generative adversarial network (GAN) 109
    GPT models 110
    neural network (NN) 107
    Transformer architecture 109
generative AI, use in business 157
    business insights 158
    communication 158
    customer engagement 158
    marketing content 157
    product description 158
    reporting 158
generative AI, use in creativity 135
    human–AI collaboration 147
    image generation 135
    music and sound generation 146
    slide generation 148
    video generation 145
generative AI, use in education 155
    adaptive content 156
    assessment 156
    challenges 156
    curriculum generation 155
    ethical considerations 156
    feedback 156
    lesson plan 155
    personalized learning 156
    student support 156
    tutoring 156
generative AI, use in entertainment 161
    animation 162
    game design 161
    music composition 161
    sound design 161
    visual effects 162
generative AI, use in healthcare 159
    decision support 159

diagnostics 159
medical imaging 159
patient recovery 160
radiology 159
rehabilitation 160
simulation 160
surgical planning 160
generative AI, use in research and innovation 153
    academic collaboration 154
    climate modelling 154
    drug design 153
    engineering 153
    environmental research 154
    healthcare 153
    open research platform 154
    product design 153
Google
    AI Studio 222
    DeepMind 5, 10
    Teachable Machine 225

H

HeyGen 146
human–AI collaboration 94, 147, 163, 194
human-in-the-loop (HITL) 79, 196
Hugging Face 131, 232
    challenges 132
    model hub 132
    Transformers library 132

I

IBM Watson 5, 10, 56
image generation 135
    Bing Image Creator 135
    DALL.E 142
    Stable Diffusion 144
inclusivity 96
InVideo AI 146

J

Jotform 227

K

knowledge representation techniques 27
    frame 27
    production rules 27
    semantic network 27

L

laboratory work 217–242
    bias in generative models 234
    build an image classifier using Google Teachable Machine 225
    concept map using Napkin AI 219
    create an agentic chatbot using Jotform 227
    image/video generation using DALL.E 233
    mind map using Canva 217
    model deployment using Hugging Face 232
    practising prompt engineering 235
    text analysis using Google AI Studio 222
    text generation using ChatGPT 231
    text mining using Voyant Tools 221

M

machine learning (ML) 4, 17, 30, 58, 70, 94, 189, 218
    reinforcement learning 31, 35
    supervised learning 30, 31
    unsupervised learning 31, 33
McCarthy, John 3, 7, 8
measurement bias 80
    addressing 81
mind map 27, 217
Minsky, Marvin 3, 7, 8
Mubert 147
music and sound generation 146
    AIVA 146
    Beatoven.ai 147
    Mubert 147
    Soundraw 146
MYCIN 29

N

Napkin AI 219
natural language processing (NLP) 4, 18, 40, 60, 156, 189
    applications 42
    feature extraction 41
    language model 41
    steps 40
    text processing 41
    transformer 41
neural network (NN) 6, 17, 32, 36, 37, 87, 107
    architecture 37
    backpropagation 37

convolutional 37
feedforward 37
hidden layer 33
input layer 33
output layer 33
recurrent 38
Newell, Allen 7, 9

O

OpenAI 11, 106, 112, 135, 154

P

Perplexity 133
   limitations 134
   Spaces 134
   templates 134
Pictory AI 146
prompt engineering **169–216**
   challenges 191
   chatbots 208
   creative content generation 203, 235, 236
   definition 169
   domain-specific applications 210
   future scope 194
   historical evolution 170
   impact on model performance 172
   impact on quality of AI output 172
   real-world applications 197
   role in ML/AI 189
   storytelling and fiction 206
   student support 209
   summarization applications 200, 235
   techniques 173
   why it matters 170
prompt engineering, applications 197
   business 213
   customer service 199
   education 198, 210
   healthcare 197, 211
   legal 199
prompt engineering, challenges 191
   ambiguity 191
   benchmarking 194
   bias 192
   ethical concerns 192
   evaluation 193
   generalization 193
   misinterpretation 191
   scalability 193
prompt engineering, chatbots 208
   automating response with empathy 208
   multilingual queries 208
prompt engineering, creative content generation 203, 235, 236
   article writing 203
   blogging 203
   caption generation 205
   social media 205
   style adaptation 204
   tone control 204
   trend alignment 205
   visual storytelling 205, 238, 239
prompt engineering, future scope 194
   ethical and responsible prompting 196
   human-in-the-loop (HITL) 196
   multimodal system integration 195
prompt engineering, role in ML/AI 189
   NLP and generative models 190
   supervised versus unsupervised learning 190
prompt engineering, storytelling and fiction 206
   character development 206
   genre-specific strategies 207
   plot progression 206
prompt engineering, student support 209
   clarifying queries 209
   personalized learning 209
prompt engineering, summarization applications 200, 235
   academic use 200
   professional use 202
prompt techniques 173
   advanced 182
   foundational 173
   intermediate 178
prompt techniques, advanced 182
   Chain-of-Thought (CoT) 182
   meta 188
   ReAct (reasoning and acting) 185
   self-consistency 184
   Tree-of-Thought (ToT) 187
prompt techniques, foundational 173
   contextual 175
   instruction-based 174
   role-based 176

step-by-step 177
zero-shot 173
prompt techniques, intermediate 178
   contrastive 179
   few-shot 178
   iterative 180
   scaffold 178

R

recurrent neural network (RNN) 6, 38
   long short-term memory 38
   vanishing memory problem 38
reinforcement learning (RL) 31, 35
   Markov decision process 35
reliability 97
robotics 4, 9, 19, 45
   actuators 46
   applications 48
   control system 46
   electric motors 46
   human–robot interaction 47
   navigation 47
   path planning 47
   sensors 45
RunwayML 145

S

Samuel, Arthur 3
sensors 45
   environmental 45
   fusion 47
   internal 45
   proximity 45
   touch 45
   vision 45
SHAKEY 4
slide generation 148, 237
   Beautiful.ai 152
   Gamma 148
   SlidesAI 150
   Slidesgo 152
   Tome 151
SlidesAI 150
Slidesgo 152
social inequality 98
   access to technology 99
   digital divide 99
   policy interventions 100
societal bias 83
   addressing 83
Sora 115
Soundraw 146
Stable Diffusion 144
statistical fairness 85
   demographic parity 85
   equalized odds 85
   predictive parity 85
supervised learning 30, 31
   decision tree 31
   neural network 32
   real-life applications 33
   support vector machine 32
sustainability 97

T

Tome 151
transparency in systems 87
   examples 87
   levels 87
transparency levels 87
   regulatory 88
   technical 87
   user 88
Turing test 3

U

unsupervised learning 31, 33
   dimensionality reduction 34
   hierarchical clustering 34
   K-means clustering 34
   real-life applications 35

V

video generation 145
   HeyGen 146
   InVideo AI 146
   Pictory AI 146
   RunwayML 145
   VEED.IO 146
VEED.IO 146
Voyant Tools 221

W

WABOT-1 4